2014

D1285340

CIRCLING · WINDROCK · MOUNTAIN

Augusta Grove Bell

The University of Tennessee Press / Knoxville

CIRCLING · WINDROCK · MOUNTAIN

Two Hundred Years in Appalachia

The paper in this book meets the minimum requirements of the
American National Standard for Permanence of Paper for Printed
Library Materials.

∞ The binding materials have been chosen for strength and durability.

♻ Printed on recycled paper.

Frontis. Windrock Mountain, photographed from Oliver Springs not long after
the L&N trestle was built in 1903. Photograph courtesy of C. S. Harvey Jr.

Library of Congress Cataloging-in-Publication Data

Bell, Augusta Grove, 1926–
Circling Windrock Mountain : two hundred years in Appalachia /
Augusta Grove Bell. — 1st ed.
    p.   cm.
Includes bibliographical references (p.) and index.
ISBN 1-57233-041-4 (cl.: alk. paper)
ISBN 1-57233-038-4 (pbk.: alk. paper)
1. Anderson County (Tenn.)—History, Local. 2. Anderson County (Tenn.)—
Biography. 3. Anderson County (Tenn.)—Genealogy. 4. Mountain whites—
Tennessee—Anderson County—Biography. 5. Mountain life—Tennessee—
Anderson County—History. I. Title.
F443.A5 B45 1999
976.8'73—ddc21   98-40113

In memory
John T. Smith
Snyder E. Roberts
Roy E. Brown

Contents

Illustrations

Genealogical Chart

Maps

Duncans and Frosts Prominent in *Circling Windrock Mountain*

Genealogical information from *Duncan Descendants of Frost Bottom, TN,* by Marjorie Duncan Byrd, 1995, and *Descendants of Joseph Frost, Sr. from Amherst, Bedford And Washington Counties, VA To Anderson County, TN And Elsewhere,* by Snyder E. Roberts, 1989.

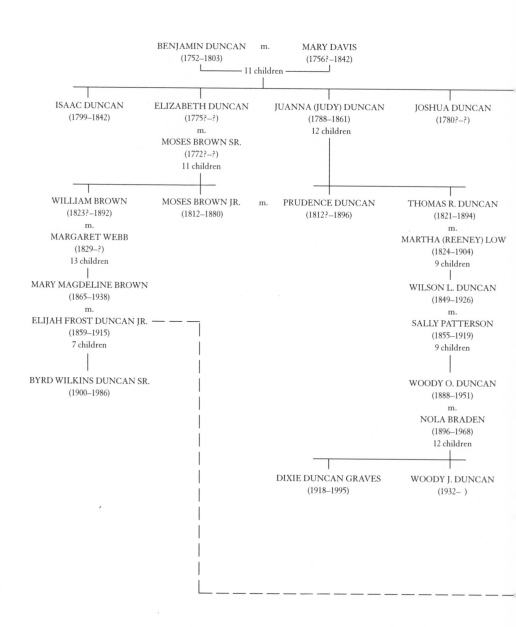

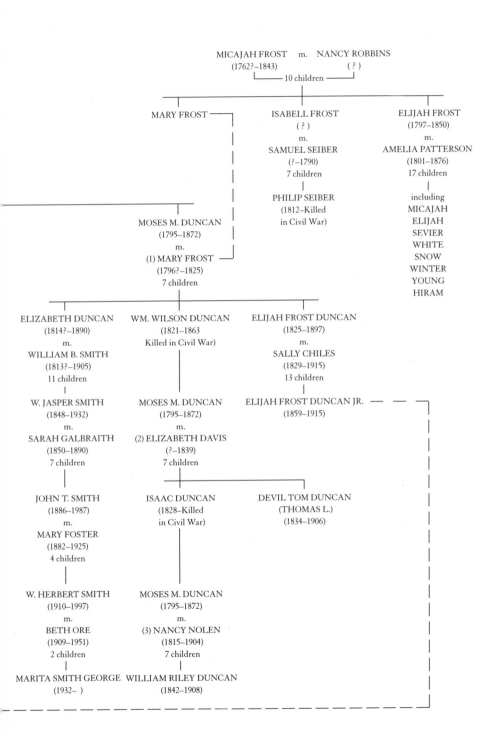

Preface

This is a book that circles around in more than two hundred years, a book that pieces together from family stories a folk history of the mountainous northwest section of Anderson County, Tennessee. Because of the Tennessee Valley Authority and the wartime Manhattan Project at Oak Ridge, the county has had more than its share of attention since the 1930s. Still, the county I got to know up in the Cumberlands was a very different place from what it has become, its memories stretching back before statehood to the time of the Southwest Territory, then on through the golden days of isolation preceding the Civil War and beyond to the tumultuous postwar exploitation of coal. It was as a newspaper reporter covering the county courthouse for the *Oak Ridger* that I first became interested in this other Anderson County. The result was over thirty long feature articles that are the basis for this book. My interviews drew me farther and farther back to a time when God-fearing mountain people were both reverent and irreverent, but always realists about everything from whiskey drinking to fatherless children.

Twenty-seven years have gone by since I moved away, and yet the impression made on me by people in places like Frost Bottom and Windrock Mountain remains surprisingly strong. Although I grew up in East Texas and have lived in such varied parts of the world as Boston and the Amazon Valley, the dozen years in Tennessee looking out toward Windrock had a special vitality because of those who lived there. Even their names had this vitality, names like Brother Church Lively. Most of those county residents, elderly when I knew them, are now dead, making me want to recapture their vanishing

stories as a celebration of their lives. John T. Smith was the most important,
for he introduced me to the old days. I first knew Uncle John when he was
in his vigorous early eighties, long retired from his job with Windrock Mine.
He lived to be over a hundred before his death in 1987 but never lost touch
after I left Tennessee, thanks to the letter-writing help of his daughter-in-
law Mary Kate Smith. John Tyler Smith inherited good longevity genes from
his father Jasper and his grandfather William B. Smith, who came to Tennessee in 1829 to marry Micajah Frost's granddaughter. From them Uncle
John must have gotten not only his long life but the Gaelic love of storytelling.
The family stories go back to 1779, when William's father left Ireland as a
stowaway.

At eighty-one, this wiry little man named John Smith was indignantly
calling me one March morning in 1968 in the newsroom at the *Oak Ridger*.

"Send a reporter down here to Oliver Springs! That big hotel did *not* burn
in 1905. I know for sure."

Actually, it wasn't Uncle John calling, but his granddaughter. He was
much too deaf to hear on the telephone. But his determination to correct what
he was certain was a gross mistake in my first feature story on county history came through. I had written about the short but fabulous life of the
Oliver Springs Hotel, a spa built near mineral springs at the turn of the century. Sweltering southerners, and more than a few Yankees, came to cool off
in the Cumberlands. People said then that Oliver Springs reminded them of
an Alpine village.

That morning when Uncle John demanded a reporter, he was even more
naive about the way the overworked reporting staff of a small daily newspaper operated than I was about the local mountain history. It would have
taken nothing short of an explosion up at Windrock Mine to have gotten me
away from my desk and the looming newsroom deadline. Covering the courthouse in nearby Clinton was my primary job. That meant reporting the
unending, byzantine doings of the squires on County Court. Anderson
County in 1968 still had eighteenth-century "squires," not county commis-
sioners, to regulate what was happening in the shadow of the U.S. Atomic
Energy Commission. And though the county's chief law enforcement officer
was not a "high" sheriff, that was what many mountain people called him.

The polite granddaughter insisted Uncle John had all kinds of information I was sure to be interested in about Frost Bottom, information from his
father Jasper Smith, who was born and grew up there in the chaos of the Civil
War. I knew where Frost Bottom was because I had recently covered a protest meeting of residents there. Unusual people like ex-miner Roy Brown had
underway a small rebellion under the leadership of Babe Edwards, a long-

ago transplanted New Yorker. Their outrage had reached clear across Walden Ridge to the Clinton courthouse because of the terrible craters in the county road made by thirty-ton coal trucks that chewed up the blacktop. Even worse than the small chasms was the ghostly limestone dust the mammoth trucks stirred up, coating every leaf of every tree, every house, every car, every person who stood still too long. The Frost Bottom Road miseries provided a good news article, but I hadn't suspected the deep valley's having any other story to tell.

Nothing could be promised on the phone that morning, but I was curious. Then one early spring day when I finally got a breather after a noon deadline, I went to Oliver Springs, not knowing I was about to meet Micajah Frost's great-great-grandson. Glad to get out in the good-smelling air, I drove down off Black Oak Ridge north toward the Cumberlands. Windrock Mountain loomed dramatically about eight miles away. There, too, were miles of bare strip mine scars from the 1950s, winding around the blue-green peaks. Just this side of the high Cumberland escarpment stood lower Walden Ridge, which sealed off Frost Bottom.

My directions said to go to Oliver Springs and after the first block on Main Street to turn east on Dutch Valley Road running along the south base of Walden Ridge. Uncle John's diminutive house, white and neat as a New England church, sat partway up the ridge. It was a mile or so from the center of the old mining town that grew up around Moses Winters's gap. The Smith home perched on what had once been the treaty boundary line that was supposed to keep white settlers out of the Cherokees' land.

John Tyler Smith was waiting for me on his front porch with a big grin. He had what he liked best in the world, a new audience. That day I knew nothing at all about this bald little man, maybe five feet five inches tall, very tidy in his ironed Big Mac overalls. His bright eyes behind glasses looked like a young man's, though he had not one tooth. Something about him reminded me of Tugboat Annie, a feisty fox terrier my sister and I once had. Uncle John immediately had me feeling at ease. Mrs. Smith, somewhat younger, said a motherly hello and disappeared into the kitchen.

"Sister, sit down, sit down"—all females were sister. "Make yoreself at home."

This would be the first of many visits in the Smiths' front room, where family photographs shared places of honor with the familiar reproduction I always called "Jesus in the Garden." That day I had no idea of the problems ahead because of Uncle John's deafness. I didn't even know for some time that he owned a hearing aid that he hated to use. Whether it worked or not remained an open question. Always strong-willed, he seemed to hear only what he "picked out" to hear, as Mrs. Smith put it. Finally, Ollie Smith had pity on me after several visits and gave away the secret of his hearing aid. This was a true sign of her acceptance of me as an outsider that, however, proved to be little help.

In a way, Uncle John probably didn't want to hear. He just wanted you to listen. He loved, literally loved, to talk and repeat the hundreds of family stories that had been sinking into his alert mind for more than eighty years. "Awright, now, I'm gonna tell you this history," he would say launching into a tale. He came by his storytelling honestly. His father, Jasper Smith, farmer, constable, once county school board chairman, a needle-thin man with flowing white beard, had filled his youngest son with tales of his life as a boy during the Civil War. Some of these Jasper wrote about for the *Anderson County News* during the 1920s. These articles also brought back the very early days of Frost Bottom long before the South's "rebellion" was caused by that first rebel Lucifer, according to Jasper's version of the war.

As Uncle John would tell me that first visit, "We're walking on the edge of two hundred years!"

Indeed we were, and I started listening very carefully.

"Law, yes, Sister, I remember my Granddaddy William. He lived to be over ninety," Uncle John said, stopping a minute to think about the old man who had lived with them. William was bald like his grandson would become and liked to keep his hat on at the table in hot weather to keep the insects off. After saying that, John Smith stopped smiling and looked dead serious. "If I live, and the Lord's willing, I want to see them early days and my family history wrote down."

There I sat, a little awed, thinking here is a man who knew very well somebody who got married in 1829. Uncle John was showing me blurry photocopies of Jasper's old newspaper columns.

Would I like them?

I most certainly would. Suddenly I became anxious to get away and read what Jasper Smith had had to say forty years earlier about what it was like on the edge of two hundred years. Besides, I was exhausted from the two-hour effort to make myself heard. Later on, I learned that sometimes it was better just to give up and write out what I wanted to know since Uncle John's stories could take off on impossibly complicated tangents. To give himself credibility, he would stop a tale and establish with his remarkable memory who was kin to whom, who married whom and when. And, maybe just as important, why. In fact, it was by using this method that he had arrived at the date the Oliver Springs Hotel burned, the reason he called me at the newspaper office to complain. For once he was wrong, although he never admitted it. He contended the magnificent hotel was not destroyed in 1905, the date I got from the eyewitness account in the Clinton newspaper. He was positive the spectacular event was in 1907, because he remembered the five-story building disappearing in flames the year he moved to Back Street when he married his long-dead first wife. And that was in 1907.

Realizing I couldn't win the hotel argument, I was glad to change the subject when he offhandedly mentioned his local fame as a walker. At eighty-one he still made his mile-plus trip into Olivers, the old name for Oliver Springs he liked to use. He would do this not once but frequently twice a day just for the pleasure of walking. But he had even more impressive walking credentials than that. After he retired from Windrock Mine in 1947, he became an official champion. Local businessmen promoted a contest to see who could make the twenty-eight miles into Knoxville the fastest. The destination was Cas Walker's grocery store on Western Avenue, the same Cas Walker whose local country music show later gave a young singer named Dolly Parton a start. That first race, Uncle John easily won the hundred-dollar prize, covering the twenty-eight miles in six hours and thirty-eight minutes. The next year, at age seventy, he defeated three other walkers just to prove the first time wasn't a fluke. This added even more luster to his title of Walkin' John.

More unusual to me, though, was the forty-five-mile hike he once made from Oliver Springs north to Petros, going over the mountain there and down into the secluded New River Valley, then up Pilot Mountain, through Graves Gap and down to Laurel Grove, finally back through Frost Bottom to Oliver Springs. This route encircles much of the mountainous part of Anderson County, a separate world of its own, a sort of miniature Appalachia. Here Micajah Frost came two hundred years ago and then the Duncans, the Browns, the Livelys, the Phillipses, the Bunches, and the Bradens, and here their children live today. This book tells their stories, their "histories," as Uncle John called them.

My saga begins in Frost Bottom, circles Windrock Mountain, and ends up at the legendary coal mine Uncle John knew firsthand from its opening in 1904. In between are other tales from Oliver Springs, New River, and Graves Gap. Farther east up the steep valley between Walden Ridge and the Cumberlands are the Coal Creek stories of terrible mine explosions and a two-year miners' insurrection. They made Anderson County unique even before the first TVA dam or the atomic bomb. An epilogue gives a look at these places today, at the sometimes surprising changes twenty-seven years have brought since I first wrote my newspaper articles.

Although these stories are glued together with "real" history, much of the content cannot be verified. I am convinced, however, that family stories and folktales are as essential as hard facts for understanding the past. In one way, such stories are truer than history itself. But working on this collection and trying to find out what I failed to learn in those days as a reporter, I have realized that this kind of book will inevitably have many omissions and mistakes, for which I apologize. Still, I am pleased to have at last written my informal history of these unusual mountain people, my own view of their two hundred years, the bad along with the good. For them I have only admiration.

I am indebted to many for help in completing this work. Over the years, all kinds of books have added to my interest in Appalachia. Although I have listed sources in the back, I want to mention three writers who especially impressed me. The first is Harry Caudill, whose *Night Comes to the Cumberlands* awakened me as it did so many others in 1962. Just as important is George Orwell, not as creator of Big Brother but as social critic, particularly his book on coal miners in the depressed north of England in the 1930s called *The Road to Wigan Pier*. And finally, Rodger Cunningham. His ideas about the twelfth-century Scottish Lowlanders and their descendants who settled our Southern Highlands have given me a new awareness. His 1987 work is *Apples on the Flood*.

As for all the people crucial to this book, there could not have been one without the original help of the three to whom this is dedicated in memory, John T. Smith, Snyder E. Roberts, and Roy E. Brown. It was my good fortune that Snyder Roberts lived to be eighty-six and, in spite of bad health, continued to assist me until his death in 1994.

I have had particular encouragement from Dick Smyser, my former editor at the *Oak Ridger,* as well as from Peter Esser, the current publisher. I am also grateful to Dave Commons, publisher, *Roane County News;* Doug Morris, publisher, the Clinton *Courier-News;* Jimmie D. Turner, owner of the *Oliver Springs Citizen* when it was published; the staff of the Clinton Public Library; Selma Shapiro, director, and Jane Alderfer, archivist, of the Children's Museum of Oak Ridge; James Overholt, former director of that museum's Regional Appalachian Center. And a special thanks to Mary S. Harris, Anderson County historian.

Many others have been generous with information and photographs. I gratefully acknowledge their help with the different sections of the book:

Frost Bottom—Lavada Brown, Marjorie Duncan Byrd, Babe Edwards, Marita Smith George, the late Dixie Duncan Graves, Wanda Kelley, Fred Smith, Harold and Mary Kate Smith, and the late W. Herbert Smith.

Oliver Springs—Ed Best, J. H. Burney, Trish Lively Cox, C. S. Harvey

Jr., Frank Juan, Ray Leamon, Curt Owens, C. H. Smith, Charles Tichy, Fred Wyatt, and Steve Wyatt.

New River—Dorothy Armes, Tim Eagle, Anne Hablas, Ron McDowell, Jerry Morehead, Nancy Phillips Patty, Scotty Phillips, and Dr. Liane Russell.

Graves Gap—Nancy Braden Byrge, Laura Duncan, Gertrude Harness, and Mary S. Harris.

Coal Creek—Edith Wilson Hutton, Ron McDowell, Bob Swisher, Gene White, Charles Winfrey, and Fred Wyatt.

Windrock—Dick Bussard, Trish Lively Cox, Tim Eagle, Frank and Helen Freels, Carl Keith, Ray Leamon, Carl Lively, Curt Owens, Ina Lea Gallaher Roe, Dr. Charles W. Sienknecht, C. H. Smith, and Earl Vickery.

And finally, I would never have finished this book without the ideas and encouragement of Dot Jackson. My friends and colleagues at Central Piedmont Community College, including Leslie Tompkins, Nancy Bryan, and James Pait, have played a special role.

But the biggest thank-you of all goes to another colleague, Cynthia Ricketson, without whose help I could not have completed circling Windrock Mountain.

My gratitude goes to you all.

Augusta Grove Bell
Charlotte, North Carolina
December 1, 1997

Part I

Frost Bottom: In the Shadow of Windrock Mountain

On the Edge of Two Hundred Years

Windrock Mountain is a mountain that does not really exist. At least not on most maps. Nevertheless, the name is every bit as real as "Anderson County." The mountain is named for a rock up on what is actually Buffalo Mountain. The opening of the famed Windrock Mine further secured the name "Windrock" in local history. The mine, which operated continuously for eighty years until the last load of coal came out of the driftmouth in 1983, not only set Tennessee records for years of operation and size, but also for safety, and unofficially for harmonious labor relations. Though nothing is perfect, today most old-timers have good memories of Windrock Mine, far different from their tragic memories of the Coal Creek mines and two disastrous explosions.

My very first night in Oak Ridge in 1958 I saw unexpected lights burning high up on the side of a mountain far across the valley. I was standing on the porch of our rented wartime house atop the town's steep ridge. It was summer, and just after the sun went down, the purple-black peaks some ten miles off seemed impressively high to my dulled Chicago eyes.

What was this mysterious place? The next day someone told me, "That's Windrock." It would be years before I learned that what I was really seeing was mostly Buffalo Mountain, including from west to east, Wolf Ridge, Little Toddy, Silvey Gap, Windrock Fields, the Pinnacle, and Sassafras Mountain. And on the other side to the north, on the unseen New River side, were Patterson Mountain and Hannah Lowe Mountain. No matter, Windrock was what almost everyone called this section of the escarpment marking the southern edge of the great upheaval that formed the coal-bearing Cumberlands.

Just as varied as these places were the people scattered around Windrock Mountain, descendants of men with Old Testament names who had fought in the American Revolution. On the south in the narrow valley between the mountain and Walden Ridge, virgin forest was cleared about 1800 by a veteran named Micajah Frost, soon to be joined by Moses Duncan, Moses Brown, Philip Seiber, and later William B. Smith. The isolated community of Frost Bottom thrived for half a century until a small-scale civil war broke out among the grandchildren of Micajah Frost during the actual Civil War.

Earlier in 1799, some miles to the west, a third Moses, Major Moses Winters, had built a mill in the gap in Walden Ridge where Oliver Springs is today. It would become a boom town after Henry Wiley returned victorious from the Union army and established a coal dynasty.

Over the mountain, however, in sealed-off New River Valley, life hardly changed for a hundred years after Isaac Phillips settled about 1812. The Bunches, Daughertys, Pattersons, and Lowes came, too, but it took World War I and the timber industry's greed for the virgin trees to bring the area into the twentieth century.

Back in the 1880s, while New River still slept, farmers like the Duncans and the Bradens at Graves Gap came down the south side of the mountain and headed east up Coal Creek Valley to burrow in the new dark tunnels with pick and shovel. Even miners from Wales arrived, as well as state convicts from Nashville. By 1891 the Coal Creek War had erupted between miners and the Tennessee militia over this convict labor. But the frenzied search for coal went on, barely slowed by the two-year conflict or by two devastating mine explosions after the turn of the century. Ernest Hill in Fraterville lived to remember these momentous events, as did Jim McCoy and Mae Martin Carroll in Briceville.

Near the top of Windrock Mountain above Oliver Springs another mine opened in 1904 with the completion of the L&N Railroad's Cow Creek Branch. This was the fabled Windrock Mine. John T. Smith, grandson of Frost Bottom's William Smith, worked for the L&N in the earliest days before signing on at the mine. He knew not only about everyone and everything along the branch line but also about all the other places and people, dead and alive, around Windrock all the way back to the very beginning, to his great-great-grandfather Micajah Frost.

Cherokees still lived up on Windrock when this Micajah Frost first went north over Walden Ridge to the foot of the mountain called "Quasi-oto" and saw his wilderness of silent giant trees. It was 1795. Fifteen years had gone by since he fought as a teenager with the legendary John Sevier against Dragging Canoe's

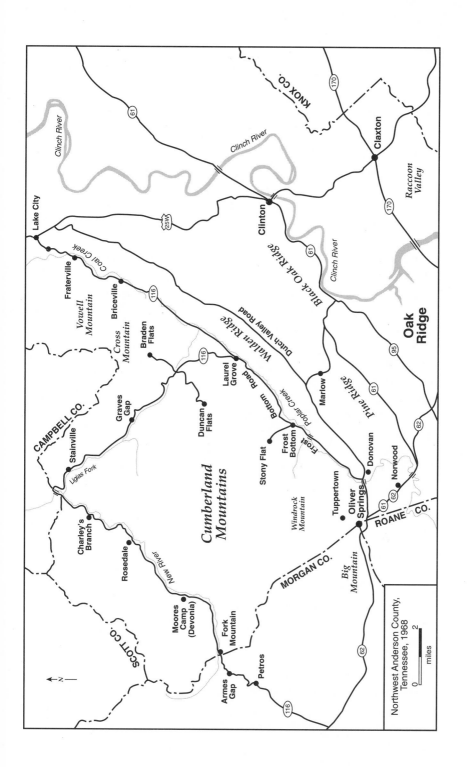

Northwest Anderson County, Tennessee, 1968

0   miles   2

N

KNOX CO.

Claxton

Raccoon Valley

170

170

Clinch River

Clinch River

Clinch River

61

61

Lake City

Clinton

25W

Black Oak Ridge

Oak Ridge

Fraterville

Coal Creek

Briceville

116

Vowell Mountain

Cross Mountain

Braden Flats

Walden Ridge

Dutch Valley Road

95

Graves Gap

116

Laurel Grove

Marlow

61

CAMPBELL CO.

Stainville

Duncan Flats

Bottom Road

Poplar Creek

Pine Ridge

62

Ugias Fork

Frost Bottom

Frost

Donovan

Norwood

62

Stony Flat

Tuppertown

62

Charley's Branch

Cumberland Mountains

Windrock Mountain

Oliver Springs

61

62

Rosedale

New River

ROANE CO.

SCOTT CO.

Moores Camp (Devonia)

Fork Mountain

MORGAN CO.

Big Mountain

62

Armes Gap

Petros

116

warriors on this frontier. The bloody running skirmishes with the Cherokees during the American Revolution gave the sturdy bearded man in buckskins good reason to respect the Indians, especially after one encounter on the Hiwassee River not far from today's Chattanooga.

Many years later, when he was seventy, Micajah Frost received an annual Revolutionary veteran's pension of $33.33. In his pension application he described as though 1780 were yesterday how his Virginia militia rendezvoused with Captain William Elliott before marching south to the Cherokee Nation to join Sevier. "We chased the Indians over the country occasionally coming in contact with them and took several of their towns," as he recollected. And young Micajah stopped an arrow, though the wound apparently made much less of an impression on him than did what happened to Captain Elliott.

It was near the bend where the Hiwassee came into the Tennessee River. The old soldier called it "a little engagement" in which the militiamen shot across the river and hit one of the warriors. "Captain Elliott rode over to scalp him, thinking he was dead. The Indian had squatted in the sage grass, and when the captain approached, he shot the captain in the head." What happened next Micajah Frost failed to say, but very likely the Cherokee's scalp was collected once the militia saw to it that the dead Indian was really dead. In those violent days when pregnant women, both brown and white, had been known to be disemboweled, scalping came quite naturally. Even as late as 1793 Indian scalps with the right ear attached would bring a bounty of $168 in the village of Cincinnati. Old Micajah couldn't recall the exact date that that particular Indian scalp cost Captain Elliott his life, but it was some time during the "warm winter" before the teenage militiaman marched with a thousand mountaineers across the Blue Ridge to the glorious victory against the Tories at Kings Mountain in October 1780.

Now, in 1795 it was different. Dragging Canoe had died and left the Cherokees retreating. Micajah Frost was starting a new life in what would become Anderson County in the soon-to-be state of Tennessee. A man in the prime of life, he had come with most of the Frost family—father, mother, uncles, aunts, his own wife Nancy and children—from up on the Holston River in Washington County, Virginia. And with his brother Elijah, he had bought a thousand forest-covered acres that backed up against Windrock Mountain, although by treaty this land still belonged to the Cherokees.

Who was this Micajah Frost?

His family numbered among the hundred thousand settlers who by 1800 had either pushed west through Cumberland Gap or, like the Frosts, followed the Holston River south. Almost certainly Micajah was the grandson of one Joseph

Frost, who received a grant of 170 acres from King George III in 1764 in present-day Amherst County, Virginia, near Lynchburg. Nothing much is known about this Joseph except that he had already lived on that land for at least eleven years before the grant. As was often the case in this vast new country where boundaries were vague, he may have just moved there and claimed the tract by squatter's rights. Certainly, it would not have been unusual for a hardworking immigrant to come to the colony as an indentured servant for seven years and then, when he had his freedom, make a new life without stigma. Joseph Sr. may have been such a man or even the son of one, since traces of Frosts in Virginia go back nearly a hundred years before that grant in 1764.

These earlier Frosts could have been among the religious Dissenters who fought with Oliver Cromwell to overthrow the English monarchy only to be betrayed by Puritan persecution. Cromwell's Parliament in 1646 passed a law calling for lifelong imprisonment of Baptists. And the Frosts were Baptists. At least it is certain Joseph Sr.'s son, the Reverend John Frost, became a well-known licensed preacher in 1780 and organized a Baptist church before the family left Virginia. Although how and when Joseph Sr. got his start is speculation, certainly his sons, the Reverend John, Thomas, and Joseph Jr., prospered. The three owned land on either side of the James River in Amherst and Bedford Counties. It was in 1764, the year of the grant, that Thomas had a second child, a son named Micajah born several miles from Lynchburg.

Only three years earlier, Elisha Wallen or Walden, with eighteen or twenty "long hunters," went from Virginia over into what is now Tennessee and Anderson County. These were the professional hunters who got their name from the long periods of time they spent in the wilderness, at least a winter, sometimes a year or more. Walden Ridge, the distinctive formation with its near-vertical rocks running all the way from Virginia to Chattanooga, was named for the long hunter Elisha. This is the same Walden Ridge where John T. Smith built his small house, where he gave me his father Jasper's Frost Bottom stories, that jumble of undated copies of newspaper clippings from the 1920s.

Two of those articles add to the local belief that Daniel Boone, the most famous long hunter of them all, knew Walden Ridge. A man named Sol Rhea told Uncle John's grandfather William how he had come with Boone though upper East Tennessee, crossed the Clinch River, and gone through Dutch Valley, stopping to rest on the south side of Walden Ridge near Duncan Springs. Daniel sat down on a rock to repair his moccasins before heading on toward Windrock Mountain. Years later, when William Smith's brother Tom followed that same route, Tom stopped to rest and found Boone's name and date cut on the very rock he was sitting on. The skeptic might unkindly ask how many thousands of rocks in the Appalachians could possibly have that name. One thing is sure: hunters did like to carve their names and Boone did hunt in Tennessee in 1771–72.

Legend aside, Boone was a real man who, like the Indians, followed the rivers and the trails beaten down by the bison. What he and the other long hunters found was a mystically beautiful land of rounded peaks and primeval forest with murmuring pines and hemlock that would later inspire the poet Longfellow. It was also a land of magnificent hardwoods like the poplars growing two hundred feet high, all but untouched by the native inhabitants. So bountiful was this country that the Cherokees and the Chickasaws put aside tribal quarrels to hunt along the Clinch River, which they called the Pellissippi. In the river bottoms, buffalo grazed while elk and deer and black bears shared the cool dark of the forests with mountain lions. The sky above the canebrakes and beaver dams often darkened with flocks of waterfowl like the great blue heron.

Even the Iroquois came down from the Great Lakes to hunt. They could cross the narrow bit of land between the upper reaches of the Clinch and the Ohio Rivers. When the first white men arrived, the Cherokees had well-organized towns on both sides of the southern Appalachian Mountains, about 160 before 1776. Only temporary hunting villages were located in what is now Anderson County, one of these in a place to be called Frost Bottom.

So valuable was the early fur trade that the British had gone to great lengths to keep the Cherokees friendly many years before Daniel Boone. Sir Alexander Cuming came to South Carolina in the 1720s and eventually took six befeathered braves, including Little Carpenter, on that famous journey back to London to visit George II. Winning over this major tribe was crucial in England's struggle with France for the new continent, a struggle that climaxed in the French and Indian War. When finally France was decisively defeated at Quebec in 1759, the British had cleared the way to settle the country clear to the Mississippi. But England had no interest in moving west, wanting only the big profits from her seaboard colonies. And certainly she wanted no more Indian wars. As a result, George III's Proclamation of 1763 declared that the land west of the crest of the Appalachians belonged to the Indians and white settlers should keep out.

It would have taken much more than the king's imaginary line and dangerous Cherokees, however, to hold back the land-hungry Europeans. Not long after 1700, waves of immigrants started pushing down from Pennsylvania, many of them Scotch-Irish. These were descendants of Presbyterians from the Scottish Lowlands that James I had resettled in Ulster as a bridgehead in his unsuccessful attempt to conquer Catholic Ireland. The Scots had found a miserable life there, facing religious persecution by the Anglican

Church. Exactly how many of these immigrants to America who were pushing into Virginia were Scotch-Irish is hard to say since experts agree that surnames are not a reliable guide. Certainly there were Protestants of all persuasions, not only from England but Germany and France.

Whether the first Joseph Frost was part of that surge in the eighteenth century or had been in Virginia even earlier, his three sons had the same restlessness of the new settlers. Although they owned a considerable amount of land near Lynchburg, deeds show that ten-year-old Micajah's father Thomas and his Uncle John sold their farms early in 1776. The American Revolution was under way in the north, but they moved across the Blue Ridge to the frontier in Washington County, Virginia, near present-day Kingsport, Tennessee. They must have been like many other adventurous settlers ready to give up security for more land, the most highly prized possession of these people. In their blood flowed that of the Celts and Saxons who centuries before had lost everything to the feudal lords of Normandy.

The Frosts resettled at Moccasin Gap not far from the Watauga settlements. These outposts in Cherokee territory had begun seven years earlier when William Bean built a cabin on Boone's Creek. Most of those who followed came from North Carolina, including some of the "Regulators" who escaped hanging after a rebellion over British taxes. These were courageous, aggressive men like Valentin Sevier and Evan Shelby, the latter the builder of a stockade and trading post near today's Bristol. Their sons John Sevier and Isaac Shelby would become famous as Indian fighters.

Just before the Revolution, these Wataugans and probably the Frosts, too, had some reason to be optimistic about relations with the Indians because of a daring North Carolina land speculator, Richard Henderson, who had grandiose plans for a new colony. This judge from Salisbury had, early in 1775, negotiated an amazing treaty with Chief Little Carpenter at Sycamore Shoals to purchase from the Cherokees most of what is now Kentucky and a big chunk of Tennessee, supposedly for ten thousand pounds. He was more than glad to resell the relatively small area wanted by the Watauga Association.

Henderson's scheme for his Transylvania colony relied on Daniel Boone, who already knew the Kentucky country and had started to hack out a way for the settlers through Cumberland Gap. Although his Wilderness Road would for years remain more trail than road, that did not dampen enthusiasm as it became the symbol of the opening of the West. Henderson's grand plan, however, suddenly came to a halt with the Minutemen's rebellion in Lexington and Concord. And war with the Cherokees was not over. Dragging Canoe, a son of Little Carpenter, refused to accept his father's deal at Sycamore Shoals, saying he would make the land "dark and bloody" as he drove the white man out of Indian hunting grounds. In a few short years, Micajah Frost would find out from an arrow that Dragging Canoe meant what he said.

With the colonists' uprising, the Cherokees allied themselves with the British in hopes of preserving their land. So the first years of the American Revolution for the Frosts and other families scattered on the Appalachian frontier meant farming with one ear always listening for an Indian attack. In the war, when the British could not stop the rebellion up north, they decided to do it through the soft underbelly of the South. By May 1780, a staggering defeat had been dealt the Continental Army in Charleston, South Carolina. Then the aggressive new leader, Lord Cornwallis, thought he could see his way clear across the Carolinas to Virginia. But ferocious war erupted in the backcountry between the patriots and their loyalist neighbors.

Cornwallis entrusted his important western flank in South Carolina to Major Patrick Ferguson, who found making Tory converts a bloody job. The British forces plundered farms, burning as they went and fighting off the hit-and-run attacks of patriots like Colonel Isaac Shelby, who gave as good as they got. It was Shelby who had first come over the mountains to fight the King's army and convinced John Sevier to help organize a force of mountaineers to cross the Blue Ridge and catch Major Ferguson. Even fears of Indian attack on their unprotected settlements would not stop them.

Colonel William Campbell was crucial to this audacious expedition destined to end at Kings Mountain. The redheaded Scotch-Irish giant, all six feet six inches, headed the militia in Micajah Frost's Washington County. The Virginian provided four hundred riflemen, the largest contingent of the makeshift army. It included a number of teenagers like Micajah since militia service usually began at sixteen, turning boys into men.

After young Private Frost's encounter with Dragging Canoe's braves on the Hiwassee, he had volunteered for a second tour of three months under a certain Captain Finley. The captain's men had the important task of guarding lead mines being worked by Hessian prisoners captured at Saratoga. Suddenly a courier arrived at the mines, near present-day Wytheville, with an urgent "express," a message to join Colonel Campbell. As many as could be spared were to rendezvous at Sycamore Shoals, that same meeting ground on the Watauga River where Henderson thought he had bought Kentucky from the Cherokees five years earlier.

So Micajah Frost found himself standing there in the warm autumn sunshine on the Watauga ready to go in fringed hunting shirt and leggings, hair tied back in a queue under a slouch hat. It was September 26, 1780. More than a thousand men, some with their families, heard the Reverend Samuel Doak urge them to go forth with the sword of the Lord. The young Virginia militiaman had no sword but a hunting knife on his belt along with a lead shot bag and a pouch of cornmeal and maple sugar. The powder horn slung over his shoulder was nearly as important as his long rifle with its thirty-inch barrel. Thanks to Pennsylvania gunsmiths like Jacob Dickert, frontiersmen could count on their accurate hunting rifles to kill a deer—or a man—three times as far as a musket could fire.

Mounting their horses after good-byes that morning at Sycamore Shoals, the backwoodsmen headed toward Roan Mountain. By October 6, the Americans camped at the Cowpens, a common grazing area in the north part of South Carolina, and got news of Ferguson's location not far to the east on the sixty-foot-high ridge called Kings Mountain. Colonel Campbell was elected commander of the combined forces, which included the militias under Isaac Shelby and John Sevier.

That night Campbell ordered the men to march. They left in drizzling rain. By midafternoon, the wet and hungry backwoodsmen encircled the base of the long ridge where about 1,100 loyalists had set up tents on the flat summit. Although the rain had finally stopped, the damp fallen leaves remained silent under foot. Even Ferguson's pickets were surprised when Colonel Campbell gave the yell to attack.

The woods came alive with noise and flame and smoke as Micajah and Campbell's other militiamen charged up the rocky ridge, many with slugs in their mouths for fast reloading. Taking cover behind trees Indian-style, the mountain men picked off their enemies. Often the Tories overshot the heads of the climbing sharpshooters, who kept up their war whoops. After a chaotic hour, a white flag went up on the loyalist side. When it was over, 157 of the enemy were killed, including Major Ferguson, who had been shot from his white horse. Another 164 were badly wounded and left to die, while nearly 700 were taken prisoner. Only 28 of the attackers lay dead, and 62 had been wounded.

That night the victorious, exhausted men from over the Blue Ridge slept there on the summit among the dead and wounded. Micajah Frost, so many years afterward, remembered Virginian James Curry, a sergeant "shot through the bowels." He carried water to Curry in his shoe and did what he could until the sergeant died at gray daylight. Among the dead he also remembered a man named Blackburn and four others all surnamed Edmonson with whom he was well acquainted.

With vultures starting to circle, the dead were quickly buried the next morning as fear of the British cavalry mounted. So hurriedly were the bodies dumped into pits and covered with earth, logs, and rocks that hogs and wolves found them even before local searching Tories did. Colonel Campbell headed the prisoners out on the long march to the Continental headquarters in Hillsborough, North

Carolina, but Micajah quite likely returned home with most of the other Virginians under Colonel Sevier. Word had arrived that Dragging Canoe planned to attack the overmountain settlements, something Sevier, now riding home with Major Ferguson's sash, was determined to stop.

Micajah had served under Sevier once before, and after Kings Mountain, he did one more tour with the militia. But it was not until 1782 that he again "marched to the frontiers." Although Cornwallis had surrendered at Yorktown in October 1781, vicious warfare continued between settlers and Indians. Micajah went out under a Captain Trimble because of trouble near Castlewoods on the Clinch River, where he served as a spy. Later that year Micajah had to return to that outpost with the same dangerous assignment as a scout and came "very near to being caught by the Indians several times."

During those years of revolution the Frost clan worked and protected their Washington County land as best they could. They had gone there in 1776, but by 1795, with the war over, they wanted to move on. The future state of Tennessee would be their destination in part because of Richard Henderson's grandiose dreams before the American Revolution. After the colonies gained their freedom, the new states of Virginia and North Carolina declared his purchase of millions of acres from the Cherokees illegal. But in 1783 Henderson won a consolation prize, a grant of two hundred thousand acres along the Powell and Clinch Rivers running down into what is now Anderson County.

A man named Stockley Donelson surveyed this huge tract for Henderson. Apparently he fell out with Henderson over rigging this so-called Big Survey in order to save some of the choice land for himself. A wheeler-dealer speculator with thousands of acres of his own, Donelson had plenty of connections, not the least of which were through his wife Elizabeth. She was the sister of James Glasgow, the North Carolina secretary of state, the official who issued land grants. And Donelson's own sister Rachel became the wife of General Andrew Jackson, the same Rachel whose unintentional bigamy played a part in more than one of the hotheaded general's duels.

It was from Donelson that Thomas Frost in 1795 bought his 640 acres in Raccoon Valley. Thomas became the first landowner to record a deed in what would become Anderson County for his land along Edgemoor Road near what is now the Tennessee Valley Authority's Bull Run Steam Plant. The Frosts must have been resolute people. Thomas was the middle son, a man of sixty, but he and his brothers, the Reverend John and Joseph, sold most of their Washington County land and for the second time uprooted themselves to move to the frontier. Thomas's six children joined the trek, including his two oldest sons Elijah and Micajah, men in their thirties with families of their own. These sons also bought from Donelson a tract of a thousand acres in what would become Frost Bottom. Such a large family migration surely took many packhorses, possibly even a wagon—in spite of there being no real roads—all loaded down with axes, saws, bedding, clothes, iron pots, flour, beans, cornmeal, and, of course, seeds for planting. Thomas's family Bible came, too, with births and deaths—every bit as important as the long rifles—and maybe even a prized piece of china tucked in with the essentials for eating.

This place called Raccoon Valley, where Thomas Frost settled in 1795, still belonged to Knox County, a part of the Southwest Territory. Only nine years before, twenty miles to the south, Captain James White had built a cabin on a bluff above the Tennessee River. More cabins and a log palisade turned the place into White's Fort, soon renamed Knoxville. It was a rowdy jumping-off place for adventurers, settlers, and all kinds of restless new Americans on the move west. A visitor named James Weir, maybe a straitlaced German Protestant, was shaken by the general uproar he found there caused by what he described as "a promiscuous throng of every denomination, blanket-clad Indians, leather-shirted woodsmen, gamblers, hardeyed and vigilant." Cheap whiskey loosened so many tongues that trading days and even Sundays became a bedlam of shouting, swearing, singing humanity. Brawling flatboatmen and soldiers added to the loud scramble of life in this frontier river settlement.

As if Indians didn't cause enough trouble, outlaws plagued the area. The most infamous were the Harpe Brothers, cruel highwaymen who enjoyed torturing their victims after robbing them. At least once they got rid of a body by ripping the man's stomach out and filling his corpse with rocks before throwing it in the Holston River. Big Harpe, whose first name, incidentally, was Micajah, met his end when a posse, including the husband of a woman the criminal had killed along with her baby, caught up with him. The story goes that the husband hacked off Harpe's head with a butcher knife while he was still alive. Little Harpe escaped but later made the mistake of trying to collect the reward for a fellow bandit. Again a severed head played a key part in the grisly story, for Little Harpe rolled up the outlaw's head in blue clay for proof to collect the money. This happened a long way off in Natchez, but unluckily for Harpe a man from Knoxville recognized him. This John Bowman had reason to remember Little Harpe because they had had a wild fight back home. And Little Harpe found himself at the end of a rope.

The Harpes were feared in Raccoon Valley, but because of the Cherokees' promise "to take hair," the Indians were feared even more. Before the arrival of the Frosts, the Treaty of the Holston had been signed in 1791. It protected the Cherokee lands north and west of the Clinch River while white settlers were allowed south of the river in places like Raccoon Valley. Nevertheless, right there in Raccoon Valley in May 1793, Thomas Gillam and his son James were scalped. The marauding Indians disappeared toward Windrock Mountain into the Cumberlands. Later that same week Holman's blockhouse, located near where the Gillams had been killed, came under attack although the Cherokees were driven off.

Amid such violence, in 1796 Tennessee gained statehood. The following year, just before leaving office, President George Washington sent out to this southwest frontier one of his trusted Valley Forge officers. Major Thomas Butler was made commander of Fort Southwest Point just a short way down the Clinch River where Kingston is today. His orders were to do a better job of preserving peace than his predecessor by keeping the white settlers on the south side of the river, the area where Thomas Frost had legally entered his deed. Captain Richard Sparks, who was replaced by Butler, had ordered illegal settlers to move or face a thousand-dollar fine and a year in jail. Outraged, they simply ignored him, protesting that Congress was making war on them when it should be subduing the Indians.

When Major Butler took over, his policies proved harsh on those unlawfully holding land. Consequently, people almost immediately started pushing for another treaty that would allow whites to move north of the Clinch River into Dutch Valley right up to the southern base of Walden Ridge. By 1798 the Cherokees yielded and signed the First Treaty of Tellico. However, even this did not make Micajah Frost's purchase legal, because his land was on the north side of Walden Ridge. Under that 1798 agreement the Cherokees got a guarantee that the rest of the territory would remain theirs forever. "Forever" hardly lasted until the ink dried. Immediately the pressure was on again from settlers itching to cross Walden Ridge and get as much of the Cumberlands as possible. And, of course, they did. By 1805 the whites won the Third Treaty of Tellico, giving them the Cumberland Plateau and much of middle Tennessee.

Where Micajah Frost was living those first years after he had bought the thousand acres in Cherokee territory is not clear. Rather than settle in what would become Frost Bottom, he may have stayed near his father Thomas in Raccoon Valley during the struggles over the treaties. Anderson County was broken off from Knox in 1801, and the following year Micajah's name appeared on the new county's first tax list as a Raccoon Valley landowner. It had been nearly twenty years since the daring rush across the mountains to defeat the Tories at Kings Mountain. Now, however, Micajah was a man with responsibilities, perhaps more cautious, not wanting to move to the foot of Windrock until the Indian question was settled.

In the meantime, various Frosts took root in Raccoon Valley. By 1798, with the revival spirit of the Second Awakening, they had started the first Baptist church in what would soon become Anderson County. It was a forerunner of the twenty-two Baptist churches that Micajah's younger half-brother Joshua would organize all over the county in the next fifty years, including one in Frost Bottom and another in Oliver Springs.

Down the river, Colonel Butler commanded the army's Fort Southwest Point until 1801. Soon after he left, he gained brief national fame because of a court-martial over his braid, or queue, as it was called. Washington's stalwart soldier ignored the order of General James Wilkinson, commander of the U.S. Army, that the hair of all officers must be "cropped without exception." Many Revolutionary veterans like Butler still wore queues. His friend Andrew Jackson vehemently appealed to President Thomas Jefferson to stop what Jackson called persecution of such an "upright" officer over his hair, one of the "gifts of nature."

But neither Jackson's fiery letter nor *The Federalist* newspaper's ridicule of the whole matter in Washington did any good, for the case got mixed up in politics. The colonel was court-martialed not once but twice, the second time in 1805. Taken off active duty, he died soon afterward still defying General Wilkinson. Butler supposedly told friends on his deathbed, "Bore a hole through the bottom of my coffin right under my head, and let my queue hang through it, so that the damned old rascal may see when dead I still refuse to obey his orders." At least that is how Washington Irving tells the story in his satirical *Diedrich Knickerbocker's History of New York*.

News about the old soldier, however, very likely never got over Walden Ridge into isolated Frost Bottom.

Mr. Frost's New Eden

That day in March 1801, when Thomas Jefferson walked from his boarding house to the unfinished Capitol to be inaugurated as president, Micajah Frost was also taking charge of a new domain. Far from Washington, Frost Bottom existed like a small forest kingdom where only a few clearings let in the sunlight. There Micajah was "king bee." At least that was what Jasper Smith called him some 125 years later in the *Anderson County News*.

Uncle John Smith gave me copies of many of Jasper's articles based on family stories. Although Jasper was not born until 1848, his father, William B. Smith, had firsthand knowledge of early-nineteenth-century life. All his life Jasper remained unusually close to his father, a poor orphan from Haywood County over in the North Carolina mountains.

William moved to Tennessee to wed Micajah Frost's granddaughter Elizabeth Duncan in 1829. As a boy, her father, Moses M. Duncan, arrived in Frost Bottom with his family not long after Micajah. The Frosts eventually moved on up to the Cumberland Plateau, but Moses stayed put until his death in 1872, marrying three wives and fathering twenty-one children. When Jasper was grown, just after the Civil War, he knew Moses as a "go-ahead" man with a fiery temper. He was the kind who left a strong impression on everyone even though, Jasper said, he "was unlearned and didn't know one letter." Moses certainly did know, however, what Frost Bottom was like when Micajah was king bee. Besides, it hadn't changed a good deal when William first visited in 1828 and decided to return and marry Elizabeth the following year. To Jasper, it seemed as though he himself had been there in those early days, so close was his

Jasper Smith, chronicler of the Duncans and the Smiths in the *Anderson County News* during the 1920s, pictured before his death in 1932. Photograph courtesy of W. H. Smith.

connection to Moses and especially to William. As an old man, William once told Jasper he wished they could die at the same time and be buried in the same coffin.

Still feeling this strong tie many years later, Jasper couldn't resist an invitation from County Agent Elrod, who one day in 1924 came by the Smith farm. He wanted white-bearded Jasper to ride with him just over Walden Ridge to Frost Bottom. At first, Micajah's great-grandson said no. He liked to remember where he was born as it had been before the Civil War, "almost a heaven" he called it, back when the soil was not worn out. Besides, as Jasper explained in his first column, "I didn't want to go up there, because all the old settlers are dead, gone to the spirit land. People are not like they used to be. People used to go barefooted 'til Christmas, now little children have to wear shoes the year round or they're nothing thought of. They have grown to be proud and haughty." Why, he could remember a man named Philip Sartin, whose bare feet were so tough he could hold down briars with them while hoeing. In his old age Jasper often found himself longing for the last century when no one in Frost Bottom could have imagined the Roaring Twenties and flappers with bobbed hair and dresses above the knee. Not to mention the Bolsheviks or Dr. Freud.

But he did finally go with Mr. Elrod, if not very enthusiastically. When they got across Walden Ridge, Mr. Henly, the mailman, rode up and started talking. He asked why this was called Frost Bottom since no Frosts lived there. Jasper told him how Micajah Frost was the first white man to build a house in the narrow valley and bury a loved one there, a small daughter named Nancy who drowned in Poplar Creek. She still rested up on Grave Hill next to the Frost Bottom Baptist Church.

Impressed, Mr. Henly interrupted him. "I guess you know all about this place."

"Yes, every inch, every groundhog hole in these mountains."

The mailman tested him, pointing down the road, "Who set out the apple trees yonder beyond the gap?"

That was easy.

"Tom Seiber about a hundred years ago, and they're bearing apples yet. I can remember lots of other trees over a hundred years old."

That reminded Jasper of the giant poplar tree that had stood near the spot where Micajah Frost built the first cabin. It was cut up into no fewer than four hundred rails by a man named Keith. "And there was another poplar that Joe Lively made a canoe out of it, it was seven feet wide. He took his family and all his house plunder in it down Poplar Creek to the Clinch River."

Jasper didn't know it at the time, but the trip with the county agent was the start of an undertaking that would last until his death in 1932. He would write some 170 short articles, preserved on microfilm of the old weekly newspaper—

not only stories of his family in Frost Bottom and Clinton but mixed in, often in the same column, obituaries of old-timers, strong opinions on the Bible, and endless warnings against the evils of the modern world. Together they make a repetitious, surprising collection, sometimes showing great intolerance and other times real wisdom.

As the years went by, Jasper's writing wandered more and more, though occasionally he would suddenly remember a wonderful story hidden away in some nook in his head, which he liked to describe as "full of brains but not cultivated." The Civil War had put an end to his formal schooling, but he read book after book by the light of a pine knot torch. Years later he served for a time as head of the county school board.

Jasper lived his last years with his son John's family. Those years were indelible in the mind of Uncle John's oldest son Herbert, who died in 1997. When he was in his eighties, Herb would describe how his grandfather Jasper spent most of his days in an office he had made for himself in the farm granary and filled with books. There he read the Bible through, something he had done forty-one times. Herb could still hear Jasper's loud praying over some sick person, "Oh, Lord, let him live one more year!" He also liked to pray outdoors at an altar he set up on an uprooted chestnut tree close to where he raised turkeys. Although his white beard made him look a little like the Moses of the Ten Commandments, the old man's mind was not always on the past or the world to come. "He was a good lawyer though he didn't have a license," Herb remembered, laughing as he told about a boy named Charlie, who got drunk and pulled a gun on somebody. "Granddad said he could get the boy off if he would follow his advice in front of the judge. First thing was to wear clean overalls, but he had to be double sure they were patched ones. And he got off, too."

So it was that at age seventy-five Jasper became a newspaper columnist, starting with what he called "Frost Bottom History" under the byline of W. J. Smith. He didn't have many exact dates and sometimes contradicted himself, but vivid pictures emerged of life in the valley between Walden Ridge and Windrock Mountain. I remember my surprise when I first read the beginning of Jasper's history shortly after Uncle John gave me some of his father's writings: "Mr. Frost had a good number of slaves and he put them to cutting poplars, oaks and walnuts and plowing with their oxens." I wasn't expecting slaves, for they were not common in the mountains. And "Mr. Frost," as Jasper referred to his great-grandfather, seemed quite formal. Apparently Micajah was respected not only as the father of the settlement but also as a man of at least some wealth. Jasper made it clear he thought Mr. Frost deserved what he and the other immigrants had taken by "push and

Fifth- and sixth-generation descendants of Micajah Frost in 1992 in Loudon, Tennessee. The late W. Herbert Smith, oldest son of Uncle John Smith, was seated in front of his daughter Marita and her husband, Darell George. Photograph by the author.

pull" from the Cherokees. Although he saw the Indians as murdering savages, Jasper admitted he still pitied them. The red men were here first and defended their homeland from the covetous white race, he once went so far as to say. The subject seemed to bother his conscience a number of times.

But in the end Jasper relied on God's mysterious ways to explain how the Indians happened to be in this new land. Where they came from couldn't be understood, he said, "and I don't think that it is any of our business." He did wonder, however, about Esau since the Bible describes him as a red man and a cunning hunter. Wasn't it possible that God had placed Esau's tribe in the American wilderness because they had been wicked? Jasper firmly believed "disobedience caused the colored races, because white is the emblem of innocence and purity." He would just as soon have not brought up the whole unpleasant subject, but he had to, Jasper explained, in order "to make my history fit together."

However it happened that the Cherokees were in this vast wilderness first and that Micajah Frost had fought them with John Sevier, the king bee now enjoyed the spoils of victory under the virgin walnuts and poplars in Frost Bottom. According to Jasper, the Frosts were soon joined by other victors of the push and pull with the Indians. Moses Duncan and Moses Brown came with their families from Yellow Creek, Kentucky, near Cumberland Gap. The two families had been through much together. Sounding like the old ballads about sailing the deep salt sea, Jasper told how Benjamin Duncan and William Brown, fathers of those two Moses, left Scotland on "a frail ship that rode the foaming water for weeks." They landed in North Carolina just before the American Revolution started. "They went to General Washington and told him they wanted to fight for freedom, and they wanted to stay together," Jasper said. They did and, after the war, married and moved their families to Yellow Creek. Finally Ben Duncan, aged and scarred from war, died in Kentucky in 1803. His widow and children, including Moses, moved to Frost Bottom. Jasper thought it was earlier, however, saying the Duncans built a log cabin there in 1799 that still stood when Jasper wrote his column over 120 years later. If the date 1799 is right, then Micajah Frost had ignored the Indian treaties and taken root in Frost Bottom well before Thomas Jefferson became president.

The location of a different log house built in those early days was what Uncle John and I were searching for one warm, sunny June afternoon in 1968 when we went to Frost Bottom. I had just read Jasper Smith's history. I was a bit confused by so many people named Moses and Isaac and Elijah, but nonetheless enthusiastic about this journey back to the edge of two hundred years. What people today call Frost Bottom runs along Poplar Creek but also up into a secluded mountain cove. We left the creek, actually a small river when heavy rains came, and headed up into the cove on Half Moon Road, then branched off to find Stony Flat at the foot of the mountain. This was where Uncle John's father, Jasper, was born in 1848.

It had been years since my guide had been in that deserted part of Stony Flat. But like a homing pigeon, Uncle John quickly found the place where the log cabin had stood. Quickly, and with great delight. In a grassy field full of foot-high clover he showed me the foundation of the fireplace near several split and rotted apple trees. The road there followed Stony Flat Creek, rushing down the mountain from high up at Peachtree Gap. Its clear water ran over slippery boulders in the cool, dark woods just as it had when Jasper Smith was born, but the road had all but vanished. Although the car groaned and rattled our bones as we left, Uncle John considered our trip a completely successful venture. "Yes, sirree, Sister, we found it!"

Earlier in the afternoon, before leaving the settled part of Frost Bottom, we had made a stop at the old Methodist cemetery. It was carefully mowed although the church was long gone, "just got weaker and weaker," according to my guide. Apparently the Baptists had gotten stronger and stronger. Uncle John wanted us to visit Moses Duncan's grave. His tombstone in the quiet glade had a kneeling angel to announce that Moses fought in the War of 1812 and died in 1872. It doesn't say so, but he was probably born in 1795. Nancy Nolen, his third wife, who is buried next to him, lived until 1903.

A second stop before reaching Stony Flat that afternoon had been at a weathered rambling house with a swing on the porch and beehives in the yard. It belonged to Frost Bottom's oldest resident, Big Andrew Duncan's widow, Sally. Ninety-six years old, she was busy cooking dumplings, though she declared she was not her usual self. "Not been right since hailstones come down the chimley and give me a cough," she said, keeping an eye on the coal burning in the front room grate, although the temperature outside was nearly eighty degrees. Sally Duncan remembered Moses Duncan's third wife, Nancy Nolen. Her first husband, Phillip, one of the Nolens, she explained, got killed in a fight long before Nancy died. We told her we were headed for Stony Flat, but Aunt Sally had no idea where to look for the location of William Smith's log house. Her house was so hot we said quick good-byes.

After our success in finding Jasper's birthplace, we headed west out of the valley toward Oliver Springs on the infamous Frost Bottom Road. I was busy navigating around the crevices while Uncle John talked about the Seibers, a German family among the earliest settlers. We were coming to the spot on Poplar Creek where John Seiber had had a gristmill.

"Them rocks're still thar," Uncle John shouted, pointing just as a monster coal truck roared past. We failed to get the car windows rolled up in time

Uncle John Smith at the tombstone of his great-grandfather Moses M. Duncan on our trip to Frost Bottom in 1968. Photograph courtesy of the *Oak Ridger*.

to keep out the storm of dust. That didn't stop him from telling one of his father's favorite stories about John Seiber. "Sister, he was a preacher but bad to drink whiskey." As the story went, Seiber would go to Clinton when court was in session and come home drunk, not an extravagant entertainment, what with whiskey only ten cents a quart. But his wife, Milly, absolutely did not approve and nagged so much that after one of the tipsy court trips on an especially wintry day John Seiber said he'd had enough of her tongue. Far gone with ten-cent liquor, he announced he was going down to his mill pond to drown himself. Milly's pleading and trying to hold him back by the coat-tail did no good. At the bank of the frozen creek, he made a solemn announcement: "Milly, you see me now, but shortly you will see me no more."

He jumped and broke a hole in the ice and hit bottom. The startling water changed his mind about suicide, but when he came up he wasn't under the hole and his head rammed into the ice. The Reverend Seiber went under again and the next time he came up he made another hole, this time with his skull. He gladly let Milly pull him to the bank.

Laughing as we bounced along the rough road, Uncle John loved telling that story. It reminded him of another one because Milly was the daughter of John Lively, another of the first settlers. In fact, his family had once owned much of the south side of Windrock Mountain. When Lively's log cabin burned, he and his wife spent the winter in a huge hollow sycamore. We passed where the legendary tree was supposed to have stood, so large a ten-foot pole could be turned around inside.

After the trip to Stony Flat, I kept thinking about how Jasper came to be born there and have William Smith for a father. William had grown up in the Smokies in Haywood County, but in 1828 came to Frost Bottom and ended up marrying Moses Duncan's daughter Elizabeth. Her mother was Micajah Frost's daughter Mary, making Micajah the great-great-grandfather of Uncle John. I wondered about William's life as a boy on Jonathan Creek near Waynesville, North Carolina. Who was his father, a man named Henry Wilson Smith?

"I don't know why my daddy didn't never write about my great-granddaddy Henry Wilson Smith," Uncle John said. That was not strictly true, for Jasper wrote more than once that Henry died in the War of 1812. The story I got from Uncle John was a very different one, and it was easy to see why he waited until Jasper was safely dead to tell it. Maybe John T. Smith got his Gaelic storytelling genes from his Irish great-grandfather Henry. To answer my questions about Henry, he gave me "A History Book of the Unknown Secret," a typed story he had dictated to his granddaughter Mary Beth some years earlier.

Although Uncle John loved to tell stories, he also had a hankering to write them in spite of very little education. Even after I moved away from Tennessee, he would send me short "histories" and sometimes poems, like his ballad about a sensational murder on Black Oak Ridge in 1921. A constable for many years, he must have been doubly interested in how "four bad men took a poor man's life." The four stole the car of a Mr. Crumley, then dumped him and his friend Mr. Lewis out for dead in an isolated spot. Part of the long poem goes

> Mr. Crumley was struck on the head.
> His throat was cut he was left for dead.
> He layed on the ground ever so still.
> Until he heard the car going up the hill.
> He had been hand in hand with death.
> So he just layed still and helt his breath.
> By the help of God on high
> His time had not yet come to die.

And because that time had not come, Mr. Crumley struggled through the dark woods for help, though it was too late for the dead Mr. Lewis, and the four murderers ended up in the electric chair.

Uncle John's history of Henry Smith and his strange disappearance is quite different from the poem but something he must have enjoyed doing. No doubt there would have been more stories like this one if his granddaughter down the hill had had the time and patience to take down what he told her and then help with the grammar. Here is part of what his granddaughter typed:

Henry Wilson Smith came from Ireland. He was born in the year 1765. As a boy he got it into his mind to come to this country. As they was loading a ship to come to this country he slipped into the ship. He left two brothers and one sister. His father and mother was dead. He was 14 years old when he left Ireland in 1779. When the ship left and got several miles out in the ocean, he came out where the captain could see him.

The captain asked the boy, "How did you get on this ship without me knowing it?"

The boy said, "I caught your back turned and I slipped in and hid between those big barrels."

So, the captain asked the boy where he wanted to go. And he said, "I want to go to the other side of this pond."

The captain said, "We're too far out in the ocean, we can't turn and go back, so I will just take you on to the other side of the pond as you called it."

So the captain fed the boy and took care of him until they landed. At the ship landing at South Carolina, the captain told the boy, "We are landed. The name of this country is South Carolina."

So the boy told him he wanted to get off. The captain said, "Hold on there just a minute. I'm going to give you 50¢." And so he did and told the boy to go and do the best he could.

So the boy started out on his journey not having any friends and no home not knowing which way to go. But he still had one friend. With his Heavenly Father to guide him, he wandered his way through the mountains of South Carolina being on Indian trails. So dark came on him, destitute of something to eat and no bed to lay on.

He turned and looked beside the trail. A little distance away he saw a big hollow log. He was talking to himself, "I will make my bed tonight in that big hollow log." It was dusty dark. He crawled into the log and was afraid to go to sleep, being wild animals of all kinds around. Along in the night he heared a noise at the end of the log. He just lay right still, then all at once something touched him. He was afraid to move, and the animal crawled up and lay down beside him, he still not knowing what it was. Being tired and sleepy he fell off to sleep. The animal kept him good and warm through the night.

When he awoke next morning, it was daylight, the animal still lying there. He didn't know what to do, so he just lay right still for a few minutes so I suppose the animal was still asleep. Then the animal awoke and crawled out of the log. He found out what it was. It was a big bear. It strolled away and didn't hurt the boy.

He crawled out of the log and went back to his path, still following the Indian trails through the mountains. He came across a mountain to the foot of it and found a little log cabin. He saw a little lady in the yard and stepped up to her and bowed his head and tipped his little red hat. He couldn't talk our language, so he made motions to her and she understood he wanted something to eat. She fixed him something to eat. He still had the 50¢ the captain gave him. While he was eating he was studying about his 50¢, "I will pay her for my meal." After he ate he told the lady in motions that he was from the old country. He offered her the 50¢. The good lady would not have it. She told him, "You may need it. You keep it as you journey on." So the boy kept it, bowed his head, and in motions thanked her for his food.

He started on his journey again, wandered his way through the mountains of South Carolina. He came out of South Carolina into Wilkes County, North Carolina. There he came to another log cabin. Just an old man and old lady lived there. The boy being hungry he wanted something to eat. The old man was beating hominy with a mallet. The old lady said to her husband, "Don't you see that boy pointing toward that kettle and then to his mouth?" The old man couldn't understand the boy. She said, "He is hungry, give him some of that hominy to eat." So the old man gave the boy the mallet and told him, "No beat, no eat." So the boy took the mallet and went to beating the hominy. After the hominy was beaten they fed the boy. The old man and his wife fell in love with the boy, took him in, and he lived with them 21 years.

He came over here in 1779 staying with them 21 years. That would make it 1800. My great-grandfather was 35 years old and he fell in love with a girl by the name of Mary Snider. Not being a long courtship, God joined them together. The old man he lived with let him build a log cabin on his farm. There were three children born into the home. He named his first child being a boy after himself, Henry Wilson Smith, born 1804. The next child was a girl. Her name was Tabitha born in 1809. The next boy, William B. Smith, was born Feb. 8, 1813. This was my grandfather.

My great-grandfather fought in the War of 1812. At the close of the war my great-grandmother got a letter from him that he would be home in about three weeks. In about another week she got a second letter telling her to do the best she could with the children, that he wouldn't never come home.

Uncle John's history goes on to explain what happened after that and how the baby boy William grew up and went to Frost Bottom. Nearly sixty years later, old William told his son Jasper, "Bud, I been studying about my father. I want you to write to Washington and see if they can find a record of him."

A lot of time went by after that letter was written in 1898 and they gave up ever hearing from the War Department. But then one day they did. The very official-looking reply said that Henry Wilson Smith had indeed fought under Andrew Jackson and gotten a "good honorable discharge." But the Washington bureaucrats knew nothing about what became of Henry afterward. A few months went by and William decided he had an answer to the secret. He told Jasper, "Bud, I been studying more about my father. He came from the old country Ireland. He was already away from home when he got his discharge so he just decided to go back to the old country where he was born."

After all those years, that may have been as good an explanation as any. However, it was far more likely that Henry Wilson Smith was one of the many new Americans with itchy feet always moving west, unlike the Duncans, who wanted nothing better than to guard their freedom in the Appalachian Mountains. If Henry had truly been the heroic adventurer of the first part of Uncle John's story, he may have headed for the turbulent frontier of Spanish Texas.

Whatever became of Henry Smith, his son William in the next sixty years led a vigorous life as a farmer and trader raising eleven children and surviving the Civil War. But in the early days things were not easy when William's mother found herself alone with three children. After a year or so, Mary Smith married a man named John McGhee and moved west from Wilkes County to Haywood County, North Carolina. Possibly she had gotten a divorce or maybe she committed bigamy. We may not take such things too seriously today, but certainly her grandson Jasper did. He wrote about McGhee, but always with the explanation that Henry Smith had died in the War of 1812. The importance of protecting his grandmother's honor must have outweighed the "sin," in the eyes of straitlaced Jasper, of telling a white lie. As I read and reread his many newspaper articles, I found this stretching of the truth rare. His usual way of dealing with family skeletons was simply to ignore them.

Jasper had plenty to say about John McGhee, all of it unflattering. Mary Smith's new husband, a one-armed schoolteacher with even more of a liking for whiskey than most mountain people, often put his wife in what Jasper called "a suffering condition."

One story stuck in Jasper's mind about his father William's early life with this hated stepfather. John McGhee would go to the county seat in Waynesville and drink himself deep in debt. His creditors would then get the law on him and auction off his property for payment. One time when this happened, a wealthy man named Colonel Sam Love showed up and made the highest bid for the family's cows.

Then the new owner said, "Here, Mrs. McGhee, you keep these cows and milk them 'til I call for them."

And when young William's pony went on the block, again the colonel was the buyer. He returned the animal to the boy, "Take her and do the best you can with her." That pony went to Tennessee when William left the Smokies, a sort of good luck talisman like Henry's fifty-cent piece.

Not without bitterness, Jasper described how his grandmother died and John McGhee married again, this time a whiskey dealer. He finally drank himself to death, but it took him until after the Civil War to do it. McGhee's dismal end brought forth one of Jasper's sharpest attacks on liquor, telling his reader, "Beware of the first drink, for whiskey is a curse to our land and in these last days the human who deals out the stuff to his fellow men is sending his own soul to hell and also the one who drinks the stuff."

William left North Carolina as a teenager for a new life in Frost Bottom. His marriage came nearly thirty years after the Frosts and Duncans and Browns and Seibers and Livelys arrived in their new Eden. Jasper Smith gave conflicting dates, so the wedding may have been in 1829 or 1831. Mr. Frost, or Grandfather Frost as Jasper occasionally called his great-grandfather, remains a shadowy figure in the stories about those earliest days around 1800. It is the Duncans who come alive in Jasper's retelling of the tales his go-ahead grandfather Moses must have told.

Moses Duncan was a boy when old Benjamin, his father, died up in Kentucky. Joshua, one of the grown sons, gathered up most of Widow Duncan's large family and moved them to Anderson County with little more than their axes and the buckskins on their backs. Joshua may have been joined by older brothers James and John, maybe even one named Samuel, as well as by other brothers and sisters, including young Moses and Isaac. All of this was unclear until recently, mainly because of a grown daughter named Juanna (Judy or Juda), who definitely did come. Judy lived and prospered in Frost Bottom until 1861, having twelve children but never a husband. How this unusual situation came about will probably never be explained, but what is certain is that for years Judy was a huge stumbling block for Duncans wanting to work on their genealogy. The descendants of some of Benjamin's other children include outstanding East Tennesseans like U.S. Representative John J. Duncan Jr. of the Second Congressional District. He holds the seat filled for many years by his father. The senior Duncan served as Knoxville's mayor before his election to Congress.

Judy Duncan was an independent woman who lived in her own two-story log house on Half Moon Road. She managed her large family well, successfully raising cattle and all their other food. Judy has been remembered as kind and always willing to help a neighbor. After she died in 1861, her first child, John R. Duncan, lived in the homeplace. It was not torn down until 1951, nearly a hundred years after she was buried up on Grave Hill. Although Judy was his grandfather Moses' sister, Jasper mentioned her only once. One sentence identified her as the great-grandmother of W. O. Duncan, the well-liked Methodist minister and Circuit Court clerk of Anderson County. Since cousins often married, I thought this Judy had married another Duncan.

"Oh, no, no, she never had a husband," Dixie Duncan Graves told me several years ago. This pleasant retired schoolteacher, a daughter of W. O. Duncan, was working on the much-delayed genealogy, which since her recent death has been completed by her longtime collaborator, Marjorie Duncan Byrd. Smiling, Mrs. Graves told how her father revealed the family's open secret before he died in 1951. "But who cares these days? Marjorie and I are going ahead with the genealogy, and the family charts will just show there was no husband." She added that people always said a surveyor out of Clinton was the father of most of the children, but that was too long ago to worry about—"It's history now!"

Still, I was surprised and downright fascinated. I had to remind myself that this was before Victorian ideas on sex. And though in colonial America fornication could bring on public whipping and heavy fines, that changed when the Revolution separated church and state. By the early nineteenth century the courts of the new republic overflowed with cases about land titles, not sexual morality. Far from towns, families in isolated forest clearings ran their lives as they saw fit. Even the appearance of a circuit-riding preacher was rare. This was the freedom the frontier offered in exchange for a hard life where every pair of hands able to work was important. That is not to say that most people didn't get married, but Widow Duncan must have welcomed all her many grandchildren, in or out of wedlock.

Nevertheless, I wonder what Micajah Frost thought about Judy Duncan. Although his half-brother Joshua was the famous Frost preacher, Micajah did some preaching himself. For sure the Reverend John Hoskins heard him because he is mentioned seven times in an early notebook Hoskins kept on religious meetings. On July 1, 1810, he wrote that Micajah preached on the Apostle Paul's strong admonition that women be obedient to men and never be allowed to speak in church, citing 1 Corinthians 14 and 1 Timothy 2. These chapters are neatly summed up in the latter epistle's verse 11: "Let the woman learn in silence with all subjection." Somehow that doesn't fit my picture of Judy Duncan, who surely had a mind of her own if she raised twelve children without a husband. In Jasper's various stories about preachers, he only once mentioned Micajah as one, and for some reason he never made clear when or why the king bee left Frost Bottom. Was there trouble over Judy, or did the old Frost urge to move on just reappear?

If Jasper wrote little about Micajah, he had much to say about the other early settlers. How, for example, Joshua Duncan managed the family's first days in the new Eden after they arrived from Kentucky. Here they would have not only freedom but plenty to eat, with corn, beans, and pumpkins soon growing to go with meat from wild animals shot for the family table without fear of gamekeepers. Of course, self-reliant Joshua knew what had to be done immediately when the family arrived, for this was not the first time the Duncans had ventured into the immense ocean of trees. "He put them to felling saplings near a spring," Jasper wrote, describing how they built a temporary shelter and covered it with pine tops as soon as they found a grindstone to sharpen their axes. After they finished the lean-to, the silence was broken again and again in the coming days by the ring of their axes. Hard chips of oak and hickory flew as a clearing for a house appeared. The smell of sap was quickly overpowered by that of smoke rising through the new opening in the canopy as the felled trees not needed for the cabin were burned. Finally a log house of about eighteen by twenty feet went up without a nail in it. Benjamin's children split logs for a puncheon floor and built a stick and clay chimney. The one-room cabin was roofed with four-foot hewn boards with rib poles on top to hold them in place.

Not too long after the Duncans arrived, Moses Brown Sr. and his family also came from Yellow Creek. He was a son of Benjamin Duncan's old friend William Brown from the days of the Revolution. This Moses had learned how to be an herb doctor from the Indians and had married Benjamin's daughter Elizabeth Duncan before leaving Kentucky. Then came Philip

Seiber, who had left Germany and settled a mile or so down Poplar Creek. It was his son John who would build the gristmill and try to drown himself in the pond. Before the mill, horses had to trample the grain. Philip put up a hewn log house like the Duncans' that was still standing when Jasper wrote about it over 120 years later: "I hope it will stand there until it rots. I love to look at an old log house. I was reared in one, I raised my family in one, it is no disgrace to live in one."

Within a few years after the arrival of Micajah's neighbors, the log homes would have upstairs lofts for sleeping, but at first all the children slept lined up in a row on a pallet of deer hides in front of a big fire—"and you can bet their families were not very small," according to Jasper. The father would keep "a good fire all night for fear the little ones would get cold or a spark jump out and burn them up and then his future would be gone."

Life was good despite wolves that could be heard in the night and ever-present bears and wildcats. In the canebrakes, cattle flourished even in the winter. Acorns two inches deep under the oaks fattened the settlers' half-wild hogs. All Joshua Duncan had to do for fresh meat was take his rifle down from above the door and shoot a turkey or deer. In addition to their garden vegetables, they had wild berries that grew everywhere—blackberries, huckleberries, elderberries, strawberries. Chestnuts covered the ground waiting to be roasted. In time they planted apple trees, providing fruit that was good to eat and essential for brandy. Over a century later the apple trees were still growing as Jasper showed the mailman the day he went with the county agent. He bemoaned how the native "sugar trees" had disappeared. These maples produced all the sugar anyone could need. But by the 1920s the weather was too warm, according to Jasper, who was convinced the winters used to be much colder. He remembered how as a boy he "helped carry hundreds of gallons of sugar water to the camp to boil off, and the snow would be one to four feet deep."

As the small settlement grew, Frost Bottom wanted a school. People pitched in to help a man from North Carolina, Levi Rice, build a hewn-log building on top of Walden Ridge. It opened with just one book, the Bible, and slate rocks with soapstone to write on. And for occasional "real" writing they used copy paper with goose quills and ink made of maple bark or pokeberries.

Learning to read and write was valued, but it was not nearly as important as the unending work necessary to produce nearly everything they ate and wore. One of Jasper's stories about clothing showed him to be more tolerant than usual on the subject of whiskey. Since deerskin clothing was too hot for summer, the settlers raised cotton and flax to weave into linsey-woolsey. Cotton was not complicated to prepare, but flax was. After the flax was pulled, it had to be spread out on the ground. When the inside rotted, the plants were bundled up and taken to a flax brake, a contraption made of split oaks lapped together like fingers, hinged in a way to separate the fibers. For fun along with the work, the boys and girls would sometimes have flax pullings. In this new Eden, where rattlesnakes and copperheads thrived, the older boys loved to tease that somebody would get bitten while they worked at the flax brake.

But no one really worried, as Jasper explained: "They always had a big gourd of corn whiskey or brandy sitting out to one side for fear of a snake bite. They'd drink a quart to kill the poison, and if a snake didn't bite them, they'd drink it anyway and think nothing of it. Every family kept it. Preachers drank it same as the rest, scarcely ever saw a man drunk. A great bottle of whiskey sat on the table at all times, beside it a bowl of sugar to sweeten the dram taken before saying grace for a meal."

Drinking distilled spirits was not something peculiar to the frontier. All Americans, including children and women, imbibed, so much so that annual per capita consumption reached five gallons by 1830, when the temperance movement began to gather momentum. Only the Swedes drank more than the citizens of this new republic, though the Scots made a contest of it.

There in Micajah's small kingdom a generation had already grown up by 1828 when William Smith came from the Smokies. Somehow Moses' brother Isaac Duncan had gotten to know William's sister Tabitha Smith over in North Carolina and married her, bringing his new bride back to Tennessee. It was for a visit with this sister that William Smith came to Mr. Frost's settlement.

The hard four-day trip from Haywood County through the mountains and down the French Broad to Knoxville and then on to Anderson County most likely took William though Clinton, the county seat. Originally called Burrville for Vice-President Aaron Burr, this small town of several hundred inhabitants had been rechristened in 1809 to honor De Witt Clinton, the New York statesman serving in the nation's second highest office. By then, no town wanted to be named Burrville. Aaron Burr had not only been labeled a murderer for killing Alexander Hamilton in a duel, he also found himself on trial for treason over a plot to create a new empire on the southwest frontier. General James Wilkinson, the same Wilkinson who had Colonel Butler court-martialed over his ponytail, was by then the army commander of the Mississippi Valley and in league with Burr. However, the general got cold feet and let President Jefferson know of the conspiracy, saving his own skin. Although friends in high places prevented Burr's conviction, Anderson County nevertheless renamed its county seat.

So it was that the town of Clinton sat on the north bank of the Clinch River in 1828, showing a few signs of progress despite the area's isolation. The log courthouse had been replaced in 1824 with a stone structure The public stocks and whipping post still in the public square would be gone the following year when William came back to marry Elizabeth. And a sweeping new state law that same year made many other changes. For one thing, a horse thief could no longer be hanged or even have his ears cropped and then be branded with an H on one cheek and a T on the other.

Penal reform in Tennessee was big news in 1829, but nothing compared to the inauguration of the state's own Andrew Jackson as the seventh president of the United States. Like Micajah Frost, a teenage veteran of the Revolution, Jackson had been the hero of the Battle of Horseshoe Bend against the Creek Indians and then superhero of the Battle of New Orleans in the War of 1812. No matter that a peace treaty had been signed in Belgium two weeks before Jackson's humiliating defeat of the British, this final military engagement helped put Old Hickory in the White House. The inauguration party when the mansion opened its doors to everyone is infamous to this day. Overexuberant country folk trampled damask sofas and smashed china and glassware before someone thought to move the barrels of whiskey punch out onto the lawn.

William and Elizabeth's marriage that same year must have also been a boisterous affair even without crystal to smash. Jasper wrote how 125 people fiddled and danced the night away while they drank up six gallons of corn liquor among other things. All this celebration came after the orphan boy in borrowed flax shirt and pants stood up with Moses Duncan's daughter before Squire William McKamey, who performed the ceremony. The squire followed it with a bit of cryptic advice, "Now, Bill, by George, honesty is the point." The party went on and on until Sim Hoskins and Ap Keith got into a fight over a keg of whiskey.

No one knows whether Elizabeth's grandfather Micajah was there that night. About that time, the old veteran of Kings Mountain left for Rockcastle County, Kentucky. Some records show him in Anderson County until 1834, but he declared on his pension application that he moved in 1828. Micajah and his wife Nancy probably had ten children there in Frost Bottom, including the small Nancy who drowned in Poplar Creek. Two of their sons died in the War of 1812. One of these was Winter (yes, that was his name) and another was Phinehas, who did not survive a British prison in Quebec. Their other sons, Thomas, Elliott, Samuel, Rolen, and Elijah, all apparently left Frost Bottom.

Son Elijah married Amelia Lonesome Patterson and had no fewer than seventeen offspring. He and Amelia moved up on the Cumberland Plateau near Crossville. Most of their children were born there before the family was swept up by the new Mormon movement, taking them to Illinois in the early 1840s and then on to Missouri. Elijah named his first son Micajah for his father, and later when he ran out of family names, he christened two sons White and Snow. And there was Sevier, pronounced "severe" in Tennessee. Later on, in a more serious time, he named two more sons Hiram and Young for the early Mormon leaders Hiram Smith and Brigham Young. Enough descendants of those seventeen children kept moving west to ensure that California eventually had its share of Micajah and Elijah Frosts. The first Micajah's half-brother Dr. Joseph Frost headed west, too. His descendants in San Antonio, Texas, shortly after the Civil War, founded what would become today's influential Frost National Bank.

Whatever happened to the first Micajah's older brother Elijah is a mystery. He had bought land in Frost Bottom with Micajah and lived there after 1809. Although he was important enough to be mentioned some twenty times in the minutes of Anderson County Court before 1814, Brother Elijah apparently either died or left the state. Not one hint of him is found in Jasper's history. So, the Frost name disappeared from Frost Bottom, although two of Micajah's daughters stayed and provided enough descendants for a community. Daughter Isabell married Samuel, son of the German immigrant Philip Seiber, and Mary became the first wife of Moses Duncan and the mother of Elizabeth Smith.

William Smith started a long and happy and often hard life with this Elizabeth in 1829. Farming from daylight until dark took great stamina, but still there was energy left for frontier pleasures like showing off one's skill as a marksman or a fighter. Sometime not long after his marriage, William played a big part in what local people still call the Shooting Match. After our trip to Stony Flat, his grandson Uncle John told the story with his usual enthusiasm, laughing and hitting his knee and ignoring any interruptions.

It is a tale of two more Moses. One was Moses Brown Jr., son of Moses the herb doctor, and the other, Moses C. Winters, son of the Moses who founded Winters's Gap. This Moses C. was an enormous man who loved a fight. As Uncle John began the tale, he wanted it clearly understood that his grandfather William was in the thick of the shooting match. "Awright, now, I know what I'm talking about. I heerd Granddaddy tell about it many a time."

The contest to see who was the best shot got a late start because the beef that was supposed to be the prize was too small. William sent for another one about twice as big, maybe six hundred pounds. "By the time the boys decided that one was all right and that they'd shoot for it, it was after night," Uncle John explained. "Now, Sister, they had fires built up so they could see to shoot the target on the tree. As usual, they had to have their drinks. They had a five-gallon keg of apple brandy with a faucet on the little keg. So during all the shooting, Brown and Winters just kept sipping brandy in their old-fashioned tin cups."

Uncle John stopped and studied a minute.

"Both them fellows was big stout men, weighed maybe I guess two hundred forty pounds. And by this time, they was pretty foxy from the brandy. Mose Brown was sitting thar on the ground leaning against a tree when Mose Winters took two sticks, one in each hand, run them under the burning brush piles and then set them right on top Brown's head. 'Course that blinded him. He couldn't see but jumped to his feet striking out at Mose Winters. Sister, he knocked the bark plumb off a pine tree with his fist instead of hitting Winters," Uncle John said laughing all the time.

Winters at last proved to be the best shot. "After that, they took the big beef up to that place we call the Blue Spring cut, but thar was no cut then cause the railroad hadn't never been thought of. They dressed it and cooked one of the hindquarters in a fifty-gallon iron kettle outside the cabin of Jim Tuggles."

The keg of brandy went along, too, with plenty of tin cups.

"Well, now after the meat got about half done, Winters took a big knife and cut himself off a slug and started walking back and forth through the house," Uncle John went on. "Brown was sitting on one of them old beds they made by nailing boards up to the log walls in a corner, you know the kind, Sister? Anyways, Winters just kept going back and forth, back and forth, chewing on that piece of beef with blood running out each corner of his mouth. All the time, growling like a dog, just to tantalize Brown."

When Brown couldn't stand it any more, he jumped up and grabbed Winters, bloody meat and all. The brawl that followed demolished not only the bed but the table and chairs and threatened the cabin itself. According to Uncle John, the end was a long time coming: "My granddaddy and the fellers watching the meat outside finally had to run in and part them. They told them they shouldn't orter be doing that way and talked them into being friends. So, Sister, the two Moses shook hands and everbody had another cup of brandy and went home peaceable."

The Duncans, the Smiths, and Old Lucifer

When I said Moses Duncan took root in Frost Bottom and stayed put, that was not the whole story. His new son-in-law in 1829 at first found himself unsatisfied in the Cumberlands. In fact, it took some years for William Smith to decide whether he really wanted to leave the Smokies for good, "the tall mountains" he called them. He would go high up on the Pinnacle above Frost Bottom on clear days and look south toward the blue ridges, wave after wave seeming to echo one another until they reached the faraway dark peaks. Finally, two years after marrying Elizabeth, William decided to move his new family back to Haywood County, where he bought a small farm and put up a gristmill on Jonathan Creek. Jasper never said what went wrong with that move, but not long afterward William returned to Anderson County, only to pull up stakes a second time and go back to his boyhood hunting grounds. This time Moses Duncan went, too, and got a farm next to William's. Mose's new wife, Nancy Nolen, came from there and wanted to return.

Despite all the moving, however, neither family had the urge to strike out west as did so many land-hungry Americans. In some ways, those who stayed in the mountains were like the dispossessed Cherokees, happy to live an unacquisitive life close to nature. Who cared if some newfangled Baltimore and Ohio Railroad had gone into operation up north while restless thousands in wagons were on the move toward the Mississippi? The Smiths and the Duncans were happy to be bypassed and isolated. They were quite un-American and did not even know it.

Once during those years while William and Moses lived in North Carolina, business called them back to the Anderson County courthouse in Clinton. It was March 1842. Snow fell the whole week and had not stopped when they headed back on horseback to North Carolina. With three large mountains to cross, Mose remained his usual go-ahead self, not one to let grass grow under his horse's feet, especially frozen grass. William never forgot that cold trip, often telling how Mose, who was leading the way, left him far behind though Mose was fifty years old. When William caught up on Mount Sterling, Mose was standing on a log stamping his feet. His black horse had turned white with lather.

Ignoring Mose's high temper, his son-in-law yelled, "Old man, you'll kill that horse!"

But Moses was unperturbed: "Better kill my horse than freeze to death!"

With the help of a bit of sunshine that finally came out and a dram of apple brandy, they made it home to learn that Moses was a father again—with number fifteen of his twenty-one children. Tiny William Riley Duncan's lusty screams were joined just four days later by those of the baby boy's new niece Polly, the fifth child of William and Elizabeth Smith. Family relationships could get very complicated in those days when a man like Moses Duncan had children from 1815 until 1858. New babies or not, the snow kept up until the mid-April. Everyone started to fear the leaves would never come out again as the Smiths and the Duncans found their hogs and sheep piled up dead. Chickens even froze and fell off their roosts.

Maybe the frigid winters in the Smokies influenced William's decision to move back to Anderson County one final time in 1846. But the immediate reason was the death of Isaac Duncan, Moses' brother who had married William's sister Tabitha. When the new widow wanted to go home to North Carolina, William sold his farm and gristmill for $150 and bought Isaac's log house and land in Frost Bottom. This was the place Uncle John and I visited in Stony Flat. Moses Duncan didn't like being left behind and soon insisted that William bring a team of horses and help move him and wife Nancy back to Tennessee, too. Either Nancy had changed her mind or got argued out of staying in North Carolina.

That five-day trip home to Frost Bottom proved to be a turning point in the life of Moses Duncan, who loved his liquor. With the wagon loaded, they took off in an unexpected light snow. William had brought a six-horse team, but following the bridgeless rivers through the mountains by way of Asheville down to Newport on primitive roads still would not be easy. Moses started out with three gallons of whiskey and stayed drunk fussing with his wife until they camped near Knoxville. Though William had real affection for his father-in-law, his patience was gone. During the night, without a sound, William got up and poured out all the liquor except for a pint. He saved that because he was afraid the old man, as he liked to call him, would be sick in the morning and need a dram to get going.

It was snowing again when William geared up the horses and got Nancy and the children in the wagon. Moses insisted on walking and dragged along in the shoe-deep snow. Finally, William burst out, "Get in the wagon! You been acting the fool long enough," probably something he had always wanted to say to his drunken stepfather, John McGhee. The starch had finally gone out of Moses so he got in. But he insisted he was deadly sick and needed some whiskey, just one swallow. William didn't give in easily, insisting he wanted all this trouble stopped. Years later William remembered how downright pitiful, to use his own word, Moses looked when he at last uncovered the hidden pint. He did indeed drink only one swallow. And to the amazement of some, not long after they arrived back home in Frost Bottom, he let his log house become a meeting place for the Methodists. His serious drinking days were over. Later Moses built a new cabin for a church where the occasional Methodist circuit rider would preach, or else that good Baptist Joshua Frost with the booming voice would come over from Raccoon Valley. Actually more Baptist preachers were available since they believed the gospel should be spread by laymen, farmers, blacksmiths, and anyone who truly got

Babe Edwards, Frost Bottom Road crusader, standing on the steps up Grave Hill, where Nancy Frost was buried in 1808. In the background is Frost Bottom Baptist Church. Photograph by the author.

the call. Baptists and Methodists worshipped together with much joyful shouting in Moses' log church. From his childhood Jasper could remember, "When John Tate, the old Negro, started singing about the Ship of Zion, they didn't think of what church they were members."

So it was that in 1846 William Smith settled for good in Anderson County. Life in Stony Flat with Elizabeth in the log home was filled with children, work, and happiness. Jasper, born there in 1848, made seven offspring. Eventually there would be eleven. That part of Frost Bottom had the right name, Jasper always said. "You have to turn a rock over to cover a grain of corn. But the soil was rich then, and it would make fine corn."

To Jasper, Stony Flat was a stony Garden of Eden in the Cumberlands. His love of the mountains made him dismiss the old idea that they had appeared as part of God's punishment at the time of the Flood. He was absolutely certain the Chief Architect, to use his words, had included mountains in his original plan for the world. I wonder if Jasper knew he was on the same side of this theological argument as that good Puritan John Calvin. Although back in the sixteenth century some called mountains "deformities" and "tumors" on the face of the earth, Calvin preached that all of Creation was good, only humanity vile. And Jasper's Scotch-Irish ancestors took Calvin seriously. So, Frost Bottom, there in the shadow of Windrock Mountain, was to Jasper a new Eden, albeit one with snakes. A rattlesnake or copperhead might appear anytime in any corner of the house or under any bed. Deer grazed right outside in the yard in front of William's cabin, while the woods still had bear and small animals, raccoon, mink, otter, and beaver, seemingly without end. Pheasants could be heard beating their wings on logs from a half mile away. A man had no trouble feeding his family with his flintlock rifle and hounds. As Jasper remembered, his daddy could stand in his door and shoot a turkey just as Joshua Duncan had been able to do more than forty years earlier.

During the growing season, the Smith family's routine was always the same. All gathered in the one room of the "big house," where William read a chapter from the Bible followed by a prayer of thanksgiving to the Creator for all the wild animals made for them to eat. Elizabeth would then go to the kitchen in the separate log cabin joined to the big house and spread the split-log table with breakfast, usually fried venison, pumpkin custard, and fatty bread along with honey and butter or homemade cheese. With everyone full, Jasper said, "Daddy would catch the horse and put on the homemade gears and line up us boys and girls for the march to the corn field." As one of the youngest, Jasper's frequent job was often to guard newly planted seed from the squirrels. Sometimes as many as twenty-five would attack in what he called a squad. Usually squirrel watch was a boring task even if one of his sisters helped, so often they "would just tumble up in the corner of the fence and go to sleep." Warm spring air filled with the scent of honeysuckle would prove too much to resist.

Mother Elizabeth stayed inside working and making sure dinner was ready when, about noontime, the sun got to the straight mark on the floor near the door. Then she would raise the ram's horn and sound the call for the family to come eat. The children had to hear that bellow only once before throwing down their hoes and scurrying to their regular places on the split-log benches. After dinner, a short rest and then back to the corn field all over again.

In the evening while William might be hammering a pair of shoes and Elizabeth making the spinning wheel fly, the young ones had fun. Neighbor boys like Fred and Jim Galbraith liked to come play snap and maybe get to kiss the girls. If they made too much fuss, Jasper said they would have to leave the big house and go to the kitchen. Out there might be popcorn or, even better, hickory sticks they could lick for the good juice until the wood made their tongues so sore they could lick no more. Bedtime meant the family gathered around for another reading from the Bible. Then came a prayer that the good Lord would keep them through the night before they sank down in their feather beds to sleep. One of Jasper's earliest memories was of being in one of those feather beds. He was so sick his mother thought he was going to die. She sat for days watching by his bedside, smoking her clay pipe. Once when she leaned over to look at the child more closely, a coal of fire fell from her pipe and burned his shoulder, leaving a small scar Jasper carried to his dying day.

In the fall when the crop was laid by, William would drop his single-bladed bull tongue plow and put a bell on each of his horses. He turned them loose in the woods filled with wild pea vine as high as the horses' backs. They could get fat on the vine although they might be hard to locate later when the fallen autumn leaves made more noise than their tinkling bells. Milk cows could stay fat all winter, too, unless the snow got too deep. And sometimes it did, up to six feet, with ice enough to turn trees up by their roots. Before the weather got bad, though, other jobs had to be done. A horse would be hitched up to some brush and one of the boys put on it to ride. His weight would beat down a path through the cockleburs and Spanish nettles making it easier to feed the farm animals. And to spot rattlesnakes. There were also eighty beehives to care for if the Smiths were to have the four hundred pounds of honey they needed on hand in the springhouse to last out the year. Once a disastrous nighttime storm swept the springhouse, honey and all, down Poplar Creek.

In those days William was not only a good farmer but a shrewd trader who

made profitable use of his time once his crops were in. He claimed wild mountain hogs to raise for trading by branding them with a unique ear notch, his
"mark." The trick to starting a herd was to find a sow with a bed of piglets and
mark them while she was off searching for food. A person's mark was registered
in the courthouse, and taking another man's hog was a serious offense. Since herds
in the wild have distinct territories and do not mix, it was simple for William to
create a herd and a hog business for himself. Long before the railroads, he and
Bart McKamey would drive about a hundred head of these semiwild creatures
to Georgia each fall, part of the way by flatboat down the Clinch River to Chattanooga. A 180-hog venture, their most successful, left William with forty-eight
dollars in gold tied up in a red bandanna.

On Sundays, after Mose Duncan returned from North Carolina and got
religion, there were regular church meetings each month when either the
Methodist circuit rider came or else a local Baptist preacher. William well
remembered the Sunday he decided to start attending the monthly preaching. It was the custom after church services for the men to hunt with their
packs of hounds, but William preferred to skip church altogether and just
hunt. That particular Sunday morning he heard a turkey gobble up on the
side of the ridge, took his rifle along with a birdcall, and went to investigate.
Tom Davis had heard the gobbling, too, and took off for the woods, not
knowing another hunter was out. William spotted the turkey and was on his
knee taking aim when Tom's dog came charging up. The turkey suddenly
turned into Tom Davis. Shaken by the near disaster, William took this as "a
sad warning" and decided never again to hunt on Sunday, morning or afternoon. The two friends promptly went down the ridge more than glad to
hear the circuit preacher.

From time to time, Frost Bottom would have what everyone called a big
meeting, much more than just a preaching. Methodists like Uncle Billy Dail from
over in Dutch Valley would come, along with Joshua Frost and other Baptists.
To get ready days beforehand, the menfolk would flock up the mountain with
their hog rifles and bring back not only hogs but deer. The women would be busy
for a week cooking chicken pies, rib pies, half moon pies, and even buckwheat
cakes. As Jasper put it, when those good religious people sat down to eat at the
rough-hewn tables, all they wanted was a sweetened dram of whiskey and a
chance to say grace before the feast began. And after the big meal, the preachers
consulted out under a tree about who would preach and on what. "They would
smoke their clay pipes, take a nap, wake up, take a dram of whiskey to cut the
cobwebs, and be off to the meeting," Jasper observed in a tolerant mood. "They
were living up to all the light they had."

Late in life, he could be anything but mild about church meetings. A self-styled John Wesley Methodist, Jasper once attended a service at his own church that he indignantly said "turned into a picture show." This was in 1927 when a visiting preacher had shown a movie trying to raise money for missionary work in Africa. Jasper neither approved of the show nor those he called the heathen, who were heathens, according to him, because they wanted to be. Complaining that his own church was becoming a "money machine," Jasper demanded to know, "Whoever heard of the Lord entertaining with a picture show?"

Picture shows were undreamed of in those days before the Civil War in Frost Bottom, although times were changing. In the sparsely populated county, schools were few and roads tortuous, but efforts had begun to bring a railroad through. Wanting a better life for his large family by 1853, William left Stony Flat for a farm at Laurel on the other side of Walden Ridge near Clinton. The land was better there, and thanks to his hard work and gifts as a trader William acquired more land and property, horses, cattle, sheep, and hogs. Soon he and his eldest sons, Moses and Henry, also had a business in town.

Always admiring his father, Jasper was nevertheless a cautious man who looked back on those wheeling-and-dealing days with a bit of I-told-you-so. At one point William had gotten to be worth maybe forty thousand dollars, or, in today's money, some six hundred thousand dollars. But as Jasper put it, "You know some men can't be satisfied in doing well; they think they can do better and consequently do worse." Still, the Smith enterprise was to be admired. It was a not easy overnight wagon trip to Knoxville, but William and his partner sons once took a load of their farm produce to this metropolis of two thousand souls to trade for tobacco, sugar, and coffee. Back home, they sold the goods at various settlements out in the county. This did not sit at all well with Clinton merchants. Squire Samuel Young, an important member of County Court, told William straightaway he would have to get a license and sell in town. That was when Moses Smith sold his good farm, bought a house in Clinton, and put up a store with brother Henry as clerk in 1856. William was busy not only farming in Laurel but also going to Knoxville to buy goods for the store.

The venture must have been a success, for soon the Smiths moved their store to a better location near the courthouse square. There across from the county's center of business stood John Jarnigan's impressive two-story mansion built in the 1830s with slave-fired red brick and elegant glass windows brought by oxen from Baltimore. As a reporter I covered a number of emotional attempts to save this historic house during one of Clinton's fits of urban renewal, but, to the city's enduring shame, it was demolished in 1969.

Back in 1856 the mansion was quite likely the most important place in Clinton as it became "railroad headquarters." Earlier efforts to get a railroad essential for developing county coal resources had failed. Then Jarnigan became president of the new Knoxville and Kentucky Railroad Company. This transplanted English businessman was another of those go-ahead people, a man who once built a wooden bridge across the Clinch River. Now he and his associates convinced Anderson County to sell a hundred thousand dollars in railroad bonds—a lot of money—to add to an equal amount from Knox County, another fifty thousand dollars from Campbell County, and eighty-eight thousand dollars put up by individuals. No wonder William Smith thought it was time to go into business in Clinton.

Rights-of-way were purchased, surveys made, and early in 1857 over two hundred laborers were working on the railroad heading north from Knoxville toward Clinton. Then a national panic set in as fear of railroad speculation swept the financial markets. It turned out to be short-lived, however, and work again resumed the following year. Construction of the railroad bridge across the Clinch River had begun when the Civil War broke out and destroyed the ambitious project and nearly everything else.

But the 1857 panic had already ruined William Smith. When the original contractors went broke, William and his sons were left with thousands of dollars in unpaid bills. Still resourceful, William had a ninety-foot boat built to take goods down the Clinch River to sell in Chattanooga. Larkin Hackworth was entrusted with steering the cargo, usually corn, wheat, oats, bacon, and lard. Maybe this trading boat would have saved the day, except that in 1858 both Moses and Henry died. Jasper, who was ten years old at the time, never explained how or why. Their deaths must have dealt a tremendous blow to their father, but the situation was made even worse by the debts they left for William to pay.

For young Jasper, however, before the family's financial calamities, life in town was exciting, mainly because of the growing importance of coal. Although he liked being a student in the Union Academy in Clinton, what he liked best were the trading trips with his father. Before the railroad came, coal had to be taken to Knoxville by wagon. In the county's mountainous area, outcroppings were everywhere, including Shoat Lick Hollow on the western edge of Frost Bottom. Moses Winters, who first settled what would become Oliver Springs, was one of the first to dig coal there. His workers would go in the shallow mines by candlelight and roll the coal out in wheelbarrows for six cents a bushel, sometimes a hundred bushels a day. Farmers, after their crops were in, would gear up their ox teams and become coal wagoners. In Knoxville coal sold for twenty-five cents a bushel, so the two-day trip was worth it.

These wagoners used a campground in the southern part of the county on the road to Knoxville. Often twenty wagons would gather there for the night in the pine thicket, a good place for trader William. One time Jasper's father hitched up his red oxen and took him and a load of supplies to the campground. After selling everything, William got ready to leave. "There were no wagon seats then or rub locks," Jasper explained, remembering the rough plank he had used for a seat. "The oxen were wild and suddenly started in a run, my father pulling back on the ropes. The front wheel hit a stump and out I went. The wheel struck me on the chin and went right over my head."

It scared William half to death, but the dazed boy recovered enough to head back home. They spent the night near Lee's Ferry at Bull Run and met up with John Russell and his son Tom headed for Knoxville with a load of coal. Both men would soon meet their end in the Civil War. John was tortured with boiling bacon grease, according to the family story, by Confederate soldiers who wanted information. When they failed to get it, they set him on fire.

Good times were coming to an end. By 1860 William was forced to sell the Clinton store and the Laurel farm and start all over. And rebellion was in the air.

It was old Lucifer who led the very first rebellion. When he became proud of his beauty, according to Jasper, he convinced other angels in heaven to help him try to dethrone God Himself. But he was cast out and man has had Satan and war to contend with ever since. It must have been this same Lucifer at work that fateful year of 1861 when Tennessee voted to secede from the union. How else could those terrible, terrible times be explained? This was the only answer that Jasper as an old man could find for the years of pillage and death he witnessed as a young teenager. Sixty-odd years after Appomattox, he began his newspaper reminiscences of the Civil War with his version of the rebellion in heaven, that first secession. His story is as artful in its own way as John Milton's ornate "Paradise Lost." Here is part of how Jasper told it:

Perilous times commenced when old Lucifer ruled against the God of Heaven and persuaded a portion of the holy angels to partake of his rebellion. He stood right up against the Son of God. He wished to be the ruler. All the host of Heaven was summoned before the court of justice, before the Judge of all the earth, the Creator of all things in heaven and earth. A part of the holy angels took Lucifer to one side to try to persuade him to recount and to take his proper position where he belonged and stop this confusion among the holy angels and get a pardon from the Holy Judge and be restored as he once was. At first he agreed and told the angels he was sorry he had acted so foolish and that he would do better. But he said this as a pretense thinking he could get a greater advantage and get a better foothold. So he went on playing his ficticious tricks as before until the Judge condemned him and took his stripes off. God had him and his angels led off and cast them all out of heaven.

Lucifer watched from afar and planned his next move against God. Jasper continued:

> Our Heavenly Father called up his son Jesus Christ and the Holy Ghost because They all agree in one and They had to all be present. He or They had already made worlds and God wanted to be doing something, for He is all wise and wanted to be busy and never idle.... So They planned to make a world, mapped it out, and made a blueprint of the work and agreed on six days for the work.... God created the heavens and the earth and all the host of the earth, the fowls of the air, and the fish of the sea, and the beasts of the field, and He called the dry land earth and He called the waters seas.... All Three agreed what They had made was not only good, but very good.

Then after God created Adam and Eve, Lucifer saw his chance for revenge and entered their Garden of Eden in the form of a serpent. However, when Adam resisted Satan's temptation to break God's commandment and eat the forbidden fruit, Jasper explained that the Devil said to himself, "All right, Mr. Adam, I'll fix you. I will visit you again and fix you proper."

Of course, Satan succeeded in tempting Eve. This fallen angel with the "sleek tongue" could lie as fast as he could talk and, after Adam and Eve's expulsion from the garden, continued to bring havoc into the world. It was this very Lucifer who caused Cain to kill his brother Abel, just as brother killed brother in the War between the States. It was also Satan's scheme to have Dutch traders uproot the poor African Negroes, as Jasper called them, and sell them as slaves in the new Eden of America. The result was civil war and death because, he explained, "when you see two brothers fall out and fight, it is conquer or die." The old man wanted to warn future generations of the "horrible deeds caused in these mountains by lifelong neighbors." Neighbors like the Duncans and the Seibers.

Some of the most savage battles of the Civil War were fought in Tennessee. Of the estimated 623,000 soldiers who died on both sides, roughly 24,000 of them perished in April 1862 on the Tennessee River in the first major engagement of the conflict. There at Shiloh, within sight of the Methodist church with that biblical name, the gigantic struggle offered a foreshadowing of the horrors to come. After two days of fighting, hogs fed on the dying as well as the dead, making what happened to the 157 Tories killed on Kings Mountain seem insignificant.

New accurate rifles meant more efficient slaughter and thousands of deaths, first from actual fighting, then from infections or disease. Amputated legs and arms piled up outside battle surgeons' tents, where they operated without anesthesia. Like the young nation itself, the war was on a grand scale never seen before. By New Year's Eve of 1862, the indecisive Battle of Stone's River at Murfreesboro caused nearly as many deaths as Shiloh. About 13,000 Union men were lost and 10,000 Confederates. Although no major engagements took place in mountainous East Tennessee, the area saw widespread devastation. Anderson County suffered as the crossroads of troops trying to keep control of Cumberland Gap and other mountain passes. Even worse were the guerrilla bands making war on each other and on farmers like William Smith. Many of these bushwhackers were mountaineers who escaped from being forced into the rebel army and then stayed in the Cumberlands. There were Confederate bands, too.

Before the war got under way with the attack on Fort Sumter in 1861, the election of Abraham Lincoln had brought years of tension to a high point. Jasper remembered the large and loud political rally in Clinton following the election. Senator Andrew Johnson of East Tennessee, who later became vice-president, appeared pleading that Lincoln be given a chance to avoid open conflict. Young Jasper remembered the excitement of the day, how a Confederate flag was nearly shot down from a housetop, and then how his father William drove his wagon and team of horses adorned with a small Union flag past the Jarnigan mansion. Its owner was a slaveholder, "a good man but he sided with the South," as Jasper said. When William rode by with his son, he saw Jarnigan standing in his doorway and hollered at the top of lungs, "Hurrah for Abraham Lincoln!"

After Fort Sumter, however, there were not enough hurrahs for Lincoln to keep Tennessee from joining the Confederacy, although the large majority of East Tennessee voted against seceding. In Anderson County, the vote was 1,278 against secession and only 97 in favor. With nearly half of the county mountainous, large farms and slaves were uncommon. Philip Seiber over in Frost Bottom did own some slaves, as had Micajah Frost before he left. His respected half-brother preacher, Joshua Frost, still had slaves in Raccoon Valley. But most farms between the ridges like those in Dutch Valley were small and worked by family members. Even those in the county's broader, more productive Big Valley to the east were mostly small. The 1850 county census showed 506 slaves and 6,391 whites; on the eve of the war ten years later, the figures had changed little. Slaves still accounted for only 9 percent of the population compared to 59 percent in South Carolina.

Anderson County also had some freed Negroes. One unusual case involved a slave named John, who came to Clinton with his master, Dr. Milton

Tate, about 1840. This bachelor physician had a fine river-bottom farm left completely under the management of John. After the doctor was elected Circuit Court clerk and became unusually busy, John would often tend the clerk's office. Apparently no eyebrows were raised by this black slave's issuing the fifty-cent marriage licenses. However, when Dr. Tate died in 1856, his will shocked the whole county. John and his wife received not only their freedom but the good farm. After the Civil War, the Reverend John G. Tate became famous as an eloquent preacher and talented singer. He was the same man that Jasper wrote about several times who could make the Methodists and Baptists in Frost Bottom forget their church differences when he sang "The Ship of Zion."

Those days of a live-and-let-live attitude toward slavery ended abruptly with Tennessee's vote to secede in June 1861. Confederate General Felix Zollicoffer quickly moved east to secure Knoxville and surrounding areas, imposing martial law and confiscating all firearms—and hanging a number of bridge burners to show he was serious about enforcing the new Enemy Alien Act against Union sympathizers. Before the war was over, more than five thousand East Tennesseans would end up in Confederate prisons, many to die there. That June, Clinton filled with Confederate soldiers arresting anyone thought to be a Lincolnite. Jasper said, "Union men began to crawl in hollow logs and lie under houses for safety." Soon General Zollicoffer advertised in a Memphis newspaper to buy fifty pairs of bloodhounds for his headquarters in Jacksboro, a few miles north of Clinton toward Cumberland Gap. Camp Goforth needed these bloodhounds "to chase those infernal, cowardly Lincoln bushwhackers of East Tennessee and Kentucky to their haunts and capture them."

Since William was a man in his late forties during the war and lived until his grandson John was sixteen, I had hoped Uncle John could untangle Jasper's stories about the Civil War. When I asked about William, he would only say, "My granddaddy didn't never talk to me about them bad times." So, it was Jasper who became the chronicler of the Civil War for the Smiths and the Duncan kinfolk. He was nearly thirteen when it started and certainly had no trouble remembering how the Smiths were ruined. They were lucky, though, not to have anyone killed in the immediate family. Moses and Henry had died just before the war, and Jasper's older brother A. T. made it through three years in the Union's Eleventh Tennessee Regiment. His sisters Mary and Sarah were married to Federal soldiers, while another, Elizabeth, was the wife of a Confederate one.

Scores, no hundreds, of cousins were quite another matter. There were Union Army stalwarts like William Riley Duncan (remember Moses

Duncan's baby boy born the winter of the big snow in North Carolina?), and there was the infamous bushwhacker Devil Tom Duncan, another of Moses' twenty-one children. Not that Jasper ever made the family relationship clear.

Of all Jasper's omissions, however, the one that truly surprised me was that William himself had been a slave owner and probably still was at the start of war. When he moved back to Anderson County for good in 1846, he had bought a slave from Moses for three hundred dollars, an eleven-year-old boy named Sam. When I came across the record of the sale recently, Jasper's idyllic picture of those early days in Stony Flat with the whole Smith brood marching to the corn field took on a different look. In my search for Jasper's writings on microfilm, I found one buried sentence about Moses having owned a slave but absolutely nothing about William. Maybe Jasper found the fact too unpleasant, since he wrote any number of times against slavery, once saying, "I don't believe Lincoln intended to free the slaves in the beginning, but he did a righteous deed, because God made animals to work and not human beings." The whole matter seemed to bother him long after the Civil War. He wondered about the Bible's saying that God created man on the sixth day and it was good. How could this be if the human race is not all the same color? It was something Jasper called "a problem to solve," something to study on. Apparently he never found the answer. Anyway, Jasper remained silent on Sam—a mystery, like Judy Duncan.

Since there is no record of Sam's being sold, at least not in Anderson County, he may have moved with the Smiths when they left Clinton in 1860 after the railroad failure put William in such deep debt. The Civil War was "breeding," Jasper said, but William was getting back on his feet on his new farm in Dutch Valley. He speeded up the process up by making whiskey, a perfectly acceptable business in those days.

But then the war started in 1861. Confederate General Zollicoffer moved into East Tennessee, and Union sympathizers headed for the Cumberlands. Although escape rapidly became dangerous, the numbers continued to grow. While men hid out waiting for a chance to get across the Clinch River, they got food and information from nearby farmers before the dash into the mountains. Down the river in Kingston, Confederate Colonel John C. Vaughn was ordered to take all available cavalry to "attack and disperse these men wherever they may be found." They needed to be caught before reaching the mountains, since the rough terrain all but stopped the cavalry. At Clinton, the colonel's regiment did a thorough job of destroying boats along the river. Those who somehow made it across the river headed for Walden Ridge, most hoping to get to Kentucky. More than once Jasper saw men slipping through the bushes of their farm on the south side of the ridge and his father taking them supplies. The first time the boy saw this, he asked William what was happening. "It's men running away," the father said. "And keep your mouth shut!" In the meantime, more men were being forced into the Confederate army. Clinton became the camp for instruction for these reluctant troops. Those who did not escape were soon sent to Savannah, Georgia, in hopes this "purer political atmosphere" would make them better soldiers for the South.

The Confederates did not have an easy time of it. Across Walden Ridge in Frost Bottom trouble soon exploded. The offspring of Micajah Frost's daughters Mary and Isabell found themselves on opposite sides. Just after the War of 1812 Mary Frost had become the first wife of Moses Duncan, while Isabell married Samuel Seiber, son of the first Philip Seiber. By the time of the Civil War, Isabell's own son Philip was the wealthiest man in the narrow valley and the owner of a number of slaves. According to Jasper, he was a good citizen and good farmer, famous as a hog trader and well on his way to owning all of Frost Bottom since "he was gaining fast." At first Philip Seiber was against seceding from the Union, but he changed his mind because his prosperity depended on his slaves.

When the war started, there were many Seiber descendants of Micajah, but even more Duncans. Jasper's mother Elizabeth Duncan was one of Mary Frost and Moses Duncan's children, as was William Wilson Duncan. Isaac Duncan was Elizabeth's half-brother. Both uncles lost their lives in that first year when the Confederates had a stranglehold on the county. Wilson Duncan lived up on Windrock Mountain and became important as a guide for the escaping Union sympathizers. "He was always ready to feed them, regardless of the number, on fresh meat, cornbread, and coffee," Jasper wrote. "They would not stay very long on account of being overtaken by the enemy. Duncan would pilot them across the mountains into Kentucky and by the time he got back home there would be another company at his house."

Feelings were running high one day when several Duncans got into an argument that turned into a fight with Solomon Disney, an old Confederate supporter. As Jasper told the story, Uncle Solomon was bleeding all over when he appeared at Philip Seiber's house. That was when Seiber wrote out a list of all the Union sympathizers in Frost Bottom and sent it to Clinton. The letter had barely gotten to the county seat before a company of gray uniformed soldiers appeared to arrest everyone Seiber had named, including Moses Duncan's son Tom. But Devil Tom, as people already called him, gave them the slip when the Confederates made the mistake of letting Tom go feed his sow and pigs. He took off to join Bill Emory's guerrilla company up in the Cumberlands. The rest were marched off to prison in Knoxville. They soon saw the light and joined the rebel army, only to go AWOL at the first chance.

Not long after Frost Bottom was supposedly cleaned out of Union men, Philip

Lavada Brown still lives in the home on Frost Bottom Road built with her late husband, Windrock miner Roy E. Brown. It is only yards from the John C. Duncan house, in the background, the site of Philip Seiber's murder during the Civil War. Photograph by the author.

Seiber returned from selling a drove of hogs with four hundred dollars in his pocket. Suddenly bushwhackers galloped up. He was shot and left for dead in his doorway. According to Jasper, Bill Emory did the shooting and then Tom Duncan stuck a bayonet in him. But Seiber lived long enough to give his daughter Margaret the money and tell what happened. Revenge was quick in coming. The guide Wilson Duncan was ambushed and killed by four men, including Seiber's brother Fred, who had already joined the Confederate army. Now the guerrilla war exploded with cousin killing cousin.

This story about Philip Seiber was one Jasper wrote about several times, and his retelling was always consistent. But questions have arisen about the much-told story of the ambush of Wilson Duncan. Marjorie Duncan Byrd's genealogical research has turned up military records showing that a William or Wilson Duncan joined the Nineteenth Regiment in the service of the Confederate States on June 6, 1861, and was killed in Sullivan County up on the Virginia border. She speculates he was forced to join the rebel army like the others taken out of Frost Bottom. But was this the same Duncan? His age on the muster roll was given as twenty, while Moses Duncan's son was a man of forty-one with nine children.

Unfortunately, exactly what happened in Frost Bottom may never be documented. Clifford Seeber, for one, apparently found it impossible when in 1928 he wrote his master's thesis on Anderson County for a degree in history at the University of Tennessee. This genial man's father came from a branch of the family in Roane County that spelled their name Seeber. Clifford Seeber served as Anderson County's school superintendent during the Depression before a long career with the Tennessee Valley Authority. Like most East Tennesseans, he loved tangled family stories—his grandmother's father was a brother of the murdered Philip Seiber—but Seeber seemed not to like trusting Jasper too much as an authority. He remembered Jasper as "a kindly old gentleman who loved the past," but when it came to the Frost Bottom killings Seeber was brief and cautious. He wrote only that Philip Seiber was killed and "some Duncans" accused before Wilson Duncan was ambushed. Nevertheless, even to this day there are enough hard feelings around that a few Duncans call the well-known 1928 master's thesis biased—even though the author's name is Seeber, not Seiber.

Regardless of who did the murdering, bushwhacking rapidly became more fearsome than the real war. The guerrilla bands, who called themselves home guards, were made up not only of Union supporters but also of Confederate ones. Although Devil Tom Duncan at first joined up with Bill Emory, he soon had a gang of his own. Henry Gibson headed up the most infamous band of renegades on the side of the South. If the small guerrilla armies were not killing each other, they were raiding villages and farms for whatever they could take. These were mountain men who knew every inch of the terrain, every good place to hide. Regular troops, neither the Confederates at first nor the Federals later on, had much success controlling the lawlessness.

Jasper Smith had no patience with the bushwhackers. "If the Devil hatches up a war, I believe in men taking the front rank and not bushwhack like some did in the Civil War," he wrote. "It would have been better for the mountain men if they had joined the regular army. They would have had better protection, for when the bushwhackers came in contact with each other, it was death with their hands up." Jasper knew about this firsthand. Not only had his mother Elizabeth's brother Wilson Duncan been killed, but his half-brother Isaac died with his hands up in a raid Gibson made on Emory's band. The Union men had camped for the night on a steep hillside in a ramshackle building with eight-foot stilts on the lower side. When the rebels' shooting started, all but three got away through a hole in the floor out into the darkness. Isaac was one of those three who didn't make it. Gabe Keith, who admitted shooting Isaac, was later captured by Union soldiers. He was unlucky to be turned over to William Riley Duncan, that younger half-brother of Isaac and Elizabeth. Ordered to take Keith to the guardhouse, Duncan instead killed him.

Devil Tom Duncan posing many years after his days as a Civil War bushwhacker in Frost Bottom. Photograph courtesy of C. S. Harvey Jr.

As for Elizabeth's half-brother Devil Tom Duncan, he became one of the most infamous bushwhackers. Jasper called him "a dangerous man" and never breathed a word about Tom's being his own uncle while telling about one of Duncan's legendary escapes from Henry Gibson. Tom had been joined by a runaway slave, Riley McKamey. The Duncan hideout was up a cliff in the Cumberlands. According to Jasper, "It was straight up like a house all around and on top was a basin. You could get up there and not be seen by anyone. They cut a tree and lodged it so they could get up there. They were well armed."

But Henry Gibson was a crafty mountain man, too. He found it and watched in hiding until the day the whole Duncan band came down and left. Then Gibson took his own men up. When Tom's guerrillas returned and started to climb up, the rebels fired away. Riley was killed. "But Devil Tom got away, his whole company running in front of him. He jumped over a bluff, grabbed a grapevine, and escaped unhurt." What Jasper never wrote was that Tom survived the war. Since the Union won, he must have been left alone to mind his own business. Tom Duncan lived to be an old man with a bad temper who somehow managed to keep it under control except, of course, the time he killed a pregnant cow with an ax.

In those murderous years, William Smith had to cope not only with bush-whackers but with foraging troops who stripped the farms in Dutch Valley of anything they wanted. One time Confederate Captain A. L. Mims's men even ventured into Frost Bottom looking for food. They were based in Olivers try-ing to stop the Union sympathizers from getting away to Kentucky. Right there on Frost Bottom Road, where John Seiber had tried to drown himself, Captain Mims ran into trouble. Supposedly it was Devil Tom, who attacked them at the pile of rocks on Poplar Creek still called Battle Bridge. I once offended Uncle John by calling the encounter a skirmish. "No-o-o-o," he said, making the word sound like a long "moo" for emphasis. "It was a battle, Sister. They's nine got killed." Maybe so, but not likely.

That first winter of the war, Jasper finally saw something besides bushwhack-ers. It was a real army, possibly ten thousand Confederate soldiers. Remember-ing January 1862, he wrote, "We were out of salt and had been making coffee out of rye, wheat, corn bran, and chestnuts. My father decided one day he would go to Scott County to try and get some salt and coffee." His mother and older brother went, too, leaving the younger children with hired hands.

Jasper said his parents had just gotten out of sight when "us children looked up the road and saw a longbearded man on a large gray horse with a sword hung to his side." He added, "We all were frightened. The hired man Bowling took to the woods and his wife crawled under the bed, but the longbearded man was General Zollicoffer, who said the soldiers would not hurt us. Two men deep they came and went all day, large cannons mounted on wagons. It was winter time, the mud was knee-deep." Then on the fifth day the long column of Confederates came back. "The tail end just barely got past our house when here came the longbearded general again. They had turned and were on their way to Fishing Creek, Kentucky, to fight the Union Army." The general would be killed there at the Battle of Mill Springs. "Old man Carroll on New River told me years later how he helped bury the dead," Jasper wrote. "The fight was in a swag. He waded in blood shoe-mouth deep and he would find dead men joined, gripping their guns with bayonets run through each other. Just wholesale murder."

That was 1862. Things were going to get much worse.

Large troop movements of eight to ten thousand men were not unusual in 1863. Federal soldiers had captured Cumberland Gap in June 1862, but the Confederates still held on to Anderson County. The rebels just moved to the south bank of the Clinch, turning the area between the river and the Cumberlands into a buffer zone where both armies foraged. When the Union soldiers came down from the north looking for provisions, they not only took what they needed but destroyed anything left over that the rebels might use. In 1863 a Federal soldier described the local devastation in his diary: "We thought we had seen desolating effects of the war before, but through this section it is the worst we have found in our travels. The people have deserted the country and the towns. Some we presume went to the South, some to the North; not a lick of improvement could we see, no new rail or board, while we could scarcely find a roof that would turn rain or a fence that would confine stock."

William Smith's farm in Dutch Valley had gotten him back on his feet only for him to watch it be picked bare. The final blow came one night in 1863 when Confederate soldiers made camp on his farm and the next day left with his last three hundred bushels of corn. He decided it was time to move over Walden Ridge into safer Frost Bottom, where it was much harder for troops to maneuver. He bought land near where Philip Seiber had been killed.

By December, the Union had control of East Tennessee, and conditions improved a little. However, the bushwhacking lasted to the very end, and Confederate raids never completely stopped. As Jasper put it, they heard the rattle of swords again in 1864 when General Joe Wheeler and some four thousand cavalrymen swept into Dutch Valley from Olivers. Farmer George Baker happened to step out of his house that day with his rifle in hopes of getting a squirrel. He was shot dead in his yard. Galloping on up the valley, the troops fired on two more men, killing a Captain Wilson, who was on leave at home, and wounding Cas Davis. "Cas jumped a fence, ran through a cornfield, and escaped in the woods," as Jasper told it. "He had a little dog in his bosom taking it home. He was bleeding from the bullet hole and had to lay down, but the dog licked his wound and stopped the blood." Wheeler's men went on still farther up the valley. In one house they found James Ross in bed. He was shot as he was putting his pants on. "The bullet knocked one eyeball out. They thought he was dead and proceeded to search for his money. But they didn't find it. It was hidden in his garden. And he recovered," Jasper related with some pleasure. Wheeler's raid ended up pillaging what remained of Clinton.

Sometime after the Smiths moved back to Frost Bottom, Jasper's brother A. T. was with the Eleventh Tennessee Regiment at Cumberland Gap. His friend Bill Larkins had a teenage slave with him named George, whom he sent to help the Smith family. As an old man, Jasper still liked to remember George playing the fiddle, saying, "I became very fond of him." One day when George was plowing, Jasper asked him how he would like to learn to read and write. He liked the idea. Before the war, Jasper was well advanced in his blue-backed spelling book, Ray's arithmetic text, and Smith's grammar, but schools had completely vanished with the war. He still loved the smell of a book so he told George he would teach him at night. "We went up on the ridge to gather pitch pine knots for torches," Jasper recalled, "and that night we started on the spelling. After lessons, George would always play the fiddle while I danced and then went to bed." A dancing Jasper Smith? What an unexpected picture to set alongside that of the cantankerous old Jasper shaking his white beard over the heathens in Africa. But I find the fiddle playing and dancing a pleasant way to end the bloody stories of the Civil War.

When peace came and Philip Seiber's brother Levi opened a log schoolhouse, he allowed Jasper to bring George. Over the course of time, George drifted over to Hawkins County and became a preacher. In 1927 Jasper Smith wrote a bit sadly, "Not long ago I got him on my mind and asked the sheriff as to his whereabouts. The reply came that he had passed on to his reward."

So George got to the spirit land before Jasper, that same place where more than six hundred thousand soldiers for the Blue and the Gray had long since gone.

Part
II

Oliver Springs: At the Gap

Two More Moses and a Wily Scot

If you head west out of Frost Bottom—actually southwest, since all East Tennessee ridges run southwest to northeast—and go through Shoat Lick Hollow, then keep going another mile or so, you're in what is today Oliver Springs. Except for the unexpected modern elevated highway that spans the mountains hemming in the old town, it is a sleepy, bypassed sort of place. You wouldn't expect that it had a famous resort hotel and any number of coal millionaires hidden in its past. Oliver Springs was once called Winters Gap, where in 1799 a public gristmill was built by Moses Winters, one of those old Indian fighters who came from Virginia like Micajah Frost.

Major Winters was one of the three men named Moses that Uncle John loved to talk about—actually four, since there were two Moses Winters. Dates are vague for the coming of the Frost Bottom two, Moses Duncan and Moses Brown, but not so the first Moses Winters. Without a doubt Knox County granted Winters the right, "the liberty" it was called, to erect a mill "where the Indian Fork of Poplar Creek breaks through Walden Ridge." This was two years before Anderson and adjoining Roane Counties were created in 1801. Winters also acquired 249 acres of land located in the center of old Oliver Springs.

The gap itself had considerable importance in what would become Anderson County since it provided the only convenient route through Walden Ridge. Two roads, which at first were hardly more than trails through the forest, joined near Winters's home and mill. One came from Jacksboro through Dutch Valley, and another from Knoxville by way of present-day Oak Ridge. After the ford at Indian Creek they divided again and continued, one north through Morgan County to Kentucky and the other along the south base of Walden Ridge. On the west the second met the main road from Knoxville headed for Nashville. From the early territorial days this Great Road was the lifeline to Fort Southwest Point at Kingston.

So Moses Winters sat at what would become a strategic county crossroads, although in the beginning it was just a clearing in the wilderness. He located his 1799 gristmill near a valuable salt well used by the Cherokees on land that was still legally theirs. Archaeological finds, including weapons and pottery, show that more than one Indian battle was fought over the salt. It was not until Major Thomas Butler, of the famous braid, or queue, negotiated the Third Treaty of Tellico in 1805 that all of Major Winters's tract got official blessing, though he had been there six years. His land had something else the Cherokees valued, the mineral springs they called Tah-hah-lehah or "healing waters." These springs eventually gave the town its name. Over two hundred years after Moses Winters settled in the gap, Jasper Smith fumed in the *Anderson County News* about the town's being called Oliver Springs and before that Olivers for the man who got the first post office in 1826. If it could not be Winters Gap, at least it could have been Winters Springs. Jasper protested, "Moses Winters buried the first white person ever buried there and the town ought to have his name."

In 1846 Moses Winters himself was buried somewhere on the hill where the American Legion Hall later stood. He had acquired still more land, some of it rich with coal that he was the first to work, though on a small scale. As Uncle John said, "Law, yes, my Granddaddy William was one of them people who bought coal off Mose Winters. He dug it out by candle right up there in Shoat Lick Holler." When the old major died, he left seven daughters and his youngest child, a son. That was Moses Charlton Winters, who made the family even better off by acquiring still more land and building a sawmill using the water power of his father's gristmill. He was the strapping Moses C. Winters of Uncle John's shooting match story. Together, Major Moses and his son saw their settlement change from an outpost in the virgin forest into a town on the verge of a coal boom after the Civil War.

That first gristmill constructed in the narrow gap must have been the work of a millwright who knew what he was doing. For at least half a century Moses Winters's mill dam withstood the tremendous surge of flood waters that could come down from the mountains. It was because of just such a flash flood that I saw Oliver Springs up close for the first time July 12, 1967. There had been five inches of rain late the previous afternoon to add to much that had fallen earlier in the week. When night came, local radio stations suddenly were pleading for Oak Ridgers with small boats to help rescue people trapped in the high waters in the valley below us. Early the next morning I found myself there in muddy boots. Nearly as fast as the waters had risen, they subsided, leaving a half million dollars' worth of damage. Houses were washed off their foundations along with the one-room Church of God jammed up against the Estabrook Street bridge. A coal truck, a tractor, and eight cars had floated right out of Hal's Radiator and Brake Shop. Cleanup was already under way, with City Hall being washed out with a fire hose. The National Guard patrolled the streets while prisoners from nearby Brushy Mountain State Penitentiary cleared sticky brown ooze from the roadways. In the middle of it all, an exhausted Mayor J. H. Burney was directing bulldozers moving heavy debris. The mayor, a full-time fire captain at the Oak Ridge nuclear installations, stood near the bridge threatened by the uprooted church. "We're just plain lucky," Burney said. "For a long time last night it looked like several rescue workers had drowned when their boat capsized, but they got out." Other than a fire truck having to rescue a woman about to have a baby, there had been no other emergencies.

After the flood, I decided to find out more about Oliver Springs and wangled time to write my story about the long-gone Oliver Springs Hotel, the article that caused Uncle John to call me. The hotel story put me in touch with Snyder Roberts, a high school history teacher and local historian who remained my good friend until his death in 1994. Tall with silver hair and black eyebrows, he still resembled the football player who graduated in 1927 from Oliver Springs High School. After finishing the University of Tennessee as a Phi Beta Kappa, he had been both a teacher and principal as well as a technical writer and editor in Oak Ridge. A precise man who sometimes seemed formal, Snyder nevertheless had a wry sense of humor. He could hardly have been a greater contrast to John T. Smith, although they shared a love of local history. Snyder was a descendant of Elias Roberts, who settled in 1798 on the good valley farmland where the Oak Ridge Gaseous Diffusion Plant would be built to separate uranium for the atomic bomb.

Snyder and Uncle John got much better acquainted after I left Tennessee in 1970, after Snyder retired to devote himself full-time to history. Doing meticulous research on families, churches, and local governments, he showed tremendous patience with the most mind-numbing legal records. He also started writing down old stories. Many of these appeared in rambling fashion in the local weekly newspapers during the American Bicentennial celebrations. The articles later came out in book form, starting in 1981. The Daughters of the American Revolution presented him their prestigious History Award Medal, only the sixth to be given in the whole country at the time.

When Snyder was in his eighties, a serious stroke greatly limited his ability to work, but not his interest in life. I told him I would like to use some of

Snyder E. Roberts, Oliver Springs historian, several years before his death in 1994. Photograph provided by Roberts.

his "real" history and stories. "Use anything," he said. "I didn't copyright them on purpose so anyone could have them. Besides, your articles were a help to me."

Although Snyder's work uncovered much information on Oliver Springs families, Moses Winters remains largely a mystery. His name first appears in Samuel Cole Williams's early account of a 1775 Indian raid in Carter's Valley in upper East Tennessee. Williams tells of further encounters involving not only Moses Winters but also the grandfather of Davy Crockett. It is also known that in 1796 Winters and his wife Elizabeth sold five hundred acres in Montgomery County, Virginia, apparently before moving south. The property was only a few miles from the mines where Hessian prisoners had been forced to dig coal during the American Revolution, just as they had in the nearby lead mines Micajah Frost guarded. Snyder speculated that the Virginia coal mines may have had something to do with Winters's knowledge of coal, which he later used in Tennessee.

However, the heyday of coal was yet to arrive in the Cumberlands. The important thing in 1800 was to domesticate this land that had so recently been Cherokee hunting grounds. Winters's durable gristmill played a big part in the strenuous undertaking—records show it operating at least seven years after his death in 1846. According to tradition, a powerful flash flood like the one in 1967 washed the mill away. Not long after the 1967 disaster, the Tennessee Valley Authority began planning a flood control channel to tame Indian Creek. Two summers later, bulldozers were about to start moving earth for the channel, the first step in an ambitious plan to turn depressed Oliver Springs into a small "model city." New public housing would be built in the flood plain along with an elevated highway to eliminate the traffic bottleneck in the old part of town. All this meant that huge earthmovers would soon destroy Back Street, where Moses Winters had built his home just above the mill in the gap. This dead-end street had once been part of the road from Knoxville to Kentucky.

I asked Snyder Roberts to go with me one early June afternoon back in 1969 to explore this place that was about to vanish. We left Tri-County Boulevard, the main thoroughfare whose name indicates that Oliver Springs is not only in Anderson and Roane Counties but also in Morgan. As for Back Street, Snyder knew every house, having lived there briefly as a boy. As we climbed up the hill, the narrow roadway lined with feathery mimosa smelled of honeysuckle. Snyder was talking. "Actually, this was once part of Main Street, and that's still its official name," he said, "but now most everybody calls it Back Street. There was even a time before livestock had to be penned up when it was called Pig Alley!" During the coal boom in the 1880s he said a bridge was built farther down Indian Creek at Estabrook Street. Fording the creek, though it was usually only a foot deep, became too much trouble. So after the bridge was built, this part of Main Street actually became a back street.

We planned to visit some of the people being uprooted from the sixteen houses condemned to the bulldozer. Once over the crest of the small hill, which was really the lower slope of Walden Ridge, we went all the way down to Indian Creek, where Back Street abruptly stopped. When Moses Winters's mill was there, this had been the spot for travelers to ford the creek. Just a few yards from the dead end stood the faded green two-story home called Preacher Brummitt's House, where I met Annie Smith Giles. At eighty-eight, she was another of the long-lived Smiths, a first cousin of Uncle John. But Mrs. Giles was not interested in talking about who her people were, what with the big move coming up.

The wispy-thin little woman didn't hesitate to say a bit indignantly, "There's not a one on this here street that wants to go, and I won't budge 'til I just have to. Been here too long, thirty-nine years."

She admitted, however, that the downpour just two days earlier "got the creek up and worried me all day!" She had good reason to worry, for Mrs. Giles and her family had had to be rescued by boat in the flood two summers earlier when everything she owned was ruined.

As Snyder and I turned back up the slope toward town, I saw that Back Street was much like the rest of Oliver Springs, a mixture of rundown houses from another era and newer, often less substantial homes. Some old ones, however, had been treated with great care, like Mrs. Theodore Smith's white Victorian two-story with a long porch running its entire length. I didn't get to meet her and find out which Smith she was, but we caught Bob and Maggie Wright out in their yard. The Wrights were already in the process of moving. Their home of forty-one years stood on the high side of Back Street, supposedly on the exact spot where Moses Winters located his log house because of an excellent spring coming out of pine-covered Walden Ridge. The couple apologized for the untidy tall grass in their yard edged with blue cornflowers and the reddest kind of poppies. Wright, retired after fifty-five years with Southern Railway, nodded toward the grass. "I just quit mowing it," he said. Mrs. Wright added sadly, "We thought it wouldn't be so hard to leave if we just let it look real ugly." She said even though Moses' spring had long been covered over, they had a well with water so good that they hated to leave it most of all.

Snyder explained as we walked on, "After the Civil War, Moses' excellent spring water was why the Russells' whiskey distillery was built right there where Winters had lived. Then later, must have been about 1900, the Oliver Springs Bottling Works got started and built on the same spot." A residence that used to be a saloon still stood across the street. Bill Potter gunned down William Walls there, but that is getting ahead of the story.

The last two houses before the intersection with Tri-County Boulevard looked impressive, both relics of the coal boom. Perched up high on the ridge, nearly hidden by magnificent peach trees, reigned a gracious white house with a wide veranda and Ionic columns. Albert Mead, owner since 1925, sat on his porch in the refreshing breeze looking out over Oliver Springs. At seventy-seven, the retired barber still cut hair three days a week but spent the rest of his time carefully tending his vegetable garden. He was philosophical about the coming upheaval: "I've seen surveyors out and I suppose it's the highway department. But even if the road does come through, we could build another house a little higher up. I own clear up to the top of Walden Ridge." A member of the Oliver Springs Businessman's Association, he had his eye on the future of his town, not on the days of Moses Winters.

"Yes, we could build again a little higher up," he said, apparently unworried. Mrs. Mead, who had just come outside, showed no enthusiasm. Like nearly everyone else on Back Street, she wanted to just stay put. Besides, she said half-jokingly, it would take days to move all her African violets.

No one was home at the elegant Ladd House, built of handmade red brick at the corner of the main thoroughfare. With its lacy white gingerbread, it was

Oliver Springs's Back Street is gone except for the Ladd House. It was built during the 1880s coal boom, a short distance from where Moses Winters settled at the gap in Walden Ridge in 1799. Photograph by the author.

and still is a landmark of Oliver Springs, the first thing you see entering the old town from Oak Ridge. Yes, it escaped the bulldozers, this house built by prosperous coal operator James K. Butler. But the Meads' Ionic columns and the rest of Back Street, hill and all, vanished. Today cars and trucks speed along the elevated highway over Moses Winters's lost spring of mountain water.

Back to Major Winters. With little more to go on than a few legal records, Snyder Roberts nevertheless had a clear picture of this man who settled in the gap in 1799.

"The old Indian fighter must have been fearless, a highly skilled millwright and craftsman, farmer, well-to-do property owner. He knew how to conduct legal matters like handling deeds, surveys, and contracts," according to Snyder's picture. He was literate, judging from his well-written signature on the petition to the Tennessee General Assembly in 1801 for the formation of Anderson County.

A question of chastity also gave more insight into Moses Winters. "Chastity" may be an all-but-unused word these days, but in 1811 that was not the case. A startling entry in the minutes of Roane County Court for January 22 of that year indicated Winters's position as a respected man of honor. One John C. Timberlake, exactly who he was no one knows, formally denied in court that he had said he saw Joseph England and Louisa Winters, the eldest of the major's seven daughters, in the act of fornication. Apparently fearing the wrath of an important man defending his family's reputation, this Timberlake formally certified before the county squires, "I never made the said charge, or called in question the chastity of the said Louisa Winters, and that any such implication on the character of the said Louisa would, if made, have been false and unfounded, and I do further certify that to the best of my knowledge and belief the said Louisa Winters is a chaste and virtuous woman."

What that was all about is hard to say. But in those early days, with little distraction from endless farm work, people paid attention when county court sat. If it were possible to attend, free entertainment might be in store. Those who could read looked on the spidery handwriting of the court minutes with real interest, for this record was the tabloid of the day. Everything was there: murder cases, endless fighting over land titles, and the names of people like Isaac Crane, who in 1804 spent two hours in the Clinton public square stocks for contempt of court. Apologies for slander, like the one involving a family accused of having "mulatoo blood," were not unusual. John C. Timberlake's 1811 denial of having made any fornication statement must have satisfied Major Winters, for the case appears to have been dropped. Illegal duels to protect one's honor were still being fought by a few hotheads like Andrew Jackson, but Winters must have been a reasonable man. And

Louisa apparently suffered no harm to her reputation, since she married in 1817.

Unlike his father, Moses Charlton Winters (Moses No. 4) left scores of stories about his exploits. The famous shooting match that Uncle John's grandfather William witnessed in the 1830s is just one. A Hercules of a man who in his early years loved to drink and brawl in the best frontier tradition, Moses C. also had lady friends in "most of the hollows in Pine Ridge and Pine Ridge had many hollows," as Snyder put it.

One famous tale about the younger Moses centered on a tough customer called Bad Bill from up in Kentucky. Headed home on the road in front of the Winters house with dark quickly settling in, Bill asked for lodging for himself and his horse. That was not uncommon then, what with travel being far from easy. Next morning out at the barn, when Bill was ready to leave, a row over the bill erupted. Either Moses didn't know or didn't care who Bad Bill was, because suddenly the bad man found himself reeling from a punch followed by a boot in the rear. The kick sent Bill sprawling face-down in the barnyard manure and that was not the end of it. Moses took Bill by the seat of the pants and threw him, manure and all, over the rail fence into the dirt of the Knoxville-Kentucky Road. He got up in no hurry, after deciding he was in one piece, weakly saying, "Mr. Mose, I'd be much obliged to ye, if'n ye will hand me my horse over the fence, and I'll be on my way."

As for Moses C. Winters, his fighting days finally came to an end when he married Leah Shaw in 1840, six years before his father died. The son proved to have real talent as a businessman and landowner. Before his death, the old major had given over the operation of his mill, farm, and "coal banks" to his son. For all his early brawling, Moses C. became a man of even more property than his father, accumulating over four thousand acres. He also got support in Knoxville for development of the salt well near his mill pond, the same deposits the Indians had fought over.

The salt project was a gigantic one. A contract was finally agreed on in 1853 by Winters and Dr. Joseph Estabrook, the president of East Tennessee University in Knoxville. A graduate of Dartmouth College in 1815, Dr. Estabrook taught Greek and Latin at Amherst College and married Nancy Dickinson, a relation of the poet Emily Dickinson. Snyder called him "a colorful character, a prodigious user of snuff with elegant ruffles and fancy boots." Dr. Estabrook unsettled the religious townspeople of Amherst by firing a gun on Sunday and even betting on lotteries. Whether all that had anything to do with his moving to Virginia and then to Tennessee is speculation. For ten years he headed the Knoxville school that would later become the University of Tennessee. But then he quit to take a big part in the salt venture. He moved his family and impressive personal library to Oliver Springs. In a day when roads often resembled quagmires and rivers had no bridges, the professor somehow got the heavy equipment moved in, including drilling rigs, boilers, furnaces, and evaporation pans for processing salt water. All this came at a time when Clinton was seized by railroad fever just before the Civil War. Winters's plans even called for building a railroad.

After the first salt well was sunk 1,100 feet deep and the ambitious drilling project seemed on the verge of success, all kinds of problems developed. In 1855 Dr. Estabrook died insolvent, and Moses C. Winters found himself struggling with lawsuits for a dozen years. Finally in 1868, after selling much of his land in the center of Oliver Springs, Winters moved Leah and family to his 453-acre farm in Roane County on the Tennessee River near Rockwood.

Winters Gap had no more people with the name of Winters. Moses C.'s last years before he died in 1874 were quite the opposite of his rambunctious early ones with the likes of Mose Brown and Bad Bill. His name is among those of the charter members of the Caney Creek Ford Baptist Church, and his tombstone shows a hand pointing upward toward heaven.

Other sons of men who fought the American Revolution also shaped the gap's history up to the Civil War, including Richard Oliver and Henry H. Wiley, whose fathers were both born in 1753. While Douglas Oliver came from Virginia, Alexander Wiley first saw the light of day on the high seas between Edinburgh, Scotland, and America. Snyder Roberts admired their outstanding sons as the aggressive, successful inheritors of this new land. Richard Oliver followed in his father's footsteps as a wealthy landholder and county politician. He died at the start of the Civil War, but Henry Wiley survived another twenty years after the upheaval to become a very rich man in the coal business.

Richard Oliver had the good fortune to be born in 1800 as one of Douglas Oliver's thirteen children. Douglas, who arrived from Virginia in 1797 just two years after the Frost family, had the wherewithal to settle in the relatively broad, fertile valley where Oak Ridge stands today. His move proved to be spectacularly successful. To the first 380 acres of land he purchased from Stockley Donelson, he soon added 600 more and then even more. Just thirteen days short of his ninetieth birthday, the old veteran, who had fought the British and Indians with George Rogers Clark, died. That was 1843. By then he was lord and master of two square miles of what is now downtown Oak Ridge. This Douglas Oliver was what Snyder Roberts called "an accumulator of wealth," a slave owner, an important member of Anderson County Court, an educated man who saw to it that his children got schooling. That meant either private tutors or the Union Academy in Clinton. Public education was a long time coming in Anderson County. It remained primitive until nearly 1900, and even then only a few free schools taught beyond the third grade because of lack of money.

So Richard Oliver was numbered among the elite for whom education could mean power on the half-tamed frontier. In 1822, long before his father died, he married and moved north over Black Oak Ridge to the flat land around Poplar Creek. Today this is Oliver Springs's newer Norwood section, which reaches the bottom of the ridge nearly to the Oak Ridge city limits. Young Richard followed his father into politics. The Olivers must have had connections in the John Quincy Adams administration, for in 1826 Richard got the first U.S. post office to serve Winters Gap, which he renamed Olivers after his family. Although Andrew Jackson had lost the presidency to Adams, it was a different story in the 1828, when Oliver helped elect Old Hickory as the first president from the frontier. Presumably Richard Oliver was impressed even before that, for he had already named his first son Andrew Jackson Oliver.

Oliver kept on making money and buying land, hundreds of acres worked by slaves. He served on county court and then in 1834 as high sheriff of Anderson County. He and his wife Mary Jane had already built a thirty-five-room brick mansion and inn on the road coming from Knoxville. Although

Richard Oliver's mansion constructed in the 1830s on his plantation in today's Norwood section of Oliver Springs. It survived the Civil War but was burned by miners during the Coal Creek War in 1892. Photograph courtesy of Snyder E. Roberts.

she died soon afterward, the inn flourished. Guests who could stay long enough were treated to a buggy ride to the mineral springs owned by the Winters family several miles north at the foot of Walden Ridge. James K. Polk once remained at the inn a week or so to drink the medicinal waters. And well-to-do Richard Oliver helped "Young Hickory," as Polk was called, in his successful campaign for the presidency in 1845.

Just a month after the Civil War started, Oliver died. His wife and younger son George were long dead. Settling his large estate would have been complicated in normal times, but with the war it became chaos. The plantation with 3,559 acres and many slaves went to ruin, as did the mansion, which both Union and Confederate troops occupied. It became a hospital and also a base for soldiers foraging the countryside for food.

Unhappily, the family fortunes were not to be rescued by the older son named for Andrew Jackson. Fifteen years before the North-South bloodletting, the adventurous Jack Oliver took off to fight in the Mexican War. When he returned to Olivers, it was not for long, what with gold discovered in California. The Civil War was well under way when in 1862 he finally headed for Tennessee on horseback. But in Salt Lake City a new gold rush in the Montana Territory easily sidetracked him. An unsentimental realist like Mark Twain, with no commitment to the war, he stayed out west and started a stage line for wild mining towns like Virginia City. Oliver and Company suffered its share of holdups and murders by the Plummer Gang and scalping of stage drivers by the Indians. Life for Jack Oliver was nearly as dangerous as it would have been had he returned to fight for the Confederacy. Years later he actually became the hero of a number of western adventure stories, facts all mixed up with fiction.

Three years after Appomattox he went to Washington, D.C., to win mail contracts for his stage lines. That was when he made a depressing trip home to Olivers. Jack Oliver's parents were dead, the estate desolate and strangled in lawsuits. Shaken by what he found, he wrote his wife, "The old mansion has been a hospital, blood stains are all over the walls and floors, the fences are all down, nothing is growing but weeds, and the Negroes are gone. I do not know how to run a plantation without slaves. I am leaving the estate to my sisters. I have cried until my eyes are as red as blood." He headed west again and eventually ended up in what would become the state of Washington. Andrew Jackson's namesake died there in 1903, never again seeing Tennessee.

Henry H. Wiley's story was completely different from that of Richard Oliver. Born in 1799, a year before Oliver, he turned out to be the man of the future, an ambitious, intelligent businessman, part of the explosion of American

Andrew Jackson Oliver, son of Richard Oliver, went out West for adventure before the Civil War and stayed because the family plantation was devastated in the conflict. Photograph courtesy of C. S. Harvey Jr.

capitalism after the Civil War. The land companies he was instrumental in setting up controlled much of Anderson County's coal deposits by the time he died in 1881. To this day, with most of the coal gone, the Coal Creek Mining and Manufacturing Company still owns the land. Somehow the mountain people whose families lost their farms could spit out "land company" like a dirty word and then in the next breath praise Henry Wiley. Local pride in this pioneer coal operator's accomplishments was large. Uncle John, for example, at the mention of Wiley would say, "Law, yes, Henry Wiley opened up a mine before the Civil War and was the first man to ship coal out of Tennessee. He hauled it by wagon four miles down thar to Poplar Creek. Then he'd float it down to the Clinch and on to the Tennessee River all the way to Georgia and Alabama."

Henry Howard Wiley must have been out of the ordinary. A glance at his photograph in Snyder Roberts' Oliver Springs book shows a fine-looking man in his fifties. Both his hair and steady-gazing eyes are dark, although his fashionable muttonchops are starting to gray. He has just the trace of a skeptical smile. His Scottish father, the baby Alexander born at sea, had grown up in North Carolina to fight the British and later moved to Tennessee. Kingston, county seat of Roane County, was where Henry was raised. The youngest of eleven children, he got a good education at the Rittenhouse Academy and then training as a surveyor and engineer. This knowledge, plus his Scottish shrewdness, was the key to his success. Both could be turned into money.

Young Henry Wiley did well as a merchant in Kingston, but he also served as the Roane County register of deeds and then as county court clerk from 1833 to 1840. In those days of log cabins, he built a fifteen-room brick mansion on Race Street, which no doubt placed him in the best society in this small but strategically located river town. And most important of all, Wiley formed a partnership with lawyer William S. McEwen to acquire and clear titles of mountain land for future coal mining in Anderson and Morgan Counties. Wiley, the savvy young county official, could hardly have been better named, even by his contemporary, the novelist Charles Dickens. In his courthouse office, he was in a position to spot good land for acquisition, although it was not an easy task to get clear titles. Confusion went back to right after the American Revolution when land speculation was a way of life. Even George Washington engaged in it. Andrew Jackson got his start that way while his brother-in-law Stockley Donelson speculated, too, until a huge land fraud nearly brought Donelson and the famed Indian fighter, Governor John Sevier, to ruin. Land title conflicts not only grew from outright fraud but also from the fact that North Carolina issued grants for Cherokee land in its western section later to become Tennessee—and often for more land than it actually had. Poor surveying and imperfect records in the near-wilderness, as well as squatters' claims often recognized in court, all added to the confusion. However, most ownership problems could be solved with enough intelligence, time, and patience. Wiley had all these and, with lawyer McEwen, worked on land titles for years.

Then one era ended and another began in 1846. Major Moses Winters died, and Henry Wiley moved to Oliver Springs. Limited mining began when Wiley opened the Poplar Creek coal seam in the Big Mountain area west of the gap despite daunting transportation problems. Wiley did indeed, as Uncle John said, ship the first coal out of Tennessee using flatboats.

But the Civil War put an end to all that. Although sixty-one, Wiley joined his five living sons in the war. They fought on both sides. One, Henry Purris Wiley, served in the Confederate army as a Texas Ranger and died of a facial wound in Baton Rouge. However, the father and his four other sons followed the path of Union sympathizers through the Cumberlands to Kentucky. The eldest son, Andrew, was killed, but Edwin was luckier as captain of Company F in the Fifth Tennessee Infantry. He survived the fighting around Cumberland Gap, then at Chickamauga and Missionary Ridge before being captured while taking part in General Sherman's push for Atlanta. His brother William, a sergeant in his company, saw action until the war ended. Henry Wiley's young son Howard joined his father in the quartermaster corps.

Unlike the Olivers, the Wileys were on the winning side with General Grant. They came back victors, soon to become very wealthy victors in the postwar coal boom.

Most East Tennesseans had not wanted to join the Confederacy, but when the war ended, most suffered like the rest of the defeated South. Although no major battles were fought in this area, crisscrossing soldiers and guerrillas left Anderson County's farmlands desolate, houses and barns burned, fences and cattle gone, fields overgrown. The rich bottomland where Richard Oliver had prospered with his slaves looked as though it had been smitten by the hand of the Old Testament God. And raiding bushwhackers kept coming down off Windrock Mountain even after the conflict was over. The few big landowners before the war eventually recovered, but small ones like Uncle John's grandfather William were devastated. The bloody walls of the Oliver Mansion told the story.

Jasper Smith wrote little about what happened after the "war of secession," as he called it. He said he had rather think about those happy days when his father William was young and game plentiful in Frost Bottom. As a young man himself after the war, Jasper briefly taught school, but there was literally no money to pay him. He eventually settled in to farm near Donovan in

Dutch Valley, just over Walden Ridge from where he was born in Frost Bottom, married Sarah Galbraith in 1872, and raised a family. His wife, Sarah, died only four years after her youngest child, John Tyler Smith, was born October 28, 1886. The Statue of Liberty was unveiled in New York Harbor that day, as Uncle John always liked to point out. Not only did his mother die in 1890, but so did his grandmother Elizabeth. Nearly seventy years had gone by since William Smith first came to Frost Bottom to marry Elizabeth Duncan, and now William was alone. After the two deaths, William would spend the rest of his life with Jasper. And little Johnny would grow up, as agricultural Anderson County entered the new industrial age, thanks to coal.

Such important changes could have come about only with the railroad. Men like Moses C. Winters and Richard Oliver and Henry Wiley had known this. Because of them, just before the Civil War the Knoxville and Kentucky Railroad had reached as far north as the Clinch River, but the conflict destroyed everything. However, East Tennessee emerged from the upheaval among the winners and suddenly got its overdue share of state railroad bonds. By 1869, the same year the golden spike of the first transcontinental railroad was driven in Utah, a Knoxville and Kentucky locomotive steamed into the just-born town of Coal Creek north of Clinton. More than thirty miles of track from Knoxville had been completed in record time as the line headed for Kentucky. It would be another fourteen years, however, before Olivers would get a railroad, so the county's coal boom arrived first in the northeast end of the valley squeezed in between Walden Ridge and the Cumberlands. There Coal Creek rumbled down off the peaks like Cross Mountain through Anderson County's only other gap in the ridge. Because of the new rail transportation, this small area of the southern Appalachians would be among the first to be extensively mined, well before Kentucky and West Virginia.

Compared to the industrialization of the North during the twenty years before the Civil War, this business activity was very late in coming. Earlier, Massachusetts had led the way as machines took over both shipyards and factories, producing not only boats but everything from shoes to farm tools. While the South remained satisfied with slaves and feudal agriculture, an American-made thresher at a Paris exhibition in 1854 showed what Yankee ingenuity could do. More important, by the start of the Civil War the North had already invested $1.5 billion in railroads, something that would have been impossible without the widespread use of corporations. Using this new type of business organization, daring financiers could raise huge amounts of capital and speculate with other people's money with moderate risk to themselves. Although panic often resulted in the markets, money could be made in amounts undreamed of by the single entrepreneur. The North's

early railroad building was just a preview of the enormous postwar industrial expansion to come.

In those days, anything went. The princes of this Gilded Age were men
like John D. Rockefeller, whose Standard Oil Company ran 90 percent of the
nation's refining business by 1879. In another dozen years Andrew Carnegie
would monopolize the manufacture of steel in the Northeast, the first step
toward giant consolidations like U.S. Steel. And by 1895, banker J. P. Morgan ran much of the financial world and literally bailed out the United States
Treasury during a gold-buying panic. His "money trust" would eventually
be worth an amazing $22 billion.

Successful as Anderson County's Henry H. Wiley would prove to be, he
was only a multimillionaire. But he could hardly have been a better example
of the American flowering of Puritan virtues inspired by reformer John
Calvin. Although Calvin would not have recognized the dizzying events in
the New World three centuries later, in a strange way his doctrine of pre-
destination had much to do with them. The all-knowing God, according to
Calvin, had already chosen his elect for heaven and good works meant nothing, but the true Christian should nevertheless glorify Him through a life of
discipline and hard work. Paradoxically, as time went on and such a life produced success in the modern world of sanctified business, this success came
to be seen as proof of salvation. Or as Rockefeller once simply put it, "The
good Lord gave me my money."

With the Civil War over, Henry Wiley and his sons returned to become small-
scale Rockefellers. Already worth $5 million in today's dollars, Wiley left Olivers
in 1869—still without a railroad—and settled in tiny Coal Creek before the first
train arrived from Knoxville. He had several mines in operation also immediately, but serious legal trouble was ahead for him and his old partner William
McEwen. Their forty years of land acquisitions ended up in federal court, challenged by a New York financier, Charles H. Bulkley. At issue were some forty
thousand acres, mostly in Anderson County. Confused land titles being what they
were, these sharp businessmen finally decided it would be much more profitable
to compromise and join forces. The result was a new land company incorporated
as the Coal Creek Mining and Manufacturing Company. The New Yorker came
out of the deal an absentee owner with half of the stock. As for Wiley, he quit
mining operations and concentrated on the even more profitable leasing of his
land to other operators. And the coal boom started gathering steam. The excep-
tional story of how the boom in Coal Creek would play out at the turn of the
century, with a miners' insurrection followed by two disastrous mine explosions,
comes later in the book.

As mine driftmouths rapidly appeared on the mountainsides around Coal Creek, back down the valley at Olivers, fortunes were waiting to be made in coal. Efforts to cash in were stymied until 1883, when Colonel John G. Scott and his partners extended the Walden Ridge Railroad from Roane County to the Big Mountain area. Six mines promptly opened there on Olivers' western edge. And the old gap showed signs of becoming a real town. Just the previous year, Colonel Scott, a go-getter from Philadelphia, bought the land where the Oliver Springs High School would eventually stand, surveyed lots, and laid out streets. About the same time, streets right up to the base of Walden Ridge took shape under the new Poplar Creek Coal and Iron Company formed by Wiley's heirs at his death in 1881. Of the $1 million in capital stock, Captain Edwin Wiley owned 55 percent. Little wonder the U.S. post office at Olivers found itself renamed Poplar Creek, though only for two years until 1884, when the town got its fourth and final name of Oliver Springs.

The Wileys' two land companies held numerous five-thousand-acre parcels, but these tracts included small areas still owned by individuals; these were called "interferences," which was often a euphemism for family farms. Ongoing efforts to buy out these interferences at cheap prices were usually successful, although today, more than a hundred years later, how this was accomplished is often not clear. Certainly, Snyder Roberts in his admiration for the Wileys gave no details and never speculated on the ethics.

To me, the most surprising of all Poplar Creek Coal and Iron Company's acquisitions was the south side of Windrock Mountain, where many millions of dollars of coal would be mined. Much of this land had originally belonged to John Lively, his sons, and grandsons (if you ignore the prior claim of the Cherokees). John's son Benjamin, along with four of Benjamin's sons in 1882, sold their part of the lower half of the mountainside to Colonel Scott, the enterprising businessman and Poplar Creek land agent. One tract of a hundred acres went for $1 an acre, or about $1,300 in today's dollars, while another seventy-five acres brought what would now amount to $7,000 because of buildings. As for the upper half of the mountain, in 1882 it belonged to John Lively's grandson John Calvin Lively, who also sold to the land company. Four of the various Livelys had served under Captain Edwin Wiley. And Scott had been Benjamin's colonel, all of which may have hastened the sale.

Trish Lively Cox, who recently compiled a Lively family history, cannot explain why the land was sold when the coal boom was already under way. Although she wonders about the authenticity of the X marks made for signatures on the deeds, she is philosophical, saying it is too late to question them now. As for the land at the top of Windrock, Trish Cox found no deed of sale. It may have originally been taken by squatter's rights, the kind of shaky title just right for a land company's taking. However the Lively land ended up belonging to the Wileys, it is certain that the Livelys became miners, not owners of the famous Windrock Mine.

Today Coal Creek Mining and Manufacturing Company is still in operation after 124 years and has absorbed Poplar Creek, although no Wileys are now involved in the corporation. Fred Wyatt, executive vice-president, pleasantly insists he knows nothing about the Livelys. He does point out, however, that predicting back then whether land had good coal seams was a risky business. And even if a small landowner had known for sure, he would have been unable to exploit the coal on his property surrounded by that of the land company. As for the prices paid, Wyatt says prices are always "relative."

Too bad Jasper Smith had next to nothing to say about the momentous changes brought by coal beginning in the 1870s. A lifelong Republican and admirer of Henry Wiley, he nevertheless could write bitterly about land companies. "Now the Northern people have our lands, Southern people are their slaves," he complained. "Our fathers should have owned it all, but Wall Street owns it and don't give a cuss for us." He took comfort, though, as he often did from the Scriptures. "The Bible says the time will come that whosoever possesses things of this world will be as though they possessed nothing. The tall, the wise, the reverent head will lie as low as ours." That was not to prove true as far as Windrock was concerned. Even when the mine finally closed in 1983, the "tall" heads of the owners were far from lying low. Ironically, one of them belonged to C. H. Smith, John Lively's great-great-great-grandson.

Henry H. Wiley and coal brought industry and jobs to Anderson County and misery, too. But then possibly the bad can never be completely untangled from the good.

Mineral Waters Plus Black Gold

When Henry Wiley and the railroad arrived in the newborn town of Coal Creek in 1869, the Knoxville Iron Company was already there. So desperate for coal was this rolling mill and foundry that the firm had opened its own mine and was hauling the coal by wagon to Clinton while laborers laid the rest of the tracks north from the county seat. Some years later, in 1881, one of the founders of this highly successful iron company left Knoxville for Anderson County, not for Coal Creek but for the much older community of Olivers. He was Joseph C. Richards, who, along with his sons, would play a big part in turning Moses Winters's village into a boomtown. "A mining mogul," Snyder Roberts called him.

While Henry Wiley and Richard Oliver were sons of men who fought in the American Revolution, Richards definitely did not fit that mold. He was a northern Yankee originally from Wales. Although he came south right after the Civil War, he was anything but a carpetbagger. Richards had arrived in America as a young man in 1848. He soon sent back to Swansea in the old country for Ann Thomas, married her, and went to work in the iron industry in Pennsylvania and later in Maine. One company he was with made munitions for the Union army. He was so certain the South would recover and prosper when peace came that he scouted the Knoxville area just after Appomattox for a new business location and relocated there with his wife, Ann, and six children. By 1869 Knoxville had nearly ten thousand souls, and Richards's initial financial venture had been reorganized into the Knoxville Iron Company with a capital stock close to $2 million in today's dollars.

Though he was no Rockefeller, Joseph C. Richards had the good businessman's eye that made him wealthy. Those years he was in Knoxville, he knew about the coal seams around Olivers, but there was no rail transportation. Knowing that would change, he started buying up the so-called Mineral Springs tract, Moses Winters's original landholding. Not only did these 1,314 acres include the springs made popular by Richard Oliver before the Civil War, this tract had coal, timber, and some low-grade iron ore in the eastern section.

Finally in 1881, the new landowner, with his four grown sons and three daughters, moved to the gap where Major Winters had put down his roots after the Revolution. And thanks to the enterprising Richards family, this village turned into a thriving coal town known nationally because of the elegant Oliver Springs Hotel.

Much of the hotel story came from Mrs. Mary Richards Sienknecht, daughter of Joseph's son John. This vigorous woman of eighty-five—called "Miss Mamie" by everyone—was still running an insurance agency when I met her in 1968. She well remembered when the five-story resort burned in 1905 and how prosperous life was then in Oliver Springs. "Oh, it was a beautiful village and residents were good-livers," Miss Mamie said in her calm, self-confident way. Some visitors even said they were reminded of Switzerland.

Historians often disparagingly label the twenty years between the 1870s and the 1890s the Gilded Age, at least in the North, where the robber barons of business changed the face of America. Of course, to admirers like Snyder Roberts they

Oliver Springs at the turn of the century, when visitors to the famous resort hotel compared the town to an Alpine village. Photograph courtesy of C. S. Harvey Jr.

were "captains of industry." To him the coming of Joseph C. Richards signaled the area's entry into a new age of prosperity, gilded not with gold but coated with thick black coal dust.

What did the Welsh patriarch and his large family find when they arrived from Knoxville in 1881, the year Henry Wiley died up in Coal Creek? It was not much more than a village. Another two years would pass before the Walden Ridge Railroad steamed in, but Colonel John Scott and Captain Edwin Wiley were already laying out lots and streets for a real town. Today it's not clear exactly who lived at the gap, but it is certain that several landmarks greeted Joseph C. Richards. One was the Baptists' large log church on land donated by Moses C. Winters near the mineral springs. It was built after the Reverend Joshua Frost, Micajah's brother, had organized the congregation in 1846. Another log structure going back to 1819, some even say 1799, stood at the corner of what today is Spring Street and Tri-County Boulevard. Nearly hidden now by giant magnolia, hemlock, and maple trees, it assumed its present white antebellum style with imposing columns about 1905. The proportions of this two-story home, relatively wide in comparison to its shallow depth, reveal the log house at its core. Called Colonial Hall, it is the only building in Oliver Springs on the National Register of Historical Places except for the much newer building put up in 1907 by the Oliver Springs Banking Company.

In addition to the log structures, the Alex Allen House stood strong and sturdy north of Indian Creek. Before it fell to bulldozers under the TVA redevelopment plan, this frame home had a long history. Made of large hewn sills, it had floor and ceiling jousts of yellow poplar put in place before the Baptists built their log church, and maybe even considerably earlier, since it was quite possibly a stage stop on the road through the gap that opened in 1809. Well before the Civil War, it was an important house there among the log ones, a house good enough for Henry Wiley when he left his brick mansion in Kingston. Alex Allen bought it not long after the Richardses arrived. A mining engineer from the University of Edinburgh, Allen was a powerful man of both wit and temper. He left behind nearly as many stories as did Moses C. Winters, including a complicated tale of his having single-handedly demolished a Knoxville saloon when somebody criticized his heavy Scottish burr. It had been a definite mistake to say what a damned shame for a man not to be able to speak English well enough to order his own whiskey.

As for the Gilded Age, when the Walden Ridge Railroad finally arrived in 1883 on the western edge of town, a half dozen mines were quickly opened in the Big Mountain area by the Richards family, William B. Wiley, and others. Unlike his brother Captain Edwin Wiley, who became part of the elite in Knoxville, Bill Wiley stayed in Olivers. J. K. Butler also jumped into mining

Uncle John Smith and his first wife, Mary Foster, posed on their wedding day in 1907. Photograph courtesy of W. H. Smith.

operations and soon built the gracious red brick house that today is all that remains of Back Street.

As the coal boom got under way, Main Street filled nearly overnight with wagons and carpenters and miners slushing through the mud in the rain and straddling the deep ruts when it dried out. A substantial new two-story store with an imposing upstairs porch and sign saying "Joseph Richards and Sons" sprang up on the corner of Mineral Springs Road. Here Mamie Richards was born in 1883. Her father John managed the business, which also served as commissary for the family's growing coal operations. And he became postmaster in 1884 when the post office was relocated in the new building and the town's name changed for the final time to Oliver Springs. Johnny Richards, as Uncle John always called him, was the eldest of the four well-organized brothers. William was the bookkeeper, Joseph the mining supervisor, and Dave the manager of Richards House, a thirty-room hotel located at the mineral springs. This highly successful establishment may have been there when the family came from Knoxville but more likely was a part of the construction boom, which even included a subscription school, the Oliver Springs Academy. By 1886, John S. Keebler had opened a real department store. Uncle John was born that year, and twenty years later he bought the pants in which he married Mary Foster in 1907 from Keebler's.

Shortly before Joseph C. Richards' death, he made two business deals destined to ensure Oliver Springs's importance in Tennessee mining. In 1888 he organized the Oliver Coal Company to exploit more efficiently his Big Mountain coal resources as well as those in Shoat Lick Hollow out near Frost Bottom. Just as important, he sold to the Walden Ridge Railroad for one dollar the right-of-way through town east to Donovan, where a station would be built for coal shipments and later timber. The train would, of course, stop at Richards House. Within six months, the railroad had completed tracks through Dutch Valley all the way to Clinton. Two-year-old Johnny Smith out on Jasper's farm near Donovan Station would grow up hearing lonesome train whistles in the night. Soon the engines belonged to the East Tennessee, Virginia, and Georgia Railroad (E. T. V. and G.), which bought out Walden Ridge. Then the E. T. V. and G. went under, and the Southern Railway took over in 1894, just a year before the grand Oliver Springs Hotel opened.

That day in 1968 when Mrs. Sienknecht, that is, Miss Mamie Richards, ushered me into her home built by Father John in the heyday of coal, she was full of friendly matter-of-factness. The very first question was whether the Oliver Springs Hotel was truly an elegant "watering place" like the famous spa in Saratoga, New York.

Indeed it was. And all 150 rooms went up in spectacular flames in 1905 after only ten glorious years.

"Oh, yes, I saw it burn," Miss Mamie said. "The hotel was big, very long, but it burned quickly. There was just no way to stop it, no fire-fighting equipment here in those days."

Although her father and his brothers already had a successful hotel operation in the popular Richards House, they had even bigger ideas. With a group of Cleveland speculators, they raised what today would be well over $2 million. A new five-story structure of Georgia pine was built in 1895 on five hundred acres, including part of Walden Ridge. There were tennis courts and croquet lawns, as well as bridle paths for riding along the wooded ridge. The establishment generated its own electricity for not only lights but the unheard-of luxury of an elevator. Steam heat and carpeting added to the comfort created by careful attention to every detail, an expensive wine cellar, damasked tables set with china and silver for gourmet dining, and bedrooms with fine hair mattresses. Each room had its own view of the Cumberlands.

"This magnificent and justly celebrated watering place is surrounded by lofty mountains whose summits are companions of the clouds." That was new manager N. F. Powel in 1899 describing the Oliver Springs Hotel in his twenty-page advertising booklet announcing the coming tourist season. His turn-of-the-century rhetoric nearly got away from him, but it was true that a number of peaks, if not actually thirty as claimed, could be seen from the fifty-foot observation

The Oliver Springs Hotel, built in 1895 by the Richards family, was a highly successful resort until it burned in 1905. Photograph courtesy of C. S. Harvey Jr.

tower rising above the rambling building and its double-decked veranda. In those days before air conditioning, the well-off arrived from sweltering cities like New Orleans, Memphis, and Chicago. Even New Yorkers came, although Saratoga Springs was much closer. For one thing, Southern Railway made Oliver Springs very easy to get to. And its Carolina Special, between Charleston and Cincinnati, had anything that high society could wish for, including Pullman sleepers and dining cars. Joseph C. Richards had indeed gotten his dollar's worth when he sold the railroad right-of-way in return for the Southern stop at the Oliver Springs Hotel.

It was a gay and pleasant time in those bustling days of moneymaking. Hundreds and hundreds of guests came. According to Miss Mamie, "They would come and stay all summer and then still more people would come from nearby places just for the big Saturday night dances at the hotel's pavilion. It was sometimes so crowded over the weekends that people couldn't find places to sleep though we took many visitors into our homes." Special trains were run on the weekends from sophisticated Knoxville. She laughed, adding, "Sometimes after the dances, young men would just have to sit up the rest

The Richards family mansion presided over Oliver Springs society in the 1890s. William Richards and his young children were pictured on the front steps. Photograph courtesy of Snyder E. Roberts.

of the night on the hotel's long porches." It had many rocking chairs, wonderful for daytime visiting, but not too comfortable for recovering from hours of dancing to the music of the Italian orchestra.

Later outside in her neat, trimmed yard, Miss Mamie pointed up on nearby Pine Ridge where her Uncle William Richards built a magnificent mansion in 1893 just before the new hotel appeared. This Victorian castle, topped with a cupola like a Prussian war helmet, may have been the finest home ever built in Anderson County. From the cupola the whole new town in its green-treed valley could be seen. A wide-eyed contemporary description in the *Clinton Gazette* pictured the living room, large enough to serve as a ballroom, with windows of curved glass as the scene of large gatherings of relatives and church organizations and singing groups so loved by the Welsh. The Richardses were sober Christians not exactly in the social whirl. But theirs was an elegant life in this house splendid with lights from the mansion's own gas plant. Handcrafted staircases imported from England led to rooms made elegant by leaded windows of stained glass and fireplaces with carved mantelpieces. Visitors stepped down from their buggies in the covered carriageway ready for entertainment in the ballroom or just enjoyment of the mountain breezes on the circular porch.

Miss Mamie explained that Uncle William and his family lived there with his unmarried sisters and also his mother, Ann, who so many years ago had left Swansea, Wales. The mansion would outlast the famous hotel across the way by nearly a half century until it, too, came to a bad end. In 1940 it was the scene of the unsolved murders of William's unmarried daughters Margaret and Ann, a crime making headlines for weeks. The elaborate old home was then sold to the Oliver Springs American Legion, and four years later it burned.

Remembering the glory days of the Richards brothers at the turn of the century, Miss Mamie said, "Uncle Will remained the bookkeeper, but the other two brothers finally moved away. Uncle Joe became a superintendent of mines in Kentucky. Uncle Dave, who was quite the ladies' man and loved all the social life at the hotel, married and went to Clinton." Dave was the one who from time to time escorted his young sisters to the big Saturday night dances at the hotel and organized exciting sleigh rides after a good snowfall.

Dave Richards was an outgoing man well liked by everyone, ideal for the job of making guests at the luxurious resort enjoy their stay. Besides the outdoor recreation and famous dance pavilion, there were bowling alleys and billiard rooms. His job of keeping people happy was unofficial since he worked as a coal dealer, but he obviously enjoyed his role helping Link Williams, the assistant manager, keep everyone entertained. Link has gone down in Oliver Springs history as one of its true characters. Snyder Roberts called him a teller of tall tales without equal, a fancy dresser who loved to fish but loved even more his pack of hounds led by Ole Blue. Snyder remembered how all this led to Link's famous "planned" foxhunt.

The so-called planning proved necessary to get Link out of the fix he had gotten himself in by bragging to hotel patrons about the aristocratic delights of riding to the hounds. Many of these big city guests, bulging from the butter-rich dishes in the dining room, asked over and over when there would be a foxhunt. Link knew getting them on horseback would end in disaster, so he planned a hunt that could be enjoyed vicariously. The always ingenious assistant manager got a number of his friends who owned hounds to round up about forty dogs. He also bought the pelt of a fox recently killed in a neighbor's pen of Plymouth Rock chickens. Then Link convinced young Tom Gilbreath to lay the scent, since he was "long-winded, fast of foot, and able to climb a ridge," according to Snyder.

On this particular evening, with the fox skin hanging over his shoulder so it would touch the ground as he ran, Tom took off in the dark up Walden Ridge to above Ab Mead's house (the one the bulldozers would get). He circled behind the hotel's reservoir and headed for Donovan Gap, where he turned back to run along the crest of the ridge to just above the hotel. When Tom had covered his route, the pack of hounds was let loose near Mead's house and the "foxhunt" was on. Hotel guests, who had just gotten comfortable for the night in their fine beds, could hear the yelping hounds and enjoy the adventure with absolutely no effort. Genteel foxhunting had arrived in the Cumberlands!

The only problem was that Link forgot to tell Tom where the trail should end. When Tom came down off the ridge, he hurriedly dragged the "fox" into the hotel basement and hung it on the wall. He left the door ajar and soon forty yelping hounds filled the basement and got tangled up with two cats in the confusion. Peace did not return until the dog owners could be located to drag the animals away. How Link talked his way out of the embarrassment is not clear, though some said his generous offerings from the wine cellar helped immeasurably.

Fake foxhunts were one thing, but the scandal of the floodlights was in an entirely different category. It would never have happened if Thomas Edison had not invented the electric light. The generator that provided the wondrous modern lighting, elevator service, and call bells for the ever-present servants was the pride of the hotel. Every night until ten o'clock floodlights played on the graceful fountains out front. The main character in this story, Alf Diggs, was the young operator of the power plant. He was also a man who loved a joke. Alf had become curious about whispers concerning unusual goings-on after the fountain lights went out. Then late one unexpectedly warm summer night, Alf quietly returned to the power plant, so quietly he could hear soft giggles coming from the manicured lawn. Suddenly he switched on the giant floodlights. There in the artificial daylight, delighting in the cool fountain water, were several very young and very nude hotel maids. And one lone clothesless man.

Shrieks, screams, and windows slamming open. For several minutes it seemed the fate of the resort lay in the hands of Alf Diggs. However, Victorian prudery did not triumph. A few guests may have checked out the next morning, but in the end hotel business was better than ever.

Of course, not everyone came just for entertainment and mountain air. The mineral springs that the Cherokees had so valued were the reason the hotel had been located there on Moses Winters's original tract of land. In Proprietor Powel's brochure, he stressed how many satisfied customers had expounded on the wonders of these waters "sufficient to relieve all the ills to which the human family is heir"—six full pages of testimonials. In those days before the U.S. Food and Drug Administration, Powel listed no fewer than seventy-eight ailments and serious diseases as being helped, if not actually cured, by the spa's nine kinds of mineral water. In addition to the smelly white, yellow, red, and black sulfur waters, there was chalybeate with its iron salts, along with manganese, lithium, magnesia, and epsom. Dr. A. K. Shelton, resident physician, promised hope for all kinds of conditions, everything from tonsillitis to what he unflinchingly called drunkard's liver. In addition, he said the mineral waters "could also improve the complexion and curing of various cutaneous eruptions," not to mention complications from gonorrhea and syphilis. The good doctor did not mince words.

And, of course, the hotel's cuisine was healthful as well as delicious. Drumming up business for the coming season, Powel emphasized how the dining experiences would be even more delightful than those of the previous year, when so many guests had wanted to come that they could not all be accommodated. "My table will be supplied with the richest milk and the best butter together with all the fruits of the surrounding country, with nice, fresh, crisp vegetables and melons in season," the manager enticed his readers. Jasper Smith of Donovan and his youngest son, Johnny, were among the suppliers of those culinary triumphs. So important to the local growers was the hotel that when it burned the farm economy was actually depressed for a time.

It is a bit hard to believe, but today it would cost only $40 for an overnight stay in the Oliver Springs Hotel and $400 to $650 for a month. If you wished to bring your own maid to add to your comfort, servants' quarters were only half price. And low rates could be arranged for families and large parties. It was indeed the day of cheap labor.

With such pleasing accommodations, the well-to-do came by the many hundreds in the ten years the resort was in operation. Elegant guests, among them young women shaped like hourglasses in their Gibson Girl costumes, stepped down from the Southern's Pullman cars ready to be pampered. Local dandies in their striped silk shirts came to dance the night away, and many people came just to look. When Sephia Cooper was a girl in nearby Harriman, the big adventure was to catch the train to visit Cousin Vannie in Oliver Springs. She remembered the highlight of the trip was going to the long veranda of the imposing hotel. What did they do? "We just sat in one of the many rocking chairs, made ourselves at home, and watched all the carryings-on!"

The story of the Richards family and their famous hotel might give the idea that the early days of coal prosperity were all harmony and progress. Far from it. During a chaotic two years, starting in 1891, there was often open warfare between miners and owners over convict labor. Virtually slaves for the owners, these convicts saved the state the cost of regular prisons, but left the jobless free miners destitute. Their fury at being deprived of work erupted in Coal Creek and spilled over into Oliver Springs several times. The new railroad made it possible for enraged Coal Creek miners to commandeer trains to Moses Winters's gap. Armed with Winchesters and anything else they could get their hands on, the miners rushed up the Big Mountain spur line and burned the state's prison stockade. How this conflict—the Coal Creek War—was finally put down by the state militia is another story told later in the book.

In Oliver Springs things had calmed down by 1895. The grand hotel had just been completed and no more commandeered trains roared through Donovan toward Big Mountain. Uncle John Smith remembered the miners' rebellion though he was only six years old. What he had much clearer memories of was the big Oliver Springs parade four years later to celebrate the election of President William McKinley. In 1896 the jovial Republican defeated the young fire-breathing orator William Jennings Bryan. Though Bryan carried Tennessee, the Republican eastern part of the state gloried in McKinley's win.

This celebration inspired one of Uncle John's "histories" that he sent me after I left Tennessee. The parade at first seemed to have nothing to do with his story as he started in his typical meandering fashion, writing as though he were talking. He must have been thinking about a visit to relatives in Haywood County, North Carolina, as he began mysteriously, "I am starting now to write a history about some people. I am beginning in North Carolina. A man there by the name of Jim Wreathbone didn't know nothing about what I wanted to know, so in my mind I was coming this way to Anderson County. I crossed Cattlelotch Mountain, Mount Sterling, Sluttie Mountain, and Chestnut Mountain."

Then he could see himself crossing the rivers at Knoxville and Clinton, finally going through Shoat Lick Hollow into Frost Bottom. There he met up with a man named Jerry Vittatoe, who also knew nothing. Uncle John wrote, "I just decided to stop doing nothing about it, but I changed my mind.

I was going to keep on until I found out what I wanted to know. You can bet your life that I found out, too."

What *was* this thing he wanted to know?

Carried away by his remembering, Uncle John didn't explain. Instead he immediately launched into a description of the McKinley parade. He was ten years old at the time. Mud "shoe mouth deep" on Main Street did nothing to slow the festivities. As he remembered, "Old Joe Nichols put a saddle on a steer for the parade and his wife Aunt Sally rode it holding a parasol." J. J. Williams, the prosperous livery stable owner and brother of Link the fox hunter, rode a big horse. Williams, over seven feet tall and weighing maybe 350 pounds, impressed the crowd by wielding a long sword that somehow demolished Aunt Sally's parasol before it was all over. This legendary businessman–deputy sheriff had a foghorn voice to go with his size. He was killed by a freight train in 1930, but for several generations many a boy toed the line when his mother threatened, "I'd whup you even if you was big as J. J. Williams!"

But the formidable Williams had nothing to do with what plagued Uncle John in his history. When he finally got back to the question, it turned out Uncle John had been studying on who Aunt Sally Nichols of the parasol was before she married Joe Nichols and not only who her father was but all her brothers. In addition, he kept wondering about Sally's sister who married Sonny Crow and had a son Frank, who lived below Oliver Springs on the Harriman Highway. Today's city dwellers rushing around anonymously probably find it hard to believe that this could be a burning question. However, for John T. Smith it was a matter of honor knowing all the families in his hometown.

So, was his mind ever put to rest? It turned out that one day Johnny Bates happened to mention Jack Wright. Of course! Uncle John remembered clear as day that Jack had had a bunch of brothers and sisters, including one named Sally. That same Jack Wright and Johnny Smith, when they were boys, once had a wild time at the Wrights' homeplace over in East Fork Valley, where Oak Ridge is today. Thanks to Johnny Bates, suddenly Uncle John could see what happened that day at the Wrights just as clearly as he saw the parade and the punctured parasol. "Jack's daddy, George, had bought fifty pounds of brown sugar. Him and his maw was gone somewheres. We got into the sugar, big lumps was in it, and we throwed them at each other like snow balls." If there was any punishment for the sticky sugar fight, he didn't say. The important thing was that Sally's father was George Wright, whom Uncle John knew and respected for fighting in the Civil War.

Sugar "snowballs" aside, William McKinley took the oath of office as president in March 1897. And just a little over one year later, the United States was in the Spanish-American War. When McKinley called for volunteers, plenty were to be had. In Oliver Springs, Church W. Lively joined up. Born on Windrock Mountain, the twenty-year-old recruit had grown up in Frost Bottom and thought he should see some of the world. In 1968 he was one of Anderson County's two remaining Spanish-American War veterans, someone Uncle John insisted I meet. They had worked together for years at Windrock Mine. Besides, they were related, sort of. Church Lively's daughter Annie married Luther Smith, grandson of Jasper Smith's brother Henry.

Finding Brother Lively was not hard to do one gray afternoon just before Christmas 1968. It just meant going through Moses Winters's gap and then along Windrock Road to a community called Tuppertown. He was waiting in his comfortable old tin-roofed house. At ninety, he stood thin and ramrod straight although he had to have some temporary help from a walker because of recent hip surgery. The strong will that kept him going all those years, first as a weighman at Windrock Mine, then as a still-smashing deputy sheriff, and finally as honored elder citizen, showed in the steady dark eyes.

Church Lively was a reserved man, probably made more so because of his difficulty in hearing, but he still talked about his long life. Yes, he lived quite independently, enjoying gardening, with Irene Bass keeping house for him. There in the yellow-curtained living room in a place of honor over the coal stove hung the commission from former governor Frank Clement making him an honorary colonel. Beside it was the certificate of appreciation from Beech Park Baptist Church to their deacon, who had barely missed a Sunday in forty years.

And also on the wall in a massive frame a Victorian face looked out from the past. Brother Lively explained, "John Calvin Lively was my father, and my family lived on a farm on the top of Windrock when I was born. It was during a big snowstorm on January 4, 1878." The new baby was really named Church for a man in Morgan County, Church Kelley. He and father John C. had been "great cronies."

Unfortunately, when I talked that day with Brother Lively, I knew little about the Livelys except Uncle John's stories of the first John Lively in the hollow sycamore tree and his daughter Milly's problems with her preacher husband who liked to drink. Today if I had a chance to talk to Church Lively, I would certainly ask how it was that his family sold their coal-laden farm to the Wileys' land company.

Whatever happened, not long after that baby was born in the snowstorm, John C. Lively moved down from the mountaintop to Frost Bottom. Life in Frost Bottom in the 1880s meant endless hard labor, even though the farmland along Poplar Creek was rich in those days, good for big corn crops. Son Church remembered all the work saying, "We only went to school three months out of the year, but when we learned something, we learned it. We had a blue speller and a pronounced speller and the McGuffey readers." He spoke in a stately cadence that belied his having attended only four years of school. Life for him in off-the-beaten-path Frost Bottom was uneventful until the war with Spain. Thinking back to why he went into the army in 1898, Brother Lively wryly explained, "President McKinley called for volunteers. When I was growing up, you worked from daylight to dark for fifty cents a day. But as a private you made fifteen dollars and sixty cents a month. So I joined up."

Many men from around Oliver Springs joined up, filling a special train. Private Lively was in the Second Regiment of Tennessee Volunteers. On the way through Knoxville, headed for training outside Washington, D.C., they saw the Fourth Regiment. It was headed by Colonel Harvey Hannah, the dashing young Oliver Springs lawyer who just two years earlier had helped elect Bob Taylor governor of Tennessee and then served as his secretary. After the short-lived war, Hannah was to become an important Democrat in Nashville, serving on the Public Service Commission for some thirty years. One of the most poplar citizens in his hometown made up mostly of Republicans, he got every vote but one in Oliver Springs in his losing battle for governor in 1922. But in 1898, young Colonel Hannah was about to ship out to Cuba. First, however, he brought his Fourth Regiment to Oliver Springs for two weeks' leave, camping near the still-new elegant resort. His soldiers drank the mineral waters and went buggy riding with the vacationing ladies from Boston and Cincinnati, thanks to J. J. Williams' livery stable. They attended hotel dances and generally set the town on its ear.

In the meantime, Church Lively had been sent to Falls Gap, Virginia, near Washington, where thirty regiments were being trained. He said, "They drilled us and drilled us hard. After a big farewell party at a Washington hotel, my regiment was sent to Columbia, South Carolina. We was all packed up, once was ready to ship out of there to Cubie," as he called their destination. "But for some reason the general canceled the order. And then peace was signed in August after only three months of war. There was no sleeping that night in those regiments, just rejoicing." Mustered out with an honorable discharge in February 1899, the young ex-private returned home and the following year married Rachel Patterson of Petros.

John T. Smith had been too young to join up, but his older brother Tom was in the First Regiment. Sent to the Philippines, that regiment had more Oliver Springs men than did all the others. "But Tom never got to the Philippines," Uncle John said, "'cause he caught the pneumonia in California. After being give up for dead three times, he recovered. But Bob Triplet, who had it, too, died."

Of those who went to those faraway islands, Uncle John especially remembered Jim Massengill. "He was one of the best sharpshooters in that regiment and told me many a time about how there'd be a shot when he was on guard duty and one of those Filipinos climbing a coconut tree would hit the ground. He'd never come right out and say he done the shooting," Uncle John recalled and grinned.

It was not long after Jim Massengill and Church Lively got back to Oliver Springs that Windrock Mine was opened in 1904 by Bessemer Coal and Coke Company of Alabama. And with it were born the now-vanished towns of Lower Windrock at the foot of the mountain and Upper Windrock at the top. Like many others, Brother Lively became a miner when he left the army. When Windrock opened, he started there, as did his friend John Smith some time later. Several years after meeting Church Lively, I would spend many hours reliving with Uncle John those days—the building of the L&N Railroad's Cow Creek Branch and the opening of Windrock Mine—as we tramped many of the twelve miles of L&N track. That story ends this book.

During all those years John Smith and Church Lively worked at Windrock, it was men with picks and shovels, not machines, that dug the coal. The work was hard, but Brother Lively found time to help build the Union Valley Baptist Church where he lived at Lower Windrock. He also served as deputy sheriff for both his district and the one over the mountain in isolated New River. He started as a lawman in addition to mining in the late 1920s during Prohibition. Mountain people considered it their God-given right to have whiskey, even if the United States Constitution had been amended to prohibit it. Cleve Daugherty, Anderson County sheriff, was killed in one moonshine raid.

Being a man who liked to hunt and walk the mountains—in fact, Church Lively never learned to drive an automobile—the new deputy took up hunting whiskey stills as something of a hobby. "We must have found several hundred over the years, the biggest one right here in Tuppertown up in the Cove. That one could produce 350 gallons, and three people went to Petros prison because of it." He was pointing up his street past Reed School into the cul-de-sac out of which Indian Creek flows.

One time a tip from New River put him and the federal authorities onto a still not far from a church. As they brought the captured apparatus out to the road, a big crowd gathered. The tipster had apparently been a competitor of the discovered moonshiner and feelings were running pretty high. "But everything finally calmed down and nobody got hurt. In all those years, I never was hurt and never had to shoot anybody, though we did have some good foot races," he added with a rare grin.

This old former deputy was even Oliver Springs's town marshal, the whole police force, for a time. Altogether he worked as a lawman for nearly twenty years following his retirement from Windrock. Although Church Lively made the job sound anything but heroic, Snyder Roberts admitted that Oliver Springs was once "a mean place," where more than one town marshal met his end. Just after the town was incorporated in 1903, the first marshal, Henry J. Cash, was killed. This tall, gangly man, whom everyone liked and called Pony, had survived the Civil War only to be shot through the heart by a drunk. It happened late one afternoon when the marshal was walking his little boy Henry up to the grand hotel to rock a bit on the long front porch for a special treat.

Killings, of course, were condemned by almost everyone, but moonshining was something else. Many did it as a sideline, but some people were real professionals. According to Snyder, the most famous and admired of the bootleggers was Alex Bunch, even though he was never convicted. Certainly he would never have denied being a moonshiner unless asked by a "revenoor." Raised in New River, Alex learned much from his father, an expert with a whiskey still appropriately named John Toddy Bunch. Alex also knew about farming and was a blacksmith as well as a popular fiddler at local dances. After he married Maggie Mills, they moved to Frost Bottom to farm and raise nine children in Shoat Lick Hollow, a most convenient spot to supplement an income with white lightning.

Maggie was a farm wife and practical nurse-midwife who wanted nothing to do with her husband's growing liquor trade. Everyone knew Alex. It was hard to miss him with his walrus mustache, astride his yellow mule, the roomy leather pockets of his saddle filled with his special snakebite medicine. Over many years customers made their way to his house on Frost Bottom Road, first by horseback and buggy, then by Model T and later Model A. As his reputation for quality grew, he expanded his business to Knoxville. He would fill two suitcases with moonshine and go over to Donovan Station to catch a train to Knoxville. In that thirsty city, he had no trouble making a quick hundred dollars. And this was when a dollar was really a dollar.

Only once in his successful career as a distiller did Alex have a close brush with the law and end up on trial. When the sober day of reckoning arrived, Alex suddenly became a sick man and had to be carried into the courtroom on a stretcher. After the damning evidence was presented, the judge asked Alex if he had anything to say for himself. Alex answered in a pained, weak voice, "I never been in trouble with the law before. I been a sick man. It's true I kept whiskey in my home, but it was for medicinal purposes. If you send me to prison, it'd be the same as a death sentence. I couldn't never live under prison conditions, and Maggie and the kids be almost sure to starve," and on and on.

The judge was skeptical, but had mercy since it was a first offense. "But," he added, "if you ever appear before me again, Alex Bunch, I'll sentence you to jail even if you die on the way!"

The stern warning did not prevent a miraculous recovery the minute the stretcher was out of the courthouse and Alex could leap with joy and go back to just plain farming in Frost Bottom, at least for several weeks.

Of all the Alex Bunch stories, the most famous and well documented, however, had to do with the time the moonshiner was truly, seriously sick. None of his home remedies, including special mountain-picked "yarbs," seemed to help although his own moonshine kept him out of pain. Wife Maggie got scared and fetched Dr. Hayes, who said Alex had double pneumonia and would probably die before the night was over. Back before antibiotics, pneumonia was indeed a death sentence more often than not.

As the day went on, Alex got weaker and weaker and finally seemed to have no pulse or sign of breath. It was then that two of his regular customers appeared, Theader Hackworth and Alf Diggs, looking for more moonshine to add to what they had already drunk. Theader was a carpenter who also worked some with John Booth, the Oliver Springs undertaker. He and Alf took one look at Alex and pronounced him dead. The two decided to get the corpse ready for Booth to pick up in the morning. This meant taking a door off its hinges and putting a chair under each end to convert it into a undertaker's cooling board. Once on the door, the corpse was undressed, bathed, and shaved, except for the handlebar mustache, and then covered with only a sheet.

By nightfall, word had gotten out in Frost Bottom and beyond that Alex Bunch had passed on. Neighbors came to sit up with the body and, as sometimes happens, tell scary tales. By midnight, a real chill was in the air and everyone on edge.

It was then that a sober Alex suddenly sat up and yelled, "What in hell you doin', tryin' to freeze me to death?"

All the amazed mourners attempted at the same time to get through the opening where the door had been, except for one giant of a man, who simply went through the wall. Snyder did admit that the part about going through the wall was not as well documented as the rest of the story.

Alex Bunch lived on and prospered until his death in the 1930s. Repeal of Prohibition had little effect on the moonshine business. With no taxes on it, white lightning was cheap. Besides, the bootleggers were always ready to provide transportation to the polls for county churches whenever a vote to make liquor legal came up. Amazingly, the situation continued until the 1960s.

Sienknechts and Doughboy Heroes

Today in Oliver Springs, if you exit the modern elevated highway and go down into the old part of town, you'll confront a pair of turn-of-the-century ghosts. These two-story brick buildings stand side by side on the main thoroughfare where it crosses the Southern tracks, separated only by the invisible line between Anderson and Roane Counties. One is the bank building, and next to it is what was once the fanciest department store this side of Knoxville, H. Sienknecht Company. The Great Depression doomed both these businesses. By the 1940s the department store had begun a series of metamorphoses into everything from a Dollar Discount Store to Copeland's Auto Parts, ending up an empty shell.

The Oliver Springs Banking Company, organized in 1907 under the enterprising William Richards, owner of the splendid mansion, barely escaped being razed for a parking lot after having served as an appliance store. Charles Tichy, a historical architect with TVA who lives in Oliver Springs, has bought and restored the bank. His personal enthusiasm for preservation brought back the elegance of the oak paneling hidden many years under layers of paint and also uncovered the decorative pressed-metal ceiling long concealed by a lower false one. The bank has been listed on the National Register of Historic Places.

In these days of shopping malls and supermarkets, nothing like the H. Sienknecht Company is likely to appear again. Henry Sienknecht's store was a place where a well-heeled vacationer could buy a tuxedo for the resort hotel's dances or a coal miner could purchase a shovel. Certainly a family like the Sienknechts would not be easy to find today. When Miss Mamie, who married Dr. Joseph A. Sienknecht, died without children in 1977, exactly fifty years after her husband, no one by that well-known name was left in Oliver Springs.

The Revolution of 1848, as it rumbled across Europe, drove this German family to America. Dr. Friedrich Sienknecht, a surgeon trained at the University of Copenhagen, fled to New York with his wife Catharina and six children. He wanted no part of compulsory military training for his young sons. This adventurous man, who had treated members of the Danish royal family, ended up in what is today Wartburg, not far from Oliver Springs in Morgan County. A German-Swiss community had been started there by George F. Gerding, another unusual man. Gerding had emigrated from Hanover much earlier in 1825 and made a New York fortune in the cut-glass and china import-export business. Gerding also served as U.S. minister to Belgium and became interested in encouraging immigration, moving to Morgan County himself in 1849. His East Tennessee Colonization Company had some 167,000 acres on the Cumberland Plateau but was in great need of a physician. Dr. Friedrich Sienknecht was just the person. When the surgeon and his family left bustling, up-to-date New York, they probably did not realize what an undertaking their new life would be. Their journey itself was daunting, going by ship to Charleston and continuing on by train, stage, wagon, and finally on foot to reach Wartburg.

The good doctor served the colony, farmed, grew his own herbs for medicine, and raised his three oldest sons to be physicians. Unluckily, his newly adopted country did not guarantee the escape from war that Friedrich Sienknecht had hoped for. Sons Theodore, Henry, and Christian all served in the Confederate army. Afterward Dr. Theodore moved his medical practice to Olivers just before the Walden Ridge Railroad arrived. He already knew the small town, for he had married Richard Oliver's daughter Charlotte and had six children before she died shortly after the Civil War. With his second wife, Matilda, the talented daughter of a Viennese music teacher, he had ten more children. Dr. Joe, who married Miss Mamie, was Matilda's second child, and Elmer her last. The genial Elmer Sienknecht served the Windrock Mining Company as business manager for over forty years before retiring in the 1950s.

Elmer's older brother, Dr. Joe, first caught the eye of young Mary Richards in something of a derring-do before the Oliver Springs Hotel burned in 1905. In fact, it had to do with putting out a fire. Miss Mamie liked to tell how a spark ignited the wooden shingle roof (foreshadowing of things to come!) and Joe Sienknecht jumped through a window out on the steep incline to smother the blaze. "He did it more to show off in front of us girls than to be a hero and keep the hotel from burning down. You know, I was young and so impressed with his bravery and his good looks that a little later I married him."

That was 1909. He and Miss Mamie lived for a while at Upper Windrock, where he was the company doctor. However, for most of their married life Dr. Joe had a practice in Oliver Springs that he first oversaw from his horse and buggy, then in a Ford Model T. In the 1920s he became the physician at Brushy Mountain State Penitentiary in Petros. He died one night on his way to see a sick prisoner, falling from a railroad trestle in an unexplained accident. The prison keys he had in his pocket were missing when his body was discovered.

It was Joe's Uncle Henry, his father's younger brother, who became the highly successful merchant. Henry Sienknecht, too, had fought for the South in the Civil War. Not having completed medical school, he served temporarily as a physician but later as a cavalryman under the famous, or infamous, General Joe Wheeler—depending on which side you were on. Wheeler's Raiders were the ones who swept so disastrously through Dutch Valley, as Jasper Smith would remember to his dying day. After the war Henry graduated from medical school in Philadelphia and returned to practice medicine in Robertsville, now part of Oak Ridge. In those hard days after Appomattox, he had to accept so much farm produce as payment from his patients that he ended up operating a grocery store on the side. Dr. Henry lived until 1890 in a two-story frame home where Oak Ridge High School now stands, but his old war injuries finally turned him into a full-time businessman. He moved to Oliver Springs and became a partner with his brother-in-law John Keebler in the latter's popular general store. But the town was booming, thanks to the coal business and the Oliver Springs Hotel, so there was more than enough business for both Keebler's and Henry Sienknecht's new department store. The doors opened early in 1902, and the business flourished for nearly half a century.

Snyder Roberts was born six years after the grand opening and grew up in the heyday of H. Sienknecht Company. He remembered how the latest fashions held the spotlight at the store entrance. A haberdashery on the right had everything for men from socks to suits, which were mainly blue serge off the rack or tailormade for the elite. To the left, women customers were enticed by that wonder of this new age, the ready-made dress, maybe a shirtwaist and skirt for those tiny around the middle, or a four-hook corset to help overcome a size problem. Bolts of piece goods nearly reached the ceiling for the large majority of women who still relied on their Singer sewing machines. So important were ladies' hats that a separate millinery department reigned on the second floor, up next to the furniture. One of those large cartwheel creations befeathered and covered in veil could be purchased from all the fashionable ones in stock or else something special made to order. A lady in a fancy buggy had to consider carefully the work of art that she wore on her head.

The noisy nerve center of Sienknecht's, the large single cash register where all purchases were completed, occupied the area past the clothing and shoes, not far from a big potbellied stove. On toward the back there was hardware in all shapes and forms, and then the grocery department with its special aroma. This was a mixture of pungent smells from the barrels of sour pickles, huge rounds of cheese, Arbuckle Coffee, onions, apples, bacon, and who knows what else. Of course, there were staples like flour and sugar, as well as barrels of soda crackers. Since Sienknecht's prided itself on being up-to-date, Jell-O stood on the shelves and even Hershey Bars, in addition to the usual stick candy. Post Toasties and Campbell's Pork and Beans would appear in 1904. Topping all this off were noisy live chickens and absolutely quiet dressed ones. At the very back of the store, feed and grain could be had while off to the side stood the tank with coal oil, that is, kerosene.

Dr. Henry and his son Fred had a flair for merchandising that meant something was always happening at the store. People would come into town just for some of the sales promotions. Once a flock of guineas was let loose from the top floor's high curved windows, a dollar bill attached to each screeching bird's leg. What followed was a wild scramble of boys up into trees and onto roof tops to retrieve the free money. Even without such doings, the store's wide front porch attracted passersby. Itinerant preachers like Charlie Hall often preached near the store entrance.

Maybe the most famous user of Sienknecht's porch was Silas Hulen, who for five decades tramped all over Anderson, Roane, and Morgan Counties, and in his younger days even parts of Kentucky and Missouri. By the time the store opened, he had been wandering no one knew how long or exactly why. A boy when the Civil War was over, Uncle Si came from a pioneer family that lost its farm in what is now Oak Ridge. He talked incessantly about imaginary thieves and robbers, telling endless tales like the one in which he killed a thousand wolves only to have them stolen by the ever-present criminals.

Today in our preoccupation with mental illness, we might not take Uncle Si and his loaded shotgun as calmly as people did back then in Oliver Springs. He was not exactly reassuring to look at. A strong man weathered from living outside, unfamiliar with baths, he always wore a wide-brimmed black hat and layer upon layer of clothes in chilly weather. Besides his gun, a tow sack was slung over his shoulder usually filled with hickory nuts or muscadines, anything he could trade for food. A pillow case served as a pouch for a few belongings and a lard can for food and cooking. Always he had a dog on a leash, the most famous being his beloved Queenie. In spite of his shotgun, the wanderer caused little trouble except when town boys teased him about his pet. If they yelled, "Turn that old sheep-killing dog loose," it was hell, not a dog, that would break loose. Uncle Si would take aim and fire, luckily with no accuracy. Nevertheless, mothers did their best to make their sons avoid such nonsense.

Of the many tales about Silas Hulen, the most unusual had to do with the killing of a tramp outside a Clinton saloon about the time Sienknecht's opened. Facts were fuzzy, but the dead man was identified as Uncle Si. An unstable young man was tried and convicted but then confined to a psychiatric hospital. The confused case was appealed to the Tennessee Supreme Court and great effort made on both sides to find new evidence. In the process, the well-known Link Williams, deputy sheriff and once assistant manager of the Oliver Springs Hotel, located Silas Hulen in Missouri. When Link appeared before the chief justices with Uncle Silas in tow, presumably without his shotgun, there was a small sensation.

"Yes, I'm Silas Hulen," he told the court, "and I ain't never been dead yit, let alone been kilt!" Witnesses, including Dr. Henry Sienknecht, agreed. Legal technicalities caused the case not to be tried again. And Uncle Si went on with his wandering until he became so ill that he was taken to the county poor farm just before his death in 1929.

Of everything Sienknecht's had to sell, soda pop was one of the most popular items. It was home-brewed, so to speak. Paul DeBlieux from New Orleans set up the Oliver Springs Bottling Works about 1900 on Back Street. He took over the building used by the Russell whiskey distillery that had flourished in the 1880s thanks to the huge thirst of coal miners and railroad construction workers. But for some reason, the business had folded. The same good water from Moses Winters's spring then went into DeBlieux's soft drinks. He called them Ironbrew, Koca Nola, Keg Cider, along with fruit names, the most popular of all being conventional strawberry.

On our visit to Back Street, Snyder pointed out what everyone called the John Vann House, which had been a saloon in the days of the distillery before the bottling works. The Reverend Elijah Vann, who was seventy-three and always called Lige, had tales to tell about Back Street. He thought back to when he was a boy: "I didn't live long in that house across from the bottling works. We had a house on down near the end of Back Street, where you forded the creek. It was close to my Granddaddy Ed Vann's two-story house." His grandfather built his home near the creek around the time of the Civil War. He was a descendant of the Cherokee chief with the same name mentioned in Ramsay's *Annals of Tennessee* in 1853. Ed Vann's grandsons included not only Lige and John but also Harry. A former mayor, Harry Vann had taken over Albert Meade's barbershop when the latter retired to sit on his veranda high up above doomed Back Street.

Grandfather Ed died when the boy Lige was only twelve. Ed Vann never talked about his Cherokee ancestor, but he loved to tell about the time his wife Nancy jumped out of bed during a thunderstorm and got bitten on her foot by a copperhead that had managed to get into their house there on Back Street. Lige

Vann laughed saying, "My granddaddy ran up the street to get Dr. Koontz and was clear back in his own yard before he thought to tell the doctor that the snake bit him, too, when he jumped up after my grandma hollered."

Three years before that, when he was only nine years old, Lige got a job washing bottles for Paul DeBlieux at the bottling works. They were nearly next-door neighbors since DeBlieux lived with his two spinster sisters, Miss Stella and Miss Octavia, across from his business. "I washed bottles for Uncle Paul for fifty cents a day. He'd hire several young boys. It was kinda hard getting the tops on the bottles, and when a lid was bent, he'd give it to me and say just drink it! Some days I'd really be full of pop!"

The bottling process was tricky and sometimes ended in flying glass as well as bent lids. DeBlieux would first put the bottle cap in the machine with his right hand. Then with his left he would pull the lever to squirt in the proper amount of syrup and at nearly the same time with his right hand release the hissing carbonated water into the bottle. He then immediately had to stamp with his foot on the pedal that secured the cap on the bottle. Too much pressure from the carbonated water, and bang would go the bottle. He wisely worked behind a shield. But even with all the problems, thousands of bottles were turned out, and today collectors pay a fancy price for the now-scarce bottles. The pop was sold not only at the elegant Oliver Springs Hotel and all over town but was hauled by wagon to the Windrock and Big Mountain commissaries. DeBlieux stayed in business until late in the 1920s when the popularity of Coca-Cola and the onset of the Depression finally proved too much. Long before that, he had moved the plant from Back Street down near City Hall, but he piped Moses Winters's spring water to the new location.

By the time the boy Lige Vann was working at the successful new bottling works, Oliver Springs had become an important part of the Southern Railway system. The railroad bought out the bankrupt E. T. V. & G. in 1894 and made the prosperous coal town into a freight distribution center. Not only was there coal to be shipped out, but also bricks from the new kilns up in the Big Mountain mining area. One of the mines there had turned out to be more valuable for the fire clay that overlay the coal seam than for the coal itself, so a brick business sprang up. Eventually seven domed kilns were constructed, looking a bit like a small city of Muslim mosques. They produced thousands and thousands of bricks and many jobs until improved technology caught up with them in the 1940s. Before that the kilns had often provided a warm sleeping spot for wandering Silas Hulen in the winter.

Those were the glory days of the coal-eating locomotives that rolled into town making incredible noise and breathing clouds of steam like so many iron dragons. Grown-ups, as well as small boys wanting to be engineers, were impressed. After the Oliver Springs Hotel burned in 1905, the center of town activities moved down to the Southern depot. With its polished spittoons, it was a showplace surrounded by a flower-edged lawn. All day freight trains pulling loaded coal gondolas and flatcars stacked high with lumber clanged through town without much notice, but the six daily passenger trains definitely got attention. Meeting the noon train headed west toward Chattanooga became a town ritual. Onlookers might see Dr. J. J. Waller climbing into the baggage car with a cot-bound patient headed for the city hospital or workmen loading glass jugs of smelly sulfur water from the mineral springs, which still flowed even after the hotel had disappeared. About 10:30 P.M. the late train heading west would arrive, often with shoppers who had been in Knoxville for the day. On Saturday nights there might be excitement when coal miners got back from spending all their money in the saloons and red-light district of the big city. They would get off at the depot "feeling no pain," according to Snyder Roberts, and generally raise hell as they made their way home up the hollows to Big Mountain and Windrock.

As the son of Samuel H. Roberts, who worked for the Southern more than fifty years, Snyder grew up with railroading. Most of that time his father had the crucial job of area maintenance foreman. Sam Roberts and his crew won many company awards for efficiency. Once they received the first motorcar to replace the old hand-lever car pumped up and down the tracks for repair work. Train accidents happened from time to time, but there was only one serious passenger train wreck that anyone can remember. Uncle John put the date at 1914. Near his home at Donovan, the noon train hit a dead animal wedged in a device at a track intersection. The locomotive went down an embankment and landed wheels up, killing the engineer, Andy Monroe. A number of cars derailed, but no one else was seriously hurt.

Oliver Springs had been brought into the new century with the roar of the iron horses. Yet it remained a small town. People still raised much of their own food in spite of the availability of Keebler's and Sienknecht's. It was not a bit unusual for a family to have a cow and a barn in their backyard near the outdoor toilet and maybe even a pigpen. The hogs were kept downwind from the house if at all possible, though one family's downwind unfortunately might be another's upwind. The cows had to graze either in J. J. Williams's pasture on Schoolhouse Hill or clear out of town. Lige Vann's teenage brother Harry became a specialist in herding cows out near Cold Springs. At two dollars a month for each cow, he became a successful young businessman. But in most families, one son was assigned that job along with cleaning out the cow shed. Late evenings as all the cows were herded back for milking, the clanging of cow bells could all but drown out a passing train.

As for the hogs, well, for the son designated as the slopper that meant a trip three times a day out to the smelly pen with a bucket of dishwater and food scraps. Only shortly before cold weather and hog-killing time were bran and corn added to fatten the squealing animals. Butchering was not a job for amateurs. The process was enough to make vegetarians out of meat eaters who today buy neatly packaged pork chops at the local A & P.

For several days after a hog killing, the eating would be so good with fresh backbones and spareribs, along with heart and liver, that a family could nearly always count on extra mouths at the dinner table. Once in a while the son who was the official slopper made the mistake of getting attached to "his" hog and the family feast left him unable to eat a bite. If he was old enough to be in high school, he had already killed rabbits and squirrels for the dinner table, maybe even a wild turkey. But eating the family hog was another matter.

So, in those years before the First World War most people in Oliver Springs had jobs thanks to mining and brickmaking, though no one was getting rich. Life generally was good even if a housewife had to do her Monday wash in a giant black cast-iron kettle in the backyard and then heat flatirons on her coal stove. Train service was convenient, although the streets were unpaved and roads in the county were not much better than they had been before the Civil War. To get across the Clinch River in Anderson County still meant going on a ferry.

Then along came Henry Ford.

Of course, there were other automobile manufacturers, but Ford was the one who changed history with mass production of his Model T. One could be bought for $850, about $12,000 in today's dollars. That was 1908, the same year the first car of any kind arrived in the county by way of the ferry at Clinton. The *Anderson County News* reported the stir as Magnet Knitting Mills employees were allowed to stop work long enough go outside to see the car toot its horn and sputter off through town. It was headed north to prosperous Coal Creek. The reporter was so impressed that he failed to find out who had purchased this amazing machine or even its make. It was one of an estimated 63,500 cars manufactured in the United States that year as Americans began their love affair with the car. By 1914 it was no longer necessary to special-order an automobile from Detroit. That year in Clinton, R. A. Moser opened the county's first car agency and was a big success selling Ford automobiles and Goodrich tires.

The year after Moser started selling Model Ts, a state law appeared requiring cars to be registered. That was 1915, the year Anderson County killed off its ferries and welcomed the twentieth century by completing four new bridges across the Clinch River. It was seventy-five thousand dollars well spent, but unfortunately taxpayers then rested on their bridge-building laurels for nearly fifty years. Until 1962, when construction of the TVA's Bull Run Steam Plant began, Oak Ridgers had to use the one-lane Edgemoor Bridge in Thomas Frost's Raccoon Valley on that popular route to Knoxville.

But in 1915 these new bridges, including Edgemoor, foretold the eventual conquest of Anderson County by the horseless carriages. Within just two years, the number of registered vehicles jumped from 18 to 117. Women may not have been allowed to vote, but no one stopped them from driving. The very first group of eighteen registered car owners included two women, both from Oliver Springs. One, Miss Annie Shelton, the schoolteacher daughter of the Oliver Springs Hotel's Dr. Shelton, bought a Metz. The other owner, Mrs. C. J. Ladd, had a Ford touring car, the open kind that demanded fashionable women wear dusters plus veils to hold on their mammoth hats as they ventured down unpaved roads. The Ladds owned the red brick Butler house still at the corner of Back Street. Their daughter Dora was to become the mother of former U.S. senator Howard Baker. The sociable Tilda Ladd was a spirited woman who was often ahead of her time, and not only as a car owner. When her husband was elected sheriff in 1926 and soon died, she served in his place until the next election.

After automobiles came the Great War. Although the United States managed to stay out until 1917, people knew all about the spectacular new-style heroes, flying aces like the famed Red Baron. It wasn't until after the war, however, that the first airplane flew over Major Winters's gap. Like many other former wartime pilots, Guy Jones was barnstorming his way across the country. When he made it to Oliver Springs and found a field large enough to land in, he was in business. He would give anyone an astonishing aerial ride over the top of Windrock Mountain for a not-cheap five-dollar ticket.

The small town had had no aviators in the war, but it did have more than its share of men living up to Tennessee's strong patriotic tradition. In 1918 two of Oliver Springs's soldier sons won the Distinguished Service Cross, an honor second only to the Congressional Medal. One, Ben Diggs, died in 1956. But the second hero, Walter Stripling, was very much alive when we met in 1969, still hardy at seventy-three and destined to live another twenty years, having survived bloody trench warfare on the Western Front decades earlier.

Both men were part of a military tradition going back before the Battle of Kings Mountain to the days of fighting the Cherokees. In the War of 1812 so many Tennesseans joined up to fight with General Andrew Jackson that Tennessee became known as the Volunteer State. This patriotism took on mythic qualities when Jasper Smith wrote how Benjamin Duncan and William Brown left Scotland only to find the American Revolution waiting for them in North

Carolina. When they heard the war drums, one said, "We better have stayed home." But the other answered, "That drum means freedom. Don't get weak, let's stand up straight and fight." They did just that, Jasper said, even helping build the "raft of logs" for General Washington to cross the Delaware!

After the revolution, Tennessee would not only produce Andrew Jackson, whose military victories made him the first frontier president, but also Davy Crockett, most famous of the heroes to die at the Alamo. And there was Sam Houston, the former governor of Tennessee who led the fight against Mexico, then became the first president of the Republic of Texas. Certainly the most celebrated American foot soldier of World War I was Sergeant Alvin York. He lived not too many miles up the road from Oliver Springs in Fentress County, which borders on Morgan County.

Morgan, of course, is one of the three counties that each claim a piece of Oliver Springs, an unusual situation brought about by attempts to avoid taxes for the railroad bonds Anderson County issued just before the Civil War. Morgan County produced a number of the town's most noted citizens like the Sienknechts and J. J. Williams and his brother Link. Another was William A. Potter, a lawman most famous for a World War I incident. He arrived in Oliver Springs during the booming 1880s sporting the name Bad Bill, maybe a latter-day relation of Moses C. Winters's Bad Bill. This Bill Potter lived up to his name, involving himself in a number of scrapes, including a shootout with William Walls that left Walls dead in the saloon destined to become the John Vann House. After that incident Potter not only reformed, but took over as the town marshal in 1905 after Pony Cash was shot to death. A picture of him and the first municipal council that hangs in City Hall shows Potter with an imposing handlebar mustache above his lawman's star.

Marshal Potter was the town's most renowned lawman. A tiny but fearless man, he was nice-looking, with dark curly hair, and very likable despite his quick temper. With his official-looking black hat and oversize dog, most people didn't want "to contrary" Bill. A niece recalled that one time he had what she called a temper tantrum and started jumping up and down. "The madder he got, the higher he jumped, and he finally started firing his pistol into the ground, which only made him jump higher," she said. "But after he ran out of ammunition, he calmed down and was as nice as you please."

When Snyder Roberts was a boy, Bill Potter gained fame because of a whipping post. During World War I, the United States was flooded with propaganda about the monstrous baby-murdering Huns. As a result, loyal German-Americans suffered as those in Oliver Springs must have when a cross-shaped contraption with fearsome leather straps appeared right across the street from Sienknecht's store, clearly a warning to German sympathizers.

Bill was as patriotic as the next man, but he nevertheless disapproved of the ten-foot-high whipping post on Main Street in front of West's Drug Store. How it got there nobody seemed to know, but everyone knew that Ed West had recently lost two sons in France. Maybe it was the American flag atop the post or maybe something else that got Marshal Potter mad. Anyway, he took a good look at it and went home for his ax. When he came back, Bill respectfully removed the flag and then furiously chopped down the whole thing. Main Street emptied as people peeked around corners of buildings and out store windows. Everyone expected a lot of shooting, but it never came. In fact, the fierce little lawman never had a genuine shootout as a police officer and died peacefully in his bed in 1926, well after the Great War was over.

As for Walter Stripling, the old hero in 1969 was still straight as a young soldier on parade. A former miner and lawman, he must have had a temper to go with his once-red hair. It flashed a little when he was asked about the draft-card burners who were then out in the streets protesting the Vietnam War. Nevertheless, Stripling wasn't inclined to talk about patriotism in the old days nor his own exploits in nine major battles in 1918. Finally, however, his pride in General John J. Pershing overcame his reticence. Even after a half century, he was enormously pleased to have served in "Black Jack" Pershing's great First Division.

He made clear what unshaken American confidence had been like in those days: "Trench warfare, we put a stop to that!" the old sergeant said, suddenly jabbing the air with his hands. He was referring to the arrival of the American Expeditionary Force that had been so important in ending the stalemate on the Western Front. "General Pershing was for open warfare, movement of troops, and moving fast. He was the best. And we need one like him now," he said forcefully. He was certain that Pershing would have known what to do about Vietnam and would not have let "the politicians" make a mess of things.

His certainty came from being one of the very first Americans to land in France in June 1917, seeing combat in October. Over a million more Americans would arrive the next spring, including Ben Diggs, to help turn the tide against the Germans and end the war on November 11, 1918.

But that's ahead of the story. Stripling and nine other Oliver Springs men came to be in the famed First Division because they had volunteered for the army in 1916, a year before America got into the First World War. They were sent to Texas, where Pershing was trying to keep Pancho Villa and his bandits on the Mexican side of the border and at the same time put together an American fighting force. The Mexican Revolution was still going on. Then German submarines sank one ship too many, and the United States entered the European conflict. The general was ready with the division that came to

Walter Stripling of Oliver Springs seen in 1969 holding his World War I uniform with his medals for bravery, the Distinguished Service Cross and the French Croix de Guerre. Photograph courtesy of the *Oak Ridger.*

glory as the Big Red One or the Bloody I. Its arrival June 26 at St. Nazaire, in spite of the submarines, caused French jubilation, so much that Black Jack Pershing complained loudly about lack of secrecy concerning troop movements, something he had always controlled in the States.

Stripling remembered that control: "We left McAllen, Texas, in June of 1917 and it took us seven whole days on that slow train to get to Hoboken, where we sailed. It was all real secret. The officers wouldn't let us off the train except for a little exercise. It was quite a change from the year of patrolling the Rio Grande River."

Texas had been hot—"a hundred degrees for days and days"—but the old East Tennessean smiled when he talked about how much he had liked the fabled army town of San Antonio. "We were stationed there first and then later sent on down to Laredo on the border and finally to McAllen, where we were patrolling ranches like the Santa Rosada to keep the Mexicans from raiding cattle. They were always right there on the other side of the river. You know, there was a revolution on." He laughed when he said how four of his eight-man squad would have to guard while the other half bathed in the Rio Grande, an occasional bullet whizzing overhead.

The story goes that it was down there on the border that American soldiers got the name "doughboy." The chalky adobe soil, the same used to make sun-dried bricks for buildings in the Southwest, covered the foot soldiers as they drilled. The men were called "adobes" and "dobies." The soldiers, who looked as though they had a coating of flour, became "doughboys."

If life on the Rio Grande had its lighter moments, there was not much to laugh about the next year when Stripling was among the initial American troops to see combat on the Western Front. This was in the southern sector of Luneville near Nancy. The young Tennessee corporal was there when the first Americans died in battle. All told, 117,000 would not survive the war, including over 53,000 killed in action. That winter the Toul sector turned out to be relatively quiet for soldiers in the wet trenches, which were filled with rats and lice as the stalemate continued. But in March 1918, the Russian Revolution resulted in a peace treaty between that country and Germany, so that the Kaiser could move all his troops in Russia back to the Western Front. Now with superior numbers of men, the Germans started their last all-out offensive to overwhelm the Allies before help arrived in full force from the United States. Paris was being pounded by Big Berthas, guns with a range of about seventy-five miles. The First Division was rushed north into the inferno at Cantigny, the point of the German salient bearing down on Paris. It was Stripling's Twenty-eighth Infantry Regiment that took over this first all-American assault, recapturing the village in May and, after five counterattacks, securing it. Stripling was in Company G. "They called us the gypsy division," he said, "because we were thrown in just anywhere we were needed."

Then came the last big German push to cross the Marne River to take Paris. It started at midnight on July 14, 1918. Corporal Stripling had been in the capital to march as part of a special American battalion in the Bastille Day parade, which was hardly over before every man was ordered back to his unit. "General Pershing counterattacked July eighteenth, when the Germans were twenty-six miles from Paris. I say that was the real turning point of the war, not the battle in the Argonne. From that day on, it all went our way," Stripling said with satisfaction.

Official records call it the Battle of Soissons, but it is remembered as the Second Battle of the Marne. And Stripling remembered it as German soldiers coming as far as the eye could see. "They were led by the Prussian Guards with their spiked helmets. There was such a hurry we were unloaded right there in the middle of the road and our guns thrown down to us. We pushed them back eleven miles that day. And you could tell where we had been." It was during those next two days of fierce fighting that he received shrapnel wounds, becoming one of seven thousand casualties in his division. After that, he was sent with Robert Haggard, another Oliver Springs man, to the south of France to recuperate. The two had been side by side flat on their bellies under fire in a wheat field. A bullet went through the front of Haggard's steel helmet. It skimmed off part of his head and came out the top of the helmet.

"At first I thought sure he was dead with all that blood. But he came to," Stripling remembered. "I always told him his head was so hard that the bullet ricocheted off it. After our wounds got pretty well healed up, we wanted to leave that rest camp, not stay six months like we were supposed to. So we just hopped a freight like back home and went back to our company. I got to stay, but Bob was sent back to the hospital."

Haggard recovered and, like Stripling, came back to Oliver Springs. He was one of those nine men who enlisted in 1916. Of the seven who survived to return home, only Stripling was left fifty years later. Tom West was killed at Cantigny and his brother George at Soissons, apparently the reason for the whipping post on Main Street. Two others not among those first volunteers, Wade Cummings and Joe Jones, also died in action that July. But luck was with Walter Stripling. He went on through the last two great battles of St. Mihiel and Meuse-Argonne. Nearly a million Americans took part in the fighting in the Argonne Forest, where one man in ten was killed or wounded. Sergeant York won the Congressional Medal there.

It was at St. Mihiel near Nonsard on September 12 that Corporal Stripling led his squad on the daring maneuver that earned him the Distinguished Service Cross. He didn't know about the decoration, however, until nearly a year later when he was in Germany in the occupation army. In fact, Stripling laughed telling how after the battle he half-expected to end up court-martialed. "After we captured those thirty Germans, one man in my squad said he was going to take one of their wrist watches. It was against the rules of war, but I said, hell, take two! My captain found out and he nearly ate me up." But there was no court-martial. Instead, General Pershing came to Montebar, Germany, after the war was over and pinned the DSC on the Tennessean. And not long afterward, Stripling was relieved one day of KP duty so that Marshall Petain could decorate him with the French Croix de Guerre.

Those two medals, still pinned to his old field jacket, were awarded for a daring wire-cutting exploit. The Americans' main line had reached the top of a small hill but couldn't advance because of a hundred yards of barbed wire entanglement and heavy fire from a German machine gun nest dug in on the top of another hill. Stripling and the seven men in his squad inched their way through the wire with insulated cutters—"that wire was juiced!"—all the time unrolling spools of tape for the soldiers to follow.

"When we got down to the bottom between the two hills we found a gully big enough for us to slip along," he explained. "We didn't have orders to do it, but we kept going along that ditch about twenty minutes, staying extra low because of the machine gun fire, and finally we came to a clump of bushes even with their right flank. We jumped them from behind and let them have it with our rifles before they could change the position of their machine guns. Three fell and the other thirty gave up." Not one of his own men was killed.

Not long afterward, when the powerful Allied offensive started pushing toward the German line, teenager Ben Diggs on October 7 proved himself a hero. His Thirtieth Division, made up of Tennesseans and Carolinians, had been sent to help the British north of Paris in the Cambrai–St. Quentin pincer action. They went down in history for being the first to puncture Germany's famous fortified Hindenburg Line. Private Diggs returned with his 117th Regiment in glorious triumph to Knoxville on April 5, 1919. Because he had lied about his age to enlist, he was only seventeen that day when thousands of welcoming Tennesseans jammed the city for a parade down Gay Street and the presentation of medals to East Tennessee's heroes.

Mrs. Vaughn Disney talked about her brother, who was always called "Little Ben" to distinguish him from his father, a lawyer who became Oliver Springs's first mayor. She said he never wanted to talk about the war. "I guess it was too terrible and he was shell-shocked. He always said he didn't deserve the medal, but I know that men in his company gave him credit for saving

At seventeen, Oliver Springs's Ben Diggs won the Distinguished Service Cross and the French Croix de Guerre in World War I. Photograph courtesy of Snyder E. Roberts.

their lives. He was just sixteen and really their pet," she explained. Mrs. Disney and Ben's two other sisters, Mrs. B. E. Ward and Miss Lula Diggs, had come over from Clinton to the Diggs' old homeplace in Tuppertown, not far from Church Lively's house. The young hero never married but lived in the spacious two-story house with the enormous magnolia tree until his death. The sisters had searched the closed-up house and found his medals.

Mrs. Disney was just a girl that tumultuous day in April 1919 when people by the thousand poured into Knoxville to welcome home the 117th Infantry Regiment. But she remembered it well. So did Lula Diggs, already a teacher in Clinton, who early that morning saw the first troop train pull into Union Station. There was a dense fog, but that didn't keep a friendly mob from covering the train tracks. Mrs. Disney added, "Ben was always so modest. He didn't let us know about the decoration, and we missed seeing it pinned on him since we weren't at the reviewing stand. We were all but trampled in the crowd."

As the 2,300 soldiers paraded down bunting-draped Gay Street over flowers thrown in their path, each of the seven heroes fell out of the ranks when he passed the reviewing stand. When they were all on the stand, General Lawrence Tyson read the citation for bravery to each soldier and pinned on his medal "in the name of General Pershing." The seventeen-year-old Oliver Springs private was decorated with the DSC for extraordinary heroism in action near Montbrehain, France, on October 7, 1918.

The general read, "Private Diggs volunteered and successfully carried a message through heavy shell and machine gun fire in plain view of the enemy after one runner had been killed and two others wounded in attempting to accomplish this mission. Although he was gassed performing this feat, he refused to seek first aid until he was wounded later in the afternoon."

How had this volunteer, just sixteen years old, found himself running through enemy lines? Little Ben had gotten to France only after months of pestering his parents to sign for him because he was under eighteen. Their resistance was hard for the teenager to understand, for his own father's father and brother had both fought bravely for the Union army and died in the infamous Confederate prison at Andersonville. Finally, Mrs. Disney said, on his sixteenth birthday, November 6, 1917, he bought a pair of long pants on the sly and secretly went to Knoxville. "He just told the recruiters he was eighteen, and they didn't question him. The birth date on his tombstone is two years off," she added.

Walter Stripling also remembered how Ben had worn knickers until that day he decided he would sign up, adding "we called them blouse breeches then." Though the two got to know each other in 1921 after the sergeant came home to Oliver Springs instead of reenlisting, they never talked about their experiences in France. Stripling grinned as he described Ben Diggs: "He was a quiet kind of boy, a good boy, but he had a fiery temper, too. He was a little like a frog in a hailstorm. But he didn't want to talk about the war."

The action near Montbrehain between Cambrai and St. Quentin apparently did not make for pleasant remembering. Ben's Company M had been attached to the British Third Army Corps and fought near Ypres in Belgium until September when the carnage of the final Allied offensive began. On October 7, the day he got through the message bringing help to his company, it had been reduced from 77 to 34 men. They had attacked 400 Germans who were strongly entrenched in a railroad cut. When it was over, 114 Germans were dead, 23 found wounded on the field, and 263 made prisoners. Then on October 9 the towns of Becquigny and Busigny fell, and the Germans' crucial railway captured.

Such were the actions that prompted Knoxville's jubilant welcome home. Glorified as the "Hindenburg Line Breakers," the Thirtieth Division sailed from France in March 1919. Knoxville saw four big parades within a week. First the 114th Machine Gun Battalion arrived March 27, followed in two days by the 114th Field Artillery. Then on April 4 came the 115th Field Artillery and the next day the huge climax when Private Ben Diggs and the rest of the 117th Infantry arrived from Charleston. Special trains brought people in from all over East Tennessee as the newspapers overflowed with stories of heroism.

Ben's 117th Regiment, "the arrowhead that broke through the Hindenburg Line," according to the Knoxville *Journal & Tribune,* left Camp Jackson in Columbia, South Carolina, in a pouring rain. But the rain dampened no one's spirits. There were six sections of the train greeted by crowds in Spartanburg and Asheville. A monumental breakfast with "chicken, ham, eggs, homemade biscuits by the thousands" awaited the soldiers in Morristown, including that town's own Private Calvin J. Ward, who had won the Congressional Medal. Ben Diggs was on the first section of the train that pulled into Knoxville's Union Station in the early morning fog of April 5. Every factory and engine in the railyards blew its whistle for ten solid minutes ahead of time.

Sister Lula remembered the excitement of it all, especially the hundreds and hundreds of soldiers hanging out the train windows. The crowd at the station kept growing, so that by the time the last section pulled in about noon, the train had to stop back at Central Avenue to get people off the tracks. Streetcars and automobiles could not run because of all the humanity. But space was found for the parade to form behind spiffy officers on high-stepping horses. After the decoration ceremonies, an enormous feast with chicken and cake appeared in the middle of Walnut Street, followed by a street dance. At midnight the infantry men boarded their train for another triumphal welcome in Nashville. Then it was on to Fort Oglethorpe, Georgia, where they were demobilized April 16.

After that, Ben went back to Maryville College's preparatory school and on to the University of Tennessee for a year. Mrs. Disney recalled how he wanted to be a reporter but had to drop out of school because of what she called hard times. He couldn't find a newspaper job and went into construction work. An expert rifle shot like Walter Stripling, Ben loved to hunt where he grew up in the mountains above his home in Tuppertown. His father had a large library, and Ben had time to read in the quiet days after the war. He liked poetry and history but was also an avid sports fan. Snyder Roberts got to know him through exchanging books. "Ben was rather small but a good athlete," according to Snyder, who was then captain of the football team. "He'd play baseball with us high school boys and scrimmage, too."

When Pearl Harbor came, Ben Diggs had turned forty-one but nevertheless volunteered. No mud trenches this time. He ended up spending most of the war in North Africa as a payroll noncom in the U.S. Army Air Force. Wonderful letters came back to his sisters in Tennessee about everything from the wildflowers in the desert to the exploits of Nazi General Erwin Rommel. After the Second World War, he worked for the Atomic Energy Commission in Oak Ridge and finally in the lab at the University of Tennessee Experimental Farm. Mrs. Disney said, "Ben wasn't very interested in science, but he got to like that job." In 1956 health problems going back to wartime caught up with him and caused his death.

Never having married, Ben Diggs had no children to whom he could leave his Distinguished Service Cross and the French Croix de Guerre, as well as the British Military Medal. But memories of the triumphant return of the 117th Regiment to Knoxville still live in Oliver Springs. On that day the town's own General Harvey Hannah came over from Nashville, where he was state public service commissioner, for Knoxville's tremendous celebration. He described it all to a local reporter, making it clear why he was called the "silver-tongued orator of Roane County": "It's been a wonderful day. It couldn't have happened anywhere except in East Tennessee. The folks over in Nashville said the reception they gave the 114th Field Artillery couldn't be equaled. And it was a great reception to gallant heroes, but I told them that in East Tennessee people would roll the mountains into the valley and splash the waters of the Tennessee River to the moon. They came pretty near to doing that very thing today. It's been a wonderful, wonderful day."

That was 1919. Seventy years later Walter Stripling, at age ninety-two, joined the general and Little Ben Diggs in the shade of Oliver Springs Cemetery.

Part
III

New River: The Other Side of the Mountain

Splendid Seclusion

New River is the closed-off mountainous part of northern Anderson County, which to this day has a mysterious isolation. It is actually not so far away as the long car trip from Oliver Springs makes it seem. If you could go over the top of Windrock Mountain, as William Smith did on horseback before the Civil War, you would eventually come down at Rosedale School. That red brick building, once vital to the vanished coal towns strung along the New River, now stands deserted. Farther on, the waters of Ligias Fork rumble down Pilot Mountain to join the river where it turns north across a tip of Campbell County and then Scott County. Near the Kentucky border it becomes part of the Cumberland River's Big South Fork. Looking at Tennessee's official highway map, cluttered with so many small towns, you'll find in this area a blank space larger than a quarter. Nothing is there—well, nearly nothing—except the Cumberlands. Narrow State Highway 116 today twists up and over Petros Mountain to get into the valley at the west end and then over Pilot Mountain at the other end to get out. Though the road is now paved, you'd better not be in a hurry.

It was not until World War I that these mountains started to wake up. For nearly a hundred years, a few families like the Phillipses, the Bunches, and the Daughertys had lived a life virtually unchanged since they replaced the Cherokees in the forest. Finally, however, this best stand of virgin trees east of California fell to the ax when the narrow-gauge Tennessee Railroad started inching its way from Scott County south into the river valley, reaching Anderson County about 1913. Just as land speculators had known of coal deposits before the Civil War, they had long coveted the wealth in the giant hardwood trees, so giant that today William P. Patterson's house near Clinton—all nine rooms—was built in the 1880s with lumber cut from only one yellow poplar. But lack of transportation, along with the Civil War, defeated efforts to exploit the resources of the New River area. The conflict halted plans for a north-south toll road following the river from Kentucky to Olivers. After the war, neither floating logs out nor pulling them over steep wagon trails was profitable, though the lumber business prospered in the rest of the county. Long before the turn of the century, the Clinch River at Clinton was lined with sawmills kept busy by endless rafts of logs. Yet no logs came out of New River.

Then the Tennessee Railroad and World War I arrived, with the timber and coal booms not far behind. By 1968, however, the New River area had long been logged and its mines shut down. In this once-prosperous part of the county, only about two hundred families were left, and many of them were in need of help from Lyndon Johnson's War on Poverty.

New River had always found itself buried at the bottom of Anderson County's social heap. Until the coming of Oak Ridge, with all its scientists and engineers during World War II, the county seat of Clinton had looked down its collective nose at smaller places like Oliver Springs. And Oliver Springs had its own prejudices. More than once I'd heard people there say smugly, "They're killin' each other again up in New River!" Well, maybe there had been a shooting, but the sheriff's daily reports showed people got shot in other places, too, even in lofty Oak Ridge. As Dixie Duncan Graves out in Dutch Valley put it, "People in Clinton go up to the top floor of the courthouse, look out as far as they can see, and that's who they're for."

As we say today, New River has had a bad press. Just one example of what outside newspapers like to run is a much reprinted photograph of Byrd Daugherty and his grown sons Fisher and Willie in their Sunday best, propped up in open coffins surrounded by Rosedale residents. An ambush of the Daughertys on Petros Mountain in the 1920s had settled some old score. If you look close, you can see a bullet hole in the father's forehead.

Typical of often-told stories in Oliver Springs was Lige Vann's account of his Uncle Dan. This particular Vann was once up in New River for a poker game when he got in a fight over moonshine. It ended when Dan gouged out his opponent's eye. Of course, to an unbiased observer this violent story could be as much a black mark for Oliver Springs as for New River with the goings-on over the mountain, since Dan was the one from "civilization."

Even Jasper Smith, who usually wrote only good things about old-timers, had unflattering words for New River. His father, William, knew Isaac Phillips, "father of all the Phillips" as Jasper called him, and knew him well. Old Isaac, or Ike as he was called, died just after the end of the Civil War. Tradition has it that he came from William's own Haywood County, North Carolina, about 1812, built a log cabin on Ligias Fork near where it joins New River, and raised a lot of sons and daughters.

"I don't know what nationality they were, but they spoke a broken language," Jasper wrote, whatever that meant. "They were a peculiar people but clever." And they loved their whiskey. In those days even the preachers were not against taking a sup, Jasper pointed out, but Isaac would often take more than a sup. When he got drunk, he would put his fingers in his ears and loudly repeat over and over, "Ole Ike will die in the mountains, Ole Ike will die in the mountains." And indeed he did, leaving everyone wondering where he had hidden his money.

One tale repeated by Jasper was how Ike at first hid his gold and silver in one of wife Nancy's old stockings. He had it in the cellar until the day she went down there for some potatoes and found it. Ike was peeping through a crack and saw it was too heavy for her to move, but he still found a safer place and apparently just kept moving it around. When William Smith came borrowing before the Civil War, the money, at least some of it, was in the cabin wall.

It was winter, and William had gotten good and cold riding the miles across Windrock Mountain. But when he reached the Phillips cabin and warmed up a bit, he told Ike his business. Could he borrow some money? When Ike said he didn't have any, William pulled out the brandy he'd had the foresight to bring along. Several long drinks later, Ike began to sing. Then he told his wife, "See if you can't find Bill some money." Nancy went to the other end of the cabin and knocked a pin out of the side of the wall to get into a money hole. Jasper ended the story saying he often thought Ike's searched-for gold was still somewhere in that house up on Ligias Fork. All this reminded Jasper of Uncle Hardy Martin, who was said to have hidden his money in the river bluff near Clinton. "I guess the first quarter he ever had is in that hole, and Uncle Hardy is in his grave," Jasper added. He could not resist reminding his readers how the Bible says the love of money is the root of all evil: "Your gold and silver will eat your flesh as a canker and shall be a swift witness against you in the court of judgment."

Well, Nancy Phillips Patty has nothing to say about money hidden by her great-great-grandfather Isaac or anything else unflattering, for that matter, although she agrees with Jasper that Isaac Phillips was the first settler in New River. She and Effie Bunch Ward recently published a collection of family photographs and stories titled *Ligas Fork,* using another spelling of the creek's name. However, a great deal of tedious searching of courthouse records still needs to be done to satisfy genealogists about New River's first families. Mrs. Patty, who is in her seventies, said that will have to be done by others. She is satisfied with the stories told by her mother. These inspired her to search the original cemetery of New Pilot Baptist Church for the field rocks she was certain had marked the graves of Isaac and Nancy Phillips. She has described locating the rocks as "digging for history under the ground." They were hard to read, but Mrs. Patty's new tombstones made her dates official until proven otherwise: Isaac Phillips, 1794–1866, and Nancy B. Phillips, 1800–1871. The "B" stands for Bunch. Nancy is thought to have been the sister of James Bunch, the head of another first family in New River and ancestor of the famous Alex Bunch. James Bunch married Isaac Phillips's sister, also named Nancy, to further confuse matters. So, Isaac and James are both Mrs. Patty's great-great-grandfathers, both married to a Nancy.

It is said the Phillips family there on Ligias Fork wanted no part of the Civil War. Whether this had anything to do with the story that Old Isaac owned slaves isn't clear. According to Mrs. Patty, an Indian cave formed by overhanging rocks was boxed in to house the slaves, a place still called Negro Cliffs. Isaac and Nancy raised three daughters and four sons. One, Little Isaac, was killed by rebels on Buffalo Mountain. Or Windrock Mountain, as most on the other side call it. This Isaac was at home mending his shoes, just waiting for his wife to finish baking sweet potatoes for supper. As Mrs. Patty tells it, "Rebels stuck a gun through a knothole, shot him, broke in and pulled him out of the house, tied him by his neck, and dragged him over the rocks. The blood was all over the rocks. No-

The New Pilot Church on Ligias Fork in New River, probably established in 1859. Isaac Phillips was likely in this photograph made soon after the Civil War. Photograph courtesy of Nancy Phillips Patty.

body knows what they did with his body, or whatever happened to his family." Her mother was taken as a child to see the bloody rocks.

Other versions of this violent story that I've heard elsewhere implicate Little Isaac's sister Hannah. Her husband, Ransom Davis, served in the Union army, as did their own son Isaac Davis, who was killed in the war. It has been said that Hannah rode with the infamous Devil Tom Duncan's bushwhackers and was herself responsible for the deaths of a woman and her baby, as well as the poisoning of several soldiers. However, although over 130 years have passed since Appomattox, no one is willing to go on record that Hannah was a renegade.

Getting to New River by car in 1968 was not easy. You left Oliver Springs headed west on much-traveled Highway 62 toward Wartburg with Thunderstruck Knob looking impressive up ahead. Then in about eight miles you turned off to the north on Highway 116. Another two miles in green farmland, with Flagpole Knob looming nearer in the Cumberlands, and you were in Petros, the old mining town now best known for the state penitentiary.

The prison was built in 1897 as a result of the Coal Creek miners' two-year war against the state's use of convict labor to replace them. Solidly backed up against Frozen Head Mountain, the Brushy Mountain State Penitentiary looked like some Victorian's idea of a neat white medieval castle, crenellated battlements ready for arrows to fly. For years, prisoners had dug coal there in a mine whose unused entrance could be easily seen up on the mountainside. The state had finally abandoned the operation after the inmates sabotaged too much equipment and took too many guards hostage. A 1959 prisoner rebellion of nearly a hundred inmates deep inside the earth made television headlines and was even reported in the *New York Times*. After officials starved the convicts into surrender with their hostages, dynamite experts found booby traps made from explosives normally used to blast the coal. However, Brushy Mountain's hostage takers were nothing like as famous as the soon-to-be prisoner James Earl Ray, confessed killer of Dr. Martin Luther King Jr.

Just past the prison entrance, State Highway 116 started its steep climb over into New River—with few guardrails. Like the penitentiary, this secondary state road had a history, though not such a long one. Roads had always been a problem for rural Anderson County, where citizens were required before the Civil War to furnish manual labor for such county projects. But in New River, no one clamored for roads. Always self-sufficient, these mountain people wanted to be left alone. The rare coming or going out of the valley posed no problem since everyone had feet and maybe a horse. There was no road over to Petros, but by 1915 Anderson County had built a primitive route from Coal Creek over Pilot Mountain into the other end of the valley. What with the timber boom, followed by the 1920s large-scale coal operations, the county tried to improve the dirt road and open its other end across the mountain to Petros. Even though it was graveled and had a new bridge in the valley, the steep grades on the mountain were too much even for Henry Ford until years later. Finally in 1937 the state took over the thirty-seven miles of Highway 116 from its junction with Highway 62 to where it ends at present-day Lake City. Even with the state as owner, though, Highway 116 remained a gravel road until 1952. At first residents refused asphalt, which was slick when ice and snow were on the many sharp curves. By 1968 the road was in poor condition, its blacktop on-again, off-again, damaged by thirty-ton coal trucks from the strip mines.

From Armes Gap at the top, the trip down the narrow highway was a dizzying descent, one curve dissolving into another. The four eye-widening miles over the mountain from Petros ended in a beautiful hemmed-in valley scattered with ruins of company coal towns. The road had barely flattened out when Fork Mountain appeared like a ghost. In 1968, most of the forlorn houses stood empty, showing only traces of the yellow paint and green trim once used by the Fork Mountain Coal Company. The train station was boarded up, as was what had been Scott's Grocery, according to its Royal Crown Cola sign. Another closed-

Barbara Leab in 1968 beside her home in Stainville, one of the now-vanished New River communities along Highway 116. Photograph courtesy of the *Oak Ridger.*

up building said "Daugherty's Furniture." Those Daughertys moved to Clinton, and today have a big business in the county seat.

The one place with a coat of bright paint was Fork Mountain Baptist Church, small and serene in its whiteness among the maples on the far side of New River. Somewhere in the vicinity the river was formed as several mountain streams joined, creeks like Sugarcamp Branch tumbling down from Panther Gap. Judging by the smoothness of the rocks, the rapid water must have been running for eons in its wandering course north to Kentucky.

Only occasionally did the valley widen out into rich-looking bottomland. Most of the time Highway 116 hugged a ledge up above the river cut out of Daugherty Ridge. On the ridge side were jagged rocks among the trees and slate outcroppings black with coal. Maples, poplar, hemlock—all kinds of trees—often lined both edges of the road, coming together in a leafy tunnel. Except for small Baptist churches with names like Shiloh—each seeming to protest its independence—there was little sign of life until "Moore's" appeared. A shoebox-size post office displayed a sign explaining it was really Devonia, Tennessee. This had once been the headquarters of Moore Coal Company, one of the largest operations in New River. In the 1920s Moore's had maybe a hundred company houses, a lodge hall, a large boarding house, and a power plant. The incline on the mountain brought down as many as twelve hundred tons of coal a day. Only the weathered three-story commissary was still there.

D. C. Richards, whose family had owned the Oliver Springs Hotel, wrote exuberantly in the *Anderson County News* on April 30, 1927, about a visit to this prosperous company town that belonged to Charlie Moore and his brother Ed. The writer was the same Dave Richards who as a young dandy had loved to dance the night away before the elegant resort hotel burned. He doubly appreciated the banquet at the Moores' clubhouse, where, he said, "beautiful women and gallant men in evening dress" feasted and then enjoyed dancing on polished floors. He was just as impressed with the modern mining equipment and the commissary with its "large storage room holding tons upon tons of beef, mutton, and pork chops."

Years after that visit, in 1953, the Moores sold out to Pocahontas Fuel Company, part of giant Consolidation Coal Company, itself a subsidiary of Continental Oil. So, in 1968 it was the Pocahontas tipple that could be seen from Highway 116 up the railroad siding at Indian Fork. Because of parent-company Consolidation's industrywide union contract, this deep mine was the only toehold the United Mine Workers had left in Anderson County. Over a hundred highly trained men worked in the automated mine.

The road passed swinging bridges as a few comfortable well-kept homes started to appear along with falling-down shacks and trailer houses perched precariously high above the road. Finally around a curve Rosedale School came in full view. Built in 1915, it now had a modern gym and cafeteria with a grassy playground leading down to the river.

Only a short distance from the school lived Lewis Coker and his wife, Belle. Coker served as unofficial mayor of the community scattered along the fifteen miles of valley. At seventy-two, he had recently retired after running the general store at Charley's Branch for half a century. Coker was still a force to be reckoned with. In 1918 he had opened one of the first two coal mines in New River but quickly got into the store business. Mrs. Coker had for years run the post office at Charley's Branch.

A friendly tall man, so tall his expanding waistline was hardly noticeable, Coker talked with pleasure about the boom days. By 1918 the New River Lumber Company, which had the rights to some sixty thousand acres of timber along the river in Anderson, Campbell, and Scott Counties, was just one of several big logging and sawmill operations. He said people with all that timber money were absolutely desperate to buy automobiles. The recent availability of these horseless carriages had all America excited, including well-heeled New Riverites. Car advertisements seemed to fill half of the Clinton newspaper each week (sometimes right next to Jasper Smith's articles railing against those modern contraptions that encouraged moral laxity).

During that first car craze, not money but roads were the big problem, Coker said. "So, we just brought the first cars in by loading them on the log trains. I guess the first car was in 1922, and I got one the next year. But we couldn't get out of the valley by road, not until the bridge was built in 1924 up there where Ligias Fork comes into New River. That was also the year we got electricity. Anyway, with the bridge, cars could go out the east end over Pilot Mountain." Laughing about how muddy and bad the road was along the valley, he added, "We'd just park those Model Ts when November came and not even try to move them 'til spring!"

Compared to those days, he said, New River in 1968 was a model of accessibility. Coker remembered how in 1918, that first year he was there, he wanted to go to Clinton. He walked the eight miles from Charley's Branch to Fork Mountain, then the four miles or so over Petros Mountain, walked some more and caught a branch line of the railroad to Harriman, where he had to change to get to Clinton.

"There was a road over to Petros," he explained, "but it was too steep for anything but wagons until the thirties, when convict labor from the prison was used to grade it down. People who wanted to go to Oliver Springs also had another way out, walking over the mountain from Rosedale to Windrock."

Lewis Coker sitting behind the wheel with his family and admiring New River children in an automobile brought into the isolated valley by logging train about 1922. Photograph courtesy of Scotty Phillips.

Fifty years later, as he sat there talking, enormous coal trucks were roaring up and down Petros Mountain from the strip mines. A large number of those trucks said Walls and Coker on the side. The partner in that big Oliver Spring trucking outfit was Lewis Coker's son Verldon. Trucks took coal out, ton after ton, but scores of railroad cars also came out of the Indian Fork siding from the underground Pocahontas Mine under its UMW banner. However, the days when union boss John L. Lewis could tell the nation's miners what to do, and sometimes even U.S. presidents, seemed to be over. Even the legendary Windrock Mine, a union stronghold, had after nearly sixty years gone out of business in 1961 and reopened as a non-union operation.

What did Coker think about the recent UMW efforts to reorganize some of its old locals like Windrock?

His answer was quick, "They've waited too long and let it get away from them. The UMW's 1950 contract calling for thirty dollars a day and portal-to-portal pay put nearly all the mine operators out of business. I hear that UMW's attempts to organize Windrock again have come to nothing, and ninety percent of the miners are against it. There's plenty of men willing to work for twenty-two dollars a day, which is guaranteed under federal regulations if there's a contract with TVA. And that's where most of the coal goes." Coker made it clear he thought the UMW's recent tactics were not smart.

Back in the late 1940s, during New River's biggest coal boom, close to a thousand men were working in the deep mines, Coker estimated. Between two and three hundred miners were probably employed by Diamond, he reckoned, and a like number at Fork Mountain plus fifty at Buffalo Mine. "And there must have been about two hundred and fifty working for Moore's before the Pocahontas Mine was sold to Consolidation," Coker added. "Moore's was really a nice place then, with good homes. There was a high school and even a clubhouse. Ed Moore, the owner, lived there and kept things in good shape."

However, things changed rapidly after World War II. Not only were union costs high, but demand for coal was down and mechanization expensive. And strip mining was turning the coal business upside down. While Pocahontas kept going after Consolidation bought it in 1953, both the Diamond and Fork Mountain Companies folded. According to Coker, they couldn't pay the minimum royalty on their land leases with the Tennessee Mining and Manufacturing Company. This land company, along with Coal Creek Mining and Manufacturing Company and Consolidation Coal Company, owned virtually all the mountainous northwestern section of Anderson County, some seventy-six thousand acres. Not getting its royalties, Tennessee Mining took over Diamond's equipment and sold it. So, Diamond's commissary stood vacant for fifteen years until its recent metamorphosis into a community center under the county's anti-poverty program.

Coker was glad to say there were some signs of a possible upswing in the coal business. Volunteer Mining Company out of Whitesburg, Kentucky, had re-opened Diamond's Rosedale mine at a new location about three miles from the huge deserted tipple high above Rosedale School. "They're using the road cut around the mountain by Paul Ross when the first strip mining started after 1950," he said. "They're hauling the coal by truck down to the old lower tipple on the railroad to ship it out. About a dozen miners are working now, and I hear a night crew may be put on, too, if the coal seam proves as good as they think." It was a six- or seven-foot seam at the new entry, a lot of coal. If the quality held up, an electrical substation would probably be put in and track laid. The beginning operation was still within the three-hundred-foot limit for shuttle cars operating on a cable without a track. Roads made by strip miners like Paul Ross had also made it easy for very small non-union operators, often families, to open the shallow mines the United Mine Workers contemptuously called "dog holes."

Coker remembered back to the thirties when the UMW had bloody pitched battles organizing the mines in places like Harlan, Kentucky. But there was little or no trouble in New River. "The big operators were all unionized then. The only real trouble we've had came later after 1950, and that was over strip miners. They were hated by the deep miners and were non-union, too. A lot of equipment belonging to Ross was blown up and nobody ever caught. He left and went to Scott County," Coker said. Lighted sticks of dynamite had a way of being thrown into the strippers' coal trucks. But things were definitely different in 1968. Tennco, the biggest strip-mine outfit, had begun operations again on Bootjack Mountain. And nothing was slowing down those trucks over Petros Mountain.

It had been fifty years since the genial Coker missed by just one day being the person who shipped the first railroad car of coal out of New River. He laughed as he remembered, "My brother and I would have been done it, but we couldn't get a drum for our incline, and H. K. Cook beat us. He was the owner of the Diamond Company."

A native of Elk Valley in adjoining Campbell County, Coker started working as a miner when he was twelve years old, but he got out of mining after only a few years in New River. Somewhat by accident he went into the grocery business. Logging by the Shea Brothers and the New River Lumber Company was still the big business before 1920, and Coker found himself ordering supplies for the loggers as well as for his own small mining business. When coal prices fell in 1924, Coker ended up as a full-time general store owner at Charley's Branch. Besides the store, Coker had run four school buses under contract with the Anderson County Schools for nearly thirty years. Neither snow nor rain would stop the buses from making their local runs to Rosedale School, or the twenty-nine-mile trip from Fork Mountain at the very western end of the valley on up over Pilot Mountain, then down through Laurel Grove and Briceville to Lake

Lewis Coker, center, apparently clowning for a traveling photographer in front of his New River general store in the 1920s. Photograph courtesy of Scotty Phillips.

City High School. Coker said, "The state highway department has always kept the road clear, and we never had one school child hurt."

He cited with pride the number of New River students finishing high school. It had risen to about 40 percent, lower than the county's average of 75 percent, but still an increase. While a forty-eight-passenger bus used to be large enough, a sixty-passenger bus currently filled up each day for the high school kids. The ones in Fork Mountain had to leave home at 6:45 A.M. and got back at 5 P.M. from Lake City. The only bad thing, Coker said, was that the students couldn't stay for after-school activities like football practice.

Though the population had dropped in the valley to maybe two hundred families and Rosedale School had only eight teachers instead of its usual twelve, Coker nevertheless felt that things were looking up. "There are fewer people on welfare now—they've moved out, and the people who are here now are going to stay. Only about half of those with good jobs in the mines live here, but some of them are building good new homes. There's a brick one going up right now back toward Moore's. And the old company houses are being torn down," Coker said.

Obviously the Cokers did not plan to move one inch.

Up the road a bit, I found someone else just as attached to the valley, Dorothy Armes. She headed up the recently organized New River Community Action Group, which was making what could be called a silk purse out of a sow's ear. That "ear" was the abandoned Diamond commissary, which was being transformed into a community center. Job No. 1 had just been completed by replacing hundreds of broken window panes.

Mrs. Armes had roots in both ends of the valley. Though born and raised at Stainville on Ligias Fork, she and her disabled miner husband, Archie, moved to Fork Mountain, where he worked as a miner when they married in 1946. They and their five children had lived there in one of the company houses through good times and bad. Only several years earlier a cave-in had killed three men when the Fork Mountain Mine briefly reopened to "rob" the old passageways of their remaining coal. Still, she was one of those optimistic souls who was always certain things would turn out for the best.

Dorothy Armes loved New River and never thought of it as isolated. It just seemed that way to outsiders, the round-faced reassuring woman said. "We go out all the time to Oliver Springs and Oak Ridge to shop, though we don't make special trips to the grocery store. It's usually easier for me to buy off the rolling store, that big truck Shelby Grocery sends over from LaFollette twice a week."

Hers was a busy life, but Dorothy Armes decided to get behind the new community center and push. The long-expected federal anti-poverty funds had not arrived to help with job training, day care, and recreation. So New River had a true pull-yourself-up-by-your-own-bootstraps program.

"My youngest, Gene, is nine, and he's the only one of my children who needs much watching these days, so I've taken this on. It's a lot of work," she said. Though her daughters Wanda and Edith had recently graduated from Lake City High School, Gary would be a senior in the fall and Patsy a sophomore, which meant catching that early morning bus over Pilot Mountain. Edith was the secretary at Rosedale School, she said, shy and proud at the same time.

Inside the old commissary, Mrs. Armes explained how essential it had been to seal off the once-deserted building from the weather as the first step in its conversion. That meant replacing 268 windowpanes. And that meant money. St. Stephen's Episcopal Church in Oak Ridge came to the rescue, along with much help from the League of Women Voters. Besides that good luck, crucial assistance came with the arrival of Arnold Groff from the Council of Southern Mountains, an interdenominational group. A recent college graduate in industrial arts, the good-looking young man seemed very serious. He was a member of the pacifist Brethren Church and a conscientious

Teenagers Gary Armes, left, and Otis Phillips working for the community action group in the summer of 1968. They were headed for Rosedale School, in the background, crossing one of the many swinging bridges over the New River. Photograph courtesy of the *Oak Ridger*.

objector, doing alternative service as a full-time community volunteer. That summer of 1968 such a status could have been a touchy subject as the war in Vietnam dragged on, but Arnold had been welcomed. He quickly succeeded in getting teenagers to help with repairs on the commissary.

Mrs. Armes was still amazed at all their work, saying, "You should have seen the dirt that accumulated through all those broken windows since Diamond closed down." Wheelbarrows had to be used just to shovel the dirt out before days of scrubbing could begin. Tables were put together from odds and ends, and the old store counter moved to the back of the cavernous single room to form a kitchen. With this accomplished, the group had just staged a spectacular rummage sale, spectacular enough to raise two hundred dollars from the sale of hundreds of items, each for just a few cents.

Their first sale had helped pay for scores of metal chairs recently bought from Reed School after it had just closed in Oliver Springs's Tuppertown. Hours of painting turned them into bright blue cheer in the old building. Next in line for a paint transformation were the inside walls and the elegant patterned metal ceiling. Then the center had to raise money for a secondhand pool table for the hardworking teenagers.

Recreation was important, Dorothy Armes said, but setting up a year-round day care center for children too young for Head Start was their main goal. Enthusiasm and manual labor would not be enough. "We've got to have some federal money for a teacher for the eighteen children under five who are waiting," she explained.

Limited funds had arrived, but only for an experiment to increase vocational motivation of sixth-, seventh-, and eighth-graders. Arnold Groff would teach part-time in this program and set up a shop to work with engines. Arnold grinned, saying, "We may even build some hot rods this fall. But right now I want some help down on the river to dredge out the swimming hole."

A walk across a nearby swinging bridge over New River made it clear why old-timers resisted moving away in hard times. Running water glinted off the silk-smooth boulders and made the only sound to be heard except for a hidden bobwhite. With a crystal ball, Dorothy Armes and Lewis Coker could have seen that American energy problems, starting in 1973 with an Arab oil embargo, would give a new importance to coal and bring better times. Nevertheless, the old boom days, when dancers in evening dress graced the polished floors of Moore's clubhouse, were gone for good.

Like Mangy Dogs

In 1968 dynamite ripped apart the upstart Southern Labor Union's headquarters in adjoining Scott County. It was just two weeks before the UMW's District 19 was to celebrate the seventieth anniversary of the eight-hour work day on April 1 in New River. The explosion in Oneida was the latest of the battles between the once-mighty UMW and the homegrown SLU, whose demands on the local coal operators were considerably less than those of the old union.

The UMW's legendary leader with the leonine head and bushy black eyebrows, John L. Lewis, had retired eight years earlier, turning the union over to feisty little Tony Boyle, who proved unable to stop the decline in membership. For four decades Lewis's roars, often eloquent with quotations from Shakespeare and the Bible, had caused U.S. presidents to stop and listen. Even presidents cannot ignore a man who once described his efforts for the union by saying, "I have pleaded your case not in the tones of a feeble mendicant asking alms but in the thundering voice of the captain of a mighty host, demanding the rights to which free men are entitled."

However, no longer could the United Mine Workers bring the country to its knees as it once did with a nationwide coal strike. From its peak membership of about six hundred thousand in the 1930s, the number of organized miners kept dwindling as the number of coal mines dwindled. The decline was obvious in Anderson County, a part of the UMW's famous District 19, which included Harlan County, Kentucky. Although it was no secret that New River's Local 8532 was the only active one in Anderson County, the district headquarters was absolutely close-mouthed about membership. The

UMW was fighting not only the postwar switch to gas and oil, but the automation that Lewis himself had pushed for. As big a problem were increased labor costs caused by the pension and health benefits Lewis had won. The welfare fund had provided a string of modern—and expensive—hospitals in southern Appalachia that earned Lewis the status of near-sainthood, despite the fact they had to be closed in the 1960s. Things were not going well for the UMW, and ugly rumors of high-level corruption kept surfacing.

And now the rival Southern Labor Union had been bombed. A trip to the district rally in New River might prove interesting, but first some background was needed. The place to get it was at Roy Brown's in Frost Bottom. He and wife Vada lived in a small white house that sat neatly up on Walden Ridge, its wide porch looking across Frost Bottom Road toward Windrock. There, almost on the very spot, Philip Seiber had been killed during the Civil War.

Roy was the likable former miner who helped Babe Edwards organize the movement to protest the abominable Frost Bottom Road. Roy looked like a tall Humphrey Bogart and had the intelligence of Bogart's famous movie detective Sam Spade, but there the similarity ended. He was born in Stainville up in New River in 1921, one of eleven children. Roy had always worked to help out with money, delivering coal by wheelbarrow during the Depression when people were just barely hanging on. Then his miner father died at forty-nine. The oldest child at home, Roy quit high school to start work in the mines, but World War II changed everything. He found himself in Baltimore as a sheet metal worker building aircraft for Martin Marietta. Though deferred as essential to war production, he volunteered for the Army Air Force.

Discharged in 1946, Roy went to work at the booming Windrock Mine, where he eventually became the popular president of the UMW local. Windrock had a good safety record, but one day a chain came loose on a coal-cutting machine, and he ended up with a pin in one arm. In 1961, the year Windrock went out of business, Roy was just back from the UMW hospital in Harlan with the same arm again in a cast as a result of a wreck on a shuttle car. This proved to be a much more serious injury, such that even a bone graft couldn't keep the arm from being an inch shorter than before. That was the end of his mining days, six months short of eligibility for a pension and a prized UMW medical benefits card. He went to work as a guard at Brushy Mountain State Penitentiary: no physical exam needed, $240 monthly take-home pay.

I knew few of these details—and wouldn't until after Roy's unexpected death from a heart attack in 1984—that day I drove out to Frost Bottom to get a crash course at the Browns' house on the union situation before my trip up to New River. Do you know, Roy asked me, that District 19 has probably had the most violent history of any district of the United Mine Workers? Considering the frequent open warfare between the union and coal operators across the United States since the turn of the century, that was saying a lot. District 19, including Tennessee and southeastern Kentucky, was the scene of the turbulent nine-year struggle to unionize Harlan County. The turmoil hadn't ended until 1939, long after most of the coal industry was unionized. In "bloody Harlan" mine owners ran the county. The sheriff's company-hired deputies held control until the federal government's crackdown under the new Wagner Act finally brought protection for the union's organizing efforts.

UMW vice-president George Titler, who would be at the April 1 rally, was the organizer who clinched the final triumph in Harlan. His boss at the time was District 19 president William J. Turnblazer, who had been trying to unionize Harlan since World War I. The current district president, William J. Turnblazer, was his son. Roy said to expect high-decibel rhetoric about the union's glory days from all the speakers, although the star would be Albert E. Pass, the district's secretary-treasurer.

"Do you know about the Jones Boys?" Roy asked.

The mysterious "Jones Boys" did dirty work like dynamiting the SLU offices in Oneida. One well-known story recounted how nearly a hundred of these so-

United Mine Workers officials before the big union rally in New River in 1968. Left to right are William J. Turnblazer, George Titler, and Albert Pass. Pass is still in prison for life for the Yablonski murders in 1969. Photograph courtesy of the *Oak Ridger.*

called boys once put pressure on a coal operator, John Van Huss, near LaFollette up north on Highway 25W not far from Lake City. When the owner kept refusing to sign a union contract, they buried him alive. Van Huss escaped, but none of the witnesses at the ensuing trial could identify even one of the defendants. Memories simply evaporated. They had no trouble, though, remembering to stay on the right side of the Jones Boys. So now in the late sixties it was again warfare, this time small-scale, and many believed that Albert Pass directed the rough stuff. People said Pass was the man who really ran District 19, not Turnblazer.

Not long after that Frost Bottom visit, over four hundred UMW miners filled New River's Rosedale School on the first day of April. It was a brilliant spring morning, the sky so blue it hurt to look at it, redbud already blooming on still-wintry Buffalo Mountain across the river. A black Cadillac pulled up. Out stepped Titler, Turnblazer, and Pass. Exuding power, they had no idea then of the turbulent days soon to come and their scandalous downfall.

Before the celebration got under way, the mild-mannered Turnblazer agreed to a short interview. No coal-dirtied face there. The union official looked more like a middle-aged professor than the lawyer he actually was. What about the Southern Labor Union? Yes, he knew the SLU headquarters in Oneida had been dynamited. Of course, he knew nothing about such violence, but anything could happen these days. Tempers were short after six years of struggles with the SLU down in Grundy and Marion Counties near Chattanooga. Yes, he quietly repeated, anything could happen.

He seemed more concerned with what was going on in Anderson County. The National Labor Relations Board had just certified the SLU as the bargaining agent for the 238 employees of Tennco Company. This certification had followed an election supervised by the board, but it was being challenged by Turnblazer for the UMW. Tennco couldn't be ignored since it was the largest coal operator in the county with both deep mines and extensive strip mines. It had a lot to do with the county's then being No. 1 among Tennessee's seventeen coal-producing counties.

While the Tennco defeat rankled, there was good news from Grundy and Marion Counties. The UMW had won the NLRB election in those two counties six weeks earlier. But the operator, Tennessee Consolidated Coal Company, refused to recognize the certification. Now Turnblazer was in federal court trying to force the company to bargain with the UMW. Turnblazer dropped his quiet tone suddenly, denouncing the SLU, "We're going to take Grundy and Marion back this spring, for sure, and eradicate that so-called union from District 19!"

Talk about eradication of the rival SLU got the rally off to an enthusiastic start. Miners had poured into the school auditorium with delegations from all over the district, but it was easy to see that many of the four hundred or so men were pensioners. When UMW vice-president George Titler got up to speak, the windows rattled with cheers. A big hulk of a man, living symbol of "Bloody Harlan County," Titler was someone to believe. He began loud and clear, "Devonia is going to be the jumping-off station where we can start gathering up non-union miners, including all those coal trucks that ought to be organized." Non-union, of course, included the Southern Labor Union.

This was the man who thirty years before had finally gotten an agreement with the coal operators bringing peace to Harlan County. It had taken years and bloodshed. By 1938, over twelve thousand miners were already under a UMW contract in Harlan, but the battle wasn't over. John L. Lewis feared the rival Progressive Mine Workers and demanded a closed shop, calling for a national strike in May 1939. This brought on a complete shutdown in Harlan County, but then one mine attempted to reopen. The worst violence since 1931 broke out, although the UMW tried to stop it because of public opinion. State troopers, and finally the National Guard, were called out. A shootout left one guardsman and two union pickets dead. Titler and his wife were among over two hundred UMW members arrested at the scene and marched nine miles to the Harlan County jail. People still called it the Battle of Stanfill.

Claiming that morning at Rosedale that fifty-eight union sympathizers had been killed during the violent nine years in Harlan County, Titler all but shouted, "We don't want to forget all the blood and sweat it took to organize this union since 1890. Those days in Harlan there were a hundred and forty company-paid thugs who were made deputy sheriffs. The fight to maintain this union today is rough, but we must reorganize the unorganized to remain strong."

Non-union mines like Windrock came in for a blasting as Enemy No. 1, while the Tennessee Valley Authority and the U.S. Atomic Energy Commission shared the title of No. 2. These were the most sacred cows in Anderson County. Titler attacked the TVA because of the low coal prices he said it forced on the small operators as virtually the sole purchaser of their coal for the TVA steam plants. The AEC ranked close behind on his enemies list because of its nuclear reactors, which Titler called both unsafe and unneeded. That was heresy in those days before the 1979 nuclear accident at Three Mile Island scared many Americans silly for the first time.

Sounding like John L. Lewis, Titler demanded to know "how long will it be before the people who dig coal in the great Volunteer State of Tennessee throw away their wishbone and get a backbone and join a real labor union instead of digging coal by the acre and giving it to the great scavenger organization known as the Tennessee Valley Authority?"

Titler charged that small non-union "kinfolk" mines sold coal to the TVA at starvation prices, causing the poverty in Appalachia. "Nowadays four or five in a family start a dog hole and only make enough to starve on with sow belly and corn bread," he said.

Titler made clear the union's argument with the AEC. He condemned what he called "the government subsidy of millions of dollars for nuclear energy in the making of electricity in peace time in competition with coal." He not only objected to the $3 million subsidy, since "we have at least five hundred years of coal in the country," but raised the issue of safety of nuclear reactors. And in connection with nuclear energy, Titler lambasted District 50, recently expelled from the UMW for supporting construction of nuclear reactors. No one was saying so at the meeting, but it was widely known that District 50 made up of chemical workers in manufacture of coal byproducts had more members than the UMW itself. Titler stressed how the union had built up District 50 with millions of dollars, adding, "George Washington had Benedict Arnold, Christ had his Judas, and now the UMW has District 50!"

When time came for Albert Pass to speak, he looked anything but imposing as he stood up in front of the worked-up audience. "Ordinary" would have described this son of a Church of Christ preacher, even though his white socks did seem to jump out against his dark business suit. He had not been in Harlan County, but this was a man people feared to cross. Though he was a gospel singer devoted to his family, Pass had the nickname of Little Hitler. And certainly the fervor of the German dictator was in his voice. The auditorium filled with "Amen!" and "Right! Right!" again and again after Pass got going. "District 50 is kicked out and it's going to stay out," he insisted, voice rising. "It was created to organize workers in the by-products of coal, but now they're hooked up with Dow Chemical Corporation!"

Pass put the amount of coal reserves in the nation even higher than Titler, "We've got ten centuries of minable coal, we've got the miners and the families who need the work, so why in hell does District 50 want to put us out of business? There'll be time enough for atomic energy when the coal is gone."

Warming up to his topic, Pass attacked the safety of nuclear reactors. With sarcasm, he charged that the AEC had no plans for safety. He accused the AEC of just saying, "We hope they won't blow up." Painting a picture of horror, Pass declared loudly, "If a big plant exploded, the disaster would be untold. I say they shouldn't be built until they are made safe."

"Amen!" "Amen!"

Pass also had strong words for critic-at-large Ralph Nader, who had just added mine safety to his growing list of safety concerns headed by the American automobile. Nader, in a letter to Stewart L. Udall, U.S. secretary of the interior, had charged that the federal Bureau of Mines was "the captive" of the coal operators and the UMW. Pass was nearly shouting, "I was amazed to read this! Amazed! We've been fighting since 1890 for safety and in 1966 finally got all mines, even those under fifteen men, put under inspection."

Whether or not the UMW had become too cozy with mine owners about safety in order to preserve jobs, the atrocious working conditions in the old days were enough to make even a cynic sympathetic to the union cause. Memories of two disastrous explosions over the mountain near Briceville at the turn of the century added to the audience's loud indignation. They could remember 1902, when Briceville's Local 2884 was fighting for survival and 184 men lost their lives in the Fraterville Mine explosion. It barely missed being the most deadly mining disaster in the United States up to that time. And that tragedy was followed in 1911 by an explosion at nearby Cross Mountain Mine that took another 84 lives. Such bad memories seemed to invade much of the music that rounded off the morning. Whether the Phillips Family Quartet was singing gospel songs or union songs, the sound was often that of melancholy, even mourning. Their homage to their old retired UMW leader rang out again and again in one hymn-like song with the refrain, "God Bless John L. Lewis."

At noon, however, an enormous spread of food in the school cafeteria had everyone in good spirits. Before the meeting adjourned, Titler had praised those in the audience from Marion and Grundy Counties, where struggles with the Southern Labor Union continued. The huge lunch crowd included a fourteen-man delegation from Palmer's Local 5881 in Grundy County. After they had finished off a mammoth meal with homemade fried pies and slabs of chocolate cake, Bill Ross talked about the trouble back home in Grundy County. He recalled the outcome of an interview with a newspaperman after violence first broke out with the SLU in 1961. "When a Chattanooga reporter asked me who burned down our local hall, I told him right off it was them damn scabs," Ross said. "That came out in the paper, and three days later my truck got blowed up in my front yard!"

Though the majority of UMW members that day showed signs of age, there was young blood there, too, like Jim Shirks. He worked at the Pocahontas Mine and headed the Devonia local. Spring was in the air, and everyone in the jammed cafeteria apparently had new hope of seeing the UMW banner flying high again. After all, UMW President Tony Boyle had just won a pay hike up to thirty dollars a day. He might not be another John L. Lewis, but who could be?

That rally in New River has always stayed with me because of what happened the following year. On New Year's Eve 1969, the dissident union leader who had seriously challenged Tony Boyle in the nationwide election for the UMW presidency was murdered. Jock Yablonski, along with his wife and daughter, were shot to death as they slept in their Pennsylvania home three weeks after the vote. The inept hired killers were soon behind bars, but it would take state and federal officials another four years to solve the complex case. However, by 1974 Albert Pass, William Turnblazer, and finally Tony Boyle himself were in prison, along with six other people involved in the banner-headline murders. Yablonski, brash son of a Polish immigrant miner and loyal union leader for years, had committed the unforgivable sin of fiercely attacking Boyle for illegal use of union funds, as well as for playing company stooge in wage negotiations and failing to push for legislation against black lung disease.

The pivotal role that Albert E. Pass played in the crime did not become clear for nearly three years. Trial after trial brought convictions of underlings like Silous Huddleston, the UMW pensioner who headed the LaFollette local near Lake City and hired the three hit men. It was Pass's ingenious scheme for laundering twenty thousand dollars to pay for the killings that led to his undoing. After Pass was found guilty, Turnblazer confessed and named Tony Boyle as the real instigator. The murder warrant for Boyle's arrest stated that Boyle had told Turnblazer and Pass that "Yablonski ought to be killed or done away with" and that Pass said District 19 would take care of it.

That warrant was in 1973, and the union election that cost Yablonski his life had already been overturned with the seventy-one-year-old Boyle convicted of misuse of union funds. By the following year, Boyle had been found guilty of murder and, despite a second trial, remained in prison until his death in 1985. Turnblazer, who had turned state's evidence against Boyle, was eventually paroled. Albert Pass, now seventy-seven, is still serving three life sentences in Pennsylvania, a state with no death penalty and no chance for parole.

After all the scandal, the United Mine Workers today has a new life. It is a democratic organization of sixty thousand highly trained miners who elect their own district officers, unlike in the days of Lewis and Boyle. It is led by another Polish immigrant's son. He is Richard Trumka, the respected miner-lawyer elected UMW president in 1982, when he was only thirty-three.

Back in Anderson County before the Yablonski murders, a strip mine was making the news in February 1969. Icicles two feet long clung to the mountainsides when old John Seiber, former deputy sheriff and deep miner, had had enough. A taciturn man, he was nevertheless outraged. He called the newspaper office protesting, "They done tore the top off Double Camp!" He meant the strip miners had literally cut the top off the peak above Moore's. People called it Double Camp Mountain, though it was actually Carroll Ridge, a spur of Patterson Mountain.

Tennessee had finally passed a law just then going into effect regulating the highly profitable surface mining of coal. But that wasn't enough to satisfy John Seiber, who had gotten the ear of his state senator, Ray Baird, with a petition from New River residents asking, or rather demanding, that the new law be made tougher.

Of course, strip mining was nothing new. It had been going on since not long after the end of World War II. The first such mining in Anderson County in 1949 targeted Pilot Mountain, where Ligias Fork started down toward New River. Soon the *Clinton Courier-News* was reporting strip miners beaten up, coal trucks overturned, and tires shot out. Angry deep miners would ambush strippers like those first ones on Pilot Mountain who got a taste of buckshot as they worked on bulldozers. Fear for their jobs, not damage to the mountains, brought out the deep miners' wrath. This relatively cheap way of snaking around the outside of a mountain, removing soil with all its vegetation to expose the coal seams, then dumping the tons of dirt down the side, could not be stopped. Within a few years, Oak Ridge residents looking north toward the Cumberlands saw so many bare places that the mountains started to resemble mangy dogs, according to Snyder Roberts. The yellow-tan circles sometime spiraled nearly to the top of a peak, leaving a strange sort of lonely crown perched on high.

The Cumberlands may have looked like mangy dogs, but up close the abandoned areas so damaged by the strippers' enormous earthmovers could give an extraordinary glimpse of a primordial world. Many Oak Ridgers were amateur fossil hunters who knew there was no better place to search than in the dark gray slate of a deserted mine. Walking along the shelf on a mountainside made by stripping, you might be amazed to see hanging exposed in the thirty-foot vertical wall the stump of a giant scale tree, once part of a swamp forest maybe three hundred million years ago. And smaller fossils lay everywhere, pieces of trunks and roots of those hundred-foot trees, some with vertical patterns of leaf scars and others with diamond-shaped outlines. Easiest of all to find were the seed ferns, often a perfect symmetrical frond with delicate oval leaflets. Layer on top of thin layer, like good pie crust, the slate could be peeled away to reveal surprises, although it took a lot of luck to find a marine fossil.

Geologists say that as shallow seas advanced and retreated, these tremendous forests became layers of peat and eventually shale and coal. Over long periods of time, mountain building began, lifting and folding the land mass into what is today the Appalachian Mountains. The older Appalachians include the Smokies, where crystalline rocks like granite were formed under greater pressure than the sedimentary rocks of the newer Appalachian Plateau. What was seen from Oak Ridge as the Cumberland Mountains, including Windrock, was actually an escarpment of that plateau, which after millions of years of erosion had turned into a rugged area of peaks and deep valleys running from New York to Alabama.

Unlike the Smokies and the Great Valley of the Tennessee River, including Walden Ridge, the plateau with its sedimentary rocks both suffered and prospered under what many called "the curse of coal."

Strip mining had produced just the latest manifestation of that curse. The wholesale destruction of the Appalachian coal country finally found an eloquent voice in a Kentuckian named Harry Caudill. In 1963 his *Night Comes to the Cumberlands* became a call to battle for the new environmental movement across the country. Everyone from U.S. secretary of the interior Stewart Udall, who wrote the book's introduction, to the newly formed Tennessee Citizens for Wilderness Planning answered that call in one way or another. The TCWP was the highly active brainchild of a husband-and-wife team of geneticists at the Oak Ridge National Laboratory, Bill and Lee Russell.

The elegiac tone of Caudill's title fit this gifted storyteller's picture of the near-death of these mountains that were first settled by Revolutionary War veterans like his ancestor James Caudill. The lanky, slow-talking lawyer—once called a mixture of John Muir, Mark Twain, and Don Quixote—had miraculously gotten strip-mining legislation passed by the Kentucky legislature. He was already well on his way to becoming a legend in 1970 when he joined Oak Ridge scientists, including John H. Gibbons (now President Clinton's science advisor) and influential Berea College graduates, to demand an end to what they called Appalachia's impoverished status as America's own Third World colony. Caudill led off the Berea conference calling for a stop to "the continuous mass hemorrhage of people and resources from these mountains."

What was needed for the region's economic development was a new Southern Mountains Authority, something like the TVA, according to Caudill. He condemned the buying up of land and mineral rights after the Civil War for next to nothing from illiterate mountaineers, setting the stage for the exploitation of timber and coal.

"Enormous sums were made in the Appalachian Mountains," Caudill filled the auditorium with his deep voice, "but no Appalachian roads, schools, or libraries came from it. I was at Yale just recently and was shown a seventy-million-dollar library building from the Mellons. We've starved while rivers of wealth have flowed out to the north."

During the 1880s and 1890s the mountains were quietly invaded by an army of agents, usually representing northern speculators, he said. Such an agent on foot or horseback searched the isolated coves and mountainsides for coal outcroppings and virgin timber. In *Night Comes to the Cumberlands,* Caudill repeatedly described unfair deals made between the unsuspecting mountaineer and the affable agent with hard cash, deals by which a half-dollar bought an acre that in years to come would produce twenty thousand tons of coal. Sometimes the land was bought outright but more often just the timber and mineral rights, thereby avoiding property taxes. A "broad-form" deed, which mountain people usually could not read, allowed use of the land surfaces for any purpose "convenient and necessary" to excavate for coal, oil, gas, or other minerals. Even worse, it exempted the mining company from liability for any damages to the land. The X mark that took the place of a signature opened the door to wholesale destruction by strip mining a half century later, according to Caudill.

As for Anderson County, exactly what methods were used in New River by the controversial Lucien Bird are not today known. But starting about 1885, this land agent and surveyor appeared on annual visits to purchase land. When he finished each year, he would go back to Pennsylvania, where he was a preacher. Bird represented investors in New York, New Jersey, and Pennsylvania, buying some fifty thousand acres mostly in his own name, then later transferring the deeds. L. Bird, as he signed himself, was a well-known figure with his long white beard, riding into Clinton on horseback from over the mountains to register land destined for the New River Coal and Coke Company.

It would be years, however, before timber and coal would finally be exploited. And many more before the earthmovers would appear in 1949 to strip the mountains. By then much of the mountainous part of the county was owned by two Knoxville-based interrelated land companies, the Tennessee Land and Mining Company and the Coal Creek Mining and Manufacturing Company. These land companies leased mining rights to large deep-mine operators like the Moores back in the boom times and years later to small strip miners like John Henley of Oliver Springs. It was Henley's stripping off of Double Camp's peak that brought me to that desolate spot in New River in February 1969.

Thanks to a four-wheel-drive Jeep, F. G. Watkins, director of the brand new strip-mining and reclamation division of the Tennessee Department of Conservation, had hauled me up the nearly vertical road from the Devonia post office. John Seiber was along, too, in the freezing weather. So was Bob Lefler, an Oak Ridge teacher and active member of the new Tennessee Citizens for Wilderness Planning conservation group. Fred Wyatt, one of the new state inspectors, and two more protesting New River residents, Byrd Phillips and Wayne Carroll, came along in a second Jeep. Carroll had been raised right below the demolished peak down on Double Camp Creek. Wyatt, incidentally, is today the Coal Creek Mining and Manufacturing Company vice-president who recently discussed the Livelys' sale of their land on Windrock in the 1880s.

All of us stood in the pale winter sunlight on the "bench," what strip miners called the shelf cut into the mountainside. A look down over the edge showed the havoc caused by dumping the so-called "overburden" down the side—topsoil, rocks, red clay, sizable boulders blasted loose with dynamite, bits of slate, small pines, and mangled trunks of what must have been poplars and oaks. Rain had eroded gullies in the upheaval of dislocated earth that was officially, and appropriately, called the "spoil bank."

"It's a horrible mess," Director Watkins, a professional forester, admitted, looking down. But he hurried to add, "It can be reclaimed and grow trees again." Watkins, at forty, appeared to be a level-headed man who realized that conservation issues often aroused strong emotions rather than the objective approach he believed necessary for reclamation. Seiber, a stoic mountain man who had lived all his life in New River, was anything but a wild-eyed conservation firebrand. But, disagreeing with Watkins, he grimly shook his head. The mountains will never be the same again, he seemed to say.

A retired UMW man who believed that plenty of coal remained in the underground mines, Seiber would have liked to stop stripping, especially since non-union operators did most of it. Standing out there in the cold wind on the very edge of the spoil bank where Double Camp's peak had been dumped, he peered down the five hundred feet of earth. It had settled some but was still slipping down the mountainside. No, he definitely did not agree. Seiber said flatly, "If the new law lets them do this, then we don't have no law. You can plant all the locust seedlings you want in that bank, but it takes ten years for them to take root and set turf, and the rains and flood won't wait that long." He was talking about the trees that would be set out when spring came, the first plantings since the law took effect.

Watkins admitted that slides were the biggest problem, but he had been unsuccessful in the face of the operators' opposition in getting a law to limit mining on steep slopes like Carroll Ridge. While Kentucky had tightened its law so that stripping was not permitted on slopes of more than 28 percent, Tennessee had no limitation other than its broad control of water quality.

It was one thing to read the new strip-mining bill along with the twenty-three-page book of detailed regulations, but quite another to grasp the size of the problem made clear by the bird's-eye view up on Carroll Ridge. Both to the north on Daugherty Ridge and to the south on Patterson Mountain could be seen miles and miles of "highwalls," the vertical cliffs left after the earth was stripped away. Just as bad were the miles of spoil banks on the lower slopes where earth had been dumped. Those were old scars, however. They were left by the first strip mining that took the cream of the coal in the 1950s. It had resulted for a time in nearly open warfare between the UMW and the non-union strippers as the latter's equipment was blown up. As Harry Caudill once said about the Cumberlands, "We have in this section a decided inclination to settle our differences with dynamite."

What was left after the initial stripping were those miles of scarred mountainsides that conservationists call "orphan mines," orphan because no one was legally responsible for them, neither the long-gone strippers nor the large land companies that owned the thousands of acres. In the late 1960s what was happening in places like Carroll Ridge could be called scavenger operations, a bit like vultures eating away at a decaying corpse. Strip miners were reworking the old areas, making new and deeper cuts for additional seams of coal along the benches left in the 1950s.

But this was good from the reclamation viewpoint, Watkins hurried to make clear. Under the new state law, the current strip operator had to regrade and replant to eliminate not only the damage he had done but also the earlier damage. This is what was scheduled to happen on Carroll Ridge, though Double Camp was flattened forever. By removing the peak, the operator John Henley had certainly profited. He had gotten to thirty-five thousand tons of coal in the rich seven-foot seam. This ridge, contour-stripped and augered in the 1950s, was well worth Henley's effort to take off the mountaintop, which had risen about six hundred feet above the old highwall. The removal had added another six or eight feet of dirt to the old spoil bank.

Because Henley had a contract with the TVA, which bought nearly all of Anderson County's coal for its Kingston Steam Plant, he was required to meet TVA's reclamation requirements, which had been in effect since 1965, two years before the state law was passed. Basically the same as the state law, they required an operator to submit a detailed mining and reclamation plan in order to get a permit and be bonded. Of prime importance was grading to level the bench, thereby eliminating pits, and covering all exposed coal seams to prevent acid water. Grading was also essential to force surface drainage toward the highwalls, so that water would go into lateral ditches at the base of the walls to be channeled off in constructed waterways. The drainage of access roads was also to be carefully controlled with ditches and culverts. All this preliminary grading had been done by Henley.

Following the Carroll Ridge trip, John Henley insisted the stir caused by Seiber had surprised him since he'd been working on the mountain nearly a year. Although he was very much in favor of the required grading, Henley believed that revegetation was too complicated for the operators and preferred to pay the state to do it. Not only would spoil banks have to be planted with trees, legumes, and grasses like *sericea lespedeza,* but so would the benches next to the highwalls. Within ten years the state hoped the black locust trees would be high enough that the miles of bare highwalls could no longer be seen from a distance.

Not all the environmental problems of the mountains could be blamed on strip mining, as a close look at Carroll Ridge made clear. Unregulated stripping, according to the state law, could cause "soil erosion, stream pollution and accumulation and seepage of contaminated water," but so could deep mining. Carroll Ridge bore the scars of both stripping and of one of the Moores' abandoned deep mines.

The Jeep climb up the ridge passed the first underground mine opened by the Moores back in the prosperous twenties. "Moore's No. 1" could barely be seen in letters above the concrete driftmouth, the dangerous old mine entrance that was only partly closed off. However, it was easy to see the nearby gigantic slag heap. It was mostly gray, though it still showed signs of the "red dog" formed when the slag was burned. This heap, plus seepage from other abandoned underground mines, added to the acid water that found its way down into New River. Silt and rocks mostly from old operations reached the bottom, too. So full of sulfur oxides was one orange-colored gully running down the mountainside that in places the oxides had actually crystallized. Rusted incline tracks along with pulley and coal cars stuck out on the cold mountain as eyesores but did little harm compared to the steady trickle of sick water. Higher up, a burned-out school bus overlooked the whole mess, apparently a victim of the "troubles" during the 1950s.

While Carroll Ridge had its twisted metal skeletons from the past, Bootjack Mountain presented a happier picture, which Watkins wanted to show off. There across the river north of Daugherty Ridge, Tennco had extensive stripping operations that were supposed to far exceed the minimum requirements of the new law. At that time the largest coal operator in Anderson County, Tennco had been organized since 1958 by the Southern Labor Union. It was the SLU's headquarters in Oneida that had been dynamited the previous year, but that hadn't slowed the Tennco operations. The access roads on Bootjack were in excellent condition and the benches already carefully graded. The spoil banks were to be planted soon with seventy thousand seedlings. Dexter Rains, Tennco manager, explained that his company had built about seventy-five miles of roads in Anderson County, "roads that will be excellent for recreation once we can open them up." Although Tennco had locked gates and no-trespassing signs, Rains insisted there had been no labor trouble.

The windy visit to Bootjack brought up the question of Cage's Creek, which runs between that mountain and Daugherty Ridge. John Seiber, who was not impressed with Tennco's operation, wanted to talk about it. He said the creek was filling with sediment from the stripping, so that during heavy rains, water came up six to eight feet over the bridge on Highway 116. That day, however, the creek was running clear, and both Watkins and Wyatt repeated their earlier strong statements that nothing was going into the creek from the Tennco operations. Still, Seiber remained unconvinced. He insisted the stripping should be stopped and was very skeptical about administration of the present strip-mine law, which he again called "no law."

After the trip, Seiber said few people in New River would speak out, though other residents opposed the stripping. "They're afraid because they'll lose their non-union jobs or else be moved out of the houses rented from the land company," he said. That was the same reason Seiber gave for the earlier lack of local support during the long battles fought in the General Assembly before the strip-mine legislation was passed.

Stop all stripping. That was what Seiber wanted. Or at the very least, stop cutting the tops off mountains. Suddenly eloquent, the retired miner said, "We were the first people in these mountains and we ought to be able to keep them like God created them. There's plenty of coal to be got from the deep mines, and it means more work for more men. Fifty men could have jobs in the deep mines where ten work as strippers."

Whatever the merits of Seiber's argument on jobs, conservationist Bob Lefler of the Tennessee Citizens for Wilderness Planning had found the trip up on Carroll Ridge especially disturbing. Afterward he said that such wholesale mutilation of mountains could seriously disturb entire watersheds. Lefler believed Tennessee needed a much stricter law so that mining would not be allowed on steep slopes, changing the topography. "But I don't think anything is going to be done right now," he explained. "The present law allows operators three years to reclaim the land and the first planting won't start 'til spring."

Bad as the strip-mining situation was, Lefler's TCWP faced an immediate crisis in its fight with the U.S. Corps of Engineers over the proposed Devil's Jump Dam just north of Oneida. The dam, to be built on the Big South Fork of the Cumberland River, would ruin hopes of saving the watershed as a national recreation area. Since New River would be included in such an area as a tributary of the Big South Fork, the success of the TCWP effort would accomplish some of what Seiber wanted. A decision by federal agencies was expected within the year.

In the meantime, strip mining was going to continue in New River, and the first seedlings, which might or might not take root on the steep mountainsides, were soon to be planted. Who would be proven right, F. G. Watkins or old John Seiber?

Part
IV

Graves Gap: Up on the Flats

On Pilot Mountain with Byrd Duncan

New River can rival the beauty of the Great Smoky Mountains, in spite of the damage done by strip mining. For brilliant fall colors, a drive from Petros through the valley and out over Pilot Mountain, say toward the end of October, is only a bit short of spectacular. Keep going east on Highway 116 from what was Lewis Coker's store at Charley's Branch, and after a mile or so you come to the bridge across New River. There the river is joined by Ligias Fork and heads north. But the highway turns south, passing nearly vanished Stainville. Houses get farther and farther apart as you start to climb Pilot Mountain in Ike Phillips's domain.

On the skinny, winding road, where trees often meet overhead, autumn foliage can be luminescent. The very air seems golden like Ike's hidden treasure. Maples range from citron yellow to the purest of orange and flame red. Some oaks will have turned a dark true red, while sweet gums are covered with star-shaped leaves, nearly maroon, often edged with gold. All this color is made more startling by the green of eastern hemlocks and somber cedars mingling with pines of all shapes and sizes. You keep going up, following the sound of water, itself headed down the mountain to New River, passing a small house of worship here and there, like New Pilot Baptist Church, built by its own members. Then unexpectedly you are on the very top at Graves Gap. There, stretched out to the south, lies all of Anderson County! Far in the distance you can see ridge after parallel ridge, the Clinch River and TVA's Bull Run Steam Plant. And farther still are the blue Smokies.

You are out of New River now, but it's still some three miles down "the

Pilot," as everyone calls the mountain. Before bottom is reached at tiny Laurel Grove, there are three unbelievably sharp switchbacks unlike any a tourist would have to maneuver in a manicured national park. This part of Highway 116 must be little changed from what it was like in 1915 when it was first blasted out of the mountainside. So steep is the grade that a car can easily roll all the way from Graves Gap to Laurel Grove, as I discovered one time when my Ford's transmission went out while I was headed up the mountain. An enormous coal truck came roaring down toward Laurel Grove and screeched to a stop. The driver jumped out, telling me to put the car in neutral and steer while he pushed it back to the very edge of the precipice and got me pointed down the mountain. Then with brake released, I was off and rolling.

This south side of Pilot Mountain is not too far from Frost Bottom and could be called Duncan Country. Although he had competition, Byrd Duncan in 1969 was probably the best known of the all the Anderson County Duncans, a sort of modern King Duncan, happily minus a murdering Macbeth. This exuberant mountain man managed to live both in the past and the present. Born and raised and still living just under the peak of Pilot Mountain, Byrd was yet another great-great-grandson of Micajah Frost. His grandfather Elijah Frost Duncan Sr. was the last child of Moses Duncan's first wife, Mary Frost. She died in 1825 at the birth of Elijah and his twin, Jacob, who like his mother did not survive. Grandfather Elijah was the brother of Elizabeth Duncan, who became William Smith's wife and the grandmother of Uncle John.

Whether this Elijah was named for the Old Testament prophet swept up into heaven in a chariot of fire—or more likely for his mother's brother Elijah Frost with the seventeen children including White and Winter—this Duncan moved his family from Frost Bottom up on Pilot Mountain to escape the guerrilla fighting during the Civil War. The place where he settled would become Duncan Flats. This was an area located on a level bench or "flat" formed millions of years earlier when the soft shale topping the mountain eroded down to the harder sandstone. Though not as productive as the bottomland below, Duncan Flats was also not as tempting to marauding bushwhackers like Elijah's half-brother Devil Tom Duncan. It must have been a good move, for Elijah prospered and lived nearly long enough to see his grandson Byrd born in 1900.

At sixty-eight this lively man, not very tall but with unusually bright brown eyes, had already lived three different lives. The first was as a coal miner in the pick-and-shovel days, and the second as a cog in the great technological complex at Oak Ridge. Retired, in 1969 he was enjoying his third life devoted to gospel singing and the Boy Scouts and other things he wanted to do. He would accomplish the nearly impossible by organizing a successful area health clinic down the mountain in Briceville. This town, the largest in the county during the twenties' coal boom, had become a depressed, forlorn shadow of its earlier self.

Of all his activities, it was the gospel singing, however, that made Byrd famous. He was known far and wide because of the Lake City Singing Convention. A hundred or more people belonged to his group that sang each weekend all over the county each January, February, and March to raise money for the Anderson County March of Dimes, and then kept right on singing most of the rest of the year at community homecomings. These so-called conventions were an outgrowth of eighteenth-century "singing schools," which by the time of the Civil War had become quite popular throughout the South. Using songbooks with notes shaped to indicate their place on the musical scale, these singers reached their heyday during the 1920s in rural areas where sometimes several hundred would gather for all-day singings with dinner on the ground. Later on, these singings changed to frequent church appearances. It was such an appearance for the March of Dimes that nearly raised the roof of New River's Free Communion Baptist Church on Palm Sunday in 1969.

"O come, let us sing unto the Lord, let us make a joyful noise to the rock of our salvation!"

The psalmist of ancient Israel would have felt right at home as the small church all but burst with joyful noise that day. It was real gospel singing, truly joyful, not the bland TV kind. And no one there was enjoying it more than the singing convention's spirited leader. When church let out, Byrd gave me a warm invitation to visit Duncan Flats soon. Though he was a mountain man, he proved to be one with a difference, one who felt nearly as much at home in Oak Ridge as up on the Pilot. And he was anything but taciturn.

"You gotta learn to cope with people, all kinds," he said grinning as he sat on his front porch with wife Laura not long after Palm Sunday. She must have been more than twenty years his junior, but Byrd looked nearly as young with only a few gray hairs. "Yep, you gotta cope."

Apparently Byrd knew not only how to cope with people, but with life in general. Living in the Cumberlands had never been easy, but the big shutdown of coal mines after World War II made it even harder. Byrd had been a miner for nearly a quarter of a century when in 1952 he started all over again in a new job in the construction warehouse at the Oak Ridge National Laboratory. He was fifty-two.

"Oak Ridge was good to me," he said, turning serious. He retired in 1965 but became busier than ever. Boy Scouting had been added to all his gospel singing activities. Oak Ridgers got him interested in the Scouts, and he ended up organizing a new troop at Briceville. After that, the abandoned one-room county schoolhouse called Flat Woods out in Duncan Flats served not only Briceville

Boy Scouts, but troops from Oak Ridge who could find near-wilderness within sight of home. Although Pilot Mountain could be seen from Oak Ridge off to the northeast of Windrock, it was still a hard, hard thirteen miles over the Walden Ridge firetower road to Laurel Grove. Then there was the climb up Highway 116 nearly to Graves Gap to get to the camping area at the old school.

Although Byrd declared that he preferred the steep gravel road over "Walnut Ridge," what many called Walden Ridge, it was not recommended to flatlanders. The unadventurous could get to Laurel Grove, in order to start up the mountain, by two other longer routes. The least exciting and longest was east through Clinton, then north to Lake City, and back west to Briceville and Laurel Grove. The other way was north to Oliver Springs and then east over the infamous Frost Bottom Road, with potholes half the size of a small car. Either route left the three-mile climb up Highway 116, with its sharp switchbacks like something out of a European road-racing movie. As a fifteen-year-old, Byrd earned his very first dollar helping build that road. It was literally one dollar for a ten-hour day.

"That was 1915, the year my daddy, Elijah Frost Duncan Jr., died. We started the road over in Dutch Valley at ole man Henry Dail's place, come across Walnut Ridge, and then up over the Pilot to Jake's Ford, where it levels out down on Ligias Fork," Byrd recalled. The timber boom was under way thanks to the new railroad into the New River valley from Scott County. But people still couldn't drive out in cars until a bridge was built across the river in 1924.

Though only fifteen, Byrd helped two men tamp holes for dynamite to blast the rock. At one spot near Graves Gap, it took eight cases of dynamite and twenty-four kegs of powder to get rid of twenty-eight feet of rock, he explained. The road helped, but life still remained isolated in the small communities like Duncan Flats and nearby Braden Flats over on the east side of the road. A few hardy souls had lived on the mountain since shortly after 1800 when the Cherokees were being pushed farther and farther north. But most people had moved up to the flats during the terrible days of the Civil War and the bad times that followed. Byrd's father, Elijah Jr., was born in 1858 in Frost Bottom and was just a boy when his father, the older Elijah, took his family to higher ground, considerably higher, just under the 3,285-foot peak of Pilot Mountain.

So on that early April day in 1969, with the weeping willows showing the first sign of spring green, Byrd Duncan was deeply rooted in Duncan Flats, a mile or so west of Highway 116. On around the winding dirt road stood the old homeplace where he grew up as one of seven children. It was just a bit farther on to the end of the road where the deserted one-room Flat Woods School sat up above Deep Hollow. There the sunlight had never entered until loggers started cutting the timber. Laura Duncan, a friendly woman who was nearly as talkative as her husband, said she grew up a Patterson down there on Harness Creek. After Byrd's first wife Malinda died, she had taken the job of housekeeper to care for the three children still at home. Daughter Beulah was twenty and already gone. Four years later Laura and Byrd married. They had three sons of their own, including two at Lake City High School. Marcus was about to graduate and go to Cumberland College to study chemistry. Wendell at fifteen thought mostly about basketball and football, while Langley, two years younger, was at Briceville Elementary School in that new scout troop. Byrd had had to quit school after the sixth grade and was determined that his children would have a better chance.

"Laura finished raising my other three and couldn't have been better to them if she'd been their own mother," Byrd said seriously. Sounding serious was unusual for him, for he loved to tease her, as he had earlier, threatening to get a divorce if she continued to wear the red plaid slacks she had on. Duncan family ties were obviously very strong in the mountain tradition, though the older sons, Ray and Byrd Jr., lived in Clinton and daughters Thelma and Beulah in Oak Ridge and Fraterville. Singing kept them together. Ray was often bass soloist with the Lake City Singing Convention, while Beulah Braden's whole family sang as a group. Even teenagers Marcus, Wendell, and Langley found time to sing along with a number of high-schoolers who helped to fill the New River church with enthusiastic gospel songs on Palm Sunday.

The home all these offspring came back to was the house Byrd had built in 1932. Before that, they had lived in a now-gone log house across the corn field from the pleasant frame one. With the chilly weather nearly gone, their yard too would be pleasant soon with its grape arbor. But that day, except for the evergreens and the pinkish haze of maples and poplars about to burst into leaf, Pilot Mountain and Duncan Flats were still winter bare. The scars of strip mining on the mountain stood out even more than usual. Spring plowing, however, was already under way despite the protesting frogs. The Duncans, with Laura in her red plaid slacks, had been busy hunting hidden turkey nests in the woods earlier in the day. Now Byrd was going to conduct an informal tour of Duncan Flats, something he obviously enjoyed.

But first he explained, "Nothing like as many people live here as used to, only maybe a dozen families now." Braden Flats, at a little lower elevation over to the east of Highway 116, had over twenty homes, in addition to Indian Bluff Baptist Church. As the tour got under way, Byrd pointed to a road, not much more than a trail, going off to the right, that was pretty well torn up by recent logging operations. On a tree a sign warned to keep open the road to the "Rose place" for the annual family gathering. "Up there a ways was where Charlie Rose and old Groundhog Mose Duncan lived. They musta been seventeen families there at one time, but they started moving away, some during the thirties, most after the war," Byrd said. "Five members of the Rose family died in just one year from TB. Groundhog Mose and his wife stayed 'til they died, but then their children left."

Groundhog Mose?

"Shore," he laughed. "Don't know why, but they's so many Mose Duncans it was hard to keep track of 'em."

The moving out had about stopped, he reckoned. There might even be people coming back who valued the isolation and quiet of the mountains. "I had a man the other day try to buy my twenty-five acres here, but I'd not leave for nothing. A lot of people who live up here now work for TVA or in Oak Ridge or Knoxville. With the chain stores, you can't make a living farming, but we raise potatoes and turkeys for people who like to buy from us," he said, sounding like a contented man.

Byrd owned another forty acres down past Deep Hollow, which he pointed toward from where the dirt road ended at the abandoned school he had helped build in 1932. "It's real beautiful down there, and some people wanted me to go in with them to build a lake, but I'm a little afraid of getting skinned," he said, grinning. A real paved road would have to be constructed. There was only a logging one used by Georgia-Pacific and the coal trucks hauling from the small deep mines belonging to Jonas Phillips. So, for the time being Flat Woods School was the end of the dusty county road. Sitting there alone in the clearing, austere with its high roof, the schoolhouse looked like a photograph from the previous century. Laura Duncan went to school there and was proud that a higher percentage of children went on to high school from Flat Woods' one-room than from any other elementary school in the county. When it was closed in 1958, all the Duncan Flats children went down to Laurel Grove. That school had three rooms, but in 1963 Laurel Grove was consolidated with the modern school in Briceville.

Still enjoying his role as guide, Byrd opened up the painted-over high windows inside the musty schoolhouse to let some light in. "Yes, sirree, this is just the place for boys. The Scouts come all winter long and sleep inside when it's really cold." Mattresses were stacked along one wall, and a few school desks remained. Oak Ridge troops had camped there a number of times, usually with some help from Byrd or with the whole Briceville Troop 123. Byrd had been serving as assistant to Scoutmaster Floyd Teno since the troop was organized. When his sons had to transfer from Laurel Grove to Briceville in 1963, he found himself president of the Briceville PTA. Bart Klima, the Oak Ridger who headed the Scouts' Pellissippi District, then convinced Byrd that a new troop should be set up in the Briceville area. "I was too old to be scoutmaster, but I helped get it going, and now we really got some plans for up here," Byrd said, pointing to the edge of the school clearing where the Scouts hoped to build four cabins.

Building things was something this active man had been doing as long as he could remember. On the way back to Byrd's house, he said to stop at the log cabin standing across from where his old homeplace once sat. The house was empty, but Byrd recalled every detail about the day when he was thirteen and the whole community came for the house-raising for his older brother Cage. Until Cage died, he lived in the sturdy log building. Hard as it was getting the logs into place, it was still simpler building that kind of house because lumber was so difficult to bring in. "We'd just cut the trees nearby, snake 'em in, and hew 'em on the spot. When the wall got higher than the men could reach to lay another log on, they'd walk the logs up, putting their feet in the cracks between the lower logs," he explained.

The timbers had been notched at the ends and carefully mortised. Split pieces of wood had been driven into the cracks between the logs and covered over with a limestone and rock mixture to make it airtight. The cabin had been empty for four or five years, ever since a family from Kentucky had moved away. Though rundown, it still had red tulips blooming on what wallpaper remained on the living room walls. Three woebegone dresses hung in the corner of the otherwise

Laura and Byrd Duncan up on Pilot Mountain in 1969 explaining how Byrd helped raise this Duncan Flats log cabin when he was a boy. Photograph courtesy of the *Oak Ridger.*

empty bedroom, apparently forgotten by the vanished Kentuckians. Just a stone's throw from an old springhouse, the log building backed up against a hill with a rocky ravine that Byrd called a "rock bar." That's what you have in the Cumberlands instead of sand bars, Byrd wryly pointed out.

Another brother Sammy and his family, plus sister Rosie Jane, lived in the comfortable-looking house on the other side of the road. It was just a couple hundred yards from the place where the house they'd all grown up in had once stood. With the help of his pony, the kind once used to haul coal inside a mine, Sammy was busy spreading manure on his garden from a sled. He stopped only long enough to say hello, but his wife talked over the fence. Pointing, she said, "Over there, down near the springhouse is where they used to butcher. We don't butcher anymore, just send it to Wampler's in Knoxville and then bring it back to our freezer." She and Laura froze everything from their gardens that would keep well, but both still did a lot of canning, too. Because electricity didn't come to the mountain until the 1950s, they appreciated it as a real blessing each and every day, she said.

Although homes out on Duncan Flats had kerosene lamps until well after the World War II, plenty of electricity was to be had over in Briceville at the New Royal Mine. Up there on Cross Mountain, Byrd once ran the electric "motor." He drove the small locomotive for more than twenty years from deep in the mine to the tipple outside. "I started the day Herbert Hoover was elected in 1928 and worked 'til the mine shut down in 1949. The juice was dangerous and there was fall-ins, but running the motor was a good job, not hard work like digging coal. I know, I dug it up in Kentucky at Blue Diamond for several years. Once won a five-dollar gold piece for pulling the most!"

The mention of Herbert Hoover got Byrd off on politics. Grinning he said, "Might nigh everbody up here's a Republican." Nevertheless, in 1935 the New Deal's Wagner Act guaranteeing labor the right to organize was more than welcome. It was during the organization drives of the United Mine Workers that the Duncan Quartet came into being. "I was raised on gospel singing, and it was then we formed the Four D's, three Duncans and one Dutchman! We sang at union-organizing rallies up at Windrock and New River," he said. Compared to the bloodletting between the UMW and the mine owners in Harlan County and other places in Kentucky, Anderson County was a quiet place, Byrd remembered. However, he did recall trouble with haulers from non-union mines for a while. "Sometimes trucks was turned over and the driver was forced to eat strong onions or got beat up. But it didn't last long. The big companies here didn't like the union, but they didn't really fight it neither."

The Democrat Franklin Roosevelt indirectly influenced another very important part of Byrd Duncan's life, the singing convention. When FDR

Free Communion Baptist Church today in New River, where Byrd Duncan and the Lake City Singing Convention raised money in 1969 for the March of Dimes. Photograph by the author.

was first organizing the March of Dimes, he asked Virgil Stamps of Texas gospel-singing fame if he would help put on a ball in Dallas to raise money. The Stamps Quartet didn't want to be associated with a dance but offered to get gospel singers across the Southeast to sing for polio victims. The Anderson County Singing Convention, which was organized during the first World War, started singing and collecting for the March of Dimes in 1938, with Byrd in on it from the very beginning. He still belonged to that group but in 1952 organized the new Lake City Singing Convention. Just the previous year an all-time record was set, with Byrd's group bringing in $1,321 from freewill offerings in the small churches where they sang. Both conventions raised a combined $2,100, an important part of the county's total.

Byrd's effectiveness for the March of Dimes could easily be seen up in New River at the Free Communion Church. With his pretty blond granddaughter Linda Belle at the piano, the singing convention's spirited music filled the attractive little church with its dark red velvet curtain behind the altar saying "Welcome." And the jovial preacher, the Reverend Dana Ward, played the guitar and harmonica at the same time while the Guy Phillips family sang "I've Seen the Light." Then the tone turned solemn with Ray Duncan's bass solo "Standing Outside." At the end of the service, when the offering was $5.62 short of the $90 that Byrd said the March of Dimes needed from the church, there was more singing and the extra bit appeared.

Everyone filed out in the bright afternoon sunshine feeling good, ready for Easter and spring and singing for annual homecomings. Whether by design or not, these gatherings appropriately would begin at the Zion Baptist Church homecoming at Claxton in Raccoon Valley. That was the oldest church in Anderson County, where Micajah's half-brother, the Reverend Joshua Frost, once held forth with his booming voice. No one was more ready for the first homecoming than Byrd Duncan, who was beaming. "Now, that was real singing!"

The Return of Hiram Braden's Offspring

Calling the south slopes below Graves Gap "Duncan Country" was stretching it a bit. The Braden clan has an equal claim. But then Braden Flats, on the east side of Highway 116, is technically not on Pilot Mountain but on Red Oak Mountain. Keeping all this straight takes careful study of a topographical map. It's much simpler to just call it Pilot Mountain. Whatever the name, the mass of Bradens coming to the all-day family reunion at Indian Bluff Baptist Church in September 1969 was a sight to behold. It took place on a Sunday under a dazzling autumn sky—with more than sixty feet of food on one long table stretching out under three tall oaks. Over two hundred people enjoyed every home-cooked morsel.

The Bradens had come from Ireland before the American Revolution and like the Frosts and the Duncans were among the first settlers in Anderson County. But it was not until after the Civil War that one Hiram Braden in 1871 bought three hundred acres out on the bench on the mountain and called his small fiefdom Braden Flats. A hundred years later his four sons and two daughters lay peacefully in the church cemetery surrounding him and his wife Susan.

Hiram's scores and scores of great-grandchildren and great-great-grandchildren, even a few great-great-great ones, had come back along the narrow gravel road leading off the not much wider highway. Goldenrod and wild purple asters were blooming in the dense woods, where the dogwood and sumac were already turning red. All the generations came and they came in everything from new white Cadillacs to late-model pickups, typical Americans but still with the special something that mountain people have.

Hiram Braden's eldest son, Isaac, and wife, Elizabeth, pictured long before Isaac's death in 1921 in Braden Flats. Photograph courtesy of Nancy Braden Byrge.

Waiting to greet them were the twenty or so families who still lived out on the flats in comfortable houses with trimmed lawns. They had produced most of the mountain of food heaped on the tremendous table—fried chicken, pinto beans, homemade sauerkraut, huge slices of tomatoes, chicken and dumplings, and dishpans full of banana pudding. Besides that, for anyone who had the room, there were coconut and chocolate pies, along with old-fashioned stack cakes, the thin layers held together with fresh-cooked fruit.

The Bradens were independent and fiercely loyal to family and homeplace. Those whose homes were there went down the mountain every day to work, some in Tennco's nearby mines, others in Oak Ridge or even in Knoxville, but they all gladly came back every night.

"Why I wouldn't live anyplace else," Mrs. Pearley Byrge said while the church was filling up. There was to be preaching and then music by Byrd Duncan's Lake City Singing Convention. The preaching would provide "spiritual food," according to the Reverend Bill Hensley, before the physical feast at noon. Not only did Mrs. Byrge not want to live anywhere else, she never had. Before she married Pearley Byrge in 1938, she was Nancy Braden, a daughter of Noah, who was a son of Isaac, oldest son of that first Hiram. How she was related to the other Bradens there that day proved too complicated to explain, what with intermarrying of different branches of the family, not to mention the Duncans, in the last hundred years. A grandmother herself, Mrs. Byrge was a most amiable woman. Nevertheless, she made it clear that she definitely did not like for mountain people to be stereotyped as ignorant and worthless. "Here in Braden Flats, we're as good as anybody in Clinton," she said, but in a good-natured way.

The Bradens could certainly brag of their offspring if they had a mind to. There were those with college degrees, including one with a doctorate in agricultural journalism, and those with heroic war records. During World War II, the family of Hiram's granddaughter Nola had become famous throughout Anderson County. Nola Braden was the wife of W. O. Duncan, longtime circuit court clerk, and the mother of eight sons, all servicemen during the war, along with her two sons-in-law. It was Nola's daughter Dixie, who told me about Judy Duncan.

After Sunday dinner under the trees, the sense of the past grew stronger. The only old building that remained was Harry Braden's home across from the church. His unpainted but neat house had stood nearly ninety years. On one end, where a bit of wooden siding was gone, hewn logs a foot wide could be glimpsed. A look inside, out of the bright sunlight, revealed low ceilings, more evidence that a log cabin was sealed inside the frame walls. No matter what the house's skeleton was made of, a modern refrigerator and stove gleamed in the kitchen, where a giant philodendron covered a whole corner. Gone were the days of kerosene lamps, days that extended into the 1950s. To have vegetables all winter, the early Bradens would dig a hole or a trench near their houses to store potatoes, carrots, and turnips, covering them with straw and planks topped by a foot or so of earth.

Outside the once-log house grew tangy yellow "hoss" apples on gnarled trees looking out toward a field edged with tall corn. It was over there that the second Andrew Braden, probably the best-known Braden, lived until his death at seventy-five in 1940. Like Nancy Byrge's grandfather Isaac, Andrew was one of Hiram's sons. He had gained fame as a coal prospector. Thirteen of Andrew's seventeen children grew up, becoming an important part of the gray-headed older generation at the family reunion that day. Bill, who had been gassed as a doughboy in the first World War, still lived in Braden Flats. So did Ernest, who rebuilt Andrew's old homeplace around the original chimney after the house burned following his father's death. He lived there and worked for Georgia Pacific Lumber Company. Other sons moved away, like Captain Jess Braden of the Clinton police force, and Joe Braden, an employee at Oak Ridge's Y-twelve weapons plant.

As loyal as any of Andrew's children was the widow of his oldest son, Wiley, who had died in 1924, long before his father. She was Beulah Brummitt Braden, at seventy-six the vigorous family historian. In recent years she had lived in Oak Ridge to be near her daughter Billie and husband, Owen Killen, a chemist. Another daughter, Rosslyn, graduated from the University of Tennessee and later received a master's degree and a doctorate in agricultural journalism at the University of Wisconsin. Rosslyn worked with her husband Aubrey Smith in the University of Georgia's extension service. Beulah Braden herself had been a teacher for many years in Anderson County. Right after her husband died, she first taught at the now-closed Braden School. Sounding like anything but a proper schoolmarm, she recalled laughing, "I don't know that I did much teaching, more just keeping school with twenty-four children from Braden Flats and another twenty-four from Brown Flats on down the mountain."

After Beulah Braden's baptism in teaching out on the flats, she moved to Shinliver School just north of Clinton. It was right there that the first Andrew Braden, a veteran of the American Revolution, settled in Anderson County. It is known that he had come at least as early as 1804, since his name is on the county's jury list that year. Andrew I, as Mrs. Braden called him, was born in 1765 in Guilford County, North Carolina. After she retired from teaching, she had time for searching courthouse records across the country and learned a great deal about the Bradens, Bredens, Brattons, and Breadens who came to this country, nearly all from Ireland. Mrs. Braden still lacked a final bit of proof but was nearly certain the first Andrew was the son of one Alexander Braden, a captain wounded in 1758 at the Battle of Ticonderoga. Alexander had been a loyal colonist fighting with the British in the French and Indian War, but twenty years later it was a different story as the colonists struggled against the British themselves in the American Revolution.

Nowhere was that struggle more savage than late in the war on the Carolina frontier. A tremendous effort by Lord Cornwallis to rally local southern Tories provoked a small but bloody civil war in 1780. That June a teenage patriot named Andrew Braden volunteered for the Guilford County militia. Alexander's son took part in the fierce encounter with loyalists at Ramsour's Mill north of Kings Mountain. Atrocities had already been committed by each side in this backwoods conflict so that neighbor took revenge on neighbor at the mill. In the smoke and confusion of the fight, men and boys used their muskets and rifles as often to smash in skulls as to shoot. But this was the first important fight the patriots would win before the fateful one at Kings Mountain in the fall. Some 150 men died on each side at Ramsour's Mill, but Andrew Braden survived. He went on to serve a total of seventeen months helping "regulate" the Tories, as he called it on his application for a veteran's pension.

That first Andrew was a determined man looking for a better life after the Revolution, for he kept moving, first north into the Blue Ridge Mountains to several counties in Virginia and finally to East Tennessee. He did well and eventually owned many acres of land, becoming active in Anderson County affairs. The Braden family must have been moderately wealthy. They had a house near Clinton that was said to be the first in the county with glass windows and an upstairs porch. Andrew, a blacksmith who probably started the first iron foundry in Tennessee, died in 1842 and was buried on the side of Black Oak Ridge. One of his sons, William, moved north on across Walden Ridge into the deep valley at the foot of the Cumberlands where Laurel Grove now stands. William fought in the War of 1812 and sired seven children. Then came the Civil War and its harsh aftermath. One of William's seven, Hiram, in 1871 took a hundred dollars and bought three hundred acres from Abraham White up on the mountain. Braden Flats was out where the Cherokees had wintered under bluffs that are nearly like caves, leaving behind hundreds of arrowheads. Tradition says they also left the graves that gave Graves Gap its name.

It was not long after Hiram's move that the killing of Isaac White took place about 1876. Beulah Braden told this story, along with all the others about the early Bradens. Jake Harness was the husband of Hiram's sister Edie. One day Jake appeared at the Bradens' log cabin and announced that he had just killed White, who owned land a bit lower down in Brown Flats. Jake not only told Hiram's wife Susan this startling news but boasted that White's head had rolled down the mountain "like a damned old pumpkin"! And indeed Isaac White was buried without a head, according to Mrs. Braden. Nearly a hundred years later, she was not sure how all this came about, but this much was certain: Jake Harness was hanged for the crime, and Susan Braden received $7.60 for appearing as a witness at his trial. Beulah Braden added that the story went that many years after the murder someone found a human skull and took it home to use for a soap dish. "But it wouldn't stay still on the table. And that was proof enough it was the lost head!"

Recent attempts to learn details about Jake Harness produced few, even with the help of Mary S. Harris, Anderson County's energetic historian. No doubt he was convicted of murder July 14, 1876, followed by a hanging after an unsuccessful appeal to the state supreme court. The county's revered Judge Xen Hicks, who served on the U.S. Court of Appeals, remembered it when he was an old man in 1951. He said there was a holiday in Clinton when Jake was hanged "in a natural amphiteatre just across from the K & O Railroad," a place where apparently everyone could get a good look. Judge Hicks, a child at the time, couldn't remember the exact date, though it was about 1880. Then Clinton had maybe five hundred citizens, muddy streets, a handful of two-story houses, and a Methodist church along with a Baptist one. Although the town also had a newspaper, the *Clinton Tribune,* it published only legal notices, and today Clinton's library has no copies. The *Clinton Gazette* started publishing in 1888, too late for an account of the hanging. A search of courthouse records did not reveal the execution date, though they show that an administrator for the estate of Jake Harness was appointed January 18, 1879, following an unsuccessful appeal of his 1876 conviction to the state supreme court. So, the hanging probably took place in January 1879.

Jasper Smith wrote briefly and vaguely about the case in 1928 for the *Anderson County News* at the request of a reader. He mistakenly recalled it as happening right after the Civil War. He also sounded a bit apologetic, possibly because he only liked to write about the good things of the past and, besides, the Harnesses were a respected family. But according to Jasper, Jake Harness "was not the man his brother John was." He knew them both. Jasper said that Jake should not have been hanged but gave no reason why nor any details at all about the case. He did make a point of saying that Jake's brother John was a Union soldier in the Ninth Tennessee Regiment and very well thought of, as were his parents, Crisley and Betsy Harness. In the same breath, Jasper calmly added that he had been told by old people that Aunt Betsy was a witch. "They said she could make a cow give bloody milk, wring buttermilk out of a dish rag, and make a dog run around and bark at its tale," Jasper said, warning his readers not to dismiss the witch story. Remember the Bible speaks of witches, he said and promptly retold the story of how King Saul went to the Witch of Endor to communicate with the dead prophet Samuel. Ignoring Samuel's prediction of the Israelites' defeat by the Philistines, Saul went to his death. Jasper also said that he himself could vouch for a boy cured of fits by a witch doctor in adjoining Morgan County. All of this was written in 1928, throwing some surprising light on ideas about witches but little on Jake Harness.

As of today, exactly why or when this Harness met his end is not known. Those who could have said are now dead. One was Gertrude Harness's father, Harvey. He was the youngest son of Jake's respected brother John. Now retired from teaching school, Harvey's daughter is a friendly woman who lives in Laurel Grove. She can look out her window and see where her great-uncle is buried on a hillside with a field stone for a marker. She, too, would like to know more about the family's history—"I've never heard anything about witches!" She is sorry she never asked her father about the murder case. "He never wanted to talk about Jake Harness," she said, "because he thought he was innocent, that one of the Vanns did it." The story persists that Dan Vann confessed on his deathbed to killing Isaac White, Gertrude Harness said, admitting there were "hard feelings" between the Harnesses and the Vanns for years. Today she is philosophical about it all and able to enjoy a story passed long from Hubo Seiber, one of

After his hanging, Jake Harness was buried on the hill behind this log house in Laurel Grove built by his brother John in the 1880s. It is still occupied. Photograph courtesy of Mary S. Harris.

Jake's great-grandsons. Seiber had recently told county historian Mary Harris, laughing the whole time, how Jake sat on his coffin and chewed tobacco before the hanging. He said making moonshine up on the mountain was probably the cause of the whole affair. And, yes, Isaac White's head did roll down the mountain like a pumpkin.

Murder aside, the big coal boom arrived down in Coal Creek Valley. Up above on Braden Flats, Hiram's family prospered and multiplied. Most of them worked in the scores of mines just down the mountain to the east near Briceville. The second Andrew—Hiram's son born in 1865 exactly a hundred years after the first Andrew—was a miner, a foreman, a prospector, and finally a coal mine operator himself. B. Rule Stout of Knoxville, manager of the Coal Creek Mining and Manufacturing Company for years, had nothing but good things to say about Andrew II, claiming the mountains were never the same after his death in 1940. Stout told Beulah Braden, "Truly, Uncle Andrew was the Wise Man of Anderson County's Cumberland Mountains. Anyone in trouble went to him and usually he could solve their problems. Many the time I asked him about difficult problems I was facing as manager for the land company."

While Andrew's schooling was very limited, his knowledge was not. He had his own system of figuring out such things as the board feet in a tract of timber and was an expert timber "cruiser" or prospector, just as he was an expert prospector of coal seams. Having grown up just after the Civil War when the county had few schools, Andrew Braden did all he could to make education possible on the flats. And he was the one that saw to the building of the Indian Bluff Baptist Church, though he never joined it. He favored the Presbyterian faith, but the Presbyterians, like the Methodists, had become almost extinct in the mountains as small independent Baptist churches multiplied.

That day of the reunion Edd Braden provided more vivid family remembrances. He was a brother of Nancy Byrge, the one who said she'd never live anywhere but Braden Flats. Edd, however, moved away in the thirties to a farm on the good valley land between Clinton and Norris. There he became an ardent beekeeper as well as a member of the security force of Stone and Webster in the early days of Oak Ridge. But he was still very much a part of the old life up on the mountain. Both his great-uncle Andrew and his own grandfather Isaac, Andrew's older brother, made strong impressions on Edd when he was a boy. "Uncle Andrew was known all over. He was a smart man and a good talker, a real money maker," Edd said. "And he had lots of friends, too, like the Cokers in New River. He wasn't quite as big as Lewis Coker is, but in ways he reminded me of him."

Edd liked to remember the story about Andrew when he was a young man working down the mountain at Minersville. He got in a fistfight with his boss. "Uncle Andrew was getting beat bad when his older brother, my Grandpa Isaac, came along and knocked the other man in a barrel of oil! Grandpa had the awfulest temper." While Andrew was a "businesslike fellow," Isaac was one of the few Bradens who never worked in the mines, according to Edd. He hewed logs and built houses. Most of all, Isaac loved to tramp the mountains and hunt with his rifle though he had a mill to take care of in addition to everything else. His grandson said, "He was a good shot. His eyesight was as good as a young man's when he died." Edd Braden recalled that about old Isaac's eyesight after he had told how his grandfather once took him way out on the scary edge of a bluff when Edd was "just a button." He wanted to show the little boy where years before he had killed his last deer with his old hog rifle. It was one with a delayed action or "long fire."

But Edd's clearest recollection was what came of the fateful time a chicken got in the kitchen and caused his grandmother to upset an oil lamp. Isaac's temper got the best of him, and he bawled out his wife. Then Edd's father Noah in turn got angry with the old man. "So Grandpa packed up and went down to my Aunt Rosie Seiber's in Frost Bottom. Finally, my daddy wanted to make up so he bought a gristmill for Grandpa. It was an awful job moving it. But when we got it moved, we sent a letter and just happened to mention the mill."

That did it.

Grandpa Isaac sent word for young Edd to saddle up the black mules and come get him.

It took all day to get down to Frost Bottom. The boy wanted to eat and go to bed, but the old man insisted on heading back immediately. And he happily ran the mill the remaining years of his life until he died in 1921.

Isaac's mill was gone, but his son Noah's house built in the 1920s was still there. It was the home of Edd's sister Nancy and her husband, Pearley Byrge. The softspoken Byrge came to Braden Flats shortly before their marriage in 1938 and, like his wife, refused to live anyplace else. He was working for Tennco in their No. 3 Walnut Mine up in the head of Beech Grove Hollow near Lake City. That Sunday afternoon while the singing convention rattled Indian Bluff Church with gospel music, Byrge talked a while out under the trees. He was one of the people responsible for the recent pleasing makeover inside the church and the new white siding on the outside, though he wanted no credit. He was just happy to be at home in Braden Flats waiting for more people to move back to the peaceful mountain.

"I predict that many of the young ones here today will come back for good," he said quietly. With that, this Braden-by-marriage pronounced a sort of benediction on the thirty-seventh family reunion.

Part
V

Coal Creek Valley:
Convicts and Disasters

The Coal Creek War

When Uncle John Smith made his grand tour walking from Oliver Springs up over Petros Mountain into New River, then through Graves Gap and down Pilot Mountain, he found Laurel Grove at the bottom. He turned right and headed back west on the Frost Bottom Road toward Oliver Springs. If, instead, he had gone left and stayed on Highway 116 another six miles east, he would have reached Briceville. Then Fraterville, the Wye, and finally Lake City.

Before the TVA was launched in 1937 with the building of Norris Dam and its reservoir lake on the Clinch River, elegantly named Lake City was a town called Coal Creek. Jasper Smith, who objected to Winters Gap becoming Oliver Springs, would certainly have complained. The name Coal Creek is a real name with a history, not something dreamed up by a public relations bureaucrat. Like Winters Gap, this town sprang up in a gap in Walden Ridge, the only other such opening in the county. But unlike Moses Winters's settlement going back to 1799, the Coal Creek area was little more than wilderness until just after the Civil War. It is here that good-sized Coal Creek—some say it was originally Cole Creek and had nothing to do with coal—comes out of the Cumberlands. This is the northeastern end of the valley squeezed in between Walden Ridge and the highest peak in the county, Cross Mountain. Here in a turbulent decade starting in 1891 the Coal Creek War raged between miners and state militia over convict labor and here two disastrous explosions killed 268 miners.

Ernest Hill, an old miner, grinned and explained in 1968, "Yes, sir, we used to have a real mean reputation. Everbody knew about Coal Creek in the old days for sure. If you said you's from Coal Creek, they stopped and listened!"

At seventy-eight, Hill still had vivid memories of the disastrous Fraterville Mine explosion in 1902. However, he was too young to remember the Coal Creek War ten years earlier. But like so many others he had a father who was in on burning the prison stockades and fighting the militia called out by Governor John "Buck" Buchanan. Young Ernest was raised on such stories.

Down at the other end of the valley in Oliver Springs, Jasper Smith's son Johnny was just six but remembered when the armed rebellion spilled over there with trains commandeered by miners who were armed to the teeth. And he remembered how later he was lucky and decided against working in the Cross Mountain Mine not long before it blew up in December 1911. That was only nine years after the Fraterville explosion. John T. Smith had been afraid of all the coal dust collecting deep in the mine for nearly forty years. He recollected how he'd walked all the way from Donovan with his brother-in-law Josh Foster to start work, but the mine foreman never sent him a coal car to start loading. "Besides, I didn't like it not one bit and told Josh I's going home," he said. "They was so much coal dust in the manways you had to wade in it, just like gunpowder. I said it'd blow before the first of the year."

That was early in 1911, and the mines were booming. But for over half a century before the Civil War, the area around Coal Creek was mostly steep forests. Only a few families were there trying to farm, like the Slovers and the Bowlings and the Vowells. It took the arrival of the Knoxville and Kentucky Railroad in 1869 to overcome the isolation of the rugged terrain. Even today the stretch of Highway 116 between Laurel Grove and Briceville has little traffic. The narrow road, which is wavy with rises never graded down, retains a dark, mysterious feeling. In places hemlock and pine join overhead to keep out the light even at noon when the sun normally gets into the deep ravines.

For all the valley's forested beauty and occasional flat places, early settlers wanted more room and good soil for farming as in Frost Bottom or, even better, wide acres like those of Richard Oliver's plantation on Poplar Creek near Oliver Springs. Since Tennessee taxed all kinds of land at the same rate until 1834, there was little incentive to populate the mountainous area where Coal Creek rushed along on its way to join the Clinch River. When the state was new, men were known to trade maybe a thousand acres of steep-sided land for a good rifle. The most heartbreaking story of all, at least to a good capitalist, is that of George Young, who in 1808 let his grant of five thousand acres near what would become the town of Coal Creek be sold for taxes. The sale brought in $25.25, the equivalent of less than $300 today.

But, even if George Young had known about the millions of dollars of coal under his rocky slopes, it would have done him little good. East Tennessee was hemmed in. Unlike Middle Tennessee with access to the Cumberland River flowing directly into the Ohio River, the eastern part of the state had the meandering Tennessee River. Its tortuous route down into Alabama, then back north across western Tennessee, and finally into the Ohio greatly impeded development. And roads, if the trails could be called that, proved even worse. Muddy in winter and rutted in summer, the Jacksboro Pike headed north from Clinton toward Kentucky but was good for little but a stage line. John Jarnigan, the energetic Clinton businessman and slave owner, spearheaded efforts during the 1830s to build a good toll turnpike to the Kentucky border but without success. Then when he and other county leaders like Oliver Springs's Richard Oliver and Henry Wiley finally got a railroad under construction from Knoxville north to Anderson County, the long-awaited project was destroyed by the Civil War. Jarnigan went off to fight for the Confederacy, and Wiley for the Union.

But when Henry Wiley and his surviving four sons returned victorious from the war, Coal Creek's time had come. The frustration of hauling coal by wagon to Knoxville or floating it down the Clinch River would end. Although the Knoxville and Kentucky Railroad had been devastated by the war, East Tennessee's luck changed. Being on the winning side meant getting state railroad bonds for immediate rebuilding. By 1869, thirty miles of new track were completed from Knoxville to Coal Creek. That same year Henry Wiley moved from Oliver Springs to this newborn town at the end of the new tracks. The rails would soon extend to Jellico and Kentucky. All of Wiley's years of accumulating land, thousands of acres going back to his partnership with lawyer William S. McEwen in 1838, were about to pay off. He arrived in Coal Creek already rich but about to become much richer, quickly building spur lines and opening new mines. Soon, however, he would get out of mining operations and form the Coal Creek Mining and Manufacturing Company to lease land to coal operators. The corporation would get a royalty on each ton of coal rumbling out through the gap in Walden Ridge, and there would be many.

Even before the tracks were completed from Clinton to Coal Creek, the Knoxville Iron Company had opened its own mine and was hauling coal by wagon to Clinton to put on the new railroad. This was the company, you remember, that Joseph C. Richards helped set up in Knoxville when Yankee capital arrived shortly after Appomattox. It would be nearly twenty more years before the Richards clan would move to Oliver Springs. Joseph Richards had come south in 1866 with four fellow Welshmen experienced in the Pennsylvania iron industry. Coal was essential for their new company's rolling mill, foundry, machine shop, nail mill, and railroad spike machine. Within a year of Richards's arrival in Knoxville, he was joined by over a hundred more Welsh men, women, and children whose livelihood would be tied to the important new mill and foundry in the city and to the company's mining in Coal Creek.

Other miners came from England and Scotland, usually by way of Pennsylvania. Coal-mining skills had developed in the British Isles going back over two hundred years, but working conditions there had been terrible, so terrible that criminals in the late seventeenth century were sentenced to five years labor in the mines instead of execution. Women worked deep in the earth by candlelight for over a hundred years, but so did children as young as six. They carried coal in baskets held in place on their backs with leather bands around their foreheads. Harnesses allowed them to pull tubs of coal on their hands and knees through the low, narrow passageways. Although the first strike took place in 1765, the British coal miners were not strong enough to form a national union until the 1840s. Then a strike of thousands of miners in 1844 was smashed and with it the union. Many headed to the United States, where the Industrial Revolution had only begun. Within several years, some thirty-seven thousand skilled miners had arrived. Though not a miner, Joseph C. Richards, too, wanted a better life and left Wales in 1848. After the Civil War he would make a fortune in both the iron and the coal businesses in Tennessee.

So, where nothing had been before, Coal Creek suddenly appeared. In 1870, Bradstreet's listing of businesses in the United States included ten establishments in the town. General stores accounted for most of them, but Wilson's Saloon, plus two nameless competitors in the whiskey business, kept over a hundred miners happy. At first they worked in the four mines less than a mile up the valley in the area called the Wye, where Beech Grove Fork joins Coal Creek. Some thirty-six thousand tons of coal rolled out over the new railroad tracks in 1871, and twice that amount in 1875.

Jobs and money were plentiful, maybe explaining why a union begun in 1873 by Coal Creek miners made no headway. Except for its official charter, next to nothing is known about this union called the Miners, Mechanics and Laborers Benevolent Association of Tennessee. It seemed to evaporate. Nevertheless, by 1876 several mines were shut down by the first major strike. Digging a bushel of coal had been bringing a miner five cents, but the price was cut to three cents or less. And loud complaints from miners having to work in water up to their knees in the mines of the Knoxville Iron Company were being heard. Little good the complaints did. The company started importing convicts to work, as was strongly encouraged by state law in order to save the expense of prisons. Miners greeted these unwanted competitors by exploding three kegs of powder as they tried to sleep their first night there. But no serious damage was done, and the prisoners stayed. It would be another fourteen years before the convict question flared into open warfare as more and more convicts replaced regular workers in the mines.

While coal rolled out of the valley, things were far from quiet across the rest of the United States. This was the start of the Gilded Age, the era of great industrial expansion by the Rockefellers, Carnegies, and Morgans. An amazing tangle of corporations unhampered by antitrust laws made millions, finally billions, in railroads, oil, steel, banking, and, of course, coal. And it was the era of militant workers demanding more of the profits that came from their labor. The so-called Molly Maguire Riots in the Pennsylvania anthracite coalfields ended with the controversial execution of ten miners. That was in 1877—the year the first convicts arrived in Coal Creek—the same year working men by the thousands took part in a railroad strike that spread across the nation, the most serious labor disturbance this country had ever seen. Pitched battles erupted between strikers and state militia backed up by federal soldiers, leaving hundreds dead. Miners and other laborers joined the rail employees as damage to railroad stations, roundhouses, freight cars, and other property reached nearly $10 million. At stake was not just the question of wages and hours but the very right to join a union, something long looked on as a conspiracy against the state. The Railroad Strike of 1877 sped up union growth despite quarreling among the young competing labor organizations. By 1886, however, the Knights of Labor, with over seven hundred thousand members, seemed the clear winner of the organizing struggles.

Still, businessmen had lost little power and believed it their God-given right to control every aspect of their private enterprise. Even among agnostics, in this land of the Puritan work ethic there was little doubt that sunup-to-sundown toil was the way to build character and keep workers out of the reach of Satan. As one manufacturer told a Massachusetts state labor board hearing testimony on shorter work hours in 1879, "Nothing saves men from debauchery and crime so much as labor 'til one is tired and ready to return to the domestic joys and duties of home."

No wonder Herbert Spencer became the unofficial spokesman for American laissez-faire after the Civil War. Although he is not taken with much seriousness today, this prolific and inconsistent English philosopher tried to apply the evolutionary ideas of Charles Darwin directly to human society in the industrial age. In fact, it was Spencer, not Darwin, who coined the phrase "the survival of the fittest." Spencer thought, for example, the state should not help the poor or regulate public health, in this way ensuring that the unfit would not survive. Without lighthouses, for instance, only the fittest sailors would make it to shore should they strike a reef. American businessmen could easily apply such an idea to working conditions. John D. Rockefeller viewed such rationalization of law-of-the-jungle capitalist practices with a religious eye: "The growth of a large business is merely a survival of the fittest . . . merely the working out of a law of nature and a law of God."

But down in the Cumberlands, even if so-called social Darwinism was at work in booming Coal Creek, nobody at first noticed. Jobs were plentiful, and life more or less peaceful. Or at least as peaceful as could be expected in a place where miners and guns and saloons were everywhere. However, there were more signs of civilization as families settled in, a Welsh church organized, and a cemetery begun. The mountains, much like those back in Wales, seemed like home. Customs going back to Celtic times found their way into the deep valley, customs like "sin-eating." To guard against damnation, a professional sin-eater would take on the guilt of the departed by eating a plate of food set on the corpse. The coins placed on the dead eyes became the payment for this service, well worth the price to keep lost souls from returning to haunt their old homes.

By 1880, something like 150,000 tons of coal had clanged along the spur lines out of the valley. By 1888, the soon-to-be U.S. senator Calvin S. Brice from Ohio saw to it that a spur extended into Slatestone Hollow at the foot of Cross Mountain and then on up into Tennessee Hollow. This former Union officer was a financier on the board of directors of the Wileys' Coal Creek land company as well as on the board of the East Tennessee, Virginia, and Georgia Railroad, which would be bought out by the Southern Railway within a few years. Naturally the town there at Slatestone Hollow was christened Briceville.

When the Tennessee Coal Mine opened in Tennessee Hollow the next year, Coal Creek was the largest town in the county. The population had jumped to over 3,000, leaving the county seat of Clinton far behind with only about 1,400 people. The very first bank in Anderson County opened. Life revolved around the railroad, the trains not only carrying miners and coal but providing a Main Street for the residents, who walked the tracks. Trees were planted to beautify the railroad grades. Close to the depot Robinson Leach built his hotel, which would become the headquarters for the traveling salesmen everyone called drummers. They set up sample rooms so customers could choose shoes or other apparel from the salesmen's large trunks. Business was so good in Coal Creek that out-of-town merchants like A. J. Queener of Oliver Springs were opening stores, according to the *Clinton Gazette* on January 20, 1888. That same year the Black Diamond Store announced in a newspaper advertisement such modern conveniences as bakery products—"finest cake that money can buy"—and refrigerated fresh meat. In addition to general stores and building contractors, Coal Creek had two drugstores. Finding Dr. Dunlop's Liver Regulator was no problem. And an opera house flourished with traveling shows, if not grand opera. Baptists and Methodists had their own churches, as did the Presbyterians, first organized by the Welsh.

Laura Kesterson, who at age ninety-five remembered the Coal Creek War, standing outside her house in Lake City in 1968. Photograph courtesy of the *Oak Ridger.*

About that same time, Laura Kesterson came to Coal Creek to work at the Leach Hotel. By 1968, she was just a wisp of a woman of ninety-five years, a survivor from the days of the turbulent miners' war that started in 1891. She lived in a small weather-beaten house on Walden Drive right where Highway 116 crosses Coal Creek in the center of Lake City. Aunt Laura had been there next to the swinging bridge since 1911. Widow of a miner named Luke Kesterson, she never had any children but had raised her nephew Marion Taylor. His father, Will, had been killed nearly in her front door during a bloody incident when the United Mine Workers tried to organize the mines in 1904, not long after the first big explosion at Fraterville in 1902. Her nephew, his wife Helen, and their grown son Jerry lived with her. They were at a prayer meeting in Fraterville, so the usually crowded little house seemed spacious. She sat in front of a coal fire in an open grate. It was early June, but she wanted to "burn that wind off the tornadoes."

Growing up in Dossett near present-day Oak Ridge, Laura Roberts was not quite sixteen when she got a cleaning job at the Leach Hotel. That was about 1889. She had worked before that for a Mrs. Shipe in Clinton, but quit. "I didn't like her little boy spitting in my face!" Thinking back all those years to the Coal Creek War, Laura Kesterson said, "That was the awfulest time ever was. A committee went to Nashville to ask the governor not to send the army. Leland Stone, J. W. Jarnigan, and Lawyer Irwin was on it. We knowed if real soldiers come, they'd be real trouble."

And real trouble was exactly what Coal Creek and Briceville got.

But why had it started in 1891? Some convicts had been used by Knoxville Iron Company for fourteen years, but jobs had been plentiful and convicts had not made much difference. Coal Creek seemed immune to work unrest while across the United States workers became more belligerent, staging a thousand strikes a year by 1886. That was the same year the Knights of Labor reached its peak membership of seven hundred thousand and organized a huge walkout in Chicago. Within several days anarchists got mixed up in it, throwing a bomb that killed a policeman. The resulting Haymarket Riot ended in ten deaths, plus the execution of four anarchists, though the bomb thrower was never found. Violent reaction across the country hurt the Knights of Labor in its competition with the new American Federation of Labor. Although the AFL rejected anything resembling socialism—the Knights' plan would have replaced private ownership with cooperatives—the Federation's organizing efforts were still resisted as strongly as those of the Knights. Several years after Haymarket, a Knights of Labor organizer named Eugene Merrill appeared in Coal Creek. The price of coal was slipping as the market was saturated with the output of the new mines in Oliver Springs's Big Mountain area.

The stage was set for the Coal Creek War of 1891–1892.

Much was written about this conflict in newspapers of the time and some in history books, but A. C. Hutson Jr.'s account of the struggle, presented to the East Tennessee Historical Society sixty years ago, is probably the fullest. While scholarly, Hutson's readable look at the insurrection gives an interesting 1930s perspective, and a quite reasonable-sounding one.

Why had the conflict come about when it did? It was not over union organizing. That would come a decade later. Unlike the northern coalfields, which were inundated with militant European immigrants, East Tennessee's relatively new mining area had workers slow to join anything, mountaineers who still valued the independence they had found in the hollows after the Revolution. Although a small number of skilled miners from the British Isles opened the mines right after the railroad came to Coal Creek, by 1890 these men had moved up to become foremen and superintendents and most certainly were not interested in fighting with the mine operators.

It was not unions but the use of convict labor that finally sparked the fire, although use of prisoners was far from new. Tennessee, like most of the other southern states right after the Civil War, set up a convict lease system. In the confusion and poverty following the war, crime escalated as the state struggled to avoid bankruptcy. Leasing prisoners not only saved the state the expense of a penal system but also brought in a profit, a total of $771,400 to Tennessee by 1890. That was not far short of all the money spent by the state on prisons since they were begun in 1829. The system was not only profitable, the idea of using convicts as virtual slave labor also fit easily into an economy that only a few years before was based on actual slavery. Just as important, convict labor offered the ultimate return on investment so crucial to the state's postwar recovery. Where else could a capitalist get a laborer for $0.28 a day? A convict was expected each day to bring out five tons of coal, which was selling at about $3 a ton, or $15, making a profit of $14.72 for the owner. There was no shortage of convicts, as each year the new Jim Crow laws were producing more and more prisoners, over half of whom were black.

Nevertheless, many in the state opposed the convict lease system as uncivilized. Charges against terrible working and living conditions, along with claims of a high death rate among the prisoners, had persisted from the time the leasing began in 1866. Legislative investigations produced divided reports, with the minority of them in 1889 calling the system "a horror and shame upon the state." And the branch prison stockades for convicts like those in Coal Creek were labeled "hell holes of rage, cruelty, despair, and vice." Frequent beatings and work in foot-deep water were just two reasons.

Knoxville Iron Company's mines near the Wye had been using some prison miners for nearly fifteen years when trouble started in Briceville at the new Tennessee Coal Company mine in April 1891. At first the trouble wasn't over the convicts. Nor were these free miners protesting the lack of safety with the daily threat of explosions and roof cave-ins—or working eleven hours often on their knees or in water for an average of $1.90 a day. But they were completely outraged at being gypped out of money they worked for by the ton. The men at the Tennessee Coal Mine demanded that the company follow a new state law allowing miners to have their own check-weighman to be sure they were paid for all they mined. They'd already hired A. H. Bradley.

And they also demanded, under another new law, to be paid in actual money, not company scrip. Scrip was just another way of profiting off the miners, since they were nearly forced to trade in the company stores, just as they had little choice but to rent the flimsy company houses without plumbing. They could get rid of the scrip only at a 20 percent discount when, for instance, they had to buy medicine. In the commissary, prices were 20 percent higher, so that miners paid $1 for their picks and $2.25 for blasting powder, while a hundred-pound sack of potatoes cost $1.40. This was all out of wages that were less than $2 a day. The miner who didn't trade at the company store was likely to find himself working in the most dangerous part of the mine, if not actually fired. He was usually in debt and often owed his soul to the company store.

Ignoring the miners' demands for compliance with the state laws, the Tennessee Coal Mine simply shut down operations for a month. When work was to resume, presumably with the miners having been taught a lesson, the operator presented the workers with an "ironclad" contract. They could forget about real money and a check-weighman. To add insult to injury, the miners were to agree to give the company any coal exceeding a ton in a miner's car. The contract also demanded there be no work stoppages over any grievance. The miners refused to sign, even though Tennessee Coal started threatening to bring in convict labor. Then suddenly it became more than a threat on July 5 when a train loaded with forty prisoners steamed into Briceville. In short order, the convicts knocked down the miners' houses and built a prison stockade for themselves and more convicts yet to arrive. Getting such labor was not a problem. A Nashville corporation called the Tennessee Coal, Iron, and Railroad Company leased all of the convicts from the state and subleased them to various mine operators.

Getting the prisoners there was not difficult, but keeping them was something else. Ten days after the stockade went up, not long after midnight, three hundred armed miners suddenly appeared out of the darkness and demanded surrender of the convicts and their guards. No one argued with the three hundred Winchesters and squirrel guns. These were men who had been toughened by the Civil War even before mining put its stamp on them. Not a shot was fired. An orderly procession of convicts and guards was marched through the night the four miles up the valley to the Coal Creek depot. Once there, the miners loaded them on a train for Knoxville. Telegraph wires jumped to life with messages going in all directions. The miners wanted Governor Buchanan to save their jobs. They pinned their hopes on "Buck" Buchanan since this new governor at his recent inauguration had called on the spirit of Andrew Jackson to help him fight for the little people.

Old Hickory forgotten, Buchanan arrived in Knoxville the next day with three companies of militia and immediately took the convicts back to Coal Creek and then up the spur toward Briceville. At Thistle Switch near Fraterville, six hundred or so miners, led by Eugene Merrill, the Knights of Labor organizer, were waiting. A famous photograph made that July 16 near the covered railroad trestle shows Merrill a self-assured young man, rather handsome in slouch hat and handlebar mustache, surrounded by determined miners. Buchanan told the crowd he had to uphold law and order. The governor hadn't been worried about upholding the law when Tennessee Coal Company refused the miners their own check-weighman and wages in real money, Merrill quickly answered. Where was the militia then? Merrill, a working miner until he was fired as a troublemaker, brought cheers when he said the contract the company tried to force on the miners meant a "modified form of slavery." Another speaker politely welcomed the gover-

Eugene Merrill (hands on knee), Knights of Labor organizer, with fellow miners waiting near Fraterville for Governor Buck Buchanan in July 1891, at the start of the two-year Coal Creek War. Photograph courtesy of Gene White.

nor, then added, pointing toward the inexperienced militiamen, "We could have done without your bringing along them dudes and boys. We wouldn't hurt them infants." Tension was high, but reason prevailed, making Merrill into something of a hero. In the past he had made little headway for the Knights of Labor, as labels of "outsider" and even "anarchist" were thrown at him.

Nothing was decided, however. Governor Buchanan spent a restless night at the stockade near the Knoxville Iron Company mine as a few scattered shots went off in the darkness. The governor wasted no time getting back to Nashville the next morning, leaving behind the poorly prepared soldiers, who had nothing against the miners. State Commissioner of Labor G. W. Ford also stayed behind to try to work out a settlement as newspapers across the state plunged into the controversy. Editors came to the side of the underdog miners, whom they portrayed as uneducated but rugged men of pioneer stock trying to protect their destitute families—and too poor to fight the operators in court to get their rights.

Although the miners accepted the labor commissioner's appeal for calm over the weekend, it proved to be the proverbial calm before the storm. As the news spread, miners from miles around, even from across the border in Kentucky, headed for Coal Creek any way they could, by train, horse, or foot. Just after sunrise Monday, July 20, they reached the Tennessee Coal Mine and spread out behind trees and rocks on the mountainsides. Then the miners' committee, headed by Merrill, appeared at the stockade gate, demanding that Colonel Granville Sevier take both the militia and convicts out of the valley. When the commanding officer moved as if to capture the committee, Merrill suddenly signaled with a handkerchief. Two thousand miners poured out of the woods. Armed with everything from shotguns and Winchester rifles to Colt pistols, they met no resistance. Colonel Sevier, grandson of the state's Indian-fighting first governor, wisely ordered his one hundred soldiers and six guards to march the forty convicts to Coal Creek to be put on the Knoxville train. It was exactly what had happened five days earlier, though this time the procession was much longer with all the new soldiers.

In the meantime, rumors flew in Knoxville as crowds gathered at the railroad station. But back in Coal Creek the miners weren't finished. They headed back to the Knoxville Iron Company's mine at the Wye and released that stockade's prisoners, sending them to join the first group. Then as good citizens, the miners took a solemn oath to protect private property and set up guards around both mines.

The next day the Knoxville *Journal* approvingly reported that the miners acted "with the resolute determination of East Tennesseans armed to fight for a just cause." And the *Clinton Gazette* warned, "The miners are a class of men who will not permit their rights to be abridged or slighted!" Up in Kentucky, the *Louisville Times* exclaimed rather smugly, "The capture of the Tennessee militia was one of the most amazing things in military tactics!"

Governor Buchanan was not amused.

He ordered General Sam T. Carnes and fourteen companies of state militia to Knoxville prepared with plenty of ammunition. Units like the Moerlin Zouaves, under an officer with the unlikely name of Captain Laughter, joined about six hundred soldiers camped on the grounds of the University of Tennessee awaiting the governor. When Buchanan got there, the miners' committee presented their petition denying that they were radicals or communists, but demanding an immediate special session of the General Assembly to end the convict lease system across the state. The governor agreed to a special session but said he could promise nothing. The miners found much more support later in the day at a mass meeting of Knoxville workers addressed by the university chancellor, Henry R. Gibson. Calling the convict labor system "a sword held over the heads of our laboring people," Gibson said the governor hadn't heard the pleas of the miners because Buchanan had "corporation cotton in his ears." (In 1891 it was the chancellor who sounded radical, not the miners!) Gibson went on to praise the restraint of the Coal Creek workers, saying they brought more honor to the state than did the people in favor of using Gatling guns on them. Later, more dickering between the governor and the miners ended in a truce until the legislators could consider the matter. As part of the agreement, the convicts were returned to the stockades, but minus the militia.

Now the state was really in an uproar as the governor brought the General Assembly back to Nashville. Calls for repeal of the convict lease law came from all quarters. The mine owners offered to give up the leased convicts but naturally wanted to be reimbursed. The money couldn't be found by the lawmakers, though the funds necessary to better equip the militia were found quickly enough. Finally, after weeks of wrangling, the legislators not only re-endorsed the convict lease system but made it a felony to interfere with the work of a convict. While newspapers across the state were calling the lawmakers stupid and unfair, the miners, with financial help from the unions, went to court, arguing that convicts were being illegally held in the mines. When their case was overturned, Eugene Merrill and his moderate committee resigned October 28, and the miners who wanted immediate action took over. No more worry about caution!

Tension built until October 31. That Halloween night, miners masked with bandannas or just plain coal dust silently surrounded the Tennessee stockade and freed 163 convicts, this time putting the place to the torch. The same thing took place at the Knoxville Mine, where 120 prisoners were turned loose and a number of buildings burned. The miners provided all the convicts with clothes for their escape by ransacking the company commissary. All four miles between Briceville and Coal Creek were covered with striped uniforms discarded by the fleeing prisoners, "everywhere, on each side, between the rails, on bushes, on rocks, in the creek bottoms cast off in the mad flight for liberty," according to the *Clinton Gazette*.

That was not the end of it. Two nights later a band of masked men quietly rode up to the Cumberland Mine stockade at Big Mountain outside Oliver Springs. They knocked down the entrance doors with a sledgehammer and released two hundred of the state's toughest criminals. No shots were fired, but this stockade also went up in flames. As convicts scattered far and wide, the miners began losing public support. The Clinton newspaper, however, still supported them, calling the miners "hardy, honest, open-hearted men." The editor blamed the law that allowed "felons, blacklegs, murderers, thieves, robbers, cutthroats—the scum of the population—into the mines in the miners' stead, taking the hard-earned bread from the mouths of their little ones."

Governor Buchanan dithered and became a laughing stock as he offered a five-thousand-dollar reward for the miners' leader, along with small rewards for the capture of the other miners and convicts. But Briceville's Tennessee Mine was losing money and decided to use no more prisoners, hiring back the free miners. Some began to think maybe the war was nearly won, though convicts were still working along with free miners at the Knoxville mine at the Wye and the Cumberland Mine in Oliver Springs.

January, however, was another story. The militia returned on New Year's Day as several hundred spectators waited at the depot in Coal Creek, wondering what would happen. Under Colonel Keller Anderson, a hard-drinking Confederate veteran, the soldiers started to rebuild the stockade at the Knoxville Iron Mine for the two hundred convicts soon brought in. And neither rain nor snow stopped the troops as they dug in on what was called Militia Hill above the mine. Fort Anderson was serious business, with its Gatling guns high enough up to be out of rifle range while the militia waited for any trouble.

Wrease Daniels, well-known county deputy sheriff, knew every foot of Militia Hill, a spur of Vowell Mountain. As boys, he and his cousin Albert Slover lived at the foot near the Wye. In fact, Slover still lived there. "We used to play all over these rocks and in the trenches the militia dug around the fort," Wrease said, climbing through underbrush choked with Virginia creeper and dogwood. Their games were based on real-life experience, for Wrease's father and Grandfather Daniels were in on all the big trouble that broke out in the summer of 1892 after the fort was built, trouble that ended with both men having to lie low in

West Virginia for a long time. His other grandfather, George Slover, had better luck until 1911, when he was killed along with eighty-three other miners in the Cross Mountain Mine explosion.

But during those cold months early in 1892 no one knew what to expect. The miners answered the militia's threat by fortifying Walden Ridge across the valley from the new military installation. What the soldiers had built on Militia Hill was a six-sided blockhouse of hewn logs complete with portholes. Shots could be heard from time to time as frustrated miners would take cover in the woods trying to get within range of Fort Anderson. The shots did no good. The soldiers would answer in turn by firing their six-pound howitzer toward Coal Creek. Though they were firing cans filled with mud, it was enough to remind the town that it could easily be flattened with real shells. As warm weather came and the demand for coal dropped, miners were laid off but convicts kept on digging. And militiamen seemed to be everywhere. Many were bored green recruits who caused trouble getting drunk when not trying to desert. One convict had been killed when several soldiers posed for a photograph pointing a gun at the "escaping" prisoner, a gun that somehow went off.

At Fraterville in 1968, retired miner Ernest Hill, who said Coal Creek had been a mean place, could tell stories of those days of the militia's occupation. So could his wife, Daisy. Although she was a very young child at the time, Mrs. Hill was sure she could remember how several soldiers once forced their way into her home during those tense months. "They was interested in my pretty sister, I always heard. We was glad they didn't do much after they got in the house except admire themselves in our big mirror." Her father, Walter Roberts, who would die in the Fraterville Mine explosion ten years later, spent a lot of time in the bull pen, where miners were punished for breaking the strict regulations imposed on the valley. Ernest Hill's father was particularly incensed at having to have a pass to move around. He found himself in the bull pen one time after he unwisely told a militiaman, patting a pistol on his hip, "My pass is right here!"

As the militia threw their weight around, Laura Kesterson was a teenager always busy with her cleaning job at the Leach Hotel. "The town was full of soldiers, and I didn't never stir out much. But I did go up to see the prisoners at the Knoxville stockade sometimes. Lots of people did. And Jody Bowling would go on Sundays to preach to them," she recalled about that spring and early summer.

The standoff continued until August, when a young miner named Dick Drummond was lynched from a railroad bridge in Briceville. No one today is sure how it came about, but many say an arrogant lieutenant named Perry Fytte forced his way into a miners' dance. There was an argument that ended up with Drummond being kicked off a train trestle with a rope around his neck. Dorsey

Ernest and Daisy Hill in 1968 remembered the Coal Creek War from their fathers' involvement when they were small children. Later as a miner, Ernest Hill was lucky and escaped the mine explosions of 1902 and 1911. Photograph courtesy of the *Oak Ridger*.

Landrum, one of Briceville's community pillars in 1968, lived barely a stone's throw from the infamous Drummond Bridge. He bemoaned how such history was lost when his father, John F. Landrum, died. Landrum said, "Whatever the reason, the militia came to my grandfather's house and took the young miner out of the room he shared with my father, who was a teenager at the time and right there when it happened." Remembering and shaking his head, he went on, "My father always said that Drummond was a fine-looking man and just as strong as an ox, but he didn't have a chance against those four men. Drummond had one of those little Owl's Head pistols. My father examined it later and said it wouldn't have fired, even if he'd had a chance to use it, because it had tobacco in it from being carried around in his pocket."

Drummond was left swinging from the railroad bridge. Ernest Hill told how his good friend Dave Davis was out looking for his milk cow the next morning and got the scare of his life when he was walking along the track and came up on the miner's body dangling there.

After that killing, no one was surprised when a hundred miners appeared the morning of August 15 outside the rebuilt stockade at the Cumberland Mine near Oliver Springs. However, this time there was no surrender as the well-prepared guards hollered, "Come and yet us!" The miners started firing, but after half an hour left with their wounded, yelling they would be back.

The war was on again. Miners once more poured into Coal Creek to join the fight from miles around, hundreds of them from Kentucky commandeering a freight train at Jellico. By midnight hundreds more had arrived. Telegraph wires were cut, two trains captured, and the engineers ordered to Oliver Springs with shotguns to their heads. This time the warden didn't argue. Just after dawn, he and his guards, along with newly arrived militiamen, marched out of the stockade between two lines of miners, who gathered up their guns and ammunition. The blockhouse was burned, and the convicts loaded on freight cars for Knoxville. The militia were told they could walk.

John T. Smith could remember when he was a boy and the militia was in Oliver Springs just before the stockade was burned the second time. His older brother Henry had tricked the soldiers. "Sam Hackworth wanted to take a bunch of men up to Coal Creek to help the miners, but he needed his Winchester out of his house because the soldiers was already in Oliver Springs," Uncle John said. "So he hid in the bushes and got Henry's attention when he saw my brother headed to town and asked him to help get his rifle. And Henry did just what he said, tied the gun around his middle, running the barrel down his overalls leg. The militia felt real sorry for that pore cripple boy with the wooden leg when Henry passed them on the way back to Sam Hackworth!"

After the miners' successful second attack in Oliver Springs, they kept the trains running under shotgun orders as more outside reinforcements headed toward Coal Creek. The governor was sent an ultimatum to surrender Fort Anderson on Militia Hill. Instead, Buchanan ordered General Sam Carnes to mobilize the rest of the state militia at Chattanooga and head for Coal Creek. "War correspondents" arrived to cover the situation from newspapers across the state and the nation—including the *New York World* and the *Washington Post,* even the *Denver Sun* and the *St. Louis Dispatch.* Artists came for *Harper's Illustrated Weekly* to add sketches to their war coverage.

By the next day the leaders of a thousand or so miners had organized their defense on Walden Ridge. Several attacks on Fort Anderson failed under fire from the militia's Gatling guns. While more state militiamen were on the way to the besieged fort, help was also coming from Knox County. But Major D. A. Carpenter and his detachment of Knox volunteers got lost as they tried to find a mountain road over Walden Ridge in the rain and darkness. Just as it was getting light on August 19, the volunteers stumbled into what they thought was a small army of miners, who shouted, "Surround them, boys!" Actually it was only a half dozen or so miner pickets on guard, but what followed is still called the Battle of Fatal Rock. Two of the major's men died in the first few seconds though some people still insist that nine bodies, not two, went back to Knoxville in pine boxes. The Knox County posse retreated with their exhausted major having to be hauled in a farm wagon back to the train in Clinton. This didn't keep the Knoxville *Journal,* once a strong supporter of the miners, from welcoming the volunteers back as heroes, calling the miners "wild, redhanded anarchists."

But the fighting in the valley would soon come to an end with the arrival of General Carnes and his five hundred soldiers hauling a heavy gun carriage. He encircled Coal Creek, demanding that the miners surrender the fort's Colonel Anderson, who had gotten drunk and ended up a hostage. As the general declared martial law, miners fled into the mountains, some of them to Kentucky never to return. One of the leaders of the revolt, according to tradition, got help from a physician who dressed the miner in the doctor's silk hat and long-tailed coat, sending him off well supplied with sugar pills.

The roundup and arrest of hundreds of miners in the hills and hollows continued until the temporary jails—boxcars, the schoolhouse, the Methodist church—overflowed. Even the state labor commissioner, G. W. Ford, was accused of helping the miners and arrested, but the search for Eugene Merrill turned up nothing. Although he had apparently objected to the final violent revolt, that made no difference to General Carnes. But for all the three hundred or so indictments, there were only two convictions, one of them for manslaughter. Witnesses who would testify in court were few and far between.

So the Coal Creek miners lost the war, but the real loser turned out to be Governor Buchanan, who was defeated in the election that fall. The Knoxville *Journal* said he would forever be remembered for his "indecision, imbecility and general incompetency." And though the military occupation of Coal Creek continued another year and the convict labor continued, the lease system would end in 1896 when the five-year contract expired. Brushy Mountain Penitentiary would be built at Petros and open the following year.

Explosions Deep in the Mountain

When the new century arrived in the Coal Creek Valley, the clang of coal trains echoed between Walden Ridge and Cross Mountain and then on out past Vowell Mountain. Life was better with convict labor gone, Militia Hill abandoned, and six mines going full blast. That meant 1,500 jobs. At Briceville up in Slatestone Hollow, Knoxville Iron Company operated the important Cross Mountain Mine, the mine everyone called Slatestone. The company had taken the progressive step of building a schoolhouse with the miners themselves helping pay for each year's four months of classes. Even a smallpox epidemic and the two "pest houses" built to isolate the victims did not dampen the optimism. The two-story Briceville Opera House with its elaborate clock tower challenged the Clinton courthouse for prestige throughout the county. After all, it sat four hundred people for entertainments like the Williams Concert Company's full week of appearances in March 1900. And the upstairs bustled with the meetings of secret lodges like the Odd Fellows and the Woodmen of the World. Even the Knights of Labor met there, still trying to organize the miners.

Although mine operators ran their own commissaries, Briceville was not a company town and had private merchants, as did Coal Creek. G. P. Norman's success story in the general mercantile business spoke of prosperous times. G. P., an orphan, had come from Roane County to Briceville just after the Coal Creek War, first to work in the store of his brother-in-law John Simpson and then on his own. Norman not only ran his general store but also the local bottling works and ice plant. Later he became a director of the old Citizens Bank of Coal Creek and was elected first a squire on Anderson County

Court, then county tax assessor. And he had a small coal operation, a far cry from the days when he was a nine-year-old working in a Roane County mine.

If G. P. Norman was a Horatio Alger story come to life, he was a rarity. Most people who started in the mines stayed there doing body-numbing, dangerous work. More often than not life ended in poverty, if not injury or death underground. Dramatic proof of this came just two years into the new century when disaster settled on the valley. An explosion in the Fraterville Mine sealed up 184 men and boys three miles deep in the earth. Some were killed outright but most suffocated. That catastrophe in 1902 was followed by a second in 1911 at Briceville's Cross Mountain Mine, where 84 died. No matter how today's social historians explain industry's survival-of-the-fittest ideas a hundred years ago, the lack of safety in the mines at that time is still shocking. The U.S. Bureau of Mines did not even come into being until 1910 and then could act only in an advisory capacity. The very next year 2,719 miners died, the year of the second explosion. It was not until 1941 that the bureau got the authority to enter a mine without the owner's consent.

So in 1902 Fraterville Mine "went up." It happened May 19 shortly after 7 A.M. This mine, owned by the Coal Creek Coal Company, was one of the first to go into operation after the railroad arrived in 1869. It had been accumulating coal dust more than thirty years. The next morning the Knoxville *Journal & Tribune* headlines screamed of this worst mining disaster ever in the South: NOT A SOUL LIVES TO TELL THE TALE. Smaller headlines told mine superintendent George Camp's "thrilling story"—"Heads and arms of some had been blown off, others dying of suffocation had burrowed their heads in the earth." The forty-three households that made up Fraterville, between Briceville and the Wye, had been nearly stripped of its men and boys. Only three were left, according to the front-page story, leaving every house with "a weeping wife and crying children." An unexpected note was added by one sentence in the story stating that someone named Eugene Merrill had offered the help of his Central Labor Union of Knoxville.

Ernest Hill, who liked to tell about his father's calling his revolver his "pass" during the Coal Creek War, lived in Fraterville near Perkins Store. In 1968 the community remained just a wide place in the road. It was only a short walk from the Hills' house across Highway 116 and over the train tracks to the hollow where the Fraterville Mine entrance once took in two hundred miners each day. Although the driftmouth had disappeared, it was easy to find in the shady undergrowth the concrete block where the ventilation fan once stood. It was impossible to miss a twenty-foot-high slag heap, a reminder of the old days, slowly washing away, polluting as it went. At the time of the explosion, the coal that came out of that driftmouth was produced by miners using picks and shovels, working by the open flames on their caps, often standing or kneeling in water. Ten paces from a miner's flame was total blackness. With no electricity in the Fraterville Mine, mules pulled the loaded coal cars from the side rooms to the main entry. There the cars were attached to a cable running along the main track and hoisted out by a steam engine outside the mine entrance.

At seventy-eight, Hill was one of those special good-natured people who survived half a century in the mines without losing his sense of humor. He seemed so vigorous that his sudden death the next year came as a real surprise. But that May day in 1968 as he talked, time reversed itself. It was 1902 again, and Ernest Hill was a thirteen-year-old going down in the darkness each day to work ten hours. There was nothing unusual about that. Only three years before a boy just eleven had been killed in a nearby mine when he fell under coal cars. Fathers willingly took their sons with them in order to add to the family income. Americans forget that as recently as 1922 a federal child labor law was declared unconstitutional.

Hill remembered that early Monday morning of May 19, 1902. "I'd just started working at Middle Ridge Mine down near Briceville," he said. "I was trapping, opening and closing the doors to control the air pumped in the mine. They'd let small kids no more than ten do that." But young Ernest was not happy. He wanted to quit Middle Ridge and work at Fraterville so he could trap two doors instead of just one and make over sixty cents a day. But his father was sick and his mother insisted he wait until the end of the month to quit in order not to lose that month's pay. So luck was with the young trapper, and he wasn't in Fraterville the morning the ominous black smoke came out of the mine entrance.

"We got the word at Middle Ridge," he remembered, "and I was sent to spread the news. We all come running out of the mine headed up the road to Fraterville. We wasn't even sure what an explosion meant. There'd never been one."

On the other side of Coal Creek toward the Clinch River, word was brought by another runner. A twelve-year-old named Arthur Riggs heard all the wild hollering out in the family garden in Longfield. Riggs, who became a miner and later served as Lake City town manager many years, told of the chaos that followed. "My brother George and I ran barefooted those four miles to Fraterville just as fast as we could. Our father worked there, but he was afraid of the mine and that day was up at Beech Grove trying to get another job. By the time we got as far as Coal Creek, the roads were full of people running, people on horses. Buggies were crowding the road," Riggs said. The screams of women bounced off the mountainsides as they ran. The

Riggs boys saw many of them become so exhausted that they had to stop even in their panic to rest under the beech trees on the creek.

What had happened that morning in Coal Creek Coal Company's Fraterville Mine? George Camp, the mine superintendent and son of the owner, told the Knoxville *Journal & Tribune* right after the catastrophe that the mine was in good condition. Camp said an explanation for the explosion was "unfathomable." The state mine inspector, a man named Shiflett, immediately left for Coal Creek after telling the newspaper he had inspected the mine in January and found the ventilation system much improved with a new sixteen-foot fan. "It's awful. . . . I'm surprised," the inspector said. But something had gone terribly wrong. Something set off an explosion that raced down the main entry like a bullet from a miner's Winchester, knocking heavy steel axles off coal cars, slamming loaded cars to bits against the side of the entry. The story goes that a mule was driven up against the slate roof of the mine and pinned there with a timber. A pocket of methane could have been ignited, setting off a coal dust explosion, or the combustion could have been spontaneous. Just as deadly as the explosion and fire were the gases formed in the wake of the inferno, the so-called after-damp that used up most of the oxygen, leaving behind various mixtures of nitrogen, carbon dioxide, and even carbon monoxide.

Crowds in 1902 waiting outside Thistle Mine while rescue operations were under way following the explosion in adjoining Fraterville Mine, which killed 184 miners. Photograph by W. L. Wilson.

Rescue workers loading coffins on Southern Railway box cars to be taken out on the spur line after the Fraterville explosion in 1902. Photograph by W. L. Wilson.

The morning of the explosion Superintendent Camp had been waiting until a spring rain let up before going into the mine. He was also in charge of his company's Thistle Mine that connected with Fraterville. Camp told reporters how men at Thistle saw smoke shoot out of the air shaft. They knew this meant serious trouble and called him. Camp and several men rushed in only a short distance to find the main entry blocked by a cave-in on top of a train of coal cars. They got out as quickly as possible and formed rescue teams to enter through Thistle Mine. They would have to build brattices, a kind of temporary partition, or put up heavy canvas curtains in order to direct the fresh air pumped into the mine.

Within a short time after Camp came out for help, over a thousand people had gathered at the Thistle entrance. Help came from miles around—men experienced in mining operations, like Philip Francis from Jellico. Years later Francis wrote in his autobiography about heading up one of the rescue parties. It was a dangerous job, with the ever-present possibility of further fires and explosions and, just as serious, deadly gases. Francis described early in the search, "We had to be careful about walking into gas. That would cause you to fall down and your breathing would soon cease unless someone picked you up and took you into purer air. Several of the rescuers had fallen and were taken outside and laid in the blacksmith shop unconscious."

Extra coffins had to be hurriedly built in 1902 for the bodies of the 184 miners killed in Fraterville. Photograph by W. L. Wilson.

Searching the side entries, often not more than four feet high, meant hours of stooping and carrying or dragging bodies to be loaded in mine cars. Many of them were found with no mark on them, dead from lack of oxygen, often in a praying position. Dead mules also had to be gotten out, even if it meant chopping off their legs to get through the narrow places, Francis remembered. After three days in the death-filled mine, his clothes took on what he called "a peculiar odor" that could never be gotten rid of.

Meanwhile, that first day young Arthur Riggs and his brother left the huge waiting crowd held back by ropes at the Thistle entrance. They went back to Coal Creek to search the temporary morgue for their cousins Roy and Levi Riggs and their mother's brother, Abner Dabney. "They were first bringing the bodies down by railroad to the old Farmers Supply Building where Ford's Furniture Store is today, but later the undertakers decided to move right up to Thistle. Coal Creek didn't have the hot water they needed." The initial order of sixty-one coffins from Knoxville that came in on the night train would soon be used up.

The brothers spent that first night, Monday, in Coal Creek with friends keeping vigil: "People kept hoping all night, but morning came and no one came out alive." By Wednesday most of the men's bodies had been found, and thirty-five were brought back to Longfield, including Arthur's two cousins and uncle. "I remember there wasn't much preaching at the big funeral. Everyone was still in a state of shock, I guess. All those thirty-five pine boxes were brought in the church before the service started," Riggs said.

Two of them held the bodies of Powell Harmon and Jacob Vowell, and another that of Jake's young son Elbert. With them had been found goodbye messages scribbled in small books used for recording their diggings. Six others said farewells, too, but none more movingly than Harmon, who told his wife, "My time has come to die. . . . May God bless you all, wife and children, for Jesus sake goodbye until we meet to part no more." His last thought was of his sons Henry and Condy as he told them never to work in the coal mines. But Condy would do just that and die nine years later at Cross Mountain Mine.

Today, nearly a hundred years later, Jake Vowell's letters to his beloved wife Ellen are painful to read. He first wrote at noon nearly five hours after the explosion, "We are shut up in the head of the entry with a little air and the bad air is closing in on us fast. . . . If we never live to get out we are not hurt but only perished for air. There is but a few of us here and I don't know where the other men is."

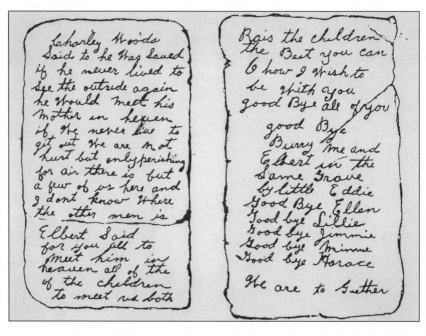

A portion of Jake Vowell's farewell letter to his family before he suffocated in the Fraterville Mine in 1902. Photograph courtesy of Edith Wilson Hutton.

Time passed, and Jake wrote again at 2:25 P.M. for the last time. His son Elbert wanted his mother to know that the Lord had saved him and that his brother Horace should wear his clothes. Jake said to look for Powell Harmon's watch in Andy Wood's hand. With only several men still alive, Jake pleaded, "Ellen, I want you to live right and come to heaven. Raise the children the best you can. Oh how I wish to be with you. Goodbye all of you, goodbye. Bury me and Elbert in the same grave by little Eddy. Goodbye Ellen, goodbye Lily, goodbye Jimmie, goodbye Horace—Jake and Elbert." After signing it, he added, "Oh God for one more breath. Ellen, remember me as long as you live. Goodbye darling."

The Vowell children were just three of scores left without fathers in 1902. Ernest Hill's wife, Daisy, lost her father, Walter Roberts. She remembered it as though it were yesterday while she sat talking on their front porch looking toward the woods where the Fraterville entrance had been. "I was fifteen and the oldest of seven girls," Mrs. Hill said quietly, "and my brother was still in the Philippines after the Spanish war. We did everything to get by. We picked berries for ten cents a gallon, did laundry for fifty cents a day, and still we went hungry sometimes."

Walter Roberts was buried along with eighty-eight other miners in old

The miners' circle of Fraterville victims seen today at Leach Cemetery near Lake City. The obelisk erected some years after the explosion by the United Mine Workers lists the names of all 184 men and boys who died. Photograph by the author.

Leach Cemetery, high up on a hill near Coal Creek. Their graves were dug in concentric circles with a view of Vowell Mountain toward the west. Although the rest of the 184 who died, among them Jake Vowell and Powell Harmon, are in other cemeteries, years later the United Mine Workers erected an impressive obelisk at Leach bearing the names of all the dead. Today, the special section on the monument for eleven names labeled "colored men" comes as a surprise there under the UMW's marble pick and shovel. If you search in the circles of tombstones, you will find many who are related to one another, including five brothers, John, David, Samuel, Car, and George Dezern. They were the sons of Catherine Dezern, a widow who was lucky that her sixth son had quit work to do the spring planting. The husbands of two of her daughters were not so fortunate; Robert Allen and James Wallace also lie in graves in the obelisk's shadow. Today in the sunshine it is a peaceful place bordered by native cedars, peaceful even though eighteen-wheel tractor trailers can be heard on Interstate 75 if the wind is right.

Criminal indictments for negligence were returned in over two hundred lawsuits filed by the dead miners' families against four defendants. Not only was Coal Creek Coal Company sued as a corporation, but legal proceedings were brought against E. C. Camp, the owner, and his son George Camp as individuals. Coal Creek Mining and Manufacturing Company and the Knoxville Iron Company were also brought into the complicated case. There was some question as to whether Knoxville Iron had once made a mine entry on the tract leased to the Fraterville Mine and then abandoned it when the roof fell in, creating a dangerous situation. Accurate maps had never been filed, since industry regulations were virtually nonexistent.

A special session of Circuit Court was called for December 1902 in Anderson County. But within three months roughly 150 of the cases had been settled out of court, averaging $320 for "each certified death," less than $5,000 today. According to the *Clinton Gazette,* the crowds resulting from the trials were the largest ever "assembled under the dome of Anderson County's beautiful courthouse." Some of the cases were appealed to the state supreme court, but there were never any convictions. The truth is that society was then mostly on the side of the mine owners, who customarily blamed the miners themselves for causing accidents by carelessness. And according to the owners, nobody was forced to become a miner. This attitude was concisely put by one mine operator before the Ohio Mining Commission in 1871: "The miner is free and can protect himself, for he can engage in mining or not."

A year after the Fraterville tragedy, the Coal Creek area was caught up in the nationwide effort of the fledgling United Mine Workers to organize the whole industry. The time following the disaster should have been ideal for organizing the Coal Creek fields, something the Knights of Labor had not been able to do. Nor had the UMW made much headway, although the union had had success in getting collective bargaining in many northern coalfields. Three years earlier, in 1900, a UMW strike had brought 127,000 anthracite miners off the job, but in the South strikes only stiffened the resistance of mine operators. With lower labor costs, the southern owners could often beat the northern competition and get an even higher return on their investment. And the profits were already enormous. Although earlier figures are not available, between 1909 and 1919 the return on coal investments was 15 to 25 percent. A quarter of the mine owners made 25 percent. In those days of low wages and little machinery, when miners had to provide their own picks and shovels, it cost relatively little to go into the mining business. So coal operators fought unionization fiercely and usually with success in the South. As Ernest Hill put it, "In those days, if you didn't like working ten hours a day in water up to your knees, you could just quit. Plenty others wanted the job."

Certainly, the Coal Creek miners joined the UMW at the risk of losing their jobs even though their number was growing. Some headway had been made among the smaller operators, but the UMW was pushing for 100 percent membership in the valley in order for the miners to have real bargaining power. The big organizing effort began with a strike called in February 1903. The union's District 19 organizers targeted the Tennessee Coal Mine near Briceville. Following a mass meeting at the opera house, a blockade of the mine was finally set up in May by two hundred men not employed by the company. They had been promised financial help from a UMW strike fund for such essentials as house rent. Briceville's 1,500 inhabitants rapidly divided into two camps, union and non-union, as company guards were hired and strikebreakers brought in. When there was not actual violence, angry disputes broke out as union supporters refused service in cafes and barber shops to non-union customers or refused to sell groceries to anyone boarding company guards.

Firebrand speeches by union men like Pat Erwin kept everyone stirred up at endless public meetings. Erwin liked to accuse Captain Nelson, one of the company bosses, of being as bad as Pharaoh in the Old Testament. Of course, the "Moses" that Erwin proposed to lead the miners out of their coal-laden land of Egypt was UMW organizer F. L. Rice. Arrests and court cases grew so rapidly that by August trials of "outside agitators" were drawing capacity crowds of four hundred spectators in the opera house.

It had been a year since the deadly explosion, and the Fraterville Mine was back in operation. By September, superintendent George Camp had also been presented a demand for higher wages by a committee of miners. When he refused to negotiate, a strike was called at Fraterville. Camp lost no time going to court for an injunction prohibiting the miners from trespassing on company property. What happened next was typical of the times. Camp described it years later saying, "I went to St. Louis and got twenty-seven men, the riff-raff of the St. Louis slums. I lost ten of 'em on the way back and got to Coal Creek with seventeen." That strike-breaking solution did not last long, however, for union men soon persuaded the outsiders that Fraterville was not the place for them. The company promptly hired more laborers and armed guards, quite likely from the Pinkerton Agency, which specialized in putting down industrial trouble. The usual practice was for the company to pay for guards, who were deputized by Sheriff G. W. Moore.

The situation led to bloodshed February 7, 1904. That Sunday morning, when Camp arrived at the Southern Railway depot in Coal Creek with more new workers and armed guards, a crowd was waiting. Maybe just waiting for the Sunday newspapers as usual or maybe looking for trouble. Exactly what happened next is unclear. One version says some boys set off firecrackers. But according to Camp, a miner brushed by him yelling, "Kill the SOB!" Judd Reeder, one of the guards, opened fire, and the others joined in. In the confusion nine spectators were wounded, four fatally. Three guards stood trial for murder, but

The bodies of Monroe Black, Will Taylor, and Jack Sharpe after they were killed in 1904 during the UMW's unsuccessful attempt to organize Coal Creek miners. Taylor was Laura Kesterson's brother-in-law. Photograph courtesy of Gene White.

the defense attorneys got the proceedings moved to Knoxville because of strong feelings in Anderson County. And after many delays, the cases were finally dropped.

Will Taylor, the brother-in-law of Laura Kesterson, was one of those men killed at the depot. She remembered how her husband Luke how been on jury duty all week but was home that day because it was Sunday. "He'd just bought me some apples so I could make a pie in the skillet when I heard all the commotion and saw them carrying Will into Squire Lindsay's office," she said. "When I heard the shooting, I just set the pie down by the stove uncooked and it set there 'til Tuesday."

The violence brought the governor to Coal Creek. By now James B. Frazier was in office, and he arrived with threats of the militia. But things calmed down as county lawmen patrolled the area. Again the union had been defeated and would have to bide its time until the 1930s.

Life went on, union or no. The backbreaking routine was accepted with stoicism as each day brought the chance of death inside the mountains. Anything as dramatic as the Fraterville explosion was rare, but day-by-day accidents certainly were not. Slate roofs would cave in, killing a miner or two, or coal cars would crush someone. In the valley, families still grieved over the many dead buried at Leach Cemetery and across the county. At least there was some comfort in thinking that lightning—and mine explosions—weren't supposed to strike in the same place twice.

Horace White was like hundreds of others who had come down off the mountain where he grew up to work in Briceville. In spite of everything, including low wages, mining provided more money than the rocky farms. At twelve he finished the fifth grade and left Braden Flats, walking down Backbone Hollow, then following Coal Creek to Briceville. Young Horace was going to live with his Aunt Mary Braden and work in one of the mines. That was 1903. For fifty cents a day he put in ten hours and took care of four mules, taking them to the mine, staying there to work as a door trapper until time to take the mules back to the barn to feed and rub them down for the night. His son, Gene White, talked about his Braden kinfolk, how his grandfather James R. White married Nancy Elizabeth Braden. She was a daughter of hot-tempered Isaac Braden, who had to be lured back to the flats from Frost Bottom with a new mill.

Isaac's great-grandson Gene, a retired Oak Ridge supervisor and history buff, in recent years has compiled two collections of family photographs and stories of Briceville. One of his earliest memories is of his mother getting his father Horace off to work as early as 4 A.M. after a big breakfast of pork chops or steak, if money wasn't skimpy. His dinner bucket would have the bottom filled with water and the top with maybe beans and bacon and cornbread. Once inside the mine, Horace White had to work and listen at the same time, listen for the creaking of roof timbers that might mean a rock slide. Even the sounds of the inevitable rats were important, for the rats left when the earth began moving, warning the workers in the darkness.

Horace was still a young miner on December 9, 1911, when the Cross Mountain Mine everyone called Slatestone exploded. He worked there but escaped being among the 84 men and boys killed because of a serious family illness. That was some years before son Gene was born, but the boy grew up hearing about the terrible day not long before Christmas. "My dad and his brother Bill stayed home that day to be with their brother John, who had a bad infection in one foot. It caused his death five days later," Gene remembers. Back up on Braden Flats, where Horace grew up, people heard the explosion, a roar, and then silence. Women who were quilting and men out in the barn shucking corn dropped everything and ran down the mountain.

Ernest Hill also just barely missed being in Slatestone that December day. Like Horace White, he had moved up from boy trapper to miner. Ernest married Daisy Roberts in 1907 and had family responsibilities. Nevertheless,

The entrance of Cross Mountain Mine in Slatestone Hollow pictured years after the explosion that killed eighty-four in 1911. Ernest Hill of Fraterville is thought to be the third miner from the left, although it may be John Wallace. Photograph courtesy of Gene White.

about a week before the explosion he let his temper get away from him. "I got in an argument with ole man Bullmer, the foreman. That's one time I was glad I got fired." Hill laughed as he explained how for the second time he had missed being in a mine when it exploded.

Unlike Fraterville, this new disaster happened on a Saturday, and fewer men were in the mine than would have been on a typical weekday. Word had also gotten out that there was a shortage of railroad coal cars. Besides, many lodges in Briceville met until late on Friday nights, and miners not in a bind for money wouldn't get up early Saturdays to go to work.

But one who did get up was Dan Martin, twenty years old and about to become a father a second time. More than half a century later, his still-pretty widow Mae lived all over again that terrible December morning. In 1968 her tidy home sat just a short way up from Dorsey Landrum's in Briceville. At seventy-six, she resembled other survivors of those bad times, confident and serene. She was proud of her well-educated children, like her son, a U.S. Air Force captain just back from two years in Labrador. A dozen years after the Slatestone explosion she married Demas Carroll and had more children.

"That morning in 1911 Jim White came by to get my husband Dan," she clearly recalled. "Jim had just set up all night with another miner who had a bar on a cutting machine go through him. Jim was in a big hurry, but Dan couldn't find his shoes. I kept hurrying him, too, saying his lunch was already packed. So they left, Dan with only one shoe tied." They had been married three years, but Dan had been working in the mines since he was twelve years old.

Mae Carroll could still hear the roar of the explosion. She said, "Right afterward, my sister and I ran up Slatestone Hollow. We saw the leaves burned off the trees near the mine entrance. It blew out and then back into the mine. When we saw that, we just went home to wait. There was nothing else to do." She said Dan and his friend Jim, who had six children, were among the last to be found, nine long days after the tremendous blast. Dan's brother Harvey was killed, too.

Just across from Slatestone Hollow lived retired miner Jim McCoy, his rickety old house literally clinging to Walden Ridge. In 1968, he was a small, fragile man of eighty, but he still enjoyed talking. He had begun work at Slatestone in 1901 when he was twelve. McCoy grew up near Donovan not far from Jasper Smith's farm. His father, W. M. McCoy, was shot to death in 1897 in an ambush growing out of arguments over timber rights. Then his mother also died, and the boy came to Briceville.

"The relatives I was staying with in Dutch Valley near let me freeze, so my sister here and her husband, Joe Rogers, a blacksmith, took me in," McCoy said. "I didn't think the superintendent, Del Nelson, was going to give me a job,

Mae Martin Carroll, seen in Briceville in 1968, was widowed by the Cross Mountain explosion in 1911. Photograph courtesy of the *Oak Ridger.*

because the law said boys was supposed to be fourteen. But he looked me in the eye finally and said he'd let me work because I was an orphan." Nelson told him he'd better be careful. So young Jim was an experienced hand the next year when Fraterville Mine blew up, but he saw none of that first disaster. "Joe wouldn't let me go up there, said I had no business in all that crowd."

Nine years later McCoy was working at Slatestone as a miner. But before December, he quit. Like John T. Smith and many others, McCoy became afraid of all the coal dust "in the old side," as people called that first mine in the hollow going back to 1888. "It was so bad you had to claw it out of your nose," as McCoy put it. In spite of the miners' fatalism mixed in with considerable machismo, memories of Fraterville must have lingered in the corners of many minds. There was so much coal dust that men couldn't see when it was stirred up, and they had to hold the tails of their mules to be led out of the side entries, McCoy said. The use of rock dusting and water sprinkling for safety was well known but seldom used. Right after the Slatestone explosion, when T. I. Stephenson, president of Knoxville Iron Company, said the mine had been sprinkled, the reaction in Briceville must have been disbelief.

Shaking his head, Jim McCoy recalled, "My father-in-law and I was working at Tennessee Mine the morning of the explosion. Our driver didn't show up. Finally the news come that Slatestone had blowed up. We said a prayer, then come out of the mine and got there fast as we could."

The ventilation fan for forcing the air three miles down into the earth had been ruined by the explosion. The superintendent immediately had a fire built over the air shaft to try to pull out the deadly after-damp, according to McCoy. Within a couple of hours a fan had been gotten from Beech Grove and installed. Then the long process of building brattices, or temporary walls, in order to enter the mine began. "We could only work about two hours at a stretch, because the air was so bad," McCoy said. "Ever scrap of lumber that could be found was brought up to the mine, and a canvas curtain was used to cover the opening just ahead of the brattices being built."

As the slow rescue work began underground, a cold December drizzle set in on the ever-growing crowd outside the mine. Hundreds, then thousands, came any way they could find, by train, automobile, horse. Or just on foot. Fires built to fight off the wet cold made an eerie scene as night came on and coffins were stacked higher and higher waiting to be filled and hauled on flatcars out of the valley. The first three bodies were brought out of the mine about midnight to the hysterical cries of waiting kinfolk. Hope began to dwindle.

The following day, Sunday, saw possibly five thousand people gathered, mostly curiosity seekers, standing any place they could get footholds on the steep mountainsides around the mine entrance. Church services were held

Former miner Jim McCoy, at his Briceville home in 1968, clearly recalled helping with the rescue operations for ten days after the Cross Mountain explosion. Photograph courtesy of the *Oak Ridger*.

out in the open winter air, the preacher asking the thousands if they were ready themselves to face death. Only two more bodies were found that day, but then Monday night a miracle seemed to happen as five miners emerged alive. William Henderson at fifty-five was the oldest and the jauntiest and refused to be carried out on a stretcher. With him were his son Milton, Irving Smith, Arthur Scott, and Dore Irish. They had been in a secondary room off to the left of Entry 19. Henderson told newspaper reporters how after the explosion they had quickly built a brattice at the entrance of the room. "With our coats we fought back the after-damp that came through cracks in the brattice, and then stuck our coats in the holes," Bill Henderson said. Then the miners waited sixty hours, sharing what little they had in their dinner pails. When the five were brought to the surface, the shouts of joy all but deafened them. And food, including hot sausages and pie, was quickly found.

Mae Carroll, along with some of the other waiting wives, was at the Hendersons' house when the rescued miners arrived. It was a scene not to be forgotten. Mrs. Henderson had never for a minute doubted that her husband and son would be found. "She kept telling everyone that they'd come out alive, and they did! Henderson was an old man, but he never even went to bed," Mrs. Carroll said, remembering it all over with pleasure. What impressed her even more, though, was how Irving Smith's mother reacted. Although he was so burned his face was "just hanging in tags," his mother literally jumped with joy. Mrs. Carroll said, "Somehow, she hit her head, and I can still see all her long hair falling down. She was an awful religious old woman." Irving Smith's mother had no way of knowing that within a few years he would go to Ducktown and be killed in a copper mine.

He and the other four were rescued on Monday, but another whole week would pass filled with feverish attempts to reach the remaining miners. Working night and day like Jim McCoy was William Stonecipher, who himself would have been in the explosion except for his wife. "She kept saying that morning she had bad dreams all night about the mine, and she wouldn't fix me no lunch. I stood around a while and then finally decided not to go and changed out of my work clothes," he said. "Not long after, all the commotion started with people out screaming in the streets. You couldn't even get along the railroad it was so crowded," he recalled, sitting in his porch swing looking toward the road up to Slatestone. In a little while he ran into his brother Joe, who had hurried from Beech Grove thinking that Bill was in the mine. Overjoyed by the surprise, Joe joined the search efforts that seemed endless as they stretched out over ten days.

By Wednesday the number of dead stood at forty-eight, and then the next day a fire started by the explosion in one of the side entries halted rescue operations for many hours. By Saturday, a week after the disaster, seventy-two bodies had been recovered. Crowds still waited as unscrupulous lawyers mingled in, trying to sign up clients among the families lined up near the mine entrance. Mae Carroll remembered how even two years later some lawyers would "come back and beg to be hired." As the days dragged on, freedom of the press also got a bad name from townspeople who complained of newsreel companies filming them in their sorrow. Finally, on Tuesday, the tenth day of the search, the last two miners were found. Eugene Ault and Alonzo Wood had scratched farewells on slate with their picks.

It was never known for certain in which room the explosion started, igniting the ankle-deep coal dust in the miles of passageways. McCoy, however, had no doubts where it began. "Jim Robbins was a careless man with his black powder and light. If we'd complain, he'd say to get out if we was afraid. It musta started in his room. When we found him, he was burned like a rooster with no arms or legs or head. The dust was all swept out of that room into drifts from the force."

Whatever the cause, the method by which each miner did his own blasting was much more dangerous than the system used in Europe. There one skilled miner, a shotfirer, set off the explosives after all the other miners had left their work shift. Europe had a much better safety record in its mines, according to the first study of mining deaths in this country done in 1907 by the U.S. Geological Survey. The American death rate was four times higher than that of France and twice that of Great Britain.

Mae Carroll's husband, Dan, and Jim White were found in a room close to Jim Robbins. McCoy told how he was helping with the cleanup several weeks later and came across a piece of scalp with Martin's hair. It had stuck to the track where his head hit. The young widow, who was expecting a baby, had not been allowed to see the body of her badly burned husband. He was buried with his brother in Pemberton Cemetery near Clinton. Mae Carroll was pleased, she said, that after several years she was able to buy him "a good rock."

Another impressive man who worked on the rescue teams was C. I. Williams. He had quit Slatestone the previous year during a mule drivers' strike. Williams, like most of the other old-timers in 1968, blamed the state for lack of proper inspection. There were two classifications of mines in those days, Class A and Class B. By definition the state said the B mines, those drift mines that entered the sides of mountains, were not "gassy" and did not need frequent inspection or many precautions for air circulation. "They said Slatestone was a Class B mine, but it still must have been a gas explosion that caught the coal dust," Williams said.

After the disaster, he went back to work at Slatestone, and things finally improved. He became a "fire boss," making daily inspections for gas. "I was

Malinda and Lee Wilson at their home in Briceville in 1968 talked about the Cross Mountain disaster and how one of the five survivors, Dore Irish, later lived with them. Photograph courtesy of the *Oak Ridger*.

never afraid after the right inspections were started," Williams added. He proudly showed off his safety lamp, whose flame was used to test for methane in the high places, and also his air circulation gauge. The days of taking canaries in the mines to test the air were finally over. Not all went well for Williams, however, because a mix-up in union records caused him to lose his pension after he retired in 1950. The UMW officer who came down from Middlesboro to investigate told Williams that he had the best safety record in District 19, but the wrong was never corrected.

At eighty-three, Williams was still trying to adjust to the recent loss of his wife Lula. With him through all those years of mining, she was "going on fourteen," and he was seventeen when they married. "She had red hair and when the preacher married us, he held us on the floor for a half-hour, because he was afraid we was too young to get married. But we never separated in all those sixty-six years."

Married sixty years, Lee Wilson and his wife also had strong memories of those wrenching days in Briceville. Wilson had been working on the "new side" of Slatestone on December 9, 1911, because he was afraid of the old side. "They was so much coal dust in the old part, it was shoe-mouth deep. Just no regulations. The owners only wanted to get ever ton out soon as possible," the tall, soft-spoken man of eighty-four said. Wilson recalled how the seam of coal that caught fire after the explosion burned for four or five weeks in spite of all efforts to put it out.

After the disaster, tiny Mrs. Wilson cooked everything in their house to help feed the hundreds of people who overflowed Briceville for two weeks. She said, "We'd just killed a hog and it was gone in three days." Both she and her husband loved to tell the story of how the two Hendersons and three other miners escaped—the amazement of "Poss" Vowell, who was bringing in a load of lumber for the brattices when he heard the miners pounding on the wall. The rescue team was about to pass them by. One of those lucky five, Dore Irish, later lived with the Wilsons. She said, "He didn't like to tell about that time, though once he did say how right after the explosion he was talking to someone next to him for a long time before he knowed the man was dead." Looking very solemn, Mrs. Wilson described how after that bad experience Dore would start talking in the dark by first asking, "You not dead?"

Wilson went to Knoxville to testify in the damage suits that were brought against the Knoxville Iron Company. But he never got to testify because the cases were compromised. Most of the widows received around $200, or about $2,700 today. Dan Martin's wife, Mae, held out, however, because she could support herself as a seamstress. Finally, after two years she received ten times as much. "I followed the advice of Dorsey Landrum's father and just held out, never got a lawyer."

As for Lee Wilson, he worked at Cross Mountain Mine several years after the catastrophe but finally went to Harlan, Kentucky. "I just never was satisfied," he said, meaning he was afraid of another explosion at Slatestone. Then a serious back injury made him quit mining in 1928. He returned to Briceville and ran a grocery store over thirty years. It was not far from the miners' circle for Slatestone victims in the cemetery at Laurel Grove Baptist Church.

The Wilsons' daughter had recently taken over the business. Still, on long afternoons at Dugger's Grocery, old retired miners sat around and remembered back a half century and more. Looking at the long list of names of those who lost their lives at Fraterville and Slatestone, Wilson summed it up simply, "When the air died, they died."

I remember what he said nearly every March 18. That was the day in 1937 when the London School in the East Texas oil field was torn apart by a gas explosion, with me inside as a sixth-grader. That explosion was at least merciful, killing 294 children and teachers within seconds. Unlike Coal Creek's miners, we had a brief moment of worldwide sympathy. It was front page news in the *New York Times,* and Adolf Hitler sent his condolences to President Franklin D. Roosevelt.

Windrock: Eighty Years of Tunneling

The L&N and the Railroad War

Although Uncle John Smith had been tempted to work at Slatestone before the explosion in 1911, he decided to stay closer to home. The Louisville and Nashville Railroad was indirectly responsible. This line started building south from Cincinnati toward Knoxville just after the turn of the century. Part of this expansion was an L&N branch line that sliced across Oliver Springs with a long trestle headed for the foot of Windrock Mountain. This Cow Creek Branch made possible the opening in 1904 of Windrock Mine, destined to become the most famous mine in Tennessee. A UMW member since the age of fourteen, Uncle John had worked for years as both a miner and farmer but at last found his niche at the Windrock tipple. There thousands upon thousands of tons of coal came down the mile-long incline to be dumped under the eyes of John Tyler Smith into the ever-waiting L&N coal cars.

In the spring of 1970, TVA's ambitious plans to help Oliver Springs rejuvenate itself into a small model town were well under way. The new flood control channel neared completion on Indian Creek, the usually unimpressive stream that had caused havoc sweeping through the heart of the old mining town in 1967. New low-cost housing and a sewer system were about to open, as plans moved ahead to reroute the bottleneck highway through downtown on to an elevated road hugging Walden Ridge. However, before the modern new highway could be constructed, the landmark L&N trestle had to go, all two thousand feet of it.

To Uncle John the demise of this monument to the coal days meant the end of an era, and rightly so. He kept the pressure on me to write what he

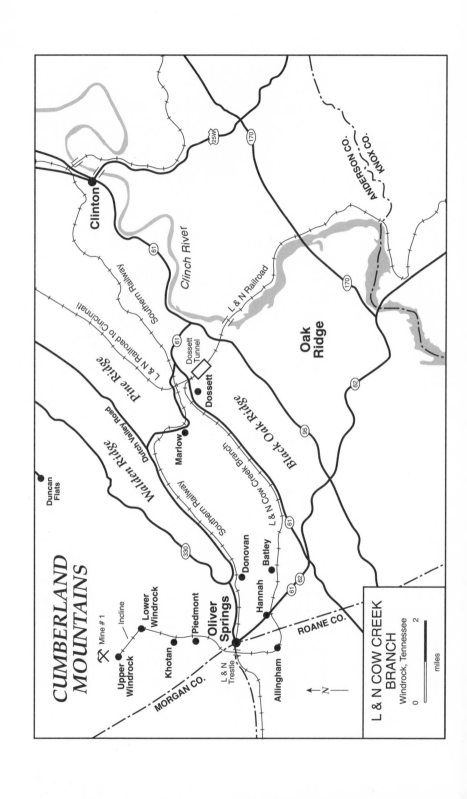

CUMBERLAND
MOUNTAINS

⚒ Mine # 1

Incline

Upper
Windrock

Lower
Windrock

Khotan

Piedmont

Oliver
Springs

Hannah

Duncan
Flats

Walden Ridge

Dutch Valley Road

Pine Ridge

Southern Railway

L & N Railroad to Cincinnati

Southern Railway

Marlow

Dossett

Dossett
Tunnel

Clinton

Clinch River

L & N Railroad

Oak
Ridge

Black Oak Ridge

L & N Cow Creek Branch

Donovan

Batley

Allingham

L & N
Trestle

ROANE CO.

MORGAN CO.

ANDERSON CO.

KNOX CO.

25W

170

61

61

170

62

95

61

61

62

330

L & N COW CREEK
BRANCH

Windrock, Tennessee

← N

0   miles   2

called a history of the L&N's Cow Creek Branch and Windrock Mine. I was definitely interested, but walking over those twelve miles of tracks and visiting many all-but-vanished places took a lot of time. One weekend, however, I finally went to talk to him about doing his history. We ended up down at the doomed trestle near where it crossed Tri-County Boulevard, Oliver Springs's main street. He was standing under the graceful red and white L&N sign hanging from the creosote timbers of the trestle where it passed over the Southern tracks. Looking sadly off toward Windrock Mountain, he said with resignation, "I shore hate to see it go."

I knew then I would have to find the time to write, if not a real history, at least all I could find out about the people and places along this railroad line to Windrock. For one thing, this was no ordinary two-thousand-foot trestle but one that had precipitated the brief but lively "Railroad War." Southern Railway, reigning supreme in Oliver Springs since Joseph C. Richards sold the right-of-way in 1887, was not at all happy about the upstart L&N crossing its tracks. In fact, things got downright nasty for a while.

At eight-three, Uncle John was still walking twice a day to Olivers, as he called Oliver Springs. The old former walking champion was delighted as we started to plan. We would visit much of the branch line from Dossett,

The L&N's trestle over the Southern Railway tracks in Oliver Springs brought about the Railroad War during the trestle's construction in 1903. Photograph courtesy of Snyder E. Roberts.

where it forked off from the main Knoxville-Cincinnati line at the east end of Oak Ridge, to the far end at the coal tipple at the foot of Windrock Mountain, where he had worked so many years. Although he didn't actually help build the Cow Creek Branch, he went to work for the L&N in 1905, the year it officially opened. He remembered the long-gone stops—Dossett, Batley, Hannah, Allingham, Khotan, and Lower Windrock—as though the year were still 1905. I would get to find out about the blasting powder plant near Dossett that operated until 1928 despite explosions. And between Oliver Springs and Lower Windrock, I would get to see where Piedmont and Khotan once prospered until the Campbell mines closed about the time of World War I. That section of the branch line hadn't been in use since 1954, when most of Windrock's coal started going to the TVA's Kingston Steam Plant, making it more economical to haul it from the tipple by truck. Those tracks between Oliver Springs and Windrock would be removed when the Oliver Springs trestle came down.

Before starting the actual trip along the Cow Creek Branch, which, incidentally, followed Little Cow Creek and not Cow Creek, I needed some official information about the L&N. I especially wanted the exact date when the trestle was built, since no one I had talked to so far seemed to know. That date turned out to be very elusive even with the help of John N. Neal, the railroad's area superintendent. I found him in the L&N's brick Victorian castle of a train station in Knoxville. He had already done some research. Neal had tried to pinpoint when "Bridge No. 167" was completed, but the railroad's dates were just as fuzzy as the others. Of course, he knew about the small war when the L&N crossed the Southern tracks. In a real understatement, he laughed about it, saying, "They didn't worry too much about legalities in those days, just went ahead!" It was no laughing matter, however, because right then in 1970 his railroad wanted to be assured of crossing rights when the old trestle came down. Earlier in the spring the whole tearing-down project had come to a halt for several months until the two railroads were both satisfied with the crossing negotiations.

The Cow Creek Branch was only part of the extensive expansion the L&N started in 1902 to lengthen its line, which earlier had run south from Cincinnati only as far as Jellico on the Kentucky border. L&N was leasing the tracks of the rival Southern from Jellico to Knoxville and wanted its own line that could be extended to Atlanta, according to Superintendent Neal. With the backing of financiers like Jay Gould and J. P. Morgan, the Louisville and Nashville would get what it wanted.

The L&N had come a long way since 1850, when the small local railroad decided to span the 187 miles between bustling Louisville on the Ohio River and much smaller Nashville. That job turned out to be harder than expected in Kentucky, what with tunnels like the two-thousand-foot one at Muldraugh's Hill to be dug and wide rivers to be crossed. The span across the Green River at eighteen hundred feet was the largest iron bridge in America at the time. In October 1859, the last spike was finally driven and the L&N was on its way to success, only to be hit by the Civil War.

The Kentucky-based line survived the chaos, including the Confederates' destroying bridges and ripping up tracks. The rebels had a bad habit of heating up rails on huge bonfires made from the white oak crossties so that they could be wrapped around convenient tree trunks. Albert Fink, the brilliant German engineer who had invented a new kind of truss essential for construction of the prewar bridges, managed to keep the railroad operating. He did such a good job under difficult wartime conditions that the Union army did not take over the L&N as it did other rail lines. It was this six-foot seven-inch German giant who headed up the expansion after the war. Within fifteen years after Appomattox, the L&N had reached Memphis, Birmingham ("Pittsburgh of the South"), Mobile, and New Orleans. Numerous railroad improvements sped up the whole process, as air brakes and automatic couplers in the 1870s made possible the development of economical large trains. Steel tracks replaced the old iron ones that had a disastrous way of snapping in cold weather and puncturing the floors of wooden passenger cars. Finally, standard time zones and standard-gauge tracks in the 1880s hastened the development of a unified rail system across the country, including the L&N.

So in 1902 the grading on the Cow Creek Branch began. It was a prosperous time in the heyday of the Oliver Springs Hotel, even though the mining industry had just suffered the shock of the Fraterville Mine explosion. The L&N started similar grading all along the seventy-five miles between Jellico and Knoxville. A new company was set up just to build the line with one of those three-city railroad names like the famous Atchison, Topeka, and Santa Fe. This was the Knoxville, LaFollette, and Jellico. Although not officially open until April 3, 1905, the line was actually in partial use in 1904. Unexpected problems with the tunnel at Dossett caused so many delays that in 1904, the first year Windrock Mine was in operation, coal had to be shipped from Oliver Springs over Southern tracks. Apparently the Southern decided it made good business sense to let bygones be bygones, if the Railroad War could be called a bygone.

Uncle John wanted to start retracing the past with a visit to Charlie Davis, who had watched the grading get under way. His home stood just off the L&N tracks in Norwood, the new part of Oliver Springs near the foot of Black Oak Ridge. It was close to his house that a work camp of log huts sprang up for the families of some thirty Negroes brought in from North

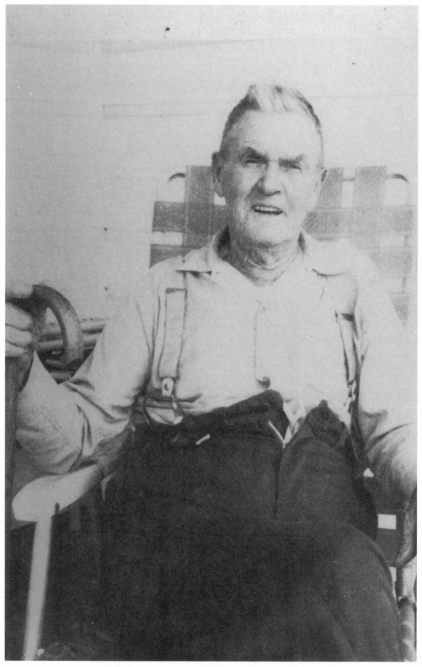

Charlie Davis at his Oliver Springs home in 1970 remembered seeing the L&N drive piles for the trestle through an overturned Southern box car in 1903. Photograph courtesy of the *Oak Ridger*.

Carolina and Alabama to do the grading. At eighty-seven, Charlie Davis had plenty of time and was more than glad to talk. It was a hot July day, and he was trying to catch a breeze on his porch, comfortable in his blue galluses, waist unbuttoned. He knew about the Railroad War, as well as the grading, but that comes later in the story. He and Uncle John greeted each other warmly but almost immediately got into a long, drawn-out debate about Lonas Cross of Clinton. Charlie Davis said Cross was the man with the contract for the grading, something Uncle John disputed, though after lots of talk he could never come up with another name. He agreed, however, when Davis said, "It was awful hard work, heavy grading and slow. Had to be done with mules. You can move as much dirt now in one day as it took a week then."

Later on, Uncle John recalled more about that fall of 1902. His recollections of the imported black laborers' lives were much more pleasant than the horror stories told about railroad building in the Kentucky coalfields. There the rolling commissaries sold not only groceries and cheap whiskey but then-unregulated cocaine and morphine, the same pacifiers the Chinese coolies got during construction of the transcontinental railroads. Uncle John did, however, remember one gory surprise. "Me and Brother Henry found a short-cut through the woods to Batley. We come to a muddy place, a fresh pile of dirt, and it was a darky. They musta been gambling and kilt him. We kept our mouths shut, but then decided we best tell."

Mostly, though, he wanted to talk about the time that fall when he was sixteen and had been across Black Oak Ridge to visit with the G. W. Foster family in East Fork Valley, where Oak Ridge is today. He probably already had his eye on Mary Foster, whom he married several years later. But on that particular visit young Lee Foster came back home with Johnny to the Smiths' farm near Donovan. After the boys crossed Poplar Creek, they saw a lively dance at the railroad work camp. "Joe Cross and his brother Ray was making the music, and Lindsay Moore from Tuppertown calling the sets. He stayed 'til midnight, Sister, and musta called five hundred dances," he grinned and said, jumping up on his front porch to show me how two couples danced a set. He was convinced the white fiddler and caller were essential because it was so complicated that "not just anyone could do it," as he diplomatically put it.

The two boys stayed late watching the fun. It was October and pretty cold when they started home. "We was on Uncle Joel Long's land and they was lots of haystacks. So I told Lee, let's just pull out some hay and stay. Lee got in under there. Then I got in last and pulled the hay in behind me. Next morning, the sun was shining, but what a frost we'd got! We went on home but had to wade Poplar Creek before we got to Brother Henry's. Yes, sirree, it was cold!"

Work went on as grading the Cow Creek Branch inched on toward

Windrock. But the L&N's biggest problem on the whole construction project between Jellico and Knoxville turned out to be the Dossett Tunnel through Black Oak Ridge. It was a big project, the tunnel itself some 3,500 feet, nearly two miles counting the approaches. The project would not have been necessary if the L&N had gotten the right-of-way through Clinton as originally planned. What with the Southern Railway already through the county seat, the town had hoped to become a rail center, complete with a handsome new L&N passenger depot. City fathers wanted to catch up with booming Coal Creek. But something went wrong in the backrooms where business deals were struck. Clinton was bypassed, and the tunnel became essential.

When the blasting and excavation got under way in steep Black Oak Ridge, the contractors were in for a bad surprise. Not solid rock but pockets of quicksand-like mud mixed with boulders completely disrupted the construction schedule. More laborers had to be called in, along with experts from the Harper's Ferry Tunnel up north. One contractor, G. H. Cole, went bankrupt. By the time the job was completed three years later, a small town was in operation, mostly on the north side of the ridge. Up on the very top perched a tiny house where workers made sure a pump continuously forced air through two shafts drilled down into the tunnel work area. Outside on the slopes, barns for an army of essential mules had to be built, as well as workshops for blacksmiths to keep the animals shod and the construction tools sharpened. An electric power plant was set up along with storehouses for everything from food to blasting powder. So many blasts rocked the ridge, probably more than two thousand, that people lost count. Since workers had to eat and sleep, a cookhouse, laundry, and sleeping quarters appeared early on. Two full-time butchers stayed busy slaughtering steers and hogs, while nearby farmers came in to sell milk and eggs and fresh vegetables. The temporary tunnel town, like the fashionable Oliver Springs Hotel, meant cash in the pockets of farmers like Jasper Smith and his son John.

All that was long gone the day Uncle John and I started our actual trek along the tracks of the Cow Creek Branch. We were at Dossett, or rather where Dossett had once been north of Black Oak Ridge, where the tracks split off for Windrock from the main L&N line. Several houses remained, but the depot and the hotel and everything else had vanished. Two freight cars sat on a siding just a short distance from a small building missing much paint, only big enough for two side-by-side doors.

"Look yonder!" Uncle John was pointing toward the outhouse. On the ground, leaning against it was proof of the past, the old depot sign with DOSSETT in foot high letters. "Law, yes, Sister, this was Dossett, awright."

He wanted me to see the rocky entrance of the tunnel better, so we walked a way up the tracks of the main line. Kudzu overwhelmed trees large and

Uncle John Smith pointing toward the pinpoint of light at the end of the mile-long L&N tunnel at Dossett as we started our trek along the Cow Creek branch line in 1970. Photograph courtesy of the *Oak Ridger*.

small with a strange green blanket above the curved tunnel opening. But he wouldn't let us start out of the tracks until he carefully put his ear down on a metal rail to listen. One of those fast diesel engines might be headed toward us from Knoxville on the other side of the ridge. We had no trouble seeing what was coming from Cincinnati—the view to the north clear with the Cumberlands looming blue and beautiful in the distance.

Walking along the track between the high walls of blasted rock, we could see a pinpoint of light at the end of the tunnel, the better part of a mile. I was in favor of not getting too close to the entrance. As for Uncle John, he stood there "studying" back to May 1905. He had started work for the L&N not long after the first train passed through the tunnel in April. Doing repairs as a section hand meant wages paid in gold, not mining company scrip. But the Dossett Tunnel nearly did him in, along with his friend Jim Brummett. "We was scaling the roof, putting ladders up from the flat car to chip off the loose rock," he remembered. "I was at one end of the flat car and Jim on the other one when a big rock fell out the top of the tunnel. Never felt such a jar in my life. Musta weighed a ton!"

The day he went to work for the railroad he had been on another of his visits to East Fork Valley. He had come down off Black Oak Ridge and was headed home toward Donovan, about to cross the new L&N tracks at Batley. A station was there, that is, a flag stop without a depot. The eighteen-year-old came up on Alf Magee's section hands eating lunch. Bill Key, who knew young John, yelled for him to come over.

"Alf Magee, he was an awful tall feller from Kentucky, he wanted to know if I'd like to go to work. I asked him if he meant right then. He said shore, but I said I didn't have no dinner." Magee pointed to his double-decker lunch pail saying, "Help yoreself right here!" With some of Magee's food under his belt, Johnny Smith started running the jacks. That meant jacking up the rails that needed gravel tamped under them.

Uncle John grinned, standing there on the tracks. "Bill Key said they'd only pulled six rails before I started, but when we quit that day we'd done eighteen, though I's just a little feller. I'd already worked some for the Southern. We used to farm in the summer and work for the railroads in the winter."

While the rock in the tunnel missed him, Uncle John wasn't so lucky a little later on when he fell off a handcar between Dossett and Batley. Headed back from the tunnel entrance, he started explaining. "We was working on the tracks right along there where Claude Galbreath lives now, you know, Sister, that house with the deer statues in the yard. It started a drizzling rain, so we loaded up to go back to Batley. I's on the front end of the handcar and my hands was wet and slipped when he backed up. I saw I was going to fall, and I sprung my foot trying to miss one of those old sawteeth cattleguards, but it cut me up pretty bad on the leg." Just how bad I could see from the mean-looking long scar he suddenly displayed.

Hurriedly, big Alf Magee loaded Johnny Smith back on the handcar and sent a man ahead with a red flag in case a train was coming. They got him to Jim Brummett's house in Batley, the same Jim Brummett the rock missed in the tunnel, and the car rushed on to Oliver Springs for the doctor. That was Dr. A. K. Shelton, who was, among other things, the physician at the Oliver Springs Hotel before the recent fire.

"They had me laying on a small iron bedstead at Jim's when the doctor got thar and got out his sewing needles and told three men to hold my feet. Sam Brummett held my hands. The doctor just went to sewing on my leg but I told him to hold on thar!" Uncle John got indignant telling the story, though sixty-five years had gone by. "Couldn't he put something on it to keep from hurting, I wanted to know? But he just went on sewing with what looked to me like an ole spaying needle you'd sew up hogs with. By the time he was through, I nearly had that bedstead pulled over my head and the man with it! Afterward Brother Henry had to come get me in the buggy."

A much more serious incident happened that summer several miles down the line toward Oliver Springs. It was between Allingham Station and Hannah Station, where the four-lane highway today crosses the L&N tracks in Norwood.

Uncle John Smith was not on this particular L&N hand-lever car, but it was the kind he worked on when injured as a section hand in 1905. Photograph courtesy of Snyder E. Roberts.

After the trip to Dossett, Uncle John and I walked the crossties one afternoon for half a mile or so, looking for where Allingham had been. One of those big water tanks that looked like a fat pagoda on stilts had stood there to supply the steam locomotives. It had been there for years, yet it took some searching in the high undergrowth before we found one of the concrete blocks that the tank had been mounted on. But suddenly there it was, right at the curve where the tracks turned north into Oliver Springs. It was not far from that curve on June 9, 1905 (Uncle John had the date firmly in mind), that he and the rest of his section were shoveling cinders to repair the roadbed. It was a hot day to start with, and things got even hotter.

"A train brung about fifteen cars of cinders from Knoxville right from the ovens, and, believe me, it was powerful hot, burned yore shoes. Fay Jett and Harry Hall was in an end of one of the cars pushing the cinders down through the hoppers, and Bill Brice in the other end with me. Ole Uncle Bill said for us boys not to drink no water or it'd go agin us. I was sweating, so it was like I jumped in the creek," he recalled. "All at once the trainmaster commenced beating on our car, and I went up and looked over the top. Running yonder in the woods out of the sun was several men," he said pointing toward some tall oaks.

And six of them died, apparently from heat prostration, though they were taken to the hospital in Knoxville. "I knowed one of them, Noah Gray. He was from North Carolina, and they shipped him back to his native home. They was about thirty men on that crew and about half got sick. They shouldn't orter drunk so much water."

I can't remember now why Uncle John could not come with me the day I visited Marlow, the small community between Dossett and Batley. It was actually on the Southern at the place where the older line came within sight of the L&N. But it was the new line and the booming coal business that apparently prompted the building of Marlow's claim to local fame. The Rand Powder Company came into being in 1905 to supply the surrounding mines, like the new one at Windrock, with essential blasting powder. After the Hercules Powder Company of Delaware bought out Rand in 1916, production of the dangerous black powder zoomed up to a thousand kegs a day.

"It's the powder plant blowed up!"

That cry went up nobody knows how many times before Hercules left Marlow in 1928. Mining techniques changed and ended the need for black powder, causing the Marlow plant to close, yet today Hercules is still very much in business. It made headlines in 1989 with an explosion in a gunpowder plant in New Jersey. Despite the company's good safety record, it only took one spark to break it.

Earlier, before I went to Marlow, Uncle John had told me about what he thought was the first explosion at the plant in 1906. "John Giles got kilt. It shook the globe off our lamp clear down nearly to Oliver Springs. My daddy Jasper knowed right off it was the powder plant and lit out for Marlow, but I had to work and couldn't go."

I was wondering about John Giles that Sunday afternoon as I circled a stand of graceful, tall pines on Powder Mill Road looking for Lonas Long. I passed several deserted buildings, one of which, I would find out later, had been the Hercules "soda house." Then I came to red brick ruins overgrown with vines and small trees, downright Gothic-looking. But there was nothing unusual about Lonas Long when I located him in his well-kept two-story home, which had once been owned by Hercules' superintendent Arthur Reynolds. It was on Marlow Circle, at the center of what had once been a prosperous town with its own hotel and even a physician, Dr. Roland Reed.

Long was a brisk but pleasant man recently retired from over forty years as a telegraph man with the L&N. In 1938, ten years after Hercules left, Long sold his sixty acres over where downtown Oak Ridge now stands and bought the deserted powder plant. It was just as well he moved then, for he would have had to anyway in a few years when work on the atomic bomb started. After the war, the sprawling administration building of the Atomic Energy Commission would sit on his old farm. The Hercules property that he purchased covered roughly 175 acres, a large area so that the different steps in the production would be carried out in widely spaced buildings for safety.

As we walked over to the brick ruins nearly covered by Virginia creeper, Long explained that the power plant needed a lot of electricity and had generated its own direct current in the two-story brick building. "I wanted to sell the large boiler for scrap metal, and the only way to get it out of the building was to blast it out. That's what we did. The rest of the walls are still standing because the bricks were put together with concrete and not mortar to make them stronger in case the boiler blew up."

Standing under the elms and tulip poplars shading the ruined building, we saw what used to be the wash house with showers for the employees, now a white cottage. We walked past a sheet iron building that turned out to be the "soda house," and finally we were in a depression Long said had been the cooling pond for the boiler.

Long remembered back through his forty-four years with the L&N. "I worked as a telegraph man all the way from Etowah down near Chattanooga to Corbin, Kentucky, mostly as a relief man. I did spend the last ten years, though, in West Knoxville and would go by train each day from Dossett." Passengers boarded at that depot by the tunnel until after World War II, Long explained. "But those were just locals. If you wanted a fast train you went to Knoxville to catch it, a train like the Flamingo Special to Florida."

Later I went across the street from Long's home to see Ed Henderson. He lived in another nice, turn-of-the-century house shaded by silver maples. It was next door to the grocery store he had run until he decided to close it and retire a year or so before. With fewer people around, Sam Brock's General Store could keep the people in Marlow supplied as it had been helping to do since 1902.

Henderson was the man who could explain how to make black powder, since he had worked a year for Hercules in 1921, when he was a teenager. He was waiting for me with a faded snapshot of seven men sitting on the pipe out over the cooling pond. That was where boiling water from the generating plant's boiler was sprayed out. Looking at the photograph, Henderson said, "Except for my brother Oscar, not a man I knew who worked here is still around. Some of them went up north to Illinois and other places to work when Hercules shut down."

And were there explosions?

"Yes, sir, there were explosions," he said, thinking back to when he was fifteen. "Altogether musta been explosions at least five or six times, and men like Garrett Whitaker got killed. I worked in what we called the packhouse, putting the powder in kegs with funnels. Working there was the same as having a gun drawn on you! And it was hard work, too, just had to keep stirring with shovels."

Things could go wrong in any of the many different steps in making the black powder, but trouble came most often with the wheel mill, according to Henderson. That step in the process came after the first two ingredients, charcoal and brimstone, had been through the pulverizing mill and broken up in the mill's revolving barrels by small metal balls. Something called a soda beater was used to add the third ingredient, nitrate of soda.

"After all that, it went to the wheel mill," Henderson said. "It was rolled out flat on concrete by two wheels, and this was when most of the explosions happened." But if all went well, the mixture was next dampened and pressed into flat cakes about thirty inches square. The corning mill put the cakes through screens to make the powder, which was then sent to the glaze mill for a graphite coating of each fine particle before being packed in kegs. And that was when young Ed Henderson did his job filling the barrels with a funnel.

The teenager quit after 1921, but Hercules continued to turn out a thousand or so kegs a day until 1928. It closed because the equipment could not be adapted to make the new pellet-type explosive the company wanted. The employees could have transferred to other plants in Illinois or Delaware, but many didn't, possibly tired of always working on the brink of disaster. If Marlow didn't become a ghost town, it certainly became a far quieter and slower-moving place.

On down the tracks some seven miles, on the edge of Oliver Springs, lived Mable Daugherty. This was not far from the Allingham curve where the hot cinders brought death to the L&N section hands the summer of 1905. Uncle John wanted me to meet Mrs. Daugherty, since she was the widow of Ab Williams, one of his good railroad friends. For many years, well into the 1930s, Williams was in charge of the giant water tanks at Allingham and Dossett. Those were the days of the incredibly noisy steam locomotives that needed not only lots of coal but plenty of water. The steam-spewing Consolidation engines were then the workhorses pulling tons of coal from Windrock. Williams and his wife Mable lived in Dossett, frequently going back and forth to Allingham on a homemade contraption Uncle John called a "railroad bicycle." Before our visit, he had tried without success to explain what it was like.

Nearly as soon as the talkative, round-faced Mrs. Daugherty opened the screen door of the rundown house, we were off on the subject of the bicycle thing. We had quickly met her second husband, John, who sat quietly listening in the front room. Years of mining coal at Fork Mountain up in New River had left him gaunt with black lung disease, a frail man with enormous eyes.

No, no, she told Uncle John. It wasn't a railroad bicycle but a "three-wheel speeder." She laughed as she tried to explain the speeder. She finally gave up and borrowed my ballpoint pen to draw a picture of the three-wheeler she

Mable Williams Daugherty, on the porch of her Oliver Springs house, remembered keeping the giant water tanks filled on the L&N's Cow Creek Branch until in the 1930s. Photograph courtesy of the *Oak Ridger.*

and Williams used to pedal on the railroad tracks. Between two connected wheels that ran on one track were two seats, while rods from each of those two wheels connected with a third smaller balancing wheel on the other track.

"We'd usually go down to Allingham ever other day from our house in Dossett to fill the water tank," she explained. "But, holy cow, during the peach season with all them boxcars coming through from Georgia, we had to go ever day!" It was not easy work keeping the tanks full of water pumped from nearby creeks. "We went rain or shine. The water pumps was run by steam boilers, and that meant we just kept shoveling coal. Them was fifteen-foot tanks and it taken all day to fill one."

Mable Daugherty remembered how when she was only eight years old in 1912 she moved to Dossett with her mother Lizzie Chandler, a young widow who wanted to be near her sister. The little girl's father, who had built concrete railroad abutments, died of typhoid fever in Atlanta. "Mother finally remarried, and we lived in a big old sixteen-room house close to Bacon Springs nearer Allingham." Her aunt in Dossett was married to Garrett Whitaker, the man whose death Ed Henderson remembered. When Mable was a teenager, Whitaker was killed in an explosion in the wheel mill, that especially dangerous part of the process for making blasting powder. "I saw the smoke and saw them go up," she said thinking back all those years. "I remember Will Owens getting killed, too. They found him with his arms wrapped around a tree."

Outside on her porch covered with potted plants and vines like the flowering widow's tears, Mrs. Daugherty seemed to long for her old active outdoors life. She had not only liked the railroad job but later enjoyed farming across the ridge where Oak Ridge would be built during the war. "That was on out past Robertsville toward the Clinch River. Oh, I done everthing, plowing, shocking hay. Except Ab wouldn't never let me run the mowing machine cause the team might run away. I liked it, but we had to move like everbody else when Oak Ridge came."

Over and over I had heard that story of having to move. In 1903, however, as the L&N construction crew reached Oliver Springs on its way to Windrock, who would have thought that four decades later the railroad would be pulling hundreds of freight cars through the Dossett Tunnel in the gigantic effort to build an atomic bomb?

The L&N could not have reached Windrock without building that Oliver Springs trestle over the Southern Railway, which caused such an uproar the summer of 1903. When the construction crews reached Allingham, they turned sharply north to follow Indian Creek through the gap in Pine Ridge into town. They skirted the woods thick with hickory and beech trees at the foot of the ridge, cleared chinquapin bushes and muscadine vines, passed where the high school now stands, and arrived in sight of the Southern Railway depot—scene of the Railroad War. After my stories on the Cow Creek Branch appeared, without an exact date for the so-called war, Joseph Nichols read them and wrote me from retirement in Fresno, California, that the furor was in July. He remembered because it was when his sister was born.

When Uncle John and I first discussed our L&N "history," I thought I was going to get an eyewitness account of the trestle trouble from him. But unfortunately he was a teenager still living at home on the Smith farm out east of town. He missed seeing the showdown, something that still keenly disappointed him after sixty-seven years.

The official history of the Louisville and Nashville Railroad by Kincaid Herr tells the story of extending the main line from Cincinnati through Knoxville on to Atlanta but offers few details about the Oliver Springs trestle. A number of branch lines were also constructed at the time in nearby Campbell and Claiborne Counties to open up lucrative coalfields. According to Herr, not only the Southern Railway but some local people in those counties—he called them "mountain feudists"—were not always happy about the arrival of the railroad. But the L&N had survived the Civil War and was not to be stopped by such minor problems. It sent out "special agents" to accompany the construction crews, apparently tough customers. The railroad's police chief in 1903 was J. B. Harlan, who had his headquarters at Pruden near Cumberland Gap. Maybe he wasn't expecting trouble in Oliver Springs, but whatever the reason, Harlan was not there when the Southern made what Herr calls an attack on the L&N construction crew. Herr diplomatically does not name the Southern, mildly saying, "The competing line hindered the progress of the work by blocking the railroad sidings with empty cars until finally, in exasperation, the L&N's chief engineer of construction, J. E. Willoughby, instructed his forces to drive the pilings right through the empty cars." Giving no more details, Herr admits that such encounters were always followed by "legal hangovers" and company lawyers were busy for years settling the differences.

Charlie Davis there in Norwood remembered it in less polite terms. "I just happened to be walking down the Southern tracks that day. I could see something going on. They was into it pretty heavy. A boxcar had been turned over and I seen a pile run right through it, nailed it right to the ground!" His brother John had been working on the trestle, but he decided that very day he'd had enough. "John come off that bridge and next day left Oliver Springs to join the army. Never come back neither," Davis said, laughing and slapping his knee.

It was not until I met Elmer Sienknecht, however, that I got a fuller version of the goings-on. I had been very anxious to get to know this youngest child of

Dr. Theodore Sienknecht, who had come to America in 1848. Elmer Sienknecht would tell me about his many years as business manager at Windrock, but unexpectedly he turned out to be an eyewitness to the railroad conflict. He was thirteen at the time and worked for the Southern hanging switch lights. Unbothered by a rival since the late 1880s, the railroad was flourishing, thanks to the famous Oliver Springs Hotel and the Big Mountain coal mines.

Sienknecht grinned, saying the Southern really had no intention of trying to stop the trestle. "The reason for the fight was different from what most people thought. It was over the danger of the piles being too close to the Southern's main line. Everybody was always sticking their heads and arms out the train windows in those days."

He remembered a man named Smith had the contract to build the two-thousand-foot trestle that crossed over much of the old part of town, maybe some forty feet off the ground. "Smith started to work at the north end, and when he got to the Southern tracks quickly crossed over instead of dismantling his pile driver and moving it to the south end in the usual way. His strategy worked to perfection. The Southern had overturned three boxcars, but they did nothing to slow down the L&N since the piles were driven right through the car that was in the way."

Joe Hannah, the big boss at the Southern depot, filled the air with four-letter words as hot as the engine he had earlier fired up by the overturned cars. The unexpected move across the tracks caused some quick improvisation. According to Sienknecht, the fireman on the Southern engine added sand to the firebox as the engineer force-drafted the fire to make more smoke. It was smoke with a real punch.

Sienknecht said, "Andy Duggins up on the L&N pile driver was the man on the hot seat, and believe me, it was hot. And so smoky Andy could hardly see, but it didn't take long to put the piles right through the old boxcar and move out of the way of the engine." He laughed, pointing out how the Southern section hands had outsmarted themselves by turning over the other two boxcars since they made it impossible to get on the adjoining side track to continue giving the pile driver the hot treatment.

So the trestle triumphed and the way was clear to Windrock.

Stories about the Railroad War persist, like the one about how the L&N paid men $1.25 a day to hug each pile to keep the timbers from being cut down. According to Snyder Roberts, the trestle in time became a center of community life with courting couples using it for a promenade in the evenings, even if mothers worried about possible flashes of their daughters' ankles as they paraded up so high. The trestle also served as grandstand from time to time to view snake-handling preachers from New River. And then there was Luther Abston, who bought one of the first Model Ts in Oliver Springs. He converted Henry Ford's sober black car into a brilliant red racer. It was already the talk of the town when one Sunday afternoon Luther went down in history. Most of the town gathered to watch "that boy kill himself," according to Snyder. Luther drove out to the middle of the long, high trestle. Instead of killing himself as everyone expected, he calmly backed the Ford, bumpity-bump, off the railroad bridge.

Uncle John loved all the stories. However, he did admit one important thing about the Railroad War, "It warn't no war at all cause nobody got kilt, but they sure drove piles through that boxcar awright."

On to Windrock Mine

Uncle John and I were on our way out Windrock Road to see his first cousin, Annie Smith Giles. As we bounced along the rough asphalt crowded with giant coal trucks, I wondered how many of those truckloads would equal the twenty-one million tons that had already come out of Windrock Mine. Since 1904 the mountain had been honeycombed with well over a thousand miles of tunnels, helping to make Anderson County in that year of 1970 the largest coal producer in the state. In the early days, coal was needed for the operation of railroads and factories, but it then became essential to run electric power plants. Bessemer Coal, Iron, and Coke Company from Birmingham, Alabama, wanted to tap Windrock Mountain's rich seams of coal, some up to ten feet thick. The L&N cooperated by building its Cow Creek Branch. However, during the 1950s, when coal prices were depressed, it became more economical to truck the coal from the tipple at Lower Windrock, and the section of the L&N line from Oliver Springs to the mine went out of use. Then in 1961 Windrock Coal and Coke Company, Bessemer's subsidiary, also went out of business, but the mine reopened not long afterward for a second life under the Oliver Springs Mining Company. So here we were that summer day meeting one noisy WACO truck after another on our way to Annie Smith Giles' house.

Although eighty-nine, she had recently uprooted herself to move back to Piedmont, one of the ghost stops along the Cow Creek Branch. It was half a century since she had had lived there. Mrs. Giles was one of the Back Street residents who had been forced to move because of TVA's flood control channel in Oliver Springs. She could have had her pick of the attractive new low-

Annie Smith Giles in her front yard on Windrock Road in 1970 across from where the Piedmont coal commissary stood during World War I. Photograph courtesy of the *Oak Ridger*.

cost housing units just completed along Indian Creek, right there in the gap where Moses Winters had settled. But she wanted none of that.

"Lord 'a mercy, no, the water'll get up agin," Mrs. Giles said showing little faith in TVA's expertise. She'd had a real scare when Indian Creek went on that rampage in 1967 and she had to be rescued by boat. So, now Annie Giles was back where she had lived when Piedmont, or Campbell Town as many called it, was a prosperous place. Although the Cow Creek Branch's destination was Windrock, it served other new coal operations along the four-mile stretch from the Oliver Springs trestle. R. O. Campbell opened several mines that operated until just after World War I. About the same time they shut down, the school closed, although the Piedmont Commissary lingered on empty for a number of years. A depot at Khotan had stood between Piedmont and the end of the line at the foot of Windrock Mountain.

Birdlike Annie Giles had on her sunbonnet and was inspecting the bright pink petunias in her yard when we pulled up. She was standing directly across the road from where the Piedmont Commissary had served as the center of the community that was now reduced to only three houses. Motioning across the way, she said, "They was houses on both sides of the road from here at the commissary and the doctor's office plumb down to the creek." That was Cow Creek, actually Little Cow Creek, which the L&N line followed instead of the main Cow Creek that meandered through Hoskins Hollow to Frost Bottom.

"Piedmont School was up the other way toward Windrock near Khotan, where Dr. Shelton's daughter Ann taught," she explained. "You know he was the doctor at the big hotel. The train stopped there regular at the Khotan depot. That's where the superintendent lived, in a nice house I visited many times. He was Uncle Ned Renwick." She smiled thinking about her husband Billy Giles, who was the drum man responsible for letting the cars down the short incline at the Round Mountain Mine. "We moved away several times, but Uncle Ned always wanted Billy back, called him on the telephone one time when we was in Mountain Ash. Billy was a good worker, even if he was my man!" Renwick, according to Mrs. Giles, was "not of this country." The superintendent came from England, a "mine expert" as she called him.

We had moved up on her cool porch out of the summer sun, but conversation was a problem because we sat just a few feet back from Windrock Road. The coal trucks made an incredible noise as they passed in rapid succession headed for TVA's Kingston Steam Plant. Mrs. Giles admitted she didn't like being back in Piedmont very much and still mourned her old home of so many years on Back Street. "Them trucks come all day, ever day of the week seems like. I'll be glad when they get all the coal out," she said quite seriously as though she'd live to see the day.

As we talked, Uncle John remembered how he had helped open Campbell's first mine. "My daddy Jasper's brother Johnny was already out here at Piedmont. He was Annie's daddy. Me and my brother Henry boarded with Uncle Johnny when we drove the opening in the Round Mountain Mine, the first one. R. O. Campbell come and started building houses about 1904 when the railroad was finished."

Both Uncle John and Mrs. Giles wanted to talk about Dr. Kyker, who worked for the company. She said he was a good doctor and wished the present-day ones were more like him. "Now it costs seven dollars to see one and still you got to go to the drugstore!" It was not his doctoring, good or bad, that got Uncle John to laughing as he remembered how Dr. Kyker was famous for his bathtub and how he'd jump in it filled with icy water in the winter. "He'd say a cold bath kept him from getting cold when he went outside."

It must have been about 1912 when Campbell sold out and a man named Buffat took over. Uncle John recalled him as a slightly mysterious figure, "a Spaniard and a little bitty feller." Unlike Windrock Mine, which from the beginning had its own generating plant and electric locomotive, the Piedmont mines had used mules. According to Uncle John, Buffat right off ordered a four-ton "motor" as everyone called a mine locomotive. "I remember when Pleas Jones pulled it to the mine from the depot with mules," he said. Things didn't go well in spite of the motor and Buffat left, too. Uncle John added, "He just took up his Winchester one day and went over the mountain, nobody knew where'bouts, though they tried to trace him up," Uncle John told us.

O'Dell Lively, who lived just a short piece on past Mrs. Giles toward Windrock, wasn't so sure about Buffat. He said he thought Buffat had just gone to work over in Morgan County. Of course, that made a much less interesting story. Though Lively was only seventy-five years old compared to Uncle John's eighty-three, he knew a lot about Campbell Town, for he had started working in Piedmont when he was fourteen, in 1909. His father was one of the Livelys who had sold the lower part of Windrock Mountain, including some of the Piedmont area, to Henry Wiley's land company.

We found him near the log house he had built himself some twenty years earlier within sight of Windrock Road. It was also just yards from one of several trestles L&N had constructed to accommodate the terrain along the bed of Little Cow Creek. It would be torn down like the other trestles when the rails came up in a month or two.

Still sharp-eyed, the old squirrel hunter came out of the shadowy woods when we honked. Lively was expecting us, ready to talk about these hollows where he had lived and mined coal all his life. "William Lively was my father and I was borned up Khotan Hollow in 1895," he explained. "But when I was five, we moved up on Windrock Mountain close to where they opened the mine. Then

O'Dell Lively outside his log house on Windrock Road in 1970 built when he retired as a miner twenty years earlier. Photograph courtesy of the *Oak Ridger.*

we moved again to the Cove, and that's when I started in the mines. They'd let a boy start when he was ten working with his daddy."

The family was living in the Cove, that cul-de-sac in Tuppertown near Church Lively's house, when all the excitement started with the construction of L&N's Cow Creek Branch. O'Dell would join other boys in rounding up discarded tin kegs that had held blasting powder so they could roll them down the hill for noisy fun. He even got in on a bit of the Railroad War. Laughing out loud, Lively said, "Ever time they'd get a post put down, the Southern would cut it down. Finally the L&N hired men just to stand and hug them posts to keep them from being cut. It was comical but a little skeery, too. I feered they was going to be some shooting!"

But nobody got shot, and when the Cow Creek Branch was completed in 1904, R. O. Campbell came from Atlanta to open three mines. O'Dell Lively worked in them off and on, ending up in the one called Khotan Mine, which finally flooded out when they cut under Wright Creek. "Right now, they's a pipe with water running out of it. Must be an ocean of water in that mountain."

Not long after that mine flooded, Lively started in 1921 as a brattice man at Windrock, building those walls essential to control ventilation. He retired in 1946 and built his log house. After all those years as a miner, Lively ended up without a union pension, though he said the local United Mine Workers representative tried hard to get the UMW headquarters to approve one. "Because of all the shutdowns when things was slack at Windrock in the 1930s, sometimes we'd only get in three or four days a month. And to get a pension, you had to work so many full months all added up out of thirty years. Others like me got a pension, and I guess I shoulda got a lawyer, but I didn't," he said.

A mountain stoic, Lively obviously wasn't bitter. After all, he said, he had his Social Security. Besides, the woods up behind his house were full of rabbits and squirrels, and as soon as he could locate some new coon dogs hunting would be even better. Lively wanted it understood that he remained a strong union man and believed that miners deserved the same seven dollars an a hour in pay that his electrician son-in-law got.

As we headed back to Oliver Springs, Uncle John pointed out the high trestle where Andy Duggins was fatally injured. Andy was the man in the hot seat on the pile driver that day when the L&N crossed over the Southern locomotive in the Railroad War. Duggins was still working for the L&N in 1920 when the accident happened. "It was January and come a shower rain and froze. His feet flew off and he fell right off that trestle," according to Uncle John.

Before the trip out to Piedmont, I had heard a lot about those early days from Elmer Sienknecht. For forty years he was the office manager and purchasing agent for the Windrock Coal and Coke Company. Among other duties, he oversaw the commissaries at both Lower Windrock at the foot of the mountain and Upper Windrock near the mine entrance. He was just a year younger than Uncle John but every bit as young and chipper, in some ways more so; his hearing was quite good. When he retired in 1952, the Sienknechts had moved to Knoxville, but both of them could still conjure up vivid scenes from up on the mountain even long after leaving. They could look out from the veranda of their comfortable house onto a panoramic view, ridge after misty blue ridge finally reaching the Smokies sixty miles to the south.

"We could see the fireworks each fall at the Tennessee A&I Fair in Knoxville nearly thirty miles off," Mrs. Sienknecht said, a little wistfully. "It was such a nice community, such good people. But it's all gone now." Their son, Dr. Charles Sienknecht, had recently driven them back up on the mountain where life had been good. Not only had their son become a medical doctor in the family tradition begun by Elmer Sienknecht's surgeon grandfather, but so had their grandson named Charles.

It was 1912 when young Elmer took his bride to live at Upper Windrock. She was a Gallaher, a flatlander, so to speak, raised in the Wheat community in the valley where K-25—the Oak Ridge Gaseous Diffusion Plant— would be built to separate uranium for the first atomic bomb. He had been

Elmer Sienknecht's family out on the steps of their home at Upper Windrock in the 1940s. Photograph courtesy of Charles W. Sienknecht.

Upper Windrock residents waiting for a ride up the mine's mile-long incline, probably in the early 1930s.
Photograph courtesy of Ina Lea Gallaher Roe.

working for the Southern Railway those years after the L&N trestle was built, but 1912 changed all that. The rest of his working life would be intertwined with that of the late W. C. Hutcheson, Bessemer's vice-president who was in charge of all the company's mines but chose to live at Windrock. Hutcheson was general superintendent there.

Showing a photograph of "Pat" Hutcheson, he said, "You couldn't find a better man or a finer engineer. He was like a brother and when he married, our wives were close friends." I had already heard about Hutcheson from a number of people, and only good things. In fact, he must have been in large part responsible for Windrock's benevolent paternalism that left so many positive memories alive, even in 1997. The two communities, Lower Windrock and Upper Windrock, were actually mining camps, but I never heard them referred to in that somewhat derogatory way. The term "camp" did not seem to fit the two small towns of clean houses with their frequent coats of whitewash. They were surrounded by virgin oak and hickory and nearly every flower known from lilacs to roses. Residents considered them homes, not houses, having little in common with the typical shanties thrown up by the Tennessee Coal Company at Briceville before the Coal Creek War.

Sienknecht said that even before the L&N's branch line was completed in 1904, a wagon road was cut up to the 2,500-foot elevation where the driftmouth of Windrock Mine No. 1 would be blasted out of solid rock. A mule train carried up a sawmill to cut the timber on the spot to build the houses and other company buildings. But that first trip with the sawmill was one of the few times the wagon road was ever used. A rail incline was soon finished that became the community's lifeline to the world. The steep 4,900 feet of track looked like a railroad from a distance, but up close you could see there were three rails in this system for moving coal cars or "monitors" on a wire cable up and down the mountain all by the force of gravity. The main job of "the drum man"—Billy Giles had been one at Piedmont—was to control the crucial brakes on the cable wrapped around big cylinders ("drums"). Attached to this cable, a loaded monitor would head down the mountain using an outside rail plus the middle one. At the same time another car would head up the mountain in like fashion, maybe loaded with goods for the commissary. Midway on the forty-five-degree slope was the passing point, a short section of track with four rails that allowed the cars to get by each other.

"A trip took about three minutes," Sienknecht said. When a car loaded with coal reached the bottom, Uncle John would be waiting at the tipple. After he put a wooden block under a wheel, he disconnected the monitor from the cable. Then came the tricky part, especially on cold mornings if the rails had ice or snow. He had to kick out the block, then jump on the monitor

Dr. and Mrs. Clinton Gallaher, visiting relatives in Windrock after World War II, tried out a double "railhorse" on the mile-long incline. Photograph courtesy of the *Oak Ridger*.

and lower it into the main tipple by using a hand brake. After that, the coal could be dumped into the train below.

Not only coal and mining supplies went up and down the incline. People did, too. Sienknecht said that in the early days nearly every family at Upper Windrock had its own homemade "rail horse." On it a ride down the mountain took just one breathtaking minute, including slowing down at the passing point. Although the contraption had a seat and balanced on wheels on two rails, that was about all it had in common with the Williams's "three-wheel speeder." Certainly no pedaling was needed coming down the mountain, just a strong arm for the brake. At the bottom, the rail horse could be thrown into an empty monitor for a free trip back up the incline, the same way a person could get a ride up. Although rail horses and the competition to break speed records with them were good for many Windrock stories, the "horses" weren't used so much by residents after the company started regular "man cars" that resembled San Francisco's open-air cable cars. But one way or another, everybody rode the incline. Even if there had been a passable road up the mountain, automobiles with four cylinders didn't have the power to pull such a steep grade. Sienknecht said it was the 1930s before the WPA built a real road to the top. A whole generation had lived without one.

In 1912 when Sienknecht left his job in Oliver Springs with the Southern the two Windrock communities were booming. "There were 105 company houses at the top and 65 at the bottom," the old manager recalled. "I

Mrs. Bill Fox, far left, joining other ladies of Upper Windrock probably on a Sunday in 1920 for a ride on the "man car" up the incline. Photograph courtesy of Charles W. Sienknecht.

was in charge of the commissaries at both places and also collected house rent as part of my job. We had fine stores with cold storage and fresh meats, better than in Oliver Springs at the time. Miners wanted nothing but the best!" He said that, even though his Uncle Henry owned the Sienknecht store popular throughout the area.

The miners' typical eat-drink-and-be-merry philosophy inevitably resulted in "Blue Monday," Sienknecht remembered. It followed after payday because everyone was broke. That was when the company scrip came in handy, allowing miners to draw against their future paychecks. In spite of the widespread complaint about owing your soul to the company store, I was surprised never to hear that about Windrock, although prices must have been higher than in Oliver Springs. Fatalistic miners usually lived for the day, somewhat as we do now with our credit cards. Not only did the convenient commissaries have fresh food, they had niceties like oysters and the intriguingly named soda pop from the Oliver Springs Bottling Company. The owner, P. J. DeBlieux, made certain that many of those empty coal monitors returned filled with his soft drinks, like Koca Nola and Ironbrew.

Elmer Sienknecht saw the boom times continue through World War I. During those years it took 350 miners with picks and shovels to blast loose and load the coal from the thick seams. The workers and their families totaled about 700 people in the two camps. The company took pride in keeping the houses in good condition and provided with plenty of electricity from the company plant that

Ina Lea Gallaher on her bike in front of Windrock Company's commissary at Lower Windrock about 1946. Photograph courtesy of Ina Lea Gallaher Roe.

operated until TVA came into being with Norris Dam in 1937. In good humor, Sienknecht explained, "We sold the generating plant then. We could buy cheaper from TVA, since the taxpayers were helping pay! We sold it to Japan for junk, and I guess they shot it right back at us after Pearl Harbor."

He proudly talked about the schools. "The county used to pay teachers only forty-five dollars a month, but the company made up the difference between that and a hundred and twenty-five dollars. So we had good teachers, some even with master's degrees." And the benevolent Windrock Company even took care of funeral expenses for its families. Over the years there were natural deaths, but few fatalities in the mine and never any explosions.

But the good times at Windrock did not last forever.

"In 1929 the bottom just fell out," the old manager recalled. "Factories shut down, and we ran little coal, sometimes just a day or two a month during the 1930s." Those were the days when the United Mine Workers fought bloody battles in places like Harlan, Kentucky. In contrast, Anderson County had little trouble, certainly nothing like the Coal Creek shootout when the UMW tried to organize in 1904. The New Deal's Wagner Act protected workers' right to organize, but Windrock miners were well paid and not too interested in a union, as many old UMW members remember even to this day. But they did set up Local 3908. Afterward, Sienknecht said that many times the Windrock men wouldn't want to strike when union headquarters called one, but Superintendent Hutcheson would insist they join the strike. "He didn't want anyone to get shot!"

Sienknecht didn't say so, but the company would give miners credit at the commissaries during strikes. Roy Brown of Frost Bottom told about such credit, saying, "Don't think that wasn't unusual. Most companies tried to starve us out." Once head of the Windrock local and still a strong union man, Roy said, "There'll never be another company like the old Windrock one. It was the most honest company I ever worked for."

After the Depression, according to Sienknecht, times got better again with a brief coal boom after World War II. But postwar mechanization increased union demands, and strip mining hit the deep mines hard. That was when Windrock houses started to deteriorate. The union contract would allow only $1.75 monthly rent per room for the company houses. "For a three-room house that meant only $5.25 a month, and we couldn't keep them up for that. So they were just given away or eventually fell down."

By 1954, Windrock was selling all of its coal to Duke Power's electric-generating plants in the Carolinas. But then rail freight went up, and Duke started buying cheaper coal from West Virginia strip mines. That spelled the end for L&N's branch line between Windrock and Oliver Springs. Trucks

Former miner Roy Brown in 1970 holding old Windrock commissary records and a 1904 light bulb. Photograph courtesy of the *Oak Ridger.*

started coming to the tipple at the bottom of the mountain when a TVA contract was won for the new Kingston Steam Plant. Sienknecht retired the next year, but the tracks remained. Now in the summer of 1970, the rails were about to be torn up. TVA had bought the 3.6 miles of right-of-way, and the L&N was planning to take its rails back after nearly seventy years.

Until 1963, Oak Ridge fossil hunters adventurous enough to drive the rutted dirt roads on Windrock Mountain were rewarded with a look at the deserted, somehow menacing, old commissary. But in that year Roy Brown bought the building put up when the mine opened. He paid a hundred dollars for it to tear down for salvage. As a former Windrock miner, he was nearly as interested in what he found in the store's attic as in what he got for the twenty-foot beams of virgin poplar.

His biggest find was an unopened carton of handblown light bulbs made in 1904 by the Incandescent Lamp Company of St. Louis. They had somehow gotten stuck in a dark corner of the attic for over half a century. The graceful, clear glass bulbs would still burn with an orange glow in the filament, enough to delight Thomas A. Edison himself. Another person who was pleased was President Lyndon Johnson. Roy laughed when he showed me two of the light bulbs still in their original corrugated paper wrappers, the same kind you get in the supermarket today. For a joke, his son Chris sent several of the antique bulbs to Washington after newspapers kidded Johnson for trying to reduce the national debt by turning off lights in the White House. "He got back a nice letter from the president, too," Roy said. After all, there were few of those fragile items around anymore except in museums like the Smithsonian.

When Windrock Coal and Coke Company officially went out of business in 1961, important records kept all those years by Elmer Sienknecht were taken by the parent company Bessemer back to Birmingham. But box after box of old bills and other papers had been left in the abandoned building for Roy to rummage through. He was showing some of the most interesting ones the day I went to see him and wife Vada in Frost Bottom. Their house up on Walden Ridge, surrounded by orange and yellow zinnias, appeared downright cheerful next to the solemn-looking John C. Duncan place. Just across Frost Bottom Road, Big Butte was not really so tall a knob, but it did block the Browns' view of Windrock mine. It was hot, and they had brought boxes of stuff out on the porch.

"Look at this," Roy said, giving me a stack of reports from a man named J. A. Byers. In 1906 this Byers carried the mail from Oliver Springs to Windrock and reported to the U.S. Post Office bureaucrats the exact hour and minute of his departure and arrival each day of the month. He also spelled out the reasons when the mail was not on time—"train late" or "mail carried by F. C. Alexander," whatever that implied. He also listed the mode of carrying the mail, usually "horseback" but sometimes "walking," plus the condition of the road, frequently just plain "bad."

Then there was the agreement Roy found that was reached on July 1, 1906, with one Dr. W. H. Eblen to run the market section of the commissary. He was to give Windrock Coal and Coke Company 10 percent of the sales, "either check or cash" would do. Dr. Eblen had to assure the company that he would handle "fresh meats, fish and oysters, soda water, loaf bread, butter, chickens, eggs, fruit and vegetables." It was also there in black and white that he would not "throw trash, empty boxes, bones or paper within a hundred yards of the building and that the market not be open on Sundays." In spite of the contract, I found hundreds of old broken beer bottles thrown under the commissary, pale blue with bubbles in the glass. Several hours of digging finally turned up two intact bottles, one with "AB" on the bottom. Anheuser-Busch? I have never found out, though the bottles, plus one of the 1904 light bulbs, are prized reminders of my years in Tennessee.

As for other merchandise sold in the commissary, there was a bit of everything. The only requirement was that it fit in an empty coal car for the ride up the incline. Children's oxfords sold at eighty cents a pair from the Haynes-Henson Shoe Company, a firm calling itself the Knoxville Million Dollar Shoe House. One of their bright yellow invoices, dated April 16, 1909, listed 193 pairs of shoes for men, women, and children shipped by L&N for a grand total of $163. Less mundane items like solid walnut coffins could be gotten through the commissary with no trouble. T. N. Deatherage would furnish one for $21. Those were the days before the loggers took most of the virgin timber.

Time went on, however, and two world wars later, life at Windrock dramatically changed. After looking through the aging records, Roy brought out several small snapshots taken with a box Kodak. The pictures were neither clear nor impressive, but in fact they were of the first equipment that arrived at Windrock in 1947 to turn the big operation into a "mechanical mine." It was the end of the pick and shovel. The new cutting and loading machines provided a system by which the coal, after being blasted loose, was picked up by the mechanical "arms" of a Joy loader that conveyed it to a shuttle car. (Joy was the name of the company, incidentally, though the loader was literally a joy to the miners.) The shuttles in turn carried the coal to the mine cars waiting on the tracks to be hauled out of the mine by the small locomotive, then dumped into the monitors for the swoosh down the incline to the waiting L&N coal cars.

But even that changed, too, when Duke Power Company said it was going to buy West Virginia coal, and nothing more from Windrock. Roy had been operating one of the new cutting machines before the big shutdown. He said it was a shock. So did affable Carl Keith, who was back from the Korean War and had taken over as business manager from Elmer Sienknecht. Though Keith grew

Lunchtime in the newly mechanized Windrock Mine about 1950 for Enoch Breeding, roof bolter (far left); Richard Ward, spray man; Ramsey Lively, cutting-machine man; Ernest Lively, shot fireman; and Roy Brown, also a cutting-machine man. Photograph courtesy of Lavada Brown.

up in Big Valley's farmland east of Clinton, he and his wife Virginia had been glad to move to their new home looking out toward the Smokies. That shutdown a couple years after the Keiths went up on the mountain was typical of the trouble the coal areas were in throughout the Appalachians.

Keith said, "It was in July 1954, when one day I got a call from Duke Power, who had been buying all our coal. I was told that as of Friday, the next day, they wanted no more coal. Period. The L&N freight rate had been raised to $4.14 a ton, while the coal itself was bringing only $3.83 a ton! We were caught with fifteen cars of coal waiting on the track. We just had to unload it and get rid of it anyway we could." Windrock was completely shut down until November. But then, Keith explained, the company got a contract with TVA's Kingston Steam Plant. "That was when we stopped using the L&N and started trucking the coal straight to Kingston."

During the reprieve, life was still good at the two Windrocks. The larger store up on the mountain reflected the prosperity the rest of the United States was enjoying in the 1950s. "We had everything up there! We sold the very first television set in Anderson County," Keith enjoyed saying. "That was in 1952, before Knoxville had any TV stations. But up on the mountain we could get Atlanta." The commissaries did a hundred thousand dollars in business and were the biggest Norge dealer in the area, he said. "We even sold boats and trailers, anything you wanted." A far cry indeed from the life of the miners fighting with the militia over convict labor during the Coal Creek War. Keith was the new generation, but he got a chance to work for a while with Windrock legends like W. F. Deaderick, the mine's electrical engineer for forty years. He invented an automatic tripping device to close the doors on the monitors before they were pulled back up the incline. And then with the Sanford-Day Company in Knoxville, Deaderick developed a highly valuable automatic mine car coupler.

But the glory days of the old Windrock were coming to an end. Roy Brown remembered the turning point in the summer of 1961 when he was just back from the UMW hospital in Harlan with his arm still in a cast. The Bessemer officials called the Windrock miners together for a meeting in Oliver Springs. "Mr. Badham, the president from Birmingham was there, and told us their steel mills couldn't absorb the coal company's losses any longer," Roy said. "They didn't object to the union pay scale, about twenty-four dollars a day, but it was the UMW's forty-cent royalty on each ton of coal for the welfare fund they couldn't stand. The company wanted that reduced, but some of the hotheads refused to go along."

So in June 1961, Windrock Coal and Coke Company ceased to exist after fifty-seven years. The following year Bessemer subleased its equipment to an operator from Kentucky, Stamper Collins. Then the union local changed its mind and agreed to a "sweetheart" contract calling for only five cents a ton for the welfare fund. This was short term, local miners thought, just until times got better. But that didn't happen, and Collins went bankrupt. Then in 1965 the Windrock equipment was leased to a new outfit called the Oliver Springs Mining Company and Windrock Mine was back in business. But this time it was non-union.

Five years after the Oliver Springs Mining Company went into operation, I was in second gear headed up Windrock to the original offices near the mine's driftmouth. C. H. Smith, company president, had said he'd be glad to see me. My "history" of the L&N and Windrock would end with the story of what was currently happening on the mountain, now that the grandson of Church Lively was in charge. Things had come full circle, in a way, since the Livelys sold their land to Henry Wiley's land company after the Civil War. The Coal Creek Mining and Manufacturing Company still owned the land and got a royalty, but the rest of the profits went to C. H. Smith and Curt Owens and their Oliver Springs Mining Company. With an annual payroll of some half million dollars, the company with fifty-five miners was producing eight thousand tons of coal a week, approximately the same amount brought out by 280 miners just before the mine was mechanized in 1947.

After I passed nearly vanished Lower Windrock and started to climb, I was impressed with how the old wagon trail had been converted into more than two miles of new hardtop. It was still steep with switchbacks, but the WACO trucks that so irritated Annie Smith Giles were taking the curves with ease on their way down. According to TVA, they had carried over two million tons of coal to the Kingston Steam Plant since the Oliver Springs Mining Company went into business in 1965. That meant $12 million. And the coal had been trucked from the very top instead of from the tipple on the L&N tracks as originally planned. An unexplained fire had ruined the incline machinery when the non-union operation first started. The noise of this relentless procession of enormous coal trucks seldom let up.

C. H. Smith and Curt Owens, an experienced mining man with a good Welsh name from Hazard, Kentucky, had picked a good time to get in the boom-and-bust coal business. A growing nationwide electrical power shortage had not been relieved by the much-publicized nuclear plants, and the price of coal was up to $6.17 a ton and still rising. The unanticipated Mideast oil crisis was just around the corner, waiting to send it spiraling toward $35 a ton.

But when I arrived at the sheet iron equipment shop, the big energy crisis was still to come. The two men were waiting in the old offices of Pat Hutcheson and

A giant Walls & Coker truck getting a thirty-ton load of coal at Windrock's No. 3 mine in 1970. Photograph courtesy of the *Oak Ridger.*

wanted right off to talk about the controversial new Federal Coal Mine Health and Safety Act, which had gone into effect April 1. Owens, the company's forceful, articulate general manager, was politely indignant about this important legislation, although their own new safety program had already been approved by the U.S. Department of Labor.

Tapping on a map, Owens pointed to the 2,500 feet of entries already opened in their new No. 3 mine. They had tunneled through the mountain to get over to the New River side to start this new operation. He said, "We've met the new requirements so far and we plan to stay in business, but I don't know about a lot of the smaller operators. It's hard even to guess right now what the cost of meeting some of the health requirements will be."

The health standards Owens referred to were aimed primarily at curbing pneumoconiosis, "black lung" disease, with devices to cut down on coal dust. Owens said, "It's taken eight years in England to bring the dust count down to eight grams per cubic meter. Now this new law expects us to have it down to two grams in eighteen months!" He was convincing, especially to someone with little technical background. Still, "coal dust" brought to mind a picture of gaunt John Daugherty, patiently sitting down there in Oliver Springs trying to get his next breath.

The new federal law had other serious safety concerns. In fact, the same argument over "gassy" and "non-gassy" mines, which old miner C. I. Williams said had taken place at the time of the 1911 Slatestone explosion, was still going on. Both Owens and Smith complained more about that aspect of the law than about regulation of coal dust. The new legislation eliminated such a classification, which had allowed less strict ventilation requirements for so-called non-gassy mines. In the past, that had included Windrock and other mines above 2,300 feet elevation, along with those that had never shown signs of gas. Now all mines would have concrete "stoppings," or walls, to block off the side entries from the main line or haulway, not wooden brattices or curtain walls as were usually used. Owens expected that concrete would take a big bite out of profits.

Smith pointed out that Windrock was 2,500 feet up and had had an outstanding safety record for sixty-six years, winning a national safety award in 1959. Over the years, he said, the mine had had only about a half dozen fatalities and no explosions. Owens added, "This new law will be the end of many small operators. Of course, that won't make the United Mine Workers unhappy. They want to see just the big mines left, the only ones still organized by the union."

Oliver Springs Mining Company was non-union, typical of the Southern coalfields in 1970. George Titler's cry at the New River union rally to raise the UMW banner over every tipple had gotten nowhere. Not long before I went up to Windrock, the last active union local in Anderson County had gone under when Consolidation Coal Company closed its Pocahontas Mine at Devonia. Most of the miners with Owens and Smith had worked at Windrock as UMW members before the original company closed in 1961. Their current pay, according to Smith, was twenty-five dollars a day plus a twenty-cent bonus on each ton. The latest UMW contract called for thirty-two dollars plus portal-to-portal pay. The latter was important in an old mine like Windrock where it might be miles from the mine entrance to the face of the coal seam. Smith said, however, his company and its fifty-five miners "split the difference" on travel time, averaging six hundred dollars a month for a forty-hour work week. The company had what Smith called an excellent hospitalization plan and planned to set up a pension plan.

What about the newest mine opened over in New River?

"We call it No. 3, though actually five entries have been made since the first one right out there," Owens said, motioning toward the original driftmouth shot out in 1904 and still in operation. Jack Hemphill, their mining engineer, estimated from mining maps that over 1,195 miles of tunnels had so far honeycombed Windrock Mountain. To be official, Owens said, the mountain is correctly referred to as Buffalo Mountain with its spurs, including Wolf Ridge, Patterson Mountain, and Sassafras Mountain. Sassafras and the Pinnacle are directly above Frost Bottom. Hemphill estimated that since 1904 roughly 20,190,720 tons of coal had been mined, with maybe another 5,000,000 still to be brought out.

The two mines then in operation were the original Windrock No. 1 extending into Wolf Ridge and the No. 3 in New River. The new one had been opened after a 3,800-foot tunnel was made through the mountain coming out on the New River side. Then another 5,000 feet of tram track was laid on the outside of the mountain to get to the new entry.

Two different seams of coal had been mined in the mountain. In No. 1 the Windrock seam at the 2,500-foot elevation, where the original driftmouth was located, had been worked out by the late 1920s. Then a mile-long tunnel angling up to the Dean seam some 60 feet higher was opened. Owens said, "We're now nearly three miles in the present heading in No. 1 and probably have another two years of work there. Then we plan to close that off and make a new entry up at the Dean level and mine a whole new area that's never been touched. In the old days the quality of the coal would not have made it economical. There's probably a million and a half tons up there and seven years' work." Smith added that in No. 3 they were maybe a half mile inside the mountain. And they expected to be mining there for another fifteen years to bring out an estimated three million tons of coal.

Before I left, Smith wanted to know if I would like to see inside No. 3. My answer was a quick yes. I would be back whenever he said.

When I returned several days later, the cordial welcome had evaporated. Not really, but a decision had been made that I should not go inside the mine. I knew about the old superstition that every time a woman went into a mine a miner would die. Or at the very least there would be bad luck and lots of it. But still I was surprised when C. H. Smith told me in as friendly a way as possible that there had been strong objections from the miners when word got around that I would be seeing inside Windrock. There might not be a union anymore up on the mountain, but there could still be a walkout. So, I was doubly glad my teen-age son Don had insisted on coming along. He could be my "leg man," as we used to say in the newspaper business, and report to me what it was like in the dark tunnels.

Before heading for No. 3, Smith showed us around the equipment shop, where the offices I had visited a few days before were located, and then went over to the driftmouth opened in 1904. It was only a few yards away. Frank Jackson, the motor man, sat on the diminutive locomotive that had just pulled fifteen loaded cars out of No. 1, each small car with five tons. Jackson's small train, attached to an overhead cable like an old streetcar, pulled the coal to a crusher. There it was dumped, broken up and then carried by conveyor belt to huge silos under which a truck could be driven.

Each vehicle would be filled with thirty tons, about a third of what a large railroad coal hopper would have held back in the days of the L&N. Asked about the arson that destroyed the incline machinery when the Oliver Springs Mining Company started up its non-union operation in 1965, Smith said no real evidence had been found. Admitting there had been hard feelings over the union, he added, "The men still wanted to go to work, and we've had no trouble since then."

Getting into Smith's yellow pickup, we headed out of what used to be the town of Upper Windrock east to the tunnel that went to Mine No. 3. All those white-washed houses that Elmer Sienknecht had been so proud of were gone like the commissary, but we passed pink and lavender hollyhocks left behind. Here and there stood an apple tree. It was only about a half mile to the new tunnel open-ing. Actually, abandoned Mine No. 2 had been partly reopened to make the tun-nel. Without the passageway, coal would have had to be trucked over the top of Windrock Mountain, a real ordeal.

A "man trip" was loading when we got out of the pickup at the tunnel en-trance. The crew of eight miners, who would work the second shift until mid-night, was already in the special car that resembled a long, open-sided coffin with the lid closed. Their seats put them in a nearly prone position. Waving, they took off for the 3,800-foot ride through the mountain and then nearly another mile around the outside to the No. 3 entry.

For us to get to the entrance of No. 3 by road meant driving over the top of Windrock Mountain past the level area called Windrock Fields I had long heard about. The dirt road all but shook our teeth loose. Just as we were nearing the top, we went under the TVA transmission line clearly seen ten miles away in Oak Ridge. Smith said, "It got pretty bad up here last winter. Curt and I were coming along here headed back down to the shop and there was a big slide, bringing trees and everything down, maybe from a strip mine. We had to radio for the bulldozer before we could get through." The company had its own radio communications system throughout the mines and on the outside with battery emergency equipment.

The road leveled out for a little way when we got to Windrock Fields at the very top. Purple phlox and sunflowers were everywhere in this Tennessee alpine meadow. But the nature lover's scene was blighted by a rusty Wiedeman Beer truck possibly left by strip miners. Then we were over the top and could see the tracks headed for the No. 3 entry. When we arrived at the driftmouth, Smith said he would be glad to walk in with Don if he still wanted to go. Sure he wanted to. Outfitted in a miner's safety helmet with light, Don and my camera took off with Smith on the trip I'd planned to make.

C. H. Smith, Oliver Springs Mining Company president, on the left, about to walk Don Bell into the No. 3 mine, which was opened in 1970 by tunneling through Windrock Mountain over to the New River side. Photograph courtesy of the *Oak Ridger.*

I had a pretty good idea what Don would see, but I still had wanted a look for myself at what Owens called a five-entry mining system. This meant that a main entry, or haulway, was first cut in the seam of coal about fourteen feet wide, and the height, depending on the thickness of the seam, was usually from five to ten feet. As the entry was cut into the mountain, a crosscut was made on either side of it every fifty feet. Then two more cuts were made on each side of the entry parallel to it. The result was the main haulway with its tracks flanked on each side by two parallel rows or pillars of fifty-by-fifty-foot blocks of coal left to help support the ceiling or roof. But the coal alone was not enough support. Roof bolts were put in by a special machine once a section of coal was cut and loaded. These bolts looked a little like giant toggle bolts, the kind used to hang pictures in plaster house walls, except these were four feet or more long. Sometimes timbers were used in addition as an extra precaution.

While I waited alone outside No. 3 in the sunshine, I got a chance to look around. There were stacks of roof bolts and concrete blocks for walls to control ventilation. And, there on a sort of workbench beside the tram track sat a surprising bit of plaster statuary. How under the sun did that cupid, maybe part of a bird bath, end up on the side of Windrock Mountain? It was enough to make me sit down and "study" about it, as Uncle John would say. Earlier storm clouds had gone, and in the late afternoon sunshine the Cumberlands were a dark blue, nearly purple. Except for the whir of the ventilating fan breathing down into the mine, there was nothing but stillness, no movement of any kind. Even the tallest poplars showed not the slightest breeze.

My mind wandered off on the women's liberation movement. I had never given it much thought, never having been slowed down in anything I wanted to do. Until today. I would have been truly furious had I known that only two years later, after I left Tennessee, my friend Maria Schenck, who took over my reporting job, would be taken on a grand tour of a deep mine at Graves Gap. And in only one more year the first woman would be hired to work underground as a miner, thanks to an equal opportunity suit that forced the hiring of women in that most macho of male occupations.

What was Don seeing besides the layout of the five-entry system, I wondered. When he and Smith reappeared, Don was surprised at how dark it was working at the coal seam with just the lights from the machinery. There at the face of the seam he got a good look at the invention of the Joy Manufacturing Company that put picks and shovels out of business after World War II. With its two mechanical arms, the Joy loader picked up the coal after it was shot loose by explosives. It could gather up about five tons a minute, putting the coal on a conveyor belt that moved it to a shuttle car that took the coal to the tram cars to be pulled out.

Don had just missed seeing the first step in the process, which involved the cutting machine. With its nine-foot cutting bar, it had been moved right up against the face of the seam—that day they were working where the coal was ten feet high—and cut a thin section about six inches thick the full width of the fourteen-foot entry. This section was removed to give the coal room to expand when it was shot with explosives detonated by an electrical charge. The charge was set off only after careful testing for possible gas that could cause an uncontrolled explosion. After the blast, the Joy loader went into action. When all the mine cars were loaded, Don and Smith rode out in one. Grinning, Don jumped out saying, "That was one dark, bumpy ride!"

Later Owens explained that their mines did not have the most up-to-date equipment because the geology would not allow it. Owens had had experience with the advanced machine called a continuous miner that eliminated explosives. This equipment had jaws like some tremendous monster that could simply bite out the coal and put it on a conveyor belt, he explained. "We've got a soft floor in this mountain that won't support such heavy machinery. Though a continuous miner might cost a million dollars, some operations can be made fully automated with no miners underground."

However, he said, the Oliver Springs Mining Company was doing just fine without the superjawed machine. We were convinced and left the mountain to Owens and Church Lively's grandson.

Soon after the trip up on Windrock, I told Uncle John how disappointed I was at not being allowed in the mine, although otherwise we'd gotten the royal treatment from his great-nephew C. H. But I got absolutely no sympathy from the old miner.

"Yes, sirree, he done the right thing!" he said without hesitation. "Why, I remember, it musta been back about 1926 when we started having some real bad luck in Windrock. And it turned out some wives of men working over at the New River Lumber Company's sawmill on Laurel Branch was riding through a tunnel with their household goods. Pat Hutcheson, the superintendent, found out and put a stop to it! And stopped the bad luck. He was shore a fine man!"

What could I say to that?

Nothing.

I decided to be satisfied that we had finished our so-called history of the Cow Creek Branch and Windrock. Now I knew about those mysterious lights I had seen up on the mountain my first night in Tennessee. Soon I would be moving to North Carolina, but I would never forget the lights.

Epilogue

I hadn't been to Windrock for years when I drove out from Oliver Springs to the foot of the mountain in 1992. What a surprise I got. Except for white-steepled Union Valley Baptist Church, which Brother Church Lively helped build, there was nothing under the dazzling fall sky except green grass edged with dense woods—and silence. It was somehow eerie and yet very pleasant. Nature had taken back Lower Windrock.

Later I discovered it was not a complete takeover. Hidden in the trees, the old schoolhouse had been made into a home by Clyde Halburnt while Kay Lively lived in a house next door. But still it was hard to remember those bustling, noisy days when the Louisville & Nashville Railroad locomotives pulled away millions of tons of coal hurtling down the mile-long incline to Uncle John's tipple. Not only were the L&N tracks gone, the railroad itself had been swallowed up by giant CSX Corporation. The very name L&N had disappeared in 1986.

After my visit to the new Windrock, I returned the following summer to the annual miners' reunion. Over two hundred people came. Helen Freels, who with husband Frank has been one of the chief reunion organizers, says the 1997 gathering in June had even more returnees, maybe three hundred. Along with gospel singing and small mountains of food, one of the main attractions is always the "board," a long display of news of Windrock people and mementos from their UMW past. Trish Lively Cox has taken over this tradition from her father, Carl, a son of O'Dell Lively. When I attended the reunion in 1993, I saw my old Windrock newspaper stories on the board and also, for the first time in twenty-three years, two men who had been so important to the coal operation before its end. One was C. H. Smith, who ran the Oliver Springs Mining Company with Curt Owens until the mine closed in 1983. And the other, Carl Keith of the old Windrock Coal and Coke Company, was there with his wife, Virginia.

The Keiths took me in their four-wheel-drive Trailblazer over the top of Windrock to Ligias Fork. Carl was telling stories about Elmer Sienknecht the whole time and saying more than once, "I love this mountain." On the way back down we overcame the ruts in the nearly abandoned side road to Windrock's original driftmouth. Only a bit of the shop's concrete floor and a few feet of rusty track could be found in the weeds. The mine entrance had disappeared after being sealed to keep sightseers out, some of whom tried driving into the dark tunnel. Everything was grown over in a tangle of black-berries and young catalpa trees with oversized heartlike leaves.

Augusta Bell in front of the original entrance of Windrock Mine blasted out of rock in 1904. This was made several years after the Oliver Springs Mining Company shut down all operations in 1983. Photograph by the author.

Lower down on the mountain, we passed the important project the Tennessee Department of Environment and Conservation had underway to relocate Windrock's eighty-year-old slag heap. Although Carl dismissed it as a "boondoggle," the refuse had been burning for years and state officials feared forest fires. Thousands of tons had to be excavated, then smothered with water and foam before finally being trucked to two new fills. Tim Eagle, the state's land reclamation director, reports that the $1.2 million project has been completed for over a year and that the oak, pine, and black locust trees planted on the new slopes are growing well.

As for C. H. Smith, Oliver Springs Mining Company was very good to him and Owens after I left Tennessee, thanks to the 1970s Middle Eastern oil embargo and energy crunch that pushed coal from less than seven dollars a ton to thirty-five dollars. They closed Windrock in 1983 and left mining after the price of oil plunged to fifteen dollars a barrel, taking coal prices with it. When I jokingly asked if the coal boom hadn't quickly made them millionaires, the affable Smith would only laugh and say, "We got in at the right time." He still lives in Oliver Springs and has helped organize the new Citizens First Bank, though he spends a lot of time on his farm in Morgan County and enjoys pheasant hunting in North Dakota.

It was Curt Owens who was the mining expert in their Windrock days, while C. H. Smith concentrated mostly on the business end. Owens says that the 1970 estimates of their mining engineer Jack Hemphill had proven to be on target. The company did make a new entry into the Dean seam as planned for Windrock Mine No. 1 and got out most of the 1.5 million tons predicted. Their No. 3 mine over on the New River side produced at least the estimated three million tons. During the 1970s coal boom, Owens had eight additional companies going in New River and helped build a $12 million coal-washing facility where Moore's had been. One of his operations, called Indian Creek Coal Company, was located near the old Pocahontas Mine. But he shut it down after being picketed for a year by the United Mine Workers. That was part of the UMW's last big effort to reorganize Anderson County. Soon afterward, a nationwide strike in 1978 caused President Carter to invoke the Taft-Hartley Act to force negotiations.

At the height of the boom, Owens's mines were producing about fifty-four thousand tons a week, compared to eight thousand from Windrock in 1970. "It was highly profitable, but the government got much of it," he said, laughing, "at least until President Reagan came into office and the seventy percent tax bracket was cut down to thirty-one."

Long before Owens and Smith left mining, they had been involved in the TVA's redevelopment plan for Oliver Springs. Today nobody has anything negative to say, at least not for the record, about why TVA pulled out in 1973. Apparently the agency was not encouraged to stay, if not outright told to leave. By that time the crucial flood control channel was completed, with low-cost housing built on the flood plain and the town's first sewer system finished. The elevated highway was assured, but the plans for an industrial park and a rejuvenated downtown got lost. As former mayor J. H. Burney has diplomatically put it, "We got some real improvements started after the flood, but businessmen had other ideas about the downtown and built that million-dollar shopping center out in Norwood." TVA's model city plan had called for Norwood—where Richard Oliver reigned before the Civil War—to become an exclusively residential area. But the new Tri-County Shopping Center on the four-lane highway went up with the backing of people like Owens and Smith. They said that suitable land for an industrial park could not be acquired and loans were unavailable for a shopping center in the old downtown. The new shopping center proved to be too close to Oak Ridge to be a success, but today it is owned by others and doing well, mostly rented as office space to Lockheed-Martin Energy Systems. This corporation recently formed by a merger between Lockheed and Martin Marietta operates the Oak Ridge facilities for the U.S. Department of Energy.

Although today everyone in Oak Ridge is edgy about layoffs and congressional budget slashing, this small city of some thirty thousand is quite prosperous, mainly because of environmental cleanup—across the country and in its own backyard. And this prosperity has a significant impact on Oliver Springs. In a roundabout way, the formation of TVA in the 1930s assured prosperity for Moses Winters's gap by way of the atomic bomb. In 1943 Anderson County could provide the Manhattan Project with tremendous amounts of essential electricity as well as an isolated location. Today, the future of Oak Ridge is definitely headed toward private "reindustrialization." British Nuclear Fuel Limited, a business consortium, has taken over Oak Ridge's K-25 complex, including the huge mile-long facility built to separate uranium for the atomic bomb. In return for a long-term lease and salvage of highly valuable metals, the consortium is responsible for the $600 million essential to complete K-25's current decontamination so that various types of modern industries can be housed there. Several are already in operation, like one for machine tooling and another for manufacture of nickel batteries.

In this nuclear age, Oliver Springs has become a sort of bedroom suburb of Oak Ridge, albeit one with its own strong identity and a bit rundown in spots. Most of its three thousand or so residents seem happy with it that way. Although Curt Owens owns extensive commercial real estate in Oak Ridge, he says, "I like Oliver Springs. It's a quiet town, but I'd rather live here."

Maybe the old downtown block where Sienknecht's department store once

shone will yet be revived. Now the buildings are mostly empty, like the drugstore of whipping post infamy. An insurance agency and a dress shop are both
gone, though upstairs above the gutted movie theater is a recording studio,
and a wholesale candy business operates behind a closed-up front. The big
news, however, is that an Oak Ridge couple, Danny and Barbara Palmer, are
planning to open an antiques business in the Sienknecht building. She, incidentally, is a grandniece of Uncle John Smith.

With the recent conversion of the unused Southern Railway depot into a library and museum, the Oliver Springs Historical Society has been revitalized
under the leadership of C. S. Harvey Jr., the town's successful, friendly furniture
businessman, whom everyone calls Sonny. A restored caboose from the glory days
of railroading has been put on the siding by the depot. Soon the town's first horse-
drawn firehose wagon will be added, along with the small ticket house used by
the Oliver Springs Hotel for its popular dance pavilion.

Charles Tichy, the TVA architect who bought and restored the old bank, and
Harvey have inspired a Main Street, USA Program under the National Trust
for Historic Preservation. While a beautification project is under way, including plans for antique streetlights, some important old homes are being restored.
The Hannah House, built by William Wiley after the Civil War and later the
home of General Hannah, has been nearly completed by Eddie Coker, grandson of New River's Lewis Coker. That should please various Richards family
ghosts who are probably walking unquietly in this weather-beaten town that was
once compared to a charming Swiss Alpine village. And I'm certain that enterprising Curt Owens will be a man after Joseph C. Richards's own heart if Owens
builds the new apartments he has planned on Ann Street. That was where the
magnificent Richards mansion once stood, on the street named for the patriarch's
wife from Swansea, Wales.

It's over in New River where the action is, after a mostly uneventful decade.
When I came down off Petros Mountain not long ago, the valley, with its morning mist, looked much as it must have before the Civil War. Those were the days
before the loggers and the miners, when William Smith rode over the top of
Windrock Mountain to borrow money from Ike Phillips. The flimsy shacks are
gone, bare spots showing where trailer houses once clung to the steep slopes on
the edge of Highway 116. The road itself was amazingly improved with resur-
facing and new steel railings for the fainthearted, although I discovered later that
the other end over Pilot Mountain was pretty much its same old narrow self.

I nearly missed Fork Mountain, gone except for its small church tucked away
under shady maples. Dorothy Armes still lives up a hollow in the only company
house left from the days of the Fork Mountain Coal Company, the same house

she moved into over fifty years ago. Always the optimist, she says, "We're just glad to keep the church as a miners' memorial and have reunion services every September." Although the New River Community Center never got any federal anti-poverty help, increased mining in the 1970s helped the depressed area for a while. Conditions never approached the terrible ones that exist even today in places like McDowell County, West Virginia. Mrs. Armes is proud of her children, including Gary, the teenager who was helping with the community center back in 1968. A longtime TVA employee until recent cutbacks, he is a Baptist deacon and commutes to work as an electrician in Oak Ridge.

Fork Mountain may have vanished, but today two giant corporations have New River's 350 inhabitants talking—Addington Enterprises and Champion International Paper Company. Addington has been using new technology called highwall mining to recover coal in the thin seams left in the abandoned strip mines like the ones above Rosedale School. This high-tech underground mining is by remote control and must meet federal requirements for planning, reclamation, and environmental monitoring. The low-quality coal is cleaned in the modernized five-story washing facility built by Curt Owens in the 1970s. Because much of Tennessee's remaining coal seams are so thin, less that twenty-four inches, this new method may bring a "significant increase in production," according to Ron McDowell in the U.S. Office of Surface Mining. Although permits for more mines in the New River watershed have been opposed by environmentalists because they are in the state-protected natural area bordering Frozen Head State Park, Addington has begun mining in the Fork Mountain area. A deep mine has also been opened.

Even the slightest possibility of more jobs is always good news at Charley's Branch, where another of Lewis Coker's grandsons now runs the New River Market. He is Scotty Phillips, a dark-haired young man in his thirties who looks nothing like I remember his mother's father, though he has Coker's pleasant self-confidence. But if a few mining jobs are welcome news, Champion Paper and its controversial clear-cutting of timber, much of it hardwood, is another story. Phillips has become the local spokesman for New River people who don't want more damage to the mountains added to that of the 1950s strip mining. In 1994 the whole county joined in an unsuccessful effort to stop the sale to Champion of eighty-five thousand acres in five counties, thirty-five thousand of them in Anderson County. Phillips said recently, "They've already clear-cut maybe six hundred acres in several places and are working now on Double Camp." This is the same Double Camp that had its peak cut off by a strip miner in 1969, so infuriating old John Seiber.

Exactly how much has been cleared in two years is hard to determine in this rugged terrain, although Phillips hopes that Anderson County's new timber severance tax may provide an estimate in the future. The log trucks have to be weighed to determine the tax.

The very active grassroots organization based in Lake City called Save Our Cumberland Mountains (SOCM) has about three thousand members in eleven chapters. They have begun air surveillance of Champion's clear-cutting, with weekend flyovers for local and state politicians in hopes of building more support for a bill regulating private timberland. It is slowly working its way through the Tennessee legislature. From her years of experience since founding Tennessee Citizens for Wilderness Planning (TCWP) in 1966, Dr. Liane Russell says it may take years. The Oak Ridge geneticist explains that such legislation is easily waylaid and often "studied to death."

The efforts of TCWP and SOCM were unable to stop Champion's new Caryville chip mill in adjacent Campbell County. They have joined other citizens' groups like the Dogwood Alliance to make an all-out push for a regional study of the impact of chip mills by the U.S. Environmental Protection Agency. Such mills are mushrooming in the Southeast because of the tightening of logging regulations in the West. A sign of the times may have been the recent demonstration by members of Earth First who chained themselves to the gate of Champion's Caryville facility.

For certain, Jasper Smith would not approve of what's happening to New River's trees, even though they are second-growth. He complained bitterly in 1926 about the disappearance of the virgin forests, saying that whatever old Lucifer hadn't gotten, Wall Street had. He demanded to know, "Where are our large poplars, oaks, and walnuts that used to wave over Frost Bottom in Micajah Frost's day?"

Although private timberland in Tennessee has virtually no regulations today, the situation with mining is quite the opposite. In 1978 the tough Federal Surface Mining Control and Reclamation Act, under the U.S. Department of Interior, went into effect. During the years after John Seiber's 1969 protest against shearing the top off Double Camp, the state's strip-mine law proved to be too weak, just as the old deep miner predicted. Operators found it cheaper to forfeit their bonds and just keep stripping in the old way. But even with the new strict federal law requiring immediate reclamation to return the land to its original contour, little was accomplished in Tennessee, where everything got snarled in politics. When Republican Lamar Alexander was elected governor, the state legislature repealed its own law. According to Tim Eagle, who directs the state's reclamation program, the result was deadlock over federal funds that lasted until 1986. Only then were efforts finally begun to do something about the so-called "orphan mines," roughly forty-six thousand abandoned sites of both strip and deep mines, eleven thousand of which are critical. Over two thousand have been worked on. Eagle says Anderson County has some eight hundred acres on the critical list, which is not much compared to more mountainous Campbell County with roughly four thousand acres. With about $2 million annually from reclamation fees, his office has a priority list based on health and safety concerns and is able to handle about fifteen projects a year. One of the biggest has been the burning slag heap of the Windrock Mine.

As for the strip-scarred mountains looking like mangy dogs, Eagle explains, "The old highwalls are ugly, but they're not our first priority. Deep mines need to be sealed to keep people out, people who want to explore or maybe just drink and party." And he also has to take care of emergencies, like the serious earth slide blocking Highway 116 near Fork Mountain caused by an old coal haul road. There the state had to excavate to bedrock and then secure the area with wire baskets of rock just above the highway. Higher up, above the rocks, fill dirt was put in and seeded.

Still, from Oak Ridge the Cumberlands don't look as bad as they did twenty-five years ago. Nature has helped some, Eagle says, and in certain areas the old benches have been graded and replanted. He says the kind of acid water I long ago saw coming down the mountain from the Moores' abandoned slag heap is a huge problem all over the state.

As for Graves Gap, the biggest event in years has been getting a new water system piped up to Duncan Flats and Braden Flats from the bottom of the mountain, thanks to reclamation funds. Mining long ago contaminated many of their wells. Byrd Duncan's widow, for one, is extremely happy about it. A resilient woman, Laura Duncan still laughs and has a busy life in Duncan Flats even without Byrd, since two sons and their families live nearby. She reports that Wendell, who works for the county highway department, teaches karate in Oak Ridge and sometimes brings his students to Flat Woods School for class and campouts. The once-gaunt old building has new siding and carpeting, which is nearly as hard for me to imagine as the karate classes themselves. Easter reunions of former Duncan Flats residents are still held there.

Just across Highway 116, Nancy Byrge has also lost her husband, Pearley, as well as brother Edd. But she has never considered for even a minute leaving Braden Flats. Hiram Braden's offspring still come back for their big annual family get-together. In fact, well over a hundred did so in September. Like Laura Duncan, she is content, surrounded by her children, grandchildren, and great-grandchildren.

While Tennessee had some 150 mining operations during the 1970s, today only 23 are under way, 4 of which are in Anderson County. Henry Wiley, should he return from the dead, would be surprised to find that his "old works" opened in 1869 have been important for several years in Beech Grove near Lake City. Beech Grove Processing Company, a subsidiary of the Williams Company, a large Oklahoma oil and gas corporation, has invested some $8 million in an ambitious project. Fred Wyatt, Coal Creek Mining and Manufacturing Company's executive vice-president, says that a solid corridor of high-quality coal between two of Wiley's original mines has been reached some nine thousand feet back inside Cross Mountain's profitable Coal Creek seam. Possibly twenty or thirty years' reserve is there. However, this is the Oklahoma company's first venture into coal mining, and they want out. They have recently suspended operations, and the mine has been put up for sale.

According to Wyatt, the Coal Creek company still owns about seventy-three thousand acres, with forty thousand in Anderson County, what he calls a "small" company compared to other public companies. Nevertheless, approximately a third of the nearly three million tons of coal being produced each year in Tennessee comes from Coal Creek's property. The company no longer has New York offices or any Wiley connections.

In addition to Addington's two New River mines, Anderson County has two other coal operations under way by Bob and Carl Swisher from their Briceville headquarters. Their S & H Mining Company is using a continuous miner in their deep mine in Cross Mountain. Their Premium Coal Company has completed extensive strip mining not far from Graves Gap, following strict federal regulations by immediate recontouring and replanting the disturbed land. They have just begun what will probably be a ten-year job stripping on New River's Ligias Fork. Swisher is typical of the nearly extinct small operator who must satisfy separate environmental and safety requirements. "The coal industry is overregulated, so that mining is hardly worth the harassment," Swisher says. His father set up Tennco, whose model stripping operation on Bootjack Mountain I saw in 1969. Back then the Swisher employees were organized by the Southern Labor Union, which went under in the 1980s when the drop in oil prices ended the coal boom.

As for Briceville itself, the old mining town is living on borrowed time. Gene White of Oak Ridge grew up there, the son of a miner. He fears that lack of students will cause the excellent elementary school to be consolidated with Lake City's. Unincorporated Briceville has never recovered from the shutdown in 1951 of Cambria Coal Company, which had bought the ill-fated Cross Mountain Mine from the Knoxville Iron Company. (Joseph C. Richards's old company, incidentally, stayed in operation in Knoxville until it was done in by the Federal Clean Air Act, according to Fred Wyatt.) As Briceville slowly fades away, the landmark Methodist church up on the hill has been reduced to a handful of members and become a community church. White says that the state transportation depart-ment is considering improvements to narrow Highway 116 between Lake City and Laurel Grove, where it joins the new Frost Bottom Road. If it is widened and its "waves" removed, that stretch will lose its feeling of pre–Civil War isola-tion. But this project is apparently a low priority with the state.

Present-day Lake City has never become the recreation area promised by its fancy name change, but it is holding its own. However, Charles Winfrey, lifelong resident and editor of the nearby *LaFollette Press,* says this town that was once wild and woolly Coal Creek remains stable, with about two thou-sand residents. It has been saved in part by Interstate 75 on the north edge of town. And a few Southern Railway gondolas are clanging out of the valley with a bit more coal, a little like the old days. The turbulent times have been remembered in Briceville by a recent state historical marker explaining the Coal Creek War, although no marker tells of the terrible Fraterville and Cross Mountain mine explosions. Gene White still has hopes that Hollywood will someday film John Rolfe Gardiner's 1974 novel about the miners' insurrec-tion, *Great Dream from Heaven.* It is an interesting book, with a fictional trans-formation of Frost Bottom into a thriving town suddenly filled with convicts freed by angry miners.

The real Frost Bottom today is far from being a town, although Micajah Frost and Moses Duncan would nevertheless find it very different from 1800. Abandoned strip mines cause a few slides, but mostly that is over.

Even after twenty-seven years, I have no trouble finding Babe Edwards, who still lives across from the Frost Bottom Baptist Church. At eighty-eight she is very much interested in life and politics, despite two broken hips and leg problems. This funny, unusual woman started life in a Catholic orphan-age in New York and followed carnivals around the country until she met her hard-drinking husband in Oliver Springs. They married and dramati-cally turned their lives around in Frost Bottom after being baptized in a creek near Petros. Lenard Edwards had died by 1967, when I first knew Babe, who was heading up the Frost Bottom Road crusade in her effective, pushy New York way. Thanks to her, the road committee made many trips to Nashville in a hearse belonging to Cox Funeral Home to lobby state legislators. Finally funds from the Appalachian Regional Commission made possible the won-derful seven miles completed after I left Tennessee. Today it is officially State Highway 330.

Although Babe has trouble walking, the sheriff recently made sure she got to Oak Ridge to help the Holiday Bureau, which annually provides Christmas toys and food for a thousand or more families. Known far and wide, Babe is essential for gathering donations, everything from money to turkeys.

Down the road a bit, pleasant, slow-talking Lavada Brown is widowed but lives in the same white house up on Walden Ridge. She and her husband, Roy, built it nearly on the spot where slave owner Philip Seiber was murdered during the Civil War. Not long ago, Vada went with me up on the Half Moon Road to locate the Methodist cemetery where Uncle John took me to find Moses Duncan's grave. It was all grown over, but the cove itself has changed for the better. Besides modest old houses and an occasional trailer, there are a number of modern new homes, even startling green city street signs, including one for Stony Flat Road. The Seibers seem to be doing well in Frost Bottom, as they did before the Civil War. Steve Seiber has a small "estate" with a large tan brick and wood house with gazebo and horizontal Kentucky-style fencing. Duncans live on the Half Moon, too, and have begun an annual Duncan Reunion. As for Roy Brown, it has been thirteen years since he was buried up on Grave Hill above Frost Bottom Church, under the trees where Micajah Frost put his small daughter Nancy in 1808 after she drowned in Poplar Creek.

To finish this story of circling Windrock Mountain, I must say that John T. Smith proved his adventurous Frost blood just a few years before his hundredth birthday. His granddaughter Marita Smith George well remembers putting him on a jetliner for California. He would spend his last years with his son Harold and wife Mary Kate in Lancaster in the Mojave Desert. But now he rests in Batley Cemetery beside Mrs. Smith, not far from where he worked for the L&N on the Cow Creek Branch.

And one last word about the Cherokees, so many years ago displaced from Frost Bottom and Windrock Mountain. They are coming back into their own in a completely modern way. Gamblers by the thousand have already visited the tribe's new $82 million Cherokee Casino built with Harrah's of Las Vegas. Under their first woman chief, Joyce Dugan, a savvy former school superintendent, annual revenues exceeding $50 million are expected for the tribe there on the reservation not far from where William Smith grew up in North Carolina's Haywood County. Today the Cherokees are busy counting their money and investing for a bright new future, leaving no time to remember all those broken treaties.

I wonder what Jasper Smith would say about all this.

Bibliographic Notes

Chapter 1. On the Edge of Two Hundred Years

I have relied on privately published histories of the Frost, Duncan, Lively, and Phillips families, along with unpublished genealogical research and several community histories, for basic information about the Cumberland Mountains area of Anderson County, Tennessee. Newspaper interviews with many elderly county citizens in 1968–70 were the source for the traditional stories I wrote about during that period in over thirty feature articles for the *Oak Ridger* newspaper in Oak Ridge, Tennessee. Recent interviews and research in old county and Knoxville newspapers have furnished material to complete this folk history of the last two hundred years in the Windrock and Cross Mountain area.

Of overall importance has been the work of the late Snyder E. Roberts. In 1981 he began publishing in book form his articles on local history, which originally appeared in the *Oliver Springs Citizen* and the *Roane County News*. His first book was *The Roots of Roane County, Tennessee 1792–* (Kingston, Tenn.: 1981). This work was followed by his four volumes of *The Story of Oliver Springs, Tennessee, and Its People* (Oliver Springs, Tenn.: 1982–85), totaling nearly eight hundred pages of invaluable details on all of the Windrock area. Unfortunately, the organization of these books is poor and the contents without an index.

Roberts's later work, *Descendants of Joseph Frost, Sr. from Amherst, Bedford & Washington Counties, VA to Anderson County, TN and Elsewhere* (1989), is the basis for my story of the Frosts. It is the source (p. 17) of the quotations about Micajah Frost's part in fighting Indians on the frontier and in the Battle of Kings Mountain. Also useful has been the ongoing genealogical research on the Frosts by Wanda Kelley.

272 **Bibliographic Notes**

For information about the first white hunters who came into the Cherokees' prized hunting grounds, see Clifford R. Seeber's *A History of Anderson County, Tennessee,* master's thesis, University of Tennessee, 1928, 3, 7–8, 18–19. What this country was like before the first Europeans arrived is well described in Federal Writers' Project, *Tennessee: A Guide to the State* (New York: Hastings, 1949), 15–19.

The story about Daniel Boone near Frost Bottom comes from W. J. (Jasper) Smith, a great-grandson of Micajah Frost and the author of some 167 short articles appearing between 1924 and 1932 in the *Anderson County News,* which was published 1905–1939, in Clinton, Tennessee. His articles on Boone are entitled "A Century Ago" (Mar. 9, 1929: 2, and Mar. 16, 1929: 1).

Robert E. Corlew, in *Tennessee: A Short History,* 2d ed. (Knoxville: U of Tennessee P, 1981), discusses relations between the Cherokees and the whites before the American Revolution (29–36) and the first permanent white settlements in Tennessee (38–51). For the location of native towns, see Betty Anderson Smith, "Distribution of Eighteenth-Century Cherokee Settlements," *The Cherokee Indian Nation: A Troubled History,* ed. Duane H. King (Knoxville: U of Tennessee P, 1979), 46–57. The information about the bounty for scalps is in Daniel J. Boorstin, *The Americans: The National Experience* (New York: Vintage-Random, 1965), 127.

I have gained additional insight into the psychology and force of the Scotch-Irish and other European settlers pushing down from Virginia into eastern Tennessee from Rodger Cunningham, *Apples on the Flood: Minority Discourse and Appalachia* (Knoxville: U of Tennessee P, 1987), 60–95.

An excellent recent book by Dan L. Morrill, *Southern Campaigns of the American Revolution* (Baltimore: Nautical & Aviation: 1993) provides background for Micajah Frost's participation in the Battle of Kings Mountain (101–12). For a concise account of this crucial encounter, see Wilma Dykeman, *With Fire and Sword: The Battle of Kings Mountain* (Washington, D.C.: National Park Service, 1978). A detailed retelling of this event is in Hank Messick, *King's Mountain: The Epic of the Blue Ridge "Mountain Men" in the American Revolution* (Boston: Little, Brown, 1976), 123–66.

The importance of land speculator Stockley Donelson is in Roberts, *Story,* 4:6–15. Roberts writes about the treaty problems in *Roots,* 21–23, 55–59. For more information on early settlers, see my article "Claxton Was Site of County's First White Settlement," *Oak Ridger,* June 25, 1968: 1+, based on interviews with Ivy Gault, Lacie Blevins, and Snyder Roberts in Claxton, Tennessee, June 1968. Also see Seeber, *History,* 10–17, 26. The quoted description of early Knoxville is from Federal Writers, *Tennessee,* 235, as is the information on the outlaw Harpe Brothers, 235–36.

The quotation from Andrew Jackson about Colonel Thomas Butler is in Michael P. Rogin, *Fathers and Children: Andrew Jackson and the Subjugation of the American Indian* (New York: Knopf, 1975), 136. Roberts quotes in *Roots,* p. 22, what Washington Irving reported that Colonel Butler said on his deathbed.

Chapter 2. Mr. Frost's New Eden

At age seventy-five Jasper Smith started writing his short articles on local history going back to 1795 for the four-page weekly *Anderson County News.* He was easily distracted from whatever plan he may have had, often interrupting his narrative to retell Bible stories or to denounce the evils of modern life. Jasper's own description of himself is in his article "Early Settlers," Jan. 18, 1930: 1. The late W. Herbert Smith's recollections of his grandfather were told me in an interview in Loudon, Tennessee, on November 28, 1992.

Beginning his newspaper history in 1924, Jasper had few firm dates and was not always consistent with those. After two years, he had written most of what he remembered but continued to produce articles until his death in 1932, adding information that he later recalled. The result is often as confusing as a jigsaw puzzle but fascinating in its details. Clifford R. Seeber, whose 1928 master's thesis on county history is still used as a reference work, once told me that Jasper Smith was a "kindly old gentleman who loved stories of the past" but made clear that he would not rely on Jasper's accuracy (telephone interview, Dec. 1969).

Although Jasper Smith's history may be nearly as much folklore as fact, it gives a picture of early life in an isolated part of the Tennessee Cumberlands, a record of people most of whom could neither read nor write. As John Mack Faragher says in the introduction to his masterful biography *Daniel Boone: The Life and Legend of an American Pioneer* (New York: Holt, 1992, xvi), many stories are "simply too good to ignore." Faragher contends that what people on the frontier told about Boone, whether true or not, reveals what they themselves and their lives were like.

Of the 167 articles by Jasper Smith that I have recently located on microfilm of the *Anderson County News,* I often had to use bits and pieces to reconstruct life in Frost Bottom starting about 1795. Some of these articles had been given me in June 1968 by his son John T. Smith during my interviews with Uncle John in Oliver Springs for my five-part series on Frost Bottom published by the *Oak Ridger* entitled "Unto These Hills." See the first in this series, "1st Settlers Went Into Frost Bottom About 1795," June 24, 1968: 1+.

An example of how I have combined details from Jasper's various articles is the story of how he came to start writing his "Frost Bottom History" (FBH). The main narrative comes from his first article (FBH, Apr. 12, 1924: 3).

However, his memories of Frost Bottom as "almost a heaven" before the Civil War come from "Clinton History," March 21, 1925: 3. His longing for the time when the soil and life there were good comes from another year (FBH, Feb. 6, 1926: 3). All the references to Jasper's writing in these bibliographic notes are to his articles in the *Anderson County News,* the source of his directly quoted words throughout my text. References are usually in the order in which they appear in each chapter.

Jasper writes of Micajah Frost's arrival in Frost Bottom (FBH, Apr. 19, 1924: 2), making clear Jasper's ambivalent attitude on the Cherokees and the supposed superiority of the white race in two other widely spaced articles (FBH, Aug. 30, 1924: 1, and "Early Settlers," Aug. 13, 1927: 4).

The tale of Benjamin Duncan and William Brown and George Washington is recounted in two articles (FBH, June 28, 1924: 3, and "A Long Time Ago," June 15, 1929: 1). The story of John Seiber that Uncle John told me on our trip to Frost Bottom is given in more detail by Jasper ("What Is Life?" July 4, 1925: 3). During that visit in June 1968, I talked with Sally Duncan.

Uncle John wrote the story of his paternal great-grandfather, Henry Wilson Smith, in his unpublished "A History Book of the Unknown Secret," given me for the second article in my Frost Bottom series. See "Duncans, Browns Were Frost Bottom Pioneers," June 25, 1968: 1+. Years later he sent me in North Carolina his long unpublished ballad "Clinton Murder."

Jasper Smith writes of his grandfather Henry and of his father William's early life in three FBH articles (Aug. 1, 1925: 2; Aug. 8, 1925: 2; and Aug. 29, 1925: 3).

Marjorie Duncan Byrd's *Duncan Descendants of Frost Bottom, TN.* (Harriman, Tenn.: 1995) provides much of the information on three of Benjamin's children who populated much of Frost Bottom: Elizabeth Duncan Brown, Juanna (Judy or Juda) Duncan, and Moses M. Duncan. My interview with the late Dixie Duncan Graves in Dutch Valley, Tennessee (Aug. 3, 1994) revealed the "problem" of Judy Duncan's having had twelve children without a husband, something never mentioned by Jasper Smith. My speculations on this unusual situation are based in part on John D'Emilio, *Intimate Matters: A History of Sexuality in America* (New York: Harper, 1988), 3–73. Snyder Roberts writes about Micajah Frost as a preacher in *Descendants,* 126.

Jasper recreates the arrival about the end of the 1700s of the Duncans and other early settlers and their lives in a number of FBH articles including Apr. 19, 1924: 2; Sept. 13, 1924: 1; May 10, 1924: 3; Feb. 13, 1926: 4; July 18, 1925: 2; and Aug. 3, 1929: 1. His description of whiskey drinking (FBH, Aug. 9, 1924: 3) is an example of the situation at that time in America. See W. J. Rorabaugh, *The Alcoholic Republic* (New York: Oxford UP, 1980), 8, 15.

For early days in Clinton, see Seeber, *History,* 40. Also see Katherine Baker

Hoskins, *Anderson County Historical Sketches* (Clinton, Tenn.: *Courier-News,* 1987), 176, and Corlew, *Tennessee,* 163.

The presidential inauguration festivities for Andrew Jackson are described in Dannye Romine Powell, "In 1829, They Had a Real Blast," *Charlotte Observer,* Jan. 20, 1993, metro final ed.: 1C. Jasper writes of the 1829 Frost Bottom wedding festivities in "The Early Settlers," Jan. 18, 1930: 1. The Frost family at the time of the wedding is in Roberts, *Descendants,* 33–34, 38–43, 53, 179.

Uncle John told me about the contest between the two Moses in an interview for the third article in my Frost Bottom series. See "Uncle John Retells Famous Shooting Match," *Oak Ridger,* June 26, 1968: 1+.

Chapter 3. The Duncans, the Smiths, and Old Lucifer

Jasper Smith's account of his father William's several moves from Frost Bottom back to North Carolina is chronologically confusing. Nevertheless, these trips through the Smokies are vividly pictured. See these FBH articles: Aug. 8, 1925: 2; Aug. 1, 1925: 2; Sept. 6, 1924: 2; Aug. 15, 1925: 2; Aug. 29, 1925: 3; Oct. 17, 1925: 3; and Aug. 23, 1924: 1.

The life of William Smith's family in Frost Bottom's Stony Flat is described in the following articles: FBH, Aug. 1, 1925: 2; "Then and Now," July 31, 1926: 4; FBH, Oct. 10, 1925: 2; "New River Settlers," Oct. 15, 1927: 2; "The Early Settlers," Jan. 18, 1930: 1; and FBH, Sept. 26, 1925: 2.

Jasper's love of the Cumberlands (FBH, Nov. 8, 1924: 3) fits John Calvin's picture of Creation as good, a picture discussed in Cunningham, *Apples,* 91–92.

William is shown to be not only a successful farmer but a shrewd trader in "The Gun and Dog," Dec. 8, 1928: 3; FBH, Sept. 26, 1925: 2; and "The Early Settlers," Jan. 18, 1930: 1.

Early church meetings in Frost Bottom are described in FBH, Oct. 24, 1925: 3, and Aug. 9, 1924: 3. For churches in general, see Malcolm J. Rohrbough, *The Trans-Appalachian Frontier: People, Societies, and Institutions, 1775–1850* (New York: Oxford UP, 1978), 144–52. Comparing Frost Bottom's early worshippers to his contemporary fellow Methodists, Jasper is quite disparaging in "Donovan News," Apr. 16, 1927, 4.

William Smith prospered in Stony Flat but even more so after he moved to a better farm in 1853 nearer Clinton at Laurel and also went into business in the county seat. See FBH, Nov. 7, 1925 (supplement): 1; "Then and Now," July 31, 1926: 4; and FBH, Nov. 14, 1925: 2. Jasper's memory of the trading trip is in FBH, Mar. 27, 1926: 3.

William's approximate worth in today's dollars has been calculated, as have all the other prices in this book, using John J. McCusker, "How Much Is That in Real Money? A Historical Price Index for Use as a Deflator of Money Values in the Economy of the United States," *Proceedings of the American Antiquarian Society* 101, pt. 2 (1992): 297–373.

The 1850s railroad boom in Clinton and the prominence of John Jarnigan are found in Hoskins, *Anderson,* 106, 121–22. See my article on Jarnigan's mansion, "Clinton Board Asked to 'Save This House,'" *Oak Ridger,* June 9, 1968: 1+. William's financial ruin in the railroad panic is in FBH, Nov. 14, 1925: 2.

Nearly thirteen years old when the Civil War began, Jasper brought his own memories to the stories of this conflict. He begins, however, with a re-telling of how that first rebel, as he calls Lucifer, fell from heaven. See "Se-cession," Apr. 13, 1929: 1; FBH, Nov. 1, 1924: 2; "The New Eden," Dec. 13, 1924: 3; and "Clinton History," May 23, 1925: 2.

Background on Tennessee in the Civil War is in Mary Beth Norton, *A People and a Nation: A History of the United States,* 3d ed., vol. 1 (Boston: Houghton, 1990), 403–4. Also see Federal Writers, *Tennessee,* 399; Seeber, *History,* 63; and James Overholt, *Anderson County, Tennessee: A Pictorial History* (Norfolk, Va.: Donning, 1989), 25–26.

Just after the election of Lincoln before the war started, Jasper tells of being with his father at the big Clinton rally ("The Houk Family," Mar. 24, 1928: 1). Soon afterward Anderson County, which had few slaves, voted against secession. See Seeber, *History,* 62; Hoskins, *Anderson,* 408; and Norton, *People,* 395. The county had an unusual freed slave, John Tate (Hoskins, *Anderson,* 13, 213), about whom Jasper writes several times ("History of Houk Fam-ily," Jan. 10, 1925: 2; "Clinton History," Mar. 21, 1925: 3; and "Four Score Years Ago," Oct. 13, 1928: 1).

For the first days of the war in East Tennessee, see Corlew, *Tennessee,* 318–19; Overholt, *Pictorial,* 30; and Seeber, *History,* 65. Jasper writes of these days in "Clinton History," Apr. 11, 1925: 2.

Just as Jasper omits Judy Duncan from his writing, he never explains that a slave owned by Moses Duncan ("Clinton History," June 13, 1925: 2) was purchased by his father William in 1846 (Anderson County, Tenn., *Register's Records, 1802–1884,* Deed book L-1: 444). Jasper did not approve of slavery ("Clinton History," Apr. 18, 1925: 4), but he was bothered by the question of racial superiority ("Winters's Gap History," Sept. 11, 1926: 2).

When the Confederates first moved into East Tennessee, William Smith had started over on a new farm in Dutch Valley following the railroad panic. See Seeber, *History,* 66–67, on Union sympathizers. Jasper writes of their at-tempts to escape through the Cumberlands in FBH, Nov. 21, 1925: 2, and in FBH, Oct. 18, 1924: 1. He describes the murders of Philip Seiber and Wil-son Duncan in "Clinton History: War of 1861," May 2, 1925: 3; FBH, Oct. 18, 1924: 1; FBH, Oct. 25, 1924: 3; and "Clinton History," June 13, 1925: 2.

For information on Wilson Duncan, see Byrd, *Duncan,* 322. Also see Seeber, *History,* 64, in addition to Seeber's letters to me (Aug. 16, 1968, and Dec. 17, 1969) and my follow-up telephone interview in December 1969.

Jasper tells of the local guerrilla war between the Confederate and Union home guards. See "Clinton History," May 23, 1925: 2; FBH, Jan. 9, 1926: 2; and "Clinton: War of 1862," June 6, 1925: 2.

Snyder Roberts, in a telephone interview (Jan. 10, 1993), told me the story of Devil Tom Duncan after the Civil War. He writes about Captain Mims's skirmish in Frost Bottom in *Story,* 3:97–98. Uncle John gave me his more flamboyant version during my visit to Oliver Springs on October 31, 1975.

Jasper Smith's seeing General Zollicoffer's army is in FBH, Nov. 28, 1925: 2. Anderson County's devastation is in Seeber, *History,* 68–69; Overholt, *Pictorial,* 25; and FBH, Oct. 10, 1925: 2.

General Wheeler's raid is described in Roberts, *Story,* 3:100, and in Jasper's recollections ("Dutch Valley Settlers," Nov. 9, 1929: 1; and "Civil War Echo," June 4, 1927: 1). Jasper's story of the slave George is in "Educating a Negro," May 28, 1927: 1.

I wrote about some of these Civil War incidents in the fourth article of my Frost Bottom series ("Walden's Ridge Divided Union and Rebels," *Oak Ridger,* June 27, 1968: 1+). It was based on the limited number of Jasper's articles given me by Uncle John in 1968.

Chapter 4. Two More Moses and a Wily Scot

For an account of the 1967 flash flood that introduced me to Oliver Springs, see the news article I helped report, "Deluge Floods Ridge, Oliver Springs," *Oak Ridger,* July 12, 1967: 1+.

Much of the information on the settling of this town is from Roberts, *The Story of Oliver Springs, Tennessee, and Its People.* All references to Roberts's writing in this and the following two chapters are to the four volumes of this work. Moses Winters and his son Moses C. are discussed in volume 4, pp. 76–94.

Uncle John Smith's recollections of the role of Moses Winters in the earliest local coal mining and, later, that of Henry Howard Wiley are in the fifth article of my Frost Bottom series, "Unto These Hills." See "McCoy Ambush Murder Roused Whole County," *Oak Ridger,* June 28, 1968: 1+.

The Tennessee Valley Authority's plan to revitalize Oliver Springs is outlined in my article "Oliver Springs Aldermen All for 'Model City' Plan," *Oak Ridger,* July 12, 1968: 1+. What the TVA flood control changes would mean to the original center of the town is told in my article "Death of Main Street Is Coming After 200 Years," *Oak Ridger,* June 25, 1969: 1+. This article was based on my interviews in June 1969 in Oliver Springs, Tennessee, with

Snyder Roberts and with Main Street residents including Annie Smith Giles, Bob and Maggie Wright, and Albert Mead.

Roberts's quoted description of the elder Winters is in volume 4, p. 80, in connection with the chastity case. The importance of county courts in the first decades of the century is made clear in Rohrbough, *Trans-Appalachian*, 52–54. See the case of Isaac Crane in *Goodspeed's History of East Tennessee*, 1886–87 (Nashville: Charles and Randy Elder, 1972), 838.

Roberts tells the stories about Moses C. Winters in volume 4, pp. 82–94, the quoted description of Dr. Estabrook being on p. 120.

Information on the Olivers is in Roberts, 4:54–75. Henry Howard Wiley, one of the outstanding men in Anderson County history, is written about in the same volume, pp. 106–19. Wiley was an excellent example of the successful collector of land titles described in Rohrbough, *Trans-Appalachian*, 54–55, a worthy successor to the earliest land speculators (Corlew, *Tennessee*, 133–35).

The economic devastation in Anderson County following the Civil War was alleviated somewhat by the arrival of the railroad in Coal Creek in 1869 and the opening there of a number of coal mines (Hoskins, *Anderson*, 122). See Ronald Eller, *Miners, Millhands, and Mountaineers: Industrialization of the Appalachian South, 1880–1930* (Knoxville: U of Tennessee P, 1982), 128–60.

The North's head start in industrialization before the Civil War is in Thomas Cochran, *The Age of Enterprise: A Social History of Industrial America* (New York: Harper, 1961), 52–83, 144–46. The exploits of J. P. Morgan are from Robert Lloyd Kelley, *The Shaping of the American Past,* 5th ed. (Englewood Cliffs, N.J.: Prentice-Hall, 1990), 508, as is his quotation on p. 410 from John D. Rockefeller. My picture of Henry Wiley as a true descendant of John Calvin partly grew out of a reading of R. H. Tawney, *Religion and the Rise of Capitalism: A Historical Study,* 1926 (Gloucester, Mass.: Peter Smith, 1962), 102–32, 227–53.

Eller, *Miners,* 39–85, gives an excellent overall view of land acquisition and formation of land companies. For a history of the Wiley family's land companies, see Hoskins, *Anderson*, 220–21. Also see Roberts, volume 4, pp. 112–14. The importance of the Wileys' associate Colonel John Scott is in Roberts's volume 2, p. 162. It is of interest how both Roberts and Hoskins completely avoid discussion of the negative aspects of these large land companies.

For information on the Lively family and the Wiley land companies, see Roberts, 2:102–3, 116–17. Also see Trish Lively Cox, *301 Years of Livelys, 1690–1991* (Oak Ridge, Tenn.: 1992), 1–8; 16–30. My telephone interview with her on April 8, 1995, provided more information. The telephone conversations I had with Fred Wyatt of Coal Creek Mining and Manufacturing Company about the Livelys were July 19, 1995, and July 20, 1995.

Jasper Smith's comment on land companies in general is in "Frost Bottom History," *Anderson County News,* Sept. 13, 1924: 1.

Chapter 5. Mineral Waters Plus Black Gold

The prominence of the Knoxville Iron Company just after the Civil War, and the role of Joseph C. Richards, is in Roberts, 2:14 and 4:137–38. Conditions in Knoxville are described in Federal Writers, *Tennessee,* 236–37. Knoxville's need for coal is in Hoskins, *Anderson,* 51.

Recollections about the Richards family's Oliver Springs Hotel are from my interview with Mary Richards Sienknecht in Oliver Springs, Tennessee, March 1968. They are the basis of my article "Lavish Resort Hotel Brought Turn of Century Swells to Oliver Springs," *Oak Ridger,* Mar. 13, 1968: 1+.

My picture of Oliver Springs in 1881 is made up of details from Roberts as noted: the Baptist Church (2:3); Colonial Hall (3:122); and Alex Allen's house (2:30–33). The coming of the railroad in 1883 and the coal boom are described in Roberts, 2:56, 163, 187, and 4:142–43.

In addition to my interview with Mrs. Sienknecht, details about the Oliver Springs Hotel are in Roberts, 2:14, 18–19, 165, and in the promotional booklet *Oliver Springs Season 1900* (Oliver Springs, Tenn.: Oliver Springs Hotel, 1899), 6, 10–12. Information on the Richards mansion is in Roberts, 4:139, and in Hoskins, *Anderson,* 103–4. Roberts's humorous stories about the hotel are from volume 2, pp. 15–16, 20–21.

Another picture of Oliver Springs at the turn of the century is in Uncle John's "history" of the victory parade for President William McKinley, an unpublished story he sent me in 1974 after I left Tennessee. More about J. J. Williams is in Roberts, 3:14.

My interview with Church Lively in Oliver Springs, Tennessee, in December 1968 was the basis for my article on him, "Meet Brother Church W. Lively, 91: Born on Mountain, Spanish-American Vet, Still Smasher," *Oak Ridger,* Dec. 18, 1968: 1+. Roberts writes of Harvey Hannah in volume 3, pp. 1–8, while Uncle John's stories about the Spanish-American War come from my interview with him in Oliver Springs, December 1968.

Oliver Springs's town marshals are described in Roberts, 4:194–97. Church Lively told me about his experiences as a lawman and a smasher of whiskey stills. However, the stories of the county's most famous moonshiner, Alex Bunch, come from Roberts, 3:33–38.

Chapter 6. Sienknechts and Doughboy Heroes

Charles Tichy described his restoration of the 1907 bank in my telephone interview with him November 19, 1994.

The history of the Sienknecht family is in Roberts, 3:126–33. Roberts's own memories of the Sienknecht department store are in volume 2, pp. 59–61. Details of new merchandise likely to have been found in the store are from Scott Derks, ed., *The Value of a Dollar: Prices and Incomes in the United States, 1860–1989* (Detroit: Gale Research, 1994). See Derks for women's clothing, p. 72; Jell-O and Hershey bars, p. 9; and Post Toasties, p. 59.

Roberts writes about Silas Hulen in volume 3, pp. 53–67.

My interviews with Elijah Vann and Snyder Roberts in Oliver Springs, Tennessee, in June 1969 are the basis for the Oliver Springs Bottling Works stories, which I included in the article "Death of Main Street." More details about the bottling process are in Roberts, 2:41–43.

Roberts describes the importance to Oliver Springs of the Southern Railway in volume 3, pp. 161–66, 169–85, 187–92. He gives many details of everyday life in Oliver Springs before World War I in volume 1, pp. 78, 84–90.

For the arrival of the county's first automobile and the growing use of these vehicles, see Hoskins, *Anderson,* 80–83, and Overholt, *Pictorial,* 74–77. The Oliver Springs women who were among the earliest owners are in Roberts, 3:125 and 2:37, as is the story of the first aviator to fly over Windrock Mountain (1:137).

Jasper Smith's quotation of Benjamin Duncan and William Brown about the American Revolution is in "Frost Bottom History," *Anderson County News,* July 5, 1924: 2. The story of Marshal William Potter, famous for cutting down the World War I whipping post, is in Roberts, 3:28–32 and 4:158–60, 195–97.

My interviews in Oliver Springs, Tennessee, in November 1969 with Walter Stripling and Snyder Roberts, along with my interview of Ben Diggs's sisters, provided the information for my article "Oliver Springs Recalls Two WWI Heroes," *Oak Ridger,* Nov. 11, 1969: 1+. When Roberts published *The Story of Oliver Springs,* he wrote in volume 3 about Diggs (pp. 111–15) and Stripling (pp. 116–19).

The story of how World War I doughboys got their name is from Jack Betts, "This Time and Place: Death of a Doughboy," *Charlotte Observer,* Oct. 16, 1993, metro final ed.: 16A. The statistics from the First World War are from "Casualities in Principal Wars of the U.S.," *The World Almanac,* 1998 ed., 161.

The four triumphant returns to Knoxville of various units of the Thirtieth Division after the war are described in the city's *Journal & Tribune.* The climax came with the arrival of Ben Diggs and the 117th Infantry ("Knoxville Receives Hindenburg Line Breakers with Unprecedented Acclaim: Veterans of 117th March in Triumph Before Huge Crowd," Apr. 6, 1919: 1+). Earlier parades were held for the 114th Machine Gun Battalion ("Thirtieth Fighting Men Loyally Received by Shouting Thousands," Mar. 28, 1919: 1+); for the 114th Field Artillery ("30,000 Knoxvillians Greet Heroes of the 114th Artillery," Mar. 30, 1919: 1+); and for the 115th Field Artillery ("115th Field Artillery Given Great Welcome as They March on Gay Street in Drizzling Rain," Apr. 5, 1919: 1+). Welcoming festivities along the train's route and in Knoxville are described in "Journey Homeward Proves One Continuous Ovation," Apr. 6, 1919: 3. The quotation from the speech of Harvey Hannah is in "'It Was a Great Day,' Says General Hannah," Apr. 6, 1919: 4.

Chapter 7. Splendid Seclusion

For information on the timber boom in the New River Valley, see Marshall McGhee and Melba Jackson, *Caryville Through the Years* (Jacksboro, Tenn.: 1988), 119–20. Additional details are in Seeber, *History,* 100, and in Hoskins, *Anderson,* 79, 192, 293, 320–21.

The quotation about Clinton's self-importance is from the Graves interview. An example of New River's "bad press" is the newspaper article about the photograph of the Daugherty coffins, "Photo Presents Reminder of 1920's 'Ambush,'" *Appalachian Observer* [Clinton, Tenn.], Mar. 28, 1984: 3. Another is Snyder Roberts's story about eye gouging in *Story,* 3:104.

Jasper Smith writes about Isaac Phillips in "New River Settlers," *Anderson County News,* Oct. 1, 1927: 2. This information first appeared in the second of my 1968 series on New River entitled "Shangri-La of Anderson County." This article is "Isaac Phillips Settled New River in 1812 Coming from N. Carolina," *Oak Ridger,* Aug. 14, 1968: 1+.

Much of the information on the Phillips family came from Nancy Phillips Patty in a telephone interview with her on October 16, 1994, and from a personal interview in Clinton, Tennessee, November 4, 1995. The quotation about Little Isaac Phillips is from her book published with Effie Bunch Ward, *Ligas Fork: A Journey Back in Time and Surrounding Areas, 1794–1992,* 115.

Background on Brushy Mountain State Penitentiary is in A. C. Hutson Jr., "The Overthrow of the Convict Lease System in Tennessee," *East Tennessee Historical Society's Publications* 8 (1936): 82–103. The 1959 rebellion in the prison is covered in the following two articles in the *New York Times:* "Convicts in Mine End Their Revolt," July 15, 1959, late city ed.: A61; and "Booby Traps in Mine," July 16, 1959, late city ed.: A27.

The history of State Highway 116 is from my telephone interviews with state engineer Jerry Morehead (Oct. 18, 1994, and Oct. 19, 1994) and with Lewis Coker in New River, Tennessee (Aug. 1968). This interview with Coker is the basis of the first article in my New River series, "New Mine, Community Spirit Rejuvenate New River," *Oak Ridger,* Aug. 13, 1968: 1+. Also see this article for my description of this valley. All quotations in this and the following chapter from New River residents originally appeared in this 1968 series.

Information about the Moore Coal Company is in Hoskins, *Anderson,* 240–

42, and in D. C. Richards, "Trip to New River," *Anderson County News,* Apr. 30, 1927: 1+.

The crucial role of the land companies in the Cumberland Mountains section of Anderson County is in Mary Smyser, "Who Owns the Cumberlands: 3 Big Firms; Stockholders Overlap," *Oak Ridger,* Mar. 25, 1971: 1+.

The conversion of the coal company commissary into a community center is described in my third article of the New River series, "Old Commissary Becoming Center," *Oak Ridger,* Aug. 15, 1968: 1+. This was based on my interviews at Rosedale in New River with Dorothy Armes and Arnold Groff in August 1968. The mine cave-in story is in "Mine Yields Body; Two Still Trapped," *Knoxville News-Sentinel,* June 25, 1961, home ed.: A1+.

Chapter 8. Like Mangy Dogs

Background on the United Mine Workers of America is found in John W. Hevener, *Which Side Are You On? The Harlan County Coal Miners, 1931–39* (Urbana: U of Illinois P., 1978), and in Trevor Armbrister, *Act of Vengeance: The Yablonski Murders and Their Solution* (New York: Saturday Review-Dutton, 1975). The quotation from John L. Lewis is in Joseph G. Rayback's article on the labor leader in *Encylopedia Americana,* 1987 ed., p. 196.

Information about the late Roy E. Brown has come from his widow, Lavada Brown, whom I interviewed in Frost Bottom, Tennessee, on March 30, 1991. My earlier interview of Roy Brown in Frost Bottom in March 1968 was shortly before the UMW rally at Rosedale School in New River. Typical of his stories about the so-called Jones Boys is the one that Armbrister tells in *Act,* p. 82.

My interview with William Turnblazer Jr. was at Rosedale School immediately before the union rally on April 1, 1968. It first appeared in my article "Mine Union Officials Plan Area Organizing Drive," *Oak Ridger,* Apr. 2, 1968: 1+. All the quotations from the rally originally appeared in this article.

The importance of the UMW's George Titler in organizing Harlan County is in Hevener, *Which Side,* 151–72.

Information on Jock Yablonski and the situation leading to his murder and that of his wife and daughter comes from Armbrister, *Act,* 35–62, 75–76, 144–52. The conviction of Albert Pass is in "Ex-Aide Convicted in Yablonski Case," *Charlotte Observer,* June 20, 1973, final ed.: 3A. Turnblazer's confession and implication of Tony Boyle is in "Boyle Charged in Murder after Ex-Aide Names Him," *Charlotte Observer,* Sept. 7, 1973, final ed.: 1A+. The outcome of the Boyle case is covered in "Jury Finds Boyle Guilty of Murder," *Charlotte Observer,* Apr. 12, 1974, final ed.: 1A+. Also see Wolfgang Saxon, "W. A. Boyle Dies; Led Miners' Union," *New York Times,* June 1, 1985, late city ed.: 29.

Armbrister, in *Act,* 331–34, discusses Turnblazer's parole. The current status of Albert Pass was verified in a telephone interview with Susan McNaughton, Pennsylvania Department of Corrections, on November 12, 1997. Information on union leader Trumka is in "Trumka, Richard L(ouis)," *Current Biography Yearbook,* 1989 ed., 565.

Early violence between strip miners and deep miners in Anderson County was reported by the *Clinton Courier-News.* See "Mine Operator and Employees Are Assaulted," July 21, 1949: sec. 1, p. 1; and "Strip Miners Wounded by Ambushers," July 28, 1949: sec. 1, p. 1.

Frank H. T. Rhodes's conveniently small *Fossils: A Guide to Prehistoric Life* (New York: Golden Press, 1962) was in my pocket and those of many other Oak Ridge amateurs looking for fossils in the abandoned strip mines. The geology of Anderson County's mountainous section is described in Hoskins, *Anderson,* 328, and in Roberts, *Story,* 2:115.

David McCullough called Harry Caudill a mixture of John Muir, Mark Twain, and Don Quixote in *Brave Companions: Portraits in History* (New York: Touchstone-Simon, 1992), 152. For Caudill's speech at Berea College, see my article "Scientists Form for Appalachia," *Oak Ridger,* Apr. 27, 1970: 1+. Information on the "broad-form deed" is in Caudill's *Night Comes to the Cumberlands: A Biography of a Depressed Area* (Boston: Atlantic Monthly-Little, 1962), 74–75. The controversial Anderson County land agent Lucien Bird is described in Overholt, *Pictorial,* 41, and Hoskins, *Anderson,* 192, 319.

My article "Whether Law Working or Not, Strip Mines Still Worry Residents," *Oak Ridger,* Feb. 19, 1969: 1+, was based on my trip to New River on February 14, 1969, and on interviews at that time with John Seiber, Bob Lefler, and F. G. Watkins. The following day I interviewed John Henley in Oliver Springs, Tennessee, and also did follow-up telephone interviews with Seiber and Lefler. All the quotations from these people first appeared in the newspaper article.

The quotation from Harry Caudill on dynamite is from McCullough, *Brave Companions,* 152.

Chapter 9. On Pilot Mountain with Byrd Duncan

The description of New River in the fall is based on my article "Who Needs the Smokies for Color?" *Oak Ridger,* Oct. 24, 1969: 1+, and on visits there in recent years.

Interviews with Byrd Duncan and his wife Laura in Duncan Flats, Tennessee, in April 1969, along with my visit to the Free Communion Baptist Church in New River, furnished information for my article "He Keeps Nearby Hills Alive with Gospel Music and Boy Scout Activity," *Oak Ridger,* Apr. 9, 1969: 1+. All the quotations from the residents come from this article.

See Seeber, *History,* 2, on the formation of mountain "flats." Evolution of the singing convention is in Jim Stokely and Jeff D. Johnson, eds., *An Encyclopedia of East Tennessee* (Oak Ridge, Tenn.: Children's Museum of Oak Ridge, 1981), 366–67. For information on Anderson County's oldest church see my article "Claxton Was Site of County's First White Settlement," *Oak Ridger,* Sept. 25, 1968: 1+.

Chapter 10. The Return of Hiram Braden's Offspring

I visited Braden Flats, Tennessee, in September 1969. Interviews at that time with Nancy Braden Byrge, her husband, Pearley, and her brother Edd provided information for my article "A Braden Always Comes Back to 'The Mountain,'" *Oak Ridger,* Sept. 17, 1969: 1+. Also important was the interview at the same time with Beulah Brummett Braden, as well as unpublished genealogical research materials she furnished me. Background on the Revolutionary battle at Ramsour's Mill is in Morrill, *Southern Campaigns,* 75–84.

The story of the hanging of Jake Harness told me by Beulah Braden is substantiated by a number of sources, including two official Anderson County volumes: *Circuit Court Record Book, 1873–1879,* 409–10, and *Circuit Court Execution Docket, 1869–1878,* 499.

Hoskins, in *Anderson,* writes of the hanging on p. 346. Jasper Smith also comments on it in "Frost Bottom History," *Anderson County News,* Sept. 22, 1928: 4.

My interview with Mary Harris in Clinton, Tennessee, Aug. 2, 1994, and my telephone interview with her on November 10, 1994, followed by her letter to me, November 16, 1994, helped clarify this case. Also important was my telephone interview with Gertrude Harness on January 8, 1995.

Chapter 11. The Coal Creek War

The town of Coal Creek's conversion to TVA-era Lake City is told in the Lake City Homecoming '86 Committee's *Coal Creek/Lake City: Visions of the Past* (1986), 39. The old name had been associated for years with the miners' Coal Creek War, which had all of Tennessee in a turmoil in 1891–1892. Uncle John first told me about this conflict when I interviewed him in Oliver Springs, Tennessee, in May 1968 for two articles about Coal Creek, one on the "war" and another on the deadly mine explosions that followed soon after. I also interviewed Ernest Hill and his wife Daisy in Fraterville at that time for both articles.

The story of George Young is in Seeber, *History,* 30, and the attempts to improve transportation in Hoskins, *Anderson,* 79, 121–22, 220–21. Details on the Knoxville Iron Company are in Hoskins, *Anderson,* 51; Corlew, *Tennessee,* 365; in Roberts, *Story,* 4:137–38.

Coal-mining conditions in Great Britain are described in Priscilla Long,

Where the Sun Never Shines: A History of America's Bloody Coal Industry (New York: Paragon, 1989), 6–19.

Details on the boom in Coal Creek come from Lake City, *Coal Creek,* 9–10; Seeber, *History,* 80–81; and Hoskins, *Anderson,* 179.

U.S. labor problems in the nineteenth century are discussed in Joseph G. Rayback, *A History of American Labor: Expanded and Updated* (New York: Macmillan, 1966), 132–37, 142–63. The opinion that unions were conspiracies is in Cochran, *Age of Enterprise,* 24. The manufacturer's statement on work hours is in Daniel T. Rodgers, *The Work Ethic in Industrial America, 1850–1920* (Chicago: U of Chicago P, 1978), 105. This book gives an excellent overview of society's attitudes toward work (pp. 1–29, 153–60), along with the position of the Knights of Labor (pp. 174–81).

The prominence of Herbert Spencer's thinking after the Civil War is in Cochran, *Age of Enterprise,* 124–28, and in Kelley, *Shaping of the American Past,* 380–82. Good discussions are also in Richard Hofstadter, *Social Darwinism in American Thought* (Boston: Beacon, 1992), 31–51, and in Robert C. Bannister, *Social Darwinism: Science and Myth in Anglo-American Social Thought* (Philadelphia: Temple UP, 1979), 34–56.

Coal Creek's early Welsh community is discussed in Gene White, *Briceville Through the Years* (Jacksboro, Tenn.: 1994), 36. Details on the coal boom are from Seeber, *History,* 80, 95; Marshall McGhee and Gene White, *Briceville: The Town That Coal Built* (Jackboro, Tenn.: 1991), 56; Lake City, *Coal Creek,* 12–13; and Hoskins, *Anderson,* 349.

I interviewed Laura Kesterson in Lake City, Tennessee, in June 1968 for my article "Miners Battle Convict Labor Plan," *Oak Ridger,* June 18, 1968: 1+.

The situation with the Knights of Labor and the American Federation of Labor when Eugene Merrill appeared in Coal Creek is in Kelley, *Shaping of the American Past,* 410–11. The saturation of the county coal market at that time is in Seeber, *History,* 81.

More background on the Coal Creek War is from A. C. Hutson Jr., "The Coal Miners' Insurrection of 1891 in Anderson County, Tennessee," *East Tennessee Historical Society's Publications* 7 (1935): 103–21. See pp. 104–5. Also see Corlew, *Tennessee,* 387–89. The low cost of convict labor is in White, *Briceville,* 114.

The miners' demand for their own check weighman is in Hutson, "Coal," 106–7. Commissary prices are from McGhee, *Briceville,* 8.

The first freeing of the convicts by the miners and the governor's reaction are from McGhee, *Briceville,* 28, and Hutson, "Coal," 108–9. The governor's claiming Andrew Jackson is from Corlew, *Tennessee,* 382, while his meeting with the miners at Thistle Switch is in Lake City, *Coal Creek,* 15–16. The quotations are from the more detailed account in Hutson, "Coal," 109–10.

Reactions from across the state are found in Hutson, "Coal," 110–15, including the quotation from the *Knoxville Journal,* on p. 115. The *Clinton Gazette's* quoted opinion is in its news article "The Briceville Affair: Latest from the Seat of Mining Troubles," July 23, 1891: 5. The quotation from the *Louisville Times* is in McGhee, *Briceville,* 30.

Governor Buchanan's return to Knoxville is in Hutson, "Coal," 115–17, and the quotation from the university chancellor is on p. 117. The subsequent actions of the state legislature are on pp. 82–86 in A. C. Hutson Jr., "The Overthrow of the Convict Lease System in Tennessee," *East Tennessee Historical Society's Publications* 8 (1936): 82–103.

The burning of the two convict stockades is in Hutson, "Overthrow," 87–90. More details are in "The Convicts at Briceville and Coal Creek Released by the Miners," *Clinton Gazette,* Nov. 5, 1891: 1+, including the quotation on the prisoners discarding their clothes. The arrival of Captain Anderson and fortification of Militia Hill are from Hoskins, *Anderson,* 74, and Lake City, *Coal Creek,* 19.

My interview with Wrease Daniels in Briceville, Tennessee, in June 1968 for my article "Miners Battle," provided his quoted remarks, as did my interviews with Mr. and Mrs. Hill and with Mrs. Kesterson.

The story of the hanging comes from Hutson, "Overthrow," 93. My interview with Dorsey Landrum in Briceville in June 1968 gave the story in his own words.

The second burning of the stockades in Coal Creek and in Oliver Springs is described in Hutson, "Overthrow," 93–95, and Lake City, *Coal Creek,* 20. The resulting arrival of General Carnes is from Hoskins, *Anderson,* 75. The conclusion of the war comes from Lake City, *Coal Creek,* 20–22, and Hutson, "Overthrow," 96–102, the quotation from the Knoxville *Journal* being on p. 100.

Chapter 12. Explosions Deep in the Mountain

Boom times in the Coal Creek Valley are described in Hoskins, *Anderson,* 250–52, 282. The dangers of coal mining and lack of regulations are in Long, *Where the Sun Never Shines,* 313–14, and in "Mine Accidents," *Anderson County News,* Nov. 16, 1912: 1. A good picture of life in a mining community is in Eller, *Miners,* 161–98, including a description of dangerous working conditions.

In Knoxville, the *Journal & Tribune* gave a sensational accounting of the 1902 Fraterville explosion in "Fraterville Mine at Coal Creek, the Tomb of 170; Not a Soul Lives to Tell the Tale of Explosion" (May 20, 1902: 1). The quotations are from that front-page story.

My interview with Ernest and Daisy Hill in Fraterville, Tennessee, in May 1968 provided information about the 1902 explosion as well as the 1911 disaster.

This interview was among a number I had with elderly residents of Briceville and Lake City for my article "184 Miners Died 66 Years Ago Sunday," *Oak Ridger,* May 17, 1968: 1+. They included Arthur Riggs, May Martin Carroll, Jim McCoy, William Stonecipher, C. I. Williams, and Mr. and Mrs. Lee Wilson. The quotations from them in this chapter are from this article.

The description of Fraterville Mine is in Vic Weals, "Old Miners Talked; Arthur Listened," *Knoxville Journal,* Feb. 21, 1980, city ed.: B1.

Use of child labor in county mines is detailed in Hoskins, *Anderson,* 201. The experience of spreading the news of the explosion was remembered vividly during my interviews by Hill, who was thirteen years old in 1902, and by Riggs, who was twelve at the time.

George Camp's statement following the Fraterville explosion is in "Mine Supt. Camp Makes a Statement," *Journal & Tribune* [Knoxville], May 20, 1902: 1. The state inspector's statement is also on the front page of that issue in the article "Interview with Inspector Shiflett."

The immediate results of the blast are described in Vic Weals, "No Profanity, Please, in Presence of Dead," *Knoxville Journal,* Feb. 7, 1980, city ed.: C1. Superintendent Camp's actions the day of the explosion come from Lee Winfrey, "Ex-Mine Operator Recalls Violent Days," *Knoxville News-Sentinel,* Aug. 30, 1959, home ed.: B10. Rescue operations are described in Vic Weals, "Francis Led Rescue Crew to Recover Miners' Bodies," *Knoxville Journal,* Jan. 31, 1980, city ed.: C1, including the quotations from Philip Francis. The growing need for coffins is in "Knoxville Called on for Many Coffins," *Journal & Tribune* [Knoxville], May 20, 1902: 1.

The memories of the funeral for thirty-five miners in the small Longfield church are from my interview with Arthur Riggs. The letters left by some of the miners are from the United Mine Workers' pamphlet "In Memory of Those Who Lost Their Lives in the Fraterville Mine Explosion and in the Cross Mountain Mine Explosion" (1940).

Mrs. Ernest Hill recalled the death of her father in my interview with her and her husband. The effect on some other families is from Vic Weals, "Mother Lost Five Sons in Fraterville Explosion," *Knoxville Journal,* Jan. 24, 1980, city ed.: C1. The outcome of lawsuits brought by survivors is in Hoskins, *Anderson,* 186; Lake City, *Coal Creek,* 25; and "Fraterville Settlement," *Clinton Gazette,* Mar. 28, 1903: 1. The quotation from the Ohio mine operator that miners are not forced to work is from Long, *Where the Sun Never Shines,* 47.

The growth of the United Mine Workers is described in Long, *Where the Sun Never Shines,* 151–65. The profitability of mining is in Eller, *Miners,* 128–32, 153–56.

The UMW's unsuccessful attempt in 1903–1904 to organize the Coal

Creek miners is in Hoskins, *Anderson,* 215–17, 394–95, and Seeber, *History,* 102–4. The quotation from George Camp is from Lee Winfrey, "Ex-Mine Operator." A description of the bloodshed in February 1904 is in Lake City, *Coal Creek,* 28–29. Laura Kesterson told of her brother-in-law's being killed in my interview with her in Lake City, Tennessee, in June 1968.

Gene White's memories of his miner father Horace are in McGhee, *Briceville,* 11–12, and White, *Briceville,* 103–4, 116. My telephone interviews with him on September 5, 1994, and February 18, 1995, added more information.

In my interviews in Briceville, Tennessee, in May 1968, Mae Martin Carroll told me the story of her husband Dan Martin's death in 1911 in the Cross Mountain Mine explosion. Jim McCoy recalled in great detail his taking part in the long rescue operations, as did William Stonecipher and C. I. Williams. The description of crowds waiting for ten days is from Vic Weals, "Mine Explosion Greatest Tragedy in Briceville, Scene of Bitter Strife," *Knoxville Journal,* Feb. 20, 1949, city ed.: D7.

The question of safety measures is discussed in Long, *Where the Sun Never Shines,* 46–47, and in "Cold, Dreary Rain Fell During the Entire Day on the Stricken Village," *Journal & Tribune* [Knoxville], Dec. 12, 1911: 2.

The Knoxville *Journal & Tribune* covered most of its front page with the rescue of the trapped miners under the huge headline "Imprisoned 60 Hours, Five Men Taken Alive from Cross Mt. Mine; Gloom Changed to Rejoicing as Men Restored to Families," Dec. 12, 1911: 1+. More information appeared on p. 2 in "Wild Demonstrations of Joy by Families of Rescued Men." Mae Carroll told me the story of her waiting with the wives.

The experiences of Lee Wilson and his wife Malinda come from my interview with them in Briceville, Tennessee, in May 1968.

Chapter 13. The L&N and the Railroad War

In August 1970 the *Oak Ridger* carried my ten-part informal history of the Louisville & Kentucky Railroad's branch line to Windrock entitled "Uncle John and the Cow Creek Branch." My trip with Uncle John to the L&N trestle in Oliver Springs is described in the first in that series, "A Saga from Dossett to Windrock," *Oak Ridger,* Aug. 12, 1970: 1+.

My interview with L&N superintendent John R. Neal in Knoxville, Tennessee, was the first of a dozen with people done for this series in July 1970, many on trips with Uncle John. All the quotations from them in this and the following chapter are from these interviews.

The history of the L&N from its founding in 1850 comes from John E. Tilford, "The Newcomen Address," unpublished manuscript, University Archives and Records Center, University of Kentucky, Feb. 1, 1951, 8–19.

Background on the extension of the main L&N line from Jellico to Knoxville is in Kincaid A. Herr, *The Louisville & Nashville Railroad, 1850–1963* (Louisville: L&N Railroad, 1964), 151–53.

My visit with Uncle John to Charlie Davis in Oliver Springs, Tennessee, is from the second series article, "Building the Dossett Tunnel," *Oak Ridger,* Aug. 13, 1970: 1+. Information about use of cocaine by construction crews is from Caudill, *Night,* 95. The story that Uncle John told me about finding the body of one of the black laborers is not in the series, but that of the dance at the work camp is in the second article.

Details about building the Dossett Tunnel are in Hoskins, *Anderson,* 206–7. My trip with Uncle John to the tunnel and his experiences working for the L&N come from the second article of my series.

The interviews in Marlow, Tennessee, with Lonas Long and with Ed Henderson were the basis of the third article, "The Powder Plant at Marlow," *Oak Ridger,* Aug. 14, 1970: 1+. Details about Marlow are in Hoskins, *Anderson,* 173–76. I used information given me and Uncle John by Mable Daugherty in Oliver Springs for the fourth article, "Tending Tanks on a Railroad Bike," *Oak Ridger,* Aug. 17, 1970: 1+.

Although the "Railroad War" over the L&N trestle built across the Southern Railway tracks is written about briefly in Herr, *Louisville,* 153, the exact date is not given. That was finally provided by a reader, Joseph L. Nichols, in a letter to me September 27, 1970, after the Windrock series was published.

Details about the actions of both railroads are from Charlie Davis and from Elmer Sienknecht in the fifth article, "The Brief but Lively 'Railroad War,'" *Oak Ridger,* Aug. 18, 1970: 1+. I interviewed Sienknecht in Knoxville, Tennessee, and received additional information from him in a letter dated July 10, 1970.

The social role of the trestle in later years in the community life of Oliver Springs is from Roberts, *Story,* 2:51–54. Uncle John's final comment on the "war" is in that volume on p. 51.

Chapter 14. On to Windrock Mine

Background on Windrock Mine comes from Roberts, *Story,* 2:116–17.

The early days of the Windrock area were remembered by Annie Smith Giles and O'Dell Lively during interviews with them on Windrock Road. They were the basis for the sixth article in the series, "Oldtimers Recall Colorful Station Names," *Oak Ridger,* Aug. 19, 1970: 1+.

My interview in Knoxville with Elmer Sienknecht provided much of the information for the seventh series article, "Windrock: Good Place to Work," *Oak Ridger,* Aug. 20, 1970: 1+. Additional details are from Roberts, *Story,* 2:126–27. Roy Brown told me about the company's helping miners during strikes when I interviewed him in Frost Bottom, Tennessee, in July 1970. That interview with Brown also provided information about postwar mechanization of the mine and his tearing down the commissary, used in the eighth article, "Windrock's Final Years," *Oak Ridger,* Aug. 21, 1970: 1+. Carl Keith gave me more details in an interview in Clinton, Tennessee, in July 1970.

The TVA's 1970 purchase of the L&N's right-of-way of the branch line from Oliver Springs to Windrock and the removal of the tracks is in Roberts, *Story,* 2:194.

The contemporary situation at Windrock Mine in July 1970 makes up the remaining two articles in the series, "Million and a Half Tons Still Left" (*Oak Ridger,* Aug. 24, 1970: 1+) and "Not Even a Woman Reporter Can Enter the Mine" (*Oak Ridger,* Aug. 25, 1970: 1+). Both are based on interviews at Upper Windrock with C. H. Smith and Curt Owens, owners of the Oliver Springs Mining Company, then operating Windrock Mine.

Shortly after my two visits on the mountain in July 1970, Uncle John told me how strongly he approved their not allowing me to go in the mine—his final word on Windrock.

Epilogue

What the mountainous section of Anderson County is like today has come from my personal interviews and follow-up telephone interviews in the last several years with thirty-one people, mostly in East Tennessee. I have not listed all the contacts, only the ones with significant information.

Extremely helpful to me in the beginning was Ray Leamon, long connected with the state's coal industry. A geologist who did the TVA's first studies on the environmental impact of strip mining starting in 1958, he later was with the Tennessee Department of the Environment until 1978. He now works as a coal consultant in areas like prospecting, most recently with Addington Enterprises. Leamon talked with me in Knoxville, Tennessee, on August 8, 1994, and then added more information in a letter dated September 23, 1994. I interviewed him by telephone on November 24, 1997.

The takeover of the L&N Railroad in 1980 by CSX Corporation was explained by Dick Bussard, CSX director of corporate communications, February 17, 1995, in a telephone interview.

When I attended the Windrock Reunion June 26, 1993, I met Helen Freels and Trish Lively Cox, later keeping up with them by telephone (Freels: Nov. 10, 1996, and Nov. 12, 1997; Cox: Apr. 8, 1995, and Nov. 12, 1997). At that reunion, I interviewed Carl Keith (telephone follow-up, Nov. 9, 1997).

Information on mine reclamation projects at Windrock, New River, and Graves Gap has come from Tim Eagle, Tennessee land reclamation director (interview in Knoxville, Tenn., Aug. 8, 1994; telephone interviews, Aug. 24, 1994; Sept. 7, 1995; Nov. 8, 1996; and Nov. 10, 1997).

C. H. Smith and Curtis Owens, Oliver Springs Mining Company owners, provided information in a number of telephone interviews (Smith: Nov. 5, 1994; Apr. 1, 1995; Nov. 10, 1996; and Nov. 9, 1997; Owens: Oct. 23, 1994; Sept. 13, 1995; Dec. 15, 1996; and Nov. 9, 1997).

Details about the TVA model city plan for Oliver Springs, Tennessee, have come from TVA's Division of Navigation Development and Regional Studies, *Synopsis of Oliver Springs Redevelopment Program,* Knoxville, Feb. 1973. Also see my articles in the *Oak Ridger:* "Unveil Plans to Make Model of Oliver Springs" (May 28, 1968: 1+); "Oliver Springs Aldermen All for 'Model City' Plan" (July 12, 1968: 1+); and "Oliver Springs Park Plan Approved" (Dec. 1, 1969). Charles Tichy has described the town today (telephone interviews, Nov. 19, 1994; Nov. 9, 1996; and Nov. 8, 1997), adding to information from my recent visits.

The future of Oak Ridge has been discussed in telephone interviews with Steve Wyatt, public information officer, U.S. Dept. of Energy, Oak Ridge (Sept. 12, 1995), and with his associate Frank Juan (Nov. 15, 1996, and Nov. 12, 1997).

C. S. Harvey Jr. has furnished information about the Oliver Springs Historical Society and the town's beautification project (telephone interviews, Nov. 10, 1996, and Nov. 2, 1997).

Residents of New River, Tennessee, have helped keep me up-to-date on what is happening in their valley since the purchase of most of the land by Champion International Paper Company. (See Fred Strohl, "Champion Buys Anderson Land," *Courier-News* [Clinton, Tenn.], July 27, 1994: A1+.) I first met and talked with Scotty Phillips in New River on August 4, 1994, and since then have had telephone interviews with him on September 1, 1994; September 9, 1995; November 9, 1996; and November 12, 1997. I have had telephone conversations with Dorothy Armes on October 23, 1994; November 9, 1996; and November 12, 1997.

Information about active mining permits in Tennessee and in Anderson County has come from Ron McDowell, U.S. Office of Surface Mining, Knoxville, in telephone interviews on September 14, 1995; November 18, 1996; and November 12, 1997.

The activities of two environmental citizens' groups have been described in telephone interviews. I discussed both Champion's clear-cutting and chip mill as well as Addington's new highwall mining with Dr. Liane Russell, Tennessee Citizens for Wilderness Planning (Nov. 9, 1996, and Nov. 9, 1997) and with Anne Hablas, Save Our Cumberland Mountains (Nov. 13, 1997).

Up at Graves Gap, news from Duncan Flats has come from telephone talks with Laura Duncan (Jan. 8, 1995; Nov. 9, 1996; and Nov. 13, 1997) and with Nancy Braden Byrge in Braden Flats (Oct. 23, 1994; Nov. 9, 1996; and Nov. 13, 1997). Mary Harris, Anderson County historian, said in a telephone conversation on November 23, 1997, that she has found no additional information on the hanging of Jake Harness.

In Lake City, Tennessee, the ambitious project reopening the 1869 mines of Henry Wiley by the Beech Grove Processing Company has been described by Fred Wyatt, Coal Creek Mining and Manufacturing Company (telephone interviews, Nov. 11, 1996, and Nov. 10, 1997). Bob Swisher gave details on his deep and strip mines in telephone interviews on September 11, 1995, and November 12, 1997.

Gene White detailed the present and uncertain future of Briceville, Tennessee, in telephone conversations on November 10, 1996, and November 13, 1997, while Charles Winfrey helped keep me current on Lake City with information in telephone talks December 15, 1996, and November 10, 1997.

Interviews in Frost Bottom, Tennessee, with Babe Edwards (Aug. 3, 1994) and with Lavada Brown (Aug. 4, 1994) have given me a picture of Micajah Frost's old settlement. More information has come from telephone conversations with Babe Edwards (Sept. 10, 1995; Nov. 17, 1996; and Nov. 17, 1997) and with Lavada Brown (Nov. 17, 1996, and Nov. 17, 1997).

Marita Smith George described her grandfather John T. Smith's jetliner trip to California in a telephone conversation April 3, 1995.

The spectacular opening of Harrah's Cherokee Casino is reported by Mark Price in the *Charlotte Observer,* Nov. 9, 1997 ("Tribe Brings Vegas' Glitz to Cherokee," metro ed.: 1A+, and "Chief Agenda: She Means Business," metro ed.: 1E+). Also see his Nov. 14, 1997, article "Casino Didn't Bet on Gridlock," metro ed.: 1A+

Bibliography

Primary Sources

Anderson County, Tennessee. *Circuit Court Execution Docket, 1869–78:* 499.

———. *Circuit Court Record Book, 1873–1879:* 409–10.

———. *Register's Records, 1802–1884. Deed Book* L-1: 444.

Armes, Dorothy. Interview by the author, New River, Tenn., Aug. 1968.

———. Telephone interview by the author, Oct. 23, 1994.

———. Telephone interview by the author, Nov. 9, 1996.

———. Telephone interview by the author, Nov. 12, 1997.

Blevins, Lacie. Interview by author, Claxton, Tenn., June 1968.

Braden, Beulah Brummett. Interview by the author, Braden Flats, Tenn., Sept. 1969.

———. Unpublished research on Braden family.

Braden, Edd. Interview by the author, Braden Flats, Tenn., Sept. 1969.

Brown, Lavada. Interview by the author, Frost Bottom, Tenn., Mar. 30, 1991.

———. Interview by the author, Frost Bottom, Tenn., Aug. 4, 1994.

———. Telephone interview by the author, Nov. 17, 1996.

———. Telephone interview by the author, Nov. 17, 1997.

Brown, Roy E. Interview by the author, Frost Bottom, Tenn., Mar. 1968.

———. Interview by the author, Frost Bottom, Tenn., July 1970.

Burney, J. H. Telephone interview by the author, Sept. 5, 1995.

Bussard, Dick. Director of corporate communications, CSX Transportation Inc. Telephone interview by the author, Feb. 17, 1995.

Byrd, Marjorie Duncan. Telephone interview by the author, Oct. 23, 1994.

———. Telephone interview by the author, Nov. 24, 1996.

———. Telephone interview by the author, Nov. 12, 1997.

Byrge, Nancy Braden. Interview by the author, Braden Flats, Tenn., Sept. 1969.

———. Telephone interview by the author, Oct. 23, 1994.

———. Telephone interview by the author, Nov. 9, 1996.

———. Telephone interview by the author, Nov. 13, 1997.

Byrge, Pearley. Interview by the author, Braden Flats, Tenn., Sept. 1969.

Carroll, Mae Martin. Interview by the author, Briceville, Tenn., May 1968.

Coker, Lewis. Interview by the author, New River, Tenn., Aug. 1968.

Cox, Trish Lively. Telephone interview by the author, Apr. 8, 1995.

———. Telephone interview by the author, Nov. 12, 1997.

Daniels, Wrease. Interview by the author, Briceville, Tenn., June 1968.

Daugherty, Mable Williams. Interview by the author, Oliver Springs, Tenn., July 1970.

Davis, Charlie. Interview by the author, Oliver Springs, Tenn., July 1970.

Diggs, Lula. Interview by the author, Oliver Springs, Tenn., Nov. 1969.

Disney, Margaret Diggs. Interview by the author, Oliver Springs, Tenn., Nov. 1969.

Duncan, Byrd and Laura. Interview by the author, Duncan Flats, Tenn., Apr. 1969.

Duncan, Laura. Telephone interview by the author, Jan. 8, 1995.

———. Telephone interview by the author, Nov. 9, 1996.

———. Telephone interview by the author, Nov. 13, 1997.

Duncan, Sally. Interview by author, Frost Bottom, Tenn., June 1968.

Eagle, Tim. Land reclamation director, Tenn. Dept. of Environment and Conservation. Interview by the author, Knoxville, Tenn., Aug. 8, 1994.

———. Telephone interview by the author, Aug. 24, 1994.

———. Telephone interview by the author, Sept. 7, 1995.

———. Telephone interview by the author, Nov. 8, 1996.

———. Telephone interview by the author, Nov. 10, 1997.

Edwards, Babe (Mary). Interview by the author, Frost Bottom, Tenn., Aug. 3, 1994.

———. Telephone interview by the author, Sept. 10, 1995.

———. Telephone interview by the author, Nov. 17, 1996.

———. Telephone interview by the author, Nov. 17, 1997.

Freels, Helen. Telephone interview by the author, Nov. 10, 1996.

———. Telephone interview by the author, Nov. 12, 1997.

Gault, Ivy. Interview by the author, Claxton, Tenn., June 1968.

George, Marita Smith. Interview by the author, Loudon, Tenn., Nov. 28, 1992.

———. Telephone interview by the author, Nov. 26, 1994.

———. Telephone interview by the author, Apr. 30, 1995.

———. Telephone interview by the author, Nov. 15, 1997.

Giles, Annie Smith. Interview by the author, Oliver Springs, Tenn., June 1969.

———. Interview by the author, Windrock, Tenn., July 1970.

Graves, Dixie Duncan. Interview by the author, Dutch Valley, Tenn., Aug. 3, 1994.

Groff, Arnold. Interview by the author, New River, Tenn., Aug. 1968.

Hablas, Anne. Save Our Cumberland Mountains (SOCM), Lake City, Tenn., office. Telephone interview by the author, Nov. 13, 1997.

Harness, Gertrude. Telephone interview by the author, Jan. 8, 1995.

Harris, Mary S. Anderson County historian. Interview by the author, Clinton, Tenn., Aug. 2, 1994.

———. Letter to the author. Nov. 16, 1994.

———. Telephone interview by the author, Nov. 10, 1994.

———. Telephone interview by the author, Nov. 24, 1996.

———. Telephone interview by the author, Nov. 15, 1997.

Harvey, C. S., Jr. Telephone interview by the author, Nov. 10, 1996.

———. Telephone interview by the author, Nov. 2, 1997.

Henderson, Ed. Interview by the author, Marlow, Tenn., July 1970.

Henley, John. Interview by the author, Oliver Springs, Tenn., Feb. 15, 1969.

Hill, Ernest and Daisy. Interview by the author, Fraterville, Tenn., May 1968.

Juan, Frank. Public information office, U.S. Dept. of Energy, Oak Ridge, Tenn. Telephone interview by the author, Nov. 15, 1996.

———. Telephone interview by the author, Nov. 12, 1997.

Keith, J. Carl. Interview by the author, Clinton, Tenn., July 1970.

———. Interview by the author, Windrock, Tenn., June 26, 1993.

———. Telephone interview by the author, Nov. 9, 1997.

Kelley, Wanda. Pellissippi Genealogical & Historical Society, Clinton, Tenn. Telephone interview by the author, Oct. 7, 1995.

———. Telephone interview by the author, Oct. 11, 1997.

————. Unpublished Frost family research.

Kesterson, Laura Roberts. Interview by the author, Lake City, Tenn., June 1968.

Landrum, Dorsey. Interview by the author, Briceville, Tenn., June 1968.

Leamon, Ray. Interview by the author, Knoxville, Tenn., Aug. 8, 1994.

————. Letter to the author, Sept. 23, 1994.

————. Telephone interview by the author, Nov. 24, 1997.

Lefler, Bob. Tennessee Citizens for Wilderness Planning (TCWP). Telephone interview by the author, Feb. 15, 1969.

Lively, Church. Interview by the author, Oliver Springs, Tenn., Dec. 1968.

Lively, O'Dell. Interview by the author, Windrock, Tenn., July 1970.

Long, Lonas. Interview by the author, Marlow, Tenn., July 1970.

McCoy, Jim. Interview by the author, Briceville, Tenn., May 1968.

McDowell, Ron. U.S. Office of Surface Mining, Knoxville, Tenn. Telephone interview by the author, Sept. 14, 1995.

————. Telephone interview by the author, Nov. 18, 1996.

————. Telephone interview by the author, Nov. 12, 1997.

McNaughton, Susan. Deputy press secretary, Penn. Dept. of Corrections. Telephone interview by the author, Nov. 12, 1997.

Mead, Albert. Interview by the author, Oliver Springs, Tenn., June 1969.

Morehead, Jerry. Engineer, Tenn. Dept. of Transportation. Telephone interview by the author, Oct. 18, 1994.

————. Telephone interview by the author, Oct. 19, 1994.

Nichols, Joseph L. Letter to the author. Sept. 27, 1970.

Owens, Curtis. Interview by the author, Windrock, Tenn., July 1970.

————. Telephone interview by the author, Oct. 23, 1994.

————. Telephone interview by the author, Sept. 13, 1995.

————. Telephone interview by the author, Dec. 15, 1996.

————. Telephone interview by the author, Nov. 9, 1997.

Patty, Nancy Phillips. Interview by the author, Clinton, Tenn., Nov. 4, 1995.

————. Telephone interview by the author, Oct. 16, 1994.

Phillips, Scotty. Interview by the author, New River, Tenn., Aug. 4, 1994.

————. Telephone interview by the author, Sept. 1, 1994.

————. Telephone interview by the author, Sept. 9, 1995.

————. Telephone interview by the author, Nov. 9, 1996.

————. Telephone interview by the author, Nov. 12, 1997.

Riggs, Arthur. Interview by the author, Lake City, Tenn., May 1968.

Roberts, Snyder E. Interview by the author, Oliver Springs, Tenn., June 1968.

————. Interview by the author, Oliver Springs, Tenn., June 1969.

———. Interview by the author, Oliver Springs, Tenn., Nov. 1969.

———. Interview by the author, Oliver Springs, Tenn., July 1970.

———. Interview by the author, Oak Ridge, Tenn., Nov. 29, 1992.

———. Letter to the author. Oct. 6, 1968.

———. Telephone interview by the author, Jan. 10, 1993.

———. Telephone interview by the author, May 2, 1993.

Russell, Liane. Oak Ridge National Laboratory, Oak Ridge, Tenn. Telephone interview by the author, Nov. 9, 1996.

———. Telephone interview by the author, Nov. 14, 1997.

Seeber, R. Clifford. Letter to the author. Aug. 16, 1968.

———. Letter to the author. Dec. 17, 1969.

———. Telephone interview by the author, Dec. 1969.

Seiber, John. Interview by the author, New River, Tenn., Feb. 14, 1969.

Sienknecht, Elmer C. Letter to the author. July 10, 1970.

———. Interview by the author, Knoxville, Tenn., July 1970.

Sienknecht, Mary Richards. Interview by the author, Oliver Springs, Tenn., Mar. 1968.

Smith, C. H. Two interviews by the author, Windrock, Tenn., July 1970.

———. Telephone interview by the author, Nov. 5, 1994.

———. Telephone interview by the author, Apr. 1, 1995.

———. Telephone interview by the author, Nov. 10, 1996.

———. Telephone interview by the author, Nov. 9, 1997.

Smith, Harold and Mary Kate. Interview, Batley, Tenn., Nov. 29, 1992.

———. Telephone interview by the author, Nov. 8, 1997.

Smith, John T. "A History Book of the Unknown Secret." Unpublished family story. Nov. 28, 1958.

———. "Clinton Murder." Unpublished poem. N.d.

———. Interviews by author for Frost Bottom series, Oliver Springs, Tenn., June 1968.

———. Interview by author, Oliver Springs, Tenn., Dec. 1968.

———. Interviews for Windrock series, Anderson County, Tenn., July 1970.

———. Unpublished story of McKinley victory parade. 1974.

Smith, W. Herbert. Interview by the author, Loudon, Tenn., Nov. 28, 1992.

Stonecipher, William. Interview by the author, Briceville, Tenn., May 1968.

Stout, B. Rule. Letter to Beulah Brummett Braden. June 6, 1969.

Stripling, Walter. Interview by author, Oliver Springs, Tenn., Nov. 1969.

Swisher, Bob. Telephone interview by the author, Sept. 11, 1995.

————. Telephone interview by the author, Nov. 12, 1997.

Tichy, Charles. Telephone interview by the author, Nov. 19, 1994.

————. Telephone interview by the author, Nov. 9, 1996.

————. Telephone interview by the author, Nov. 8, 1997.

Tilford, John E. "The Newcomen Address." Unpublished manuscript. University Archives and Records Center, University of Louisville, Feb. 1, 1951.

Turnblazer, William, Jr. President, District 19, United Mine Workers of America. Interview by the author, New River, Tenn., Apr. 1, 1968.

Vann, Elijah. Interview by the author, Oliver Springs, Tenn., June 1969.

Watkins, F. G. Reclamation director, Tenn. Dept. of Conservation. Interview by the author, New River, Tenn., Feb. 14, 1969.

White, Gene. Telephone interview by the author, Sept. 5, 1994.

————. Telephone interview by the author, Feb. 18, 1995.

————. Telephone interview by the author, Sept. 7, 1995.

————. Telephone interview by the author, Nov. 10, 1996.

————. Telephone interview by the author, Nov. 13, 1997.

Williams, C. I. Interview by the author, Briceville, Tenn., May 1968.

Wilson, Lee and Malinda. Interview by the author, Briceville, Tenn., May 1968.

Winfrey, Charles. Telephone interview by the author, Sept. 27, 1995.

————. Telephone interview by the author, Dec. 15, 1996.

————. Telephone interview by the author, Nov. 10, 1997.

Wright, Bob and Maggie. Interview by the author, Oliver Springs, Tenn., June 1969.

Wyatt, Fred. Executive vice-president, Coal Creek Mining and Manufacturing Co., Knoxville, Tenn. Telephone interview by the author, July 19, 1995.

————. Telephone interview by the author, July 20, 1995.

————. Telephone interview by the author, Sept. 8, 1995.

————. Telephone interview by the author, Nov. 11, 1996.

————. Telephone interview by the author, Nov. 10, 1997.

Wyatt, Steve. Public information officer, U.S. Dept. of Energy, Oak Ridge, Tenn. Telephone interview by the author, Sept. 12, 1995.

Secondary Sources

Armbrister, Trevor. *Act of Vengeance: The Yablonski Murders and Their Solution*. New York: Saturday Review-Dutton, 1975.

Bannister, Robert C. *Social Darwinism: Science and Myth in Anglo-American Social Thought*. Philadelphia: Temple UP, 1979.

Bell, Jimmie (Augusta). "A Braden Always Comes Back to 'The Mountain.'" *Oak Ridger,* Sept. 17, 1969: 1+.

————. "Claxton Was Site of County's First White Settlement." *Oak Ridger*, June 25, 1968: 1+.

————. "Clinton Board Asked to 'Save This House.'" *Oak Ridger*, June 9, 1968: 1+.

————. "Death of Main Street Is Coming After 200 Years." *Oak Ridger*, June 25, 1969: 1+.

————. "Flood Victims' Bodies Found Saturday, Sunday." *Oak Ridger*, July 10, 1967: 1+.

————. "He Keeps Nearby Hills Alive with Gospel Music and Boy Scout Activity." *Oak Ridger*, Apr. 9, 1969: 1+.

————. "Lavish Resort Hotel Brought Turn of Century Swells to Oliver Springs." *Oak Ridger*, Mar. 13, 1968: 1+.

————. "Meet Brother Church W. Lively, 91: Born on Mountain, Spanish-American Vet, Still Smasher." *Oak Ridger*, Dec. 18, 1968: 1+.

————. "Mine Union Officials Plan Area Organizing Drive." *Oak Ridger*, Apr. 2, 1968: 1+.

————. "Miners Battle Convict Labor Plan." *Oak Ridger*, June 18, 1968: 1+.

————. "Oliver Springs Aldermen All for 'Model City' Plan." *Oak Ridger*, July 12, 1968: 1+.

————. "Oliver Springs Park Plan Approved." *Oak Ridger*, Dec. 1, 1969: 1+.

————. "Oliver Springs Recalls Two WWI Heroes." *Oak Ridger*, Nov. 11, 1969: 1+.

————. "184 Miners Died 66 Years Ago Sunday." *Oak Ridger*, May 17, 1968: 1+.

————. "Scientists Form for Appalachia." *Oak Ridger*, Apr. 27, 1970: 1+.

————. "Shangri-La of Anderson County—1: New Mine, Community Spirit Rejuvenate New River." *Oak Ridger*, Aug. 13, 1968: 1+.

————. "Shangri-La of Anderson County—2: Isaac Phillips Settled New River in 1812 Coming from N. Carolina." *Oak Ridger*, Aug. 14, 1968: 1+.

————. "Shangri-La of Anderson County—3: Old Commissary Becoming Center." *Oak Ridger*, Aug. 15, 1968: 1+.

————. "2 Years After Flood, O. Springs Buzzes." *Oak Ridger*, July 11, 1969: 1+.

————. "Uncle John and the Cow Creek Branch—1: A Saga from Dossett to Windrock." *Oak Ridger*, Aug. 12, 1970: 1+.

————. "Uncle John and the Cow Creek Branch—2: Building the Dossett Tunnel." *Oak Ridger*, Aug. 13, 1970: 1+.

————. "Uncle John and the Cow Creek Branch—3: The Powder Plant at Marlow." *Oak Ridger*, Aug. 14, 1970: 1+.

————. "Uncle John and the Cow Creek Branch—4: Tending Tanks on a Railroad Bike." *Oak Ridger,* Aug. 17, 1970: 1+.

————. "Uncle John and the Cow Creek Branch—5: The Brief but Lively 'Railroad War.'" *Oak Ridger,* Aug. 18, 1970: 1+.

————. "Uncle John and the Cow Creek Branch—6: Oldtimers Recall Colorful Station Names." *Oak Ridger,* Aug. 19, 1970: 1+.

————. "Uncle John and the Cow Creek Branch—7: Windrock: Good Place to Work." *Oak Ridger,* Aug. 20, 1970: 1+.

————. "Uncle John and the Cow Creek Branch—8: Windrock's Final Years." *Oak Ridger,* Aug. 21, 1970: 1+.

————. "Uncle John and the Cow Creek Branch—9: Million and a Half Tons Still Left." *Oak Ridger,* Aug. 24, 1970: 1+.

————. "Uncle John and the Cow Creek Branch—10: Not Even a Woman Reporter Can Enter the Mine." *Oak Ridger,* Aug. 25, 1970: 1+.

————. "Unto These Hills—1: 1st Settlers Went into Frost Bottom About 1795." *Oak Ridger,* June 24, 1968: 1+.

————. "Unto These Hills—2: Duncans, Browns Were Frost Bottom Pioneers." *Oak Ridger,* June 25, 1968: 1+.

————. "Unto These Hills—3: Uncle John Retells Famous Shooting Match." *Oak Ridger,* June 26, 1968: 1+.

————. "Unto These Hills—4: Walden's Ridge Divided Unions and Rebels." *Oak Ridger,* June 27, 1968: 1+.

————. "Unto These Hills—5: McCoy Ambush Murder Roused Whole County." *Oak Ridger,* June 28, 1968: 1+.

————. "Unveil Plans to Make Model of Oliver Springs." *Oak Ridger,* May 28, 1968: 1+.

————. "Whether Law Working or Not, Strip Mines Still Worry Residents." *Oak Ridger,* Feb. 19, 1969: 1+.

————. "Who Needs Smokies for Color?" *Oak Ridger,* Oct. 24, 1969: 1+.

Betts, Jack. "This Time and Place: Death of a Doughboy." Editorial. *Charlotte Observer,* Oct. 16, 1993, metro final ed.: 16A.

"Booby Traps in Mine." *New York Times,* July 16, 1959, late city ed.: A27.

Boorstin, Daniel J. *The Americans: The National Experience.* New York: Vintage-Random, 1965.

"Boyle Charged in Murder after Ex-Aide Names Him." *Charlotte Observer,* Sept. 7, 1973, final ed.: 1A+.

"The Briceville Affair: Latest from the Seat of Mining Troubles." *Clinton Gazette,* July 23, 1891: 5.

"Burned Totally." *Anderson County News,* Apr. 22, 1905: 2.

Byrd, Marjorie Duncan. *Duncan Descendants of Frost Bottom, TN.* Harriman, Tenn.: 1995.

Campbell, Joseph. *The Hero with a Thousand Faces.* Princeton, N.J.: Princeton UP, 1949.

"Casualities in Principal Wars of the U.S." *World Almanac.* 1998 ed.: 161.

Caudill, Harry M. *Night Comes to the Cumberlands: A Biography of a Depressed Area.* Boston: Atlantic Monthly-Little, 1962.

Cochran, Thomas C., and William Miller. *The Age of Enterprise: A Social History of Industrial America.* Revised ed. New York: Harper, 1961.

"Cold, Dreary Rain Fell During the Entire Day on the Stricken Village." *Journal & Tribune* [Knoxville], Dec. 12, 1911: 2.

"The Convicts at Briceville and Coal Creek Released by the Miners." *Clinton Gazette,* Nov. 5, 1891: 1+.

"Convicts in Mine End Their Revolt." *New York Times,* July 15, 1959, late city ed.: A61.

Corlew, Robert E. *Tennessee: A Short History.* 2d ed. Knoxville: U of Tennessee P, 1981.

Cox, Trish Lively. *301 Years of Livelys, 1690–1991.* Oak Ridge, Tenn.: 1992.

Cunningham, Rodger. *Apples on the Flood: Minority Discourse and Appalachia.* Knoxville: U of Tennessee P, 1987.

"Deluge Floods Ridge, Oliver Springs." *Oak Ridger,* July 12, 1967: 1+.

D'Emilio, John, and Estelle B. Freedman. *Intimate Matters: A History of Sexuality in America.* New York: Harper, 1988.

Derks, Scott, ed. *The Value of a Dollar: Prices and Incomes in the United States, 1860–1989.* Detroit: Gale Research, 1994.

Dykeman, Wilma. *With Fire and Sword: The Battle of Kings Mountain, 1780.* National Park Service. Washington, DC: GPO, 1978. N.p.

Eller, Ronald D. *Miners, Millhands, and Mountaineers: Industrialization of the Appalachian South, 1880–1930.* Knoxville: U of Tennessee P, 1982.

"Ex-Aide Convicted in Yablonski Case." *Charlotte Observer,* June 20, 1973, final ed.: 3A.

Faragher, John Mack. *Daniel Boone: The Life and Legend of an American Pioneer.* New York: Holt, 1992.

Federal Writers' Project of the Work Projects Administration. *Tennessee: A Guide to the State.* New York: Hastings, 1949.

Fleeson, Lucinda. "Undermining the Obstacles: Female Coal Miners at Conference Assess the Price of Their Progress." *Charlotte Observer,* June 28, 1983, final ed.: 2A.

Flowers, Charles. "One of State's Oldest and Biggest Mines, Windrock Also Is Safest, Most Efficient." *Knoxville News-Sentinel,* Oct. 13, 1957, home ed.: C5.

"Fraterville Mine at Coal Creek, the Tomb of 170; Not a Soul Lives to Tell the Tale of Explosion." *Journal & Tribune* [Knoxville], May 20, 1902: 1.

"Fraterville Settlement." *Clinton Gazette,* Mar. 28, 1903: 1.

Gardiner, John Rolfe. *Great Dream from Heaven.* New York: Dutton, 1974.

Goodspeed's History of East Tennessee. 1886–87. Nashville: Charles and Randy Elder, 1972.

Herr, Kincaid A. *The Louisville & Nashville Railroad, 1850–1963.* Louisville: L&N Railroad, 1964.

Hevener, John W. *Which Side Are You On? The Harlan County Coal Miners, 1931–39.* Urbana: U of Illinois P, 1978.

Hofstadter, Richard. *Social Darwinism in American Thought.* 1944. Boston: Beacon, 1992.

Hoskins, Katherine Baker. *Anderson County Historical Sketches.* Clinton, Tenn.: Clinton-Courier News, 1987.

Hutson, A. C., Jr. "The Coal Miners' Insurrection of 1891 in Anderson County, Tennessee." *East Tennessee Historical Society's Publications* 7 (1935): 103–21.

———. "The Overthrow of the Convict Lease System in Tennessee." *East Tennessee Historical Society's Publications* 8 (1936): 82–103.

"Imprisoned 60 Hours, Five Men Taken Alive from Cross Mt. Mine; Gloom Changed to Rejoicing as Men Restored to Families." *Journal & Tribune* [Knoxville], Dec. 12, 1911: 1+.

"Interview with Inspector Shiflett." *Journal & Tribune* [Knoxville], May 20, 1902: 1.

"'It Was a Great Day,' Says General Hannah." *Journal & Tribune* [Knoxville], April 6, 1919: 4.

James, Simon. *The World of the Celts.* London: Thames, 1993.

"Journey Homeward Proves One Continuous Ovation." *Journal & Tribune* [Knoxville], Apr. 6, 1919: 3.

"Jury Finds Boyle Guilty of Murder." *Charlotte Observer,* Apr. 12, 1974, final ed.: 1A+.

Kelley, Robert Lloyd. *The Shaping of the American Past.* 5th ed., combined ed. Englewood Cliffs, N.J.: Prentice-Hall, 1990.

"Knoxville Called on for Many Coffins." *Journal & Tribune* [Knoxville], May 20, 1902: 1.

"Knoxville Receives Hindenburg Line Breakers with Unprecedented Acclaim: Veterans of 117th March in Triumph Before Huge Crowd." *Journal & Tribune* [Knoxville], Apr. 6, 1919: 1+.

Lake City Homecoming '86 Committee. *Coal Creek/Lake City: Visions of the Past.* 1986.

Long, Priscilla. *Where the Sun Never Shines: A History of America's Bloody Coal Industry.* New York: Paragon, 1989.

McCullough, David. *Brave Companions: Portraits in History.* New York: Touchstone-Simon, 1992.

McCusker, John J. "How Much Is That in Real Money? A Historical Price Index for Use as a Deflator of Money Values in the Economy of the United States." *Proceedings of the American Antiquarian Society* 101, pt. 2 (1992): 297–373.

McGhee, Marshall, and Melba Jackson. *Careyville Through the Years.* Jacksboro, Tenn.: 1988.

McGhee, Marshall, and Gene White. *Briceville: The Town That Coal Built.* Jacksboro, Tenn.: 1991.

Messick, Hank. *King's Mountain: The Epic of the Blue Ridge "Mountain Men" in the American Revolution.* Boston: Little, Brown, 1976.

"Mine Accidents." *Anderson County News,* Nov. 16, 1912: 1.

"Mine Operator and Employees Are Assaulted." *Clinton Courier-News,* July 21, 1949: sec. 1, p. 1.

"Mine Supt. Camp Makes a Statement." *Journal & Tribune* [Knoxville], May 20, 1902: 1.

"Mine Yields Body; Two Still Trapped." *Knoxville News-Sentinel,* June 25, 1961, home ed.: A1+.

Morrill, Dan L. *Southern Campaigns of the American Revolution.* Baltimore: Nautical & Aviation, 1993.

Norton, Mary Beth, et al. *A People and a Nation: A History of the United States.* 3d. ed. vol. 1. Boston: Houghton-Mifflin, 1990. 2 vols.

Oliver Springs Season 1900. Oliver Springs, Tenn.: Oliver Springs Hotel, 1899.

"115th Field Artillery Given Great Welcome as They March on Gay St. in Drizzling Rain." *Journal & Tribune* [Knoxville], Apr. 5, 1919: 1+.

Overholt, James. *Anderson County, Tennessee: A Pictorial History.* Norfolk: Donning, 1989.

Patty, Nancy Phillips, and Effie Bunch Ward. *Ligas Fork: A Journey Back in Time and Surrounding Areas, 1794–1992.*

Pellissippi Genealogical & Historical Society of Clinton, Tenn. *The Tennessee 200 Bicentennial History of Anderson County.* Jacksboro, Tenn.: 1997.

"Photo Presents Reminder of 1920's 'Ambush.'" *Appalachian Observer* [Clinton, Tenn.], Mar. 28, 1984: 3.

Powell, Dannye Romine. "In 1829, They Had a Real Blast." *Charlotte Observer,* Jan. 20, 1993, metro final ed.: 1C.

Price, Mark. "Casino Didn't Bet on Gridlock." *Charlotte Observer,* Nov. 14, 1997, metro ed.: 1A+.

————. "Chief Agenda: She Means Business." *Charlotte Observer,* Nov. 9, 1997, metro ed.: 1E+.

————. "Tribe Brings Vegas' Glitz to Cherokee." *Charlotte Observer,* Nov. 9, 1997, metro ed.: 1A+.

"Principal U.S. Mine Disasters Since 1900." *World Almanac.* 1998 ed.: 267.

Rayback, Joseph G. *A History of American Labor: Expanded and Updated.* 1959. New York: Macmillan, 1966.

————. "Lewis, John Llewellyn." *Encyclopedia Americana.* 1987 ed.

Rhodes, Frank H. T., and Herbert S. Zim, Paul R. Shaffer. *Fossils: A Guide to Prehistoric Life.* New York: Golden Press, 1962.

Richards, D. C. "Trip to New River." *Anderson County News,* Apr. 30, 1927: 1+.

Roberts, Snyder E. *Descendants of Joseph Frost, Sr. from Amherst, Bedford and Washington Counties, VA to Anderson County, TN and Elsewhere.* 1989.

————. *The Roots of Roane County, Tennessee, 1792—.* Kingston, Tenn.: 1981.

————. *The Story of Oliver Springs, Tennessee, and Its People.* 4 vols. Oliver Springs, Tenn.: 1982–85.

Rodgers, Daniel T. *The Work Ethic in Industrial America, 1850–1920.* Chicago: U of Chicago P, 1978.

Rogin, Michael Paul. *Fathers and Children: Andrew Jackson and the Subjugation of the American Indian.* New York: Knopf, 1975.

Rohrbough, Malcolm J. *The Trans-Appalachian Frontier: People, Societies, and Institutions, 1775–1850.* New York: Oxford UP, 1978.

Rorabaugh, W. J. *The Alcoholic Republic.* New York: Oxford UP, 1980.

Saxon, Wolfgang. "W. A. Boyle Dies; Led Miners' Union." *New York Times,* June 1, 1985, late city ed.: 29.

Schenck, Maria J. "Superstition Put Aside: Gray's Gap Mine Awes Female Reporter." *Oak Ridger,* Mar. 15, 1972: 1+.

Seeber, R. Clifford. *A History of Anderson County, Tennessee.* Master's thesis, University of Tennessee, 1928.

Smith, Betty Anderson. "Distribution of Eighteenth-Century Cherokee Settlements." In *The Cherokee Indian Nation: A Troubled History,* edited by Duane H. King. Knoxville: U of Tennessee P, 1979. 46–57.

Smith, W. J. (Jasper). "A Century Ago." *Anderson County News,* Mar. 16, 1929: 1.

————. "Century Ago." *Anderson County News,* Mar. 9, 1929: 2.

————. "Civil War Echo." *Anderson County News,* June 4, 1927: 1.

————. "Clinton History." *Anderson County News,* 1925—Mar. 21: 3; Apr. 11: 2; Apr. 18: 4; May 23: 2; June 13: 2.

————. "Clinton History: War of 1861." *Anderson County News,* May 2, 1925: 3.

————. "Clinton History: War of 1862." *Anderson County News,* 1925—May 16: 1; June 6: 2.

————. "Donovan News." *Anderson County News,* Apr. 16, 1927: 4.

————. "Dutch Valley Settlers." *Anderson County News,* Nov. 9, 1929: 1.

————. "Early Settlers." *Anderson County News,* Aug. 13, 1927: 4.

————. "The Early Settlers." *Anderson County News,* Jan. 18, 1930: 1.

————. "Educating a Negro." *Anderson County News,* May 28, 1927: 1.

————. "The Family Circle." *Anderson County News,* July 21, 1928: 1.

————. "Four Score Years Ago." *Anderson County News,* Oct. 13, 1928: 1.

————. "Frost Bottom History." *Anderson County News,* 1924—Apr. 12: 3; Apr. 19: 2; May 10: 3; May 24: 1; June 28: 3; July 5: 2; Aug. 9: 3; Aug. 23: 1; Aug. 30: 1; Sept. 6: 2; Sept. 13: 1; Sept. 20: 2; Oct. 18: 1; Oct. 25: 3; Nov. 1: 2; Nov. 8: 3; Nov. 15: 2.

————. "Frost Bottom History." *Anderson County News,* 1925—July 18: 2; Aug. 1: 2; Aug. 8: 2; Aug. 15: 2; Aug. 22: 2; Aug. 29: 3; Sept. 26: 2; Oct. 10: 2; Oct. 17: 3; Oct. 24: 3; Nov. 7: 1 (supplement); Nov. 14: 2; Nov. 21: 2; Nov. 28: 2; Dec. 5: 3.

————. "Frost Bottom History." *Anderson County News,* 1926—Jan. 9: 2; Jan. 30: 3; Feb. 6: 3; Mar. 27: 3; Apr. 3: 1 (supplement).

————. "Frost Bottom History." *Anderson County News,* Sept. 28, 1928: 4.

————. "Frost Bottom History." *Anderson County News,* Aug. 3, 1929: 1.

————. "The Gun and Dog." *Anderson County News,* Dec. 8, 1928: 3.

————. "History of Houk Family." *Anderson County News,* Jan. 10, 1925: 2.

————. "The Houk Family." *Anderson County News,* Mar. 24, 1928: 1.

————. "Long Time Ago." *Anderson County News,* June 15, 1929: 1.

————. "The New Eden." *Anderson County News,* Dec. 13, 1924: 3.

————. "New River Settlers." *Anderson County News,* 1927—Oct. 1: 2; Oct. 15: 2.

————. "Secession." *Anderson County News,* Apr. 13, 1929: 1.

————. "Then and Now." *Anderson County News,* July 31, 1926: 4.

————. "What Is Life?" *Anderson County News,* July 4, 1925: 3.

————. "Winters's Gap History." *Anderson County News,* Sept. 11, 1926: 2.

Smyser, Mary P. "Who Owns the Cumberlands: 3 Big Firms; Stockholders Overlap." *Oak Ridger,* Mar. 25, 1971: 1+.

Stokely, Jim, and Jeff D. Johnson, eds. *An Encyclopedia of East Tennessee.* Oak Ridge: Children's Museum of Oak Ridge, 1981.

"Strip Miners Wounded by Ambushers." *Clinton Courier-News,* July 28, 1949: sec. 1, p. 1.

Strohl, Fred. "Champion Buys Anderson Land." *Courier-News* [Clinton, Tenn.], July 27, 1994: A1+.

Tawney, R. H. *Religion and the Rise of Capitalism: A Historical Study.* 1926. Gloucester, Mass.: Peter Smith, 1962.

Tennessee Valley Authority. Division of Navigation Development and Regional Studies. *Synopsis of Oliver Springs Redevelopment Program.* Knoxville: Feb. 1973.

"Thirtieth Fighting Men Loyally Received by Shouting Thousands." *Journal & Tribune* [Knoxville], Mar. 28, 1919: 1+.

"30,000 Knoxvillians Greet Heroes of 114th Artillery." *Journal & Tribune* [Knoxville], Mar 30, 1919: 1+.

"Trumka, Richard L(ouis)." *Current Biography Yearbook.* 1986 ed.

United Mine Workers of America, District 19. "In Memory of Those Who Lost Their Lives in the Fraterville Mine Explosion and in the Cross Mountain Mine Explosion." 1940.

Weals, Vic. "Francis Led Rescue Crew to Recover Miners' Bodies." *Knoxville Journal,* Jan. 31, 1980, city ed.: C1.

————. "Mine Explosion Greatest Tragedy in Briceville, Scene of Bitter Strife." *Knoxville Journal,* Feb. 20, 1949, city ed.: D7.

————. "Mother Lost Five Sons in Fraterville Explosion." *Knoxville Journal,* Jan. 24, 1980, city ed.: C1.

————. "No Profanity, Please, in Presence of Dead." *Knoxville Journal,* Feb. 7, 1980, city ed.: C1.

————. "Old Miners Talked; Arthur Listened." *Knoxville Journal,* Feb. 21, 1980, city ed.: B1.

White, Gene. *Briceville Through the Years.* Jacksboro, Tenn.: 1994.

"Wild Demonstrations of Joy by Families of Rescued Men." *Journal & Tribune* [Knoxville], Dec. 12, 1911: 2.

Winfrey, Lee. "Ex-Mine Operator Recalls Violent Days." *Knoxville News-Sentinel,* Aug. 30, 1959, home ed.: B10.

Index